Georgia's Historical Recipes

Grape Conserve.

3 pt. grape pulp.
8 cups sugar
1 whole orange
grated rind + juice
½ lb. raisins
Boil 20 min. + add
1 cup nut meats.

Grape Conserve
5 lbs. grapes (concords)
5 " sugar
2 whole oranges
1 lb. raisins - 1 cup nut meats
wash grapes + pulp. Cook
P + skins seperate. Rub P.
thru fine colander to remove
seeds. Put all ingredients into
kettle, using juice + grated peal
of oranges. Cook 30 min. put
in jellie glasses.

GEORGIA'S HISTORICAL RECIPES

Seeking Our State's Oldest Written Foodways and the Stories behind Them

VALERIE J. FREY

The University of Georgia Press Athens

This publication is made possible in part through a grant from the Bradley Hale Fund for Southern Studies.

Published by the University of Georgia Press
Athens, Georgia 30602
www.ugapress.org

Designed by Erin Kirk
Set in Sentinel
Printed and bound by Friesens

The paper in this book meets the guidelines for permanence and durability of the Committee on Production Guidelines for Book Longevity of the Council on Library Resources.

Most University of Georgia Press titles are available from popular e-book vendors.

Printed in Canada
29 28 27 26 25 C 5 4 3 2 1

EU Authorized Representative
Easy Access System Europe—Mustamäe tee 50, 10621
Tallinn, Estonia, gpsr.requests@easproject.com

Library of Congress Cataloging-in-Publication Data
Names: Frey, Valerie J., 1969– author.
Title: Georgia's historical recipes : seeking our state's oldest written foodways and the stories behind them / Valerie J. Frey.
Description: Athens : The University of Georgia Press, [2024] | Includes bibliographical references and index. | Summary: "Georgia's Historical Recipes is a survey of Georgia's historical cookbooks, recipes, and related foodways from 1733 to the end of World War II. It offers many recipes while also weaving together information and some of the history and stories of Georgia's old cookbooks and their authors. As Frey puts it, "the book explores what Georgians grew, gathered, hunted, cooked, and ate. It explains various changes in technology, transportation, communication, social norms, and food science that slowly altered what could be found between the covers of Georgia's old cookbooks"— Provided by publisher.
Identifiers: LCCN 2024047866 (print) | LCCN 2024047867 (ebook) | ISBN 9780820367965 (hardback) | ISBN 9780820367972 (epub) | ISBN 9780820367989 (pdf)
Subjects: LCSH: Cooking—Georgia—History. | Cooking—Georgia—Research. | Cooking, American—Southern style—History. | LCGFT: Cookbooks.
Classification: LCC TX715.2.S68 F74 2024 (print) | LCC TX715.2.S68 (ebook) | DDC 641.59758—dc23/eng/20241205
LC record available at https://lccn.loc.gov/2024047866
LC ebook record available at https://lccn.loc.gov/2024047867

To my son, Eli.

The decade that I worked on this book overlapped your childhood, and I will forever be grateful for our history treks and culinary adventures.

You made it even more fun.

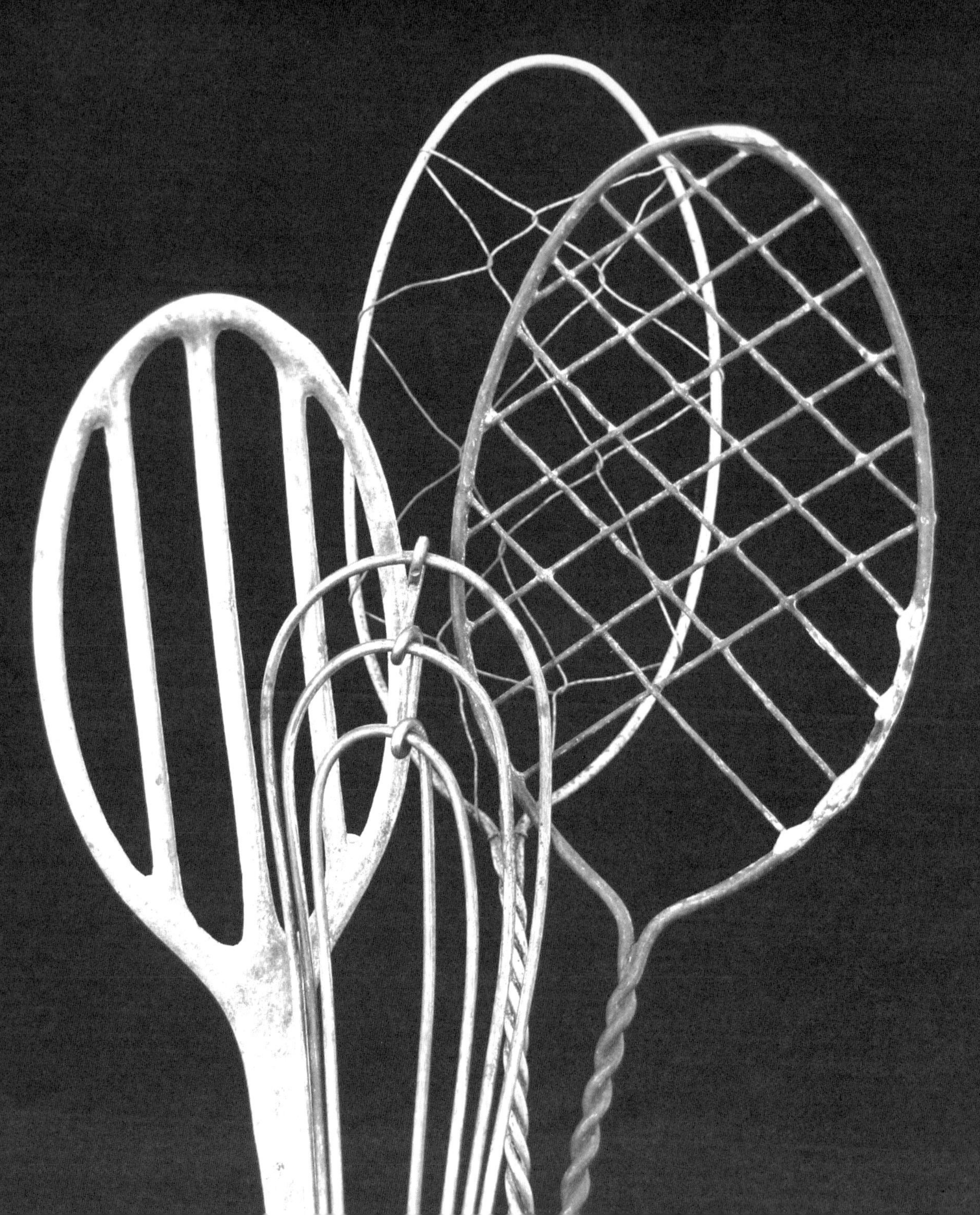

Contents

BAKERS
CALUMET
THE DOUBLE ACTING
BAKING POWDER
10 LBS

Georgia's Historical Recipes

The New Annie Dennis Cook Book

Rediscovering Georgia's Historical Recipes

Are recipes like pantry ingredients—useful, but with a shelf life?

I needed a work break one winter afternoon. I was deep into edits on my previous history-related book, *Preserving Family Recipes*, so an antique shop sounded like just the thing. I drifted through an old country store that had become a labyrinth of everything from art deco vases to scratched disco albums until a ragged paperback caught my eye. It was a cookbook handled so many times that the cardstock covers felt like soft leather—*The New Annie Dennis Cook Book*. When I saw it was published in Atlanta in 1915, my eyebrows went up. The project I was playing hooky from regularly led me to old cookbooks. I'd worked with two from Georgia, *Mrs. Hill's New Cook Book* (1867) and *Southern Cooking* (1928), yet I'd never heard of this cookbook published in between. Kitchens changed radically during that gap between publications; for some households, skipping those six decades was a leap from open-fire hearth cooking to a tidy range powered by gas or electricity. What did Georgia recipes look like between Reconstruction and the First World War? I paid the one-dollar asking price and waited while the shop clerk carefully wrapped the battered cookbook in tissue paper. Now that I know the cooking adventures and history explorations it led to, it may have been the best dollar bill I ever spent.

That evening, I curled up on the sofa and unwrapped the parcel. The book in my hands was the personal possession of some unknown cook before me. *Who owned*

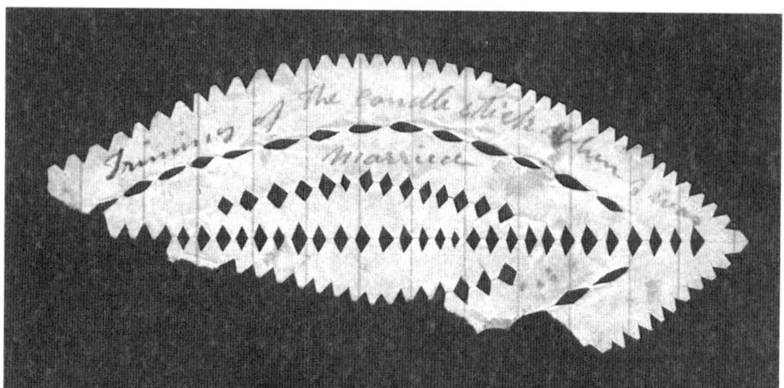

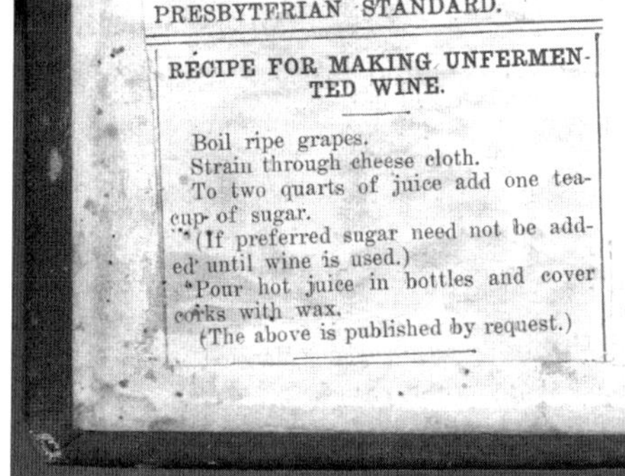

PRESBYTERIAN STANDARD.

RECIPE FOR MAKING UNFERMENTED WINE.

Boil ripe grapes.
Strain through cheese cloth.
To two quarts of juice add one teacup of sugar.
(If preferred sugar need not be added until wine is used.)
Pour hot juice in bottles and cover corks with wax.
(The above is published by request.)

Poverty Cake.
1 cup Cream
1 " Sugar
1 egg.
1 Teaspoon Cream Tartar
1 " " Soda
1 teaspoon Salt
2 cups flour
Nutmeg or Lemon

In my copy of the 1883 *Dixie Cook-Book,* I found ephemera, small clues about a life left by the previous owner, including recipes both loose and pasted inside the covers. And there was a five-inch handmade doily with a note penciled on it: "Trimming of the candle stick when I was married."

this? What did they cook and why? Sometimes an old cookbook offers clues—notes scrawled inside or loose recipes as bookmarks. With the Annie Dennis cookbook, I followed the page creases and cooking stains to find the recipes that the previous owner may have used most. Perhaps they shared my affinity for home baking, because the chocolate cake page was dotted with cocoa fingerprints.

Thankfully for chocolate cake lovers, a cookbook is a "re-createable source," one intent on reader participation. People with musical training can pick up century-old sheet music and re-create the sound of the past. For those with construction or sewing skills, old blueprints and clothing patterns can help re-create what our ancestors built or wore. Skills-wise, the most universal of these "re-createables" may be the recipe. Old cookbooks allow us to revive the chocolate cake shared at yesteryear's tables as well as other dishes so old that they seem new to us. Annie Dennis offered many familiar and classic baking recipes but also Sweet Potato Johnny Cake. Tiny cornmeal donuts called Jolly Boys. Savoy Cakes "of olden times" lightly flavored with lemon and coriander.

Hmm. What to try first?

Falling out of Favor . . . and Then Falling in Again

There's a sense of anticipation when picking up an unfamiliar cookbook. *Are these recipes I'll want to try? Will this cookbook become a favorite?* Perhaps you use a modern cookbook to make supper. If the process is smooth and the meal turns out well, you'll likely value the cookbook. It may even become "Ol' Reliable." Still, there's a slow-motion cookbook cycle. Our kitchen needs and interests evolve with changes in our lives. Food trends come and go. Technology and food science marches on. Once the recipes don't seem useful anymore, we may weed a cookbook out of our collection. Display tables at charity book sales fairly wobble under the weight of castoff cookbooks, including many that were quite popular when published. If your goal is to whip up a pleasing dinner or party food that isn't ho-hum, then using a contemporary cookbook that easily falls in line with familiar ingredients and tools in your contemporary kitchen simply makes sense. That is why even though I've lived much of my life within Georgia's borders, the name Annie Dennis was unfamiliar. State newspapers carried echoes of her cookbook, reprinted recipes or testimonials for half a century following her death, but eventually her legacy went quiet—especially in the years after World War II when much of the nation began to embrace convenience foods.

For those of us who like to cook, however, "easy peasy" or "riding the food trends" needn't be our only approaches to recipes and cookbooks. If a cookbook loses popularity, it doesn't mean that its usefulness is over. The oldest recipe in my family is for tea cakes made by my Arkansas great-great-grandmother, but it was brief and lacking detail.[1] Comparing it with similar recipes from nineteenth-century southern cookbooks helped me figure out the baking details—and opened my eyes to these sources. Largely forgotten by a society that in the mid-1900s seemingly turned toward cake mixes on the one hand or epicurean European recipes on the other extreme, older American cookbooks recorded flavors and techniques silently waiting to be rediscovered—summery rosewater instead of vanilla, homemade peach cordial brushed over pound cake, and toasted hickory nuts scattered across icing, to name a few. (If you aren't a baker, then perhaps you might explore old recipes for Sweet Apple Pickles, Scalloped Tomatoes, Hot Slaw, and dozens of takes on barbecue sauce . . .)

Every recipe I try isn't good simply because it is old, yet I do find some real pearls. Sometimes I am eager to reproduce the exact dish. At other times I use it as inspiration, trying the recipe's flavor combination or techniques to create a new dish with old roots. Whichever approach I use, there is always a pleasing sense of exploration. *How many years have passed since someone last tasted this?* It is a culinary exploit one can enjoy even while stuck at home on a rainy day. Many people love learning through international or gourmet recipes, yet never think to give historical recipes a try.

Through old cookbooks, I learned how to bake without chemical leavenings, appreciating the hard work of my foremothers even as I clicked on my stand mixer to complete what would have taken them another thirty minutes of arm-aching stirring.[2] I found that yesteryear's baked goods with quaint names like Sweet Wafers and Jumbles are unique best sellers at today's bake sale and conversation starters at tonight's dinner party. Many old recipes are refreshingly simple, calling for fewer ingredients than the recipes you'll find while thumbing through modern magazines in the grocery checkout line.[3] When I want to bake without having to go to the store first, I often reach for older cookbooks because they usually call for ingredients I already have in my pantry and fridge. And don't underestimate the charm of an old-fashioned cake atop an interesting plate from an antique store bargain bin.

Old cookbooks, however, offer more than nostalgia and curiosity. In these days of lightning-fast news sources and social media, we are used to paying attention to what is novel and groundbreaking, the latest best-selling cookbook, yet older recipes are finding their way into home kitchens again. Popular interest in foodways as a whole has taken off in recent years. Books such as David Kamp's *United States of Arugula: How We Became a Gourmet Nation* and Allen Salkin's *From Scratch: Inside the Food Network* outline how interest in food and cooking exploded in the late twentieth century. Food writers for print, podcasts, and documentary features often outline the history of specific ingredients, dishes, and food traditions. Increased interest means that many historical cookbooks are now revived as reprints, while originals tucked away in archives are being scanned and placed online so that they are just a few clicks away.[4]

In the last few years, social and ecological issues have also stirred interest. A resurgence of attention to historical cookbooks and household guides reflects modern homesteading, people craving self-reliance. The Slow Food Movement, credited to Italian Carlo Petrini in 1980, began with worries about the fast pace of modern life, respect for the links between food and health, plus an eye on sustainability for the sake of the environment and has now evolved into worldwide conferences.[5] California restaurant owner, cookbook author, and social activist Alice Waters is an example of an American working with similar ideas. Authors like Michael Pollan, Melanie Rehak, and Eric Schlosser explore the darker sides

Foodways

What are "foodways"? A simple answer is "the intersection of food and culture."[1] According to a folklore encyclopedia, "Foodways means nothing less than the full consideration of how food and culture intersect—what food says about the people who prepare and consume it and how culture shapes the dietary choices people make."[2] Foodways historian Marcie Cohen Ferris puts it this way: "Eating is a complicated activity that reveals who we are and where we come from, an activity that defines our race, gender, class, and religion."[3]

1. Brunvand, *American Folklore*, 299.
2. Green, *Folklore*, 367.
3. Ferris, *Matzoh Ball Gumbo*, 9.

of today's large-scale, mechanized food production, raising concerns that are becoming increasingly important to home cooks.[6] Also pointing toward change, articles about the future of agriculture highlight farms that embrace organics and low-impact technology—hydroponics, crop-specific LED lighting, high-yield smaller fields tended by drones, or "agritopias," suburban neighborhoods designed around garden plots supported by the latest developments in water and energy efficiency.[7] These models encourage fresh, local ingredients that work better with Annie Dennis's recipes than they do with the add-a-can-of-condensed-soup cookbooks many of us grew up with. Recipes from old cookbooks are worth bringing back into the kitchen.

History through Cookbooks

Old recipes improved my kitchen skills, but that wasn't all. They also helped me piece together how foodways in my state, region, and country evolved, creating a sense of rootedness I hadn't even realized I was missing. This began as curiosity due to the difference in publishing norms. Nowadays we expect to open a cookbook and learn details about the author's professional and personal life. In contrast, older cookbooks are often mysterious, revealing little about the people and places behind them.[8] Even with those offering lengthy passages of advice, learning more about the authors and their collections of recipes often begins with tombstones and census records.

Having become the owner of a Dennis cookbook, I was curious to understand the person behind the recipes, get a better idea of her culinary point of view. Using research skills from my days as a reference librarian and archivist, I made my way through period newspaper articles and other documents to discover that Dennis came of age just after the Civil War and her life testified to how much the social fabric of the South changed in the second half of the 1800s. Dennis not only learned to keep house with her own two hands but also traveled to enter her cooking in countless fairs, amassing over $10,000 in prize winnings worth over a quarter of a million dollars in today's money—a rare feat for a nineteenth-century woman.[9]

Cookbooks and Academia

In *The American Cookbook,* Carol Fisher lists thirty-five American institutions from Harvard to the Library of Congress actively collecting cookbooks. How are these materials used? Diane Tye and Janet Theophano are examples of scholars who have written about recipes from a folklore point of view.[1] Researcher Colleen Cotter uses them to explore linguistics.[2] Recipes preserve the cooking expertise of families, and thus are helpful to genealogists. Women's studies academics such as Elizabeth Engelhardt value cookbooks written for women by women as well as the clues they hold about women's lives back when men's pursuits were far more likely to be documented.[3] Historian Jessamyn Neuhaus examines cookbooks for changing ideas about gender.[4] Social historians may use cookbooks to explore what everyday life was like in the past. (In fact, *The Public Historian* dedicated a whole issue to foodways and recipes.[5]) As scholar Alan Grubb put it, "For historians, particularly social historians, these nineteenth-century cookery and household books may actually be most valuable, for they represent a kind of 'populist' literature and enable us to observe the household from within, as those who had the responsibility for domestic tasks experienced things, showing how industrialization altered women's work, how technology and science changed domestic economy, and how political events or wars affected new ideas about women's roles."[6]

1. Tye, *Baking as Biography*; Theophano, *Eat My Words*.
2. Cotter, "Claiming a Piece of the Pie."
3. Engelhardt, *A Mess of Greens*.
4. Neuhaus, *Manly Meals and Mom's Home Cooking*.
5. *Public Historian* 34.2 (May 2012).
6. Grubb, "House and Home in the Victorian South," 159.

THE NEW SOUTH

COOK BOOK

TESTED AND PROVED RECIPES

CONTRIBUTED BY

ROME HOUSEKEEPERS

COMPILED BY

The Ladies' Aid Society

—OF—

The First Presbyterian Church

ROME, GEORGIA

1905
T. E. CLEMENT, PRINTER,
ROME, GEORGIA.

COOK BOOK

PIES AND PASTRY

"I wish," he said, "You could make pies
Like mother use to bake."
"And I," said she, "wish that you made
The dough pa used to make."

Old cookbooks may include illustrations showing fads and fashions of yesteryear, yet many are without images. Still, the layout and typefaces of a cookbook (like this title page from the collection of Cynthia Graubart) can offer a visual "flavor" of its era. And the occasional inspirational quotation or joke (as in the *Service Star Legion Cook Book* [1927], 103) reminds us there were real people behind each cookbook.

Then there was the sense of place behind Dennis's recipes. We know that foodways aren't the same across the South; cuisine from the lowland international port of New Orleans is different in some ways from what you'll find on the secluded slopes of the Appalachians. Although the differences may be less pronounced, foodways aren't the same across the varied landscapes of Georgia, either—and that was even more true during the days of the state's early cookbooks, before easy travel and mass communication spread recipes and encouraged the blending of traditions. Thus, when a family trip took me to the western portion of the state, I made a side jaunt down Pine Mountain, through woods and past logged open spaces to visit Dennis's hometown. I found Talbotton sleepy yet appealing. The house where Dennis lived still stands, a Greek Revival with a wide porch overlooking what is now a highway. A sprinkling of historical markers led me to sites that would have been familiar to Dennis, teaching me more about my home state.

A Deeper Sense of Early Georgia

In her essay "What Is Southern?" the Virginia chef, educator, and cookbook author Edna Lewis (1916–2006), who lived in Atlanta for more than a decade, wrote:

> The world has changed. We are now faced with picking up the pieces and trying to put them into shape, document them so the present-day young generation can see what southern food was like.

Turning northward, I visited the Atlanta History Center's Clifford A. Shillinglaw Cookbooks collection to see Dennis's 1894 first edition. A long-ago-pressed flower is nestled below the Stewed 'Possum recipe on page 184. In contrast to the delicate blossom and newspaper accounts of refined Miss Dennis, she advised readers on the stark realities of preparing this live wild animal for the table.[10] I glimpsed a past somehow both genteel and no-nonsense. I also discovered additional cookbooks whose authors were closely connected with our state—lifelong Georgians, as well as cooks who spent just parts of their lives here. As with finding the Dennis cookbook, this was eye-opening. These sources preserved historical foodways by recording traditions, trends, and innovations. Once upon a time I figured that if Georgia had more old cookbooks than the previously mentioned works from 1867 and 1928, I would have found a list somewhere. Now I realized that there were enough cookbooks to make a list, and that it was up to me to compile it.

Additional early cookbooks and recipes are indeed out there, representing a wide swath of old Georgia from the Low Country to above the Piedmont, the cultured cities to the quiet back roads. Before starting this search, I'd read a good deal about Georgia history, but now my state's old recipes and household guides brought yesteryear's home life into focus. The politicians and the war generals, the front-page-of-the-newspaper events and the key dates receded into the background as I instead thought about farmer and cook, garden and blackberry thicket, hearth and mixing bowl. I tried my hand at old-fashioned kitchen tasks, re-creating the textures, scents, and tastes of a Georgia I never knew.

The book you now hold in your hands was coming together. I'd already read many old American cookbooks, so it was intriguing that foodways trends I'd seen elsewhere were echoed in my home state. And I was quickly learning that old recipes reach their full potential only with appreciation for the people, places, events, and culture attached to them. I let that guide this book project, which I can best

explain using a baker's analogy. Research can sometimes be akin to granulated white sugar—boiled down to the pure crystalline facts. Yet although white sugar is a key baking ingredient, one isn't tempted by a spoonful. Brown sugar, however, retains enough complex molasses flavor that my son appears in the kitchen to sneak a lump whenever he hears our canister snap open.[11] The cookbooks and recipes discussed in this book are carefully researched, yet I left in some of the flavor that makes these sources fun to explore—smatterings of travels across Georgia, interesting coincidences, funny quotes, mysteries to be pondered, and glimpses of long-gone cookbook authors as real, breathing human beings.

The location and date of this image, purchased at an antique store in Lavonia, are unknown, yet its unusual overview of the various outbuildings shows how complex a farm could be.

The authors of Georgia's historical cookbooks include widows, "bachelor girls," and more than one divorcée (back when such things were scandalous). Through recipes and related documents, I met a statesman-turned-chain-gang-prisoner, society ladies pondering woman's suffrage, and an orphan who grew up to be an inventor as well as a nationally published "poetess." And, of course, I found the lure that turns family history sleuths into dedicated genealogists; looking into the lives of these authors brought up intriguing side stories including Georgia's Great Locomotive Chase, lighthouse ghost tales, and the sinking of the *Titanic*, to name a few. Taking Sunday drives to retrace the steps of Georgia's early cookbook authors meant visiting out-of-the-way towns, forgotten springs still flowing, vast peach orchards blushing pink with blooms, and a child's grave high on a hill with a sweeping view of the distant blue mountains.

Although sometimes the biographical details for Georgia's early cookbook authors are a matter of clues and hints rather than concrete answers, these individuals can inspire. Neither becoming a culinary expert nor writing a book is easy. Although not all the Georgia-related authors were female, the majority were, and their publications were at a time when books written by women were relatively few and the idea of a "career woman" was questionable at best. Interestingly, most of the authors seemed to turn to the kitchen due to hardship. These authors lived by their unique versions of what my grandpa might have called "gumption." Not only was I personally inspired by their stories, but I also learned more about the history of my home state, and my baking repertoire expanded in delicious ways.

This Book as a Recipe Pathfinder

My career blended well with my kitchen interests, so let me briefly explain how that led to the book you now hold in your hands. Long before I heard of Annie Dennis, I earned a graduate degree in Information Science and my vita includes the former roles of Junior Fellow in the Manuscripts Division of the Library of Congress (Washington, D.C.), Manuscripts Archivist at the Georgia Historical Society (Savannah), and Education Coordinator at the Georgia Archives (Morrow, Atlanta area).[12] I also served as president for the Society of Georgia Archivists, with duties that took me to quite a few of the state's special collection libraries. Wherever work took me, I'd take a little free time during my lunch hour to search reading rooms for old recipes.

Once this book project was officially under way, I went about research methodically. Nevertheless, serendipity played a role. Years before the discovery of Annie Dennis, I scribbled notes whenever I stumbled upon recipes while helping researchers or processing manuscript collections. Knowing I loved historical cookery, kind colleagues shared their discoveries as well. Outside of work,

I frequented estate sales, used book sales, yard sales, and the like, discovering some amazing materials.[13] Since providence was part of the process, how can I be sure I found every key historical Georgia cookbook and recipe? I can't. Through collection-building and scanning efforts in Georgia's archival institutions as well as historians publishing new findings, the past is over and yet never finished. I am hoping this book is just the beginning; I'm looking forward to researchers and foodways lovers turning up Georgia recipe treasures not evident during my own research.

Speaking of research, let me explain the intent of this book. While serving as Education Coordinator at the Georgia Archives, I taught as a guest in many schools. I would research interesting primary sources to bring into the classroom and then guide students in the question "What can we learn from this document?" The goal was not to learn everything about the given document nor to reach conclusions, but to explore each source for something compelling or useful it could tell us about the past. This book approaches recipes and cookbooks in a similar way. It does not catalog essential ingredients, identify classic dishes, or define Georgia foodways, but it will guide you to sources you need should this be your interest.

When it comes to finding foodways sources, experience helps. The longer an archivist works at an institution, the better known its historical collections and reference sources become. For this reason, reference staff often create "pathfinders," annotated lists that lead researchers to materials on a given topic. For instance, an archives might offer a "Genealogy Pathfinder" or a "Property Records Pathfinder." Although this book isn't limited to the sources at one institution, it serves as a pathfinder for Georgia's historical recipes—while including 210 reprinted recipes to whet your appetite figuratively and literally.

The section you're reading right now serves as an introduction. The next section gives tips to help you cook with old recipes. The third section offers a historian's view of cookbooks. After that, you're into the core material—fifty sections that explore either single recipes or whole cookbooks. The latter sections are more in-depth, offering background information that make a cookbook's recipes meaningful as a collection. The fifty core sections are arranged chronologically. Some fit into a time slot better than others, but overall, this approach builds an understanding of how Georgia foodways changed over time. The final section takes us to 1944. Every book needs a cutoff point, and after World War II Georgia kitchens were impacted by a marked increase in travel, mass communication, and convenience foods. Publishing also increased, so there are wonderful Georgia cookbooks after this point, but they usually look more familiar to modern readers and are easier to find.

Whatever your interests in old recipes, this book-length pathfinder can be helpful to you as a reader, a culinary adventurer, or a foodways researcher. In the words of food historian Kay Moss, "There is so much to learn and so many delightful surprises in store through attempting to work in our ancestors' mind-set. Culinary exploration brings new joy to our palates as we seek pure flavors from an ancestral dinner plate."[14]

So come join the journey. Read on and taste Georgia's past.

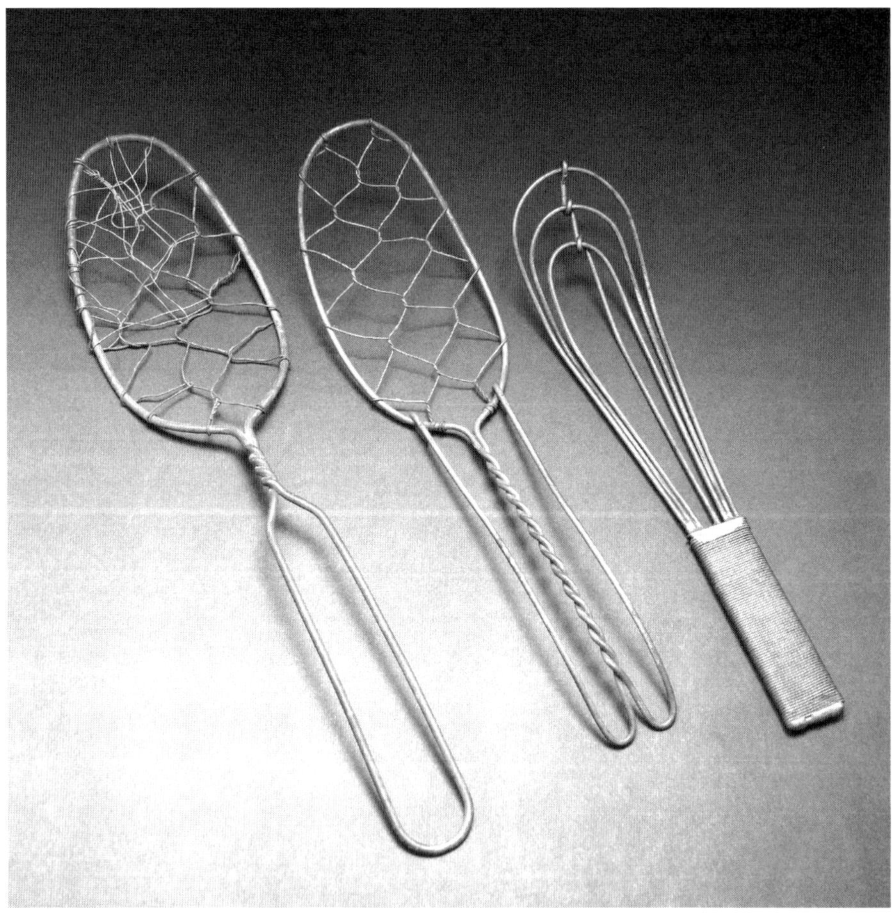

Recipes in Context I

Old Recipes in Your Modern Kitchen

Corn Starch Cake

One package corn starch, six eggs, three-fourths each butter and sugar. Flavor with lemon.
—A. Roberts, *Drummers' Home Cook Book*, 97

The recipe above, a mere eighteen words, appeared in a 1902 Georgia cookbook. Could you use it to turn out a cake? An old recipe allows us to make a dish from yesteryear reappear with all its sensory pleasures—but this is only true if you have enough information to make that recipe work in your own kitchen! Unfortunately, some older recipes read like one expert cook chatting to another over the back fence, leaving out details they feel sure the other knows. Even if you are an expert cook, outdated language or methods can be puzzling. So how do you turn a sparse or tricky old recipe into something useful?

First, explore any ingredients and cooking terms you don't know. The Internet gives old recipe lovers a huge advantage that didn't exist a few decades ago, allowing cooks to easily define recipe vocabulary, find images of old utensils, watch kitchen technique videos, and track down needed items. We can even enjoy accounts by history-buff bloggers working with older recipes.[1] As for print sources, the bibliography at the back of this book contains many helpful ones. In particular, cookbooks by contemporary Georgia authors Shirley O. Corriher and Alton Brown explore the science behind cooking and thus are great sources for understanding what is going on in a recipe.[2]

The second step is to find comparison recipes, putting the confusing recipe in a working context. For the "recipe puzzle" above, comparing it with cake recipes in general and with cornstarch cake and lemon cake recipes in particular can help you determine how much cornstarch, if the "three-fourths" measurements are pounds or cups (since early American recipes were sometimes by weight rather than volume), whether it is best to utilize the zest, juice, or both from the lemon, and the method required to successfully turn the ingredients into a cake. If the comparison process becomes unwieldy, food historian Kay Moss helpfully suggests creating a simple table, as seen in the sidebar.[3] Some testing and tweaking will likely be necessary, but many recipe mysteries can be solved in this way.

Corn Starch Cakes from Early Georgia Cookbooks

Recipe Title	*Corn Starch*	*Flour*	*Eggs*	*Butter*	*Sugar*	*Milk*	*Baking Powder*	*Flavoring*	*Instructions?*	*Source*	*Notes*
Corn Starch Cake	¾ pound	3 table-spoons	6, beaten separately	½ pound	1 pound			"to taste"	No	Hill, 1872, 287.	"Bake in small shapes or cups."
Corn Starch Cake	¾ pound		8	½ pound	¾ pound			Lemon	No	*Choice Recipes*, 1880, 71.	
Alpine Snow Cake	2 cups	2 cups	15 whites	1 cup	3 cups	1 cup sweet		Rose water	No	Tennent, 1885, 118.	
Snow Cake	1 cup	2 cups	8 whites	1 cup	2 cups		2 teaspoons		No	Dennis, 1894, 231.	
Governor Northen Cake	1 cup	2 cups	8 whites	1 cup	2 cups	1 cup sweet	2 tablespoons Horsford's		Yes	Wilson, 1895, 52.	Includes icing recipe.
Cornstarch Cake	1 cup	2 cups	7 whites	¾ cup	2 cups	1 cup sweet	1 teaspoon	Lemon	Yes	*Home Cook Book*, 1898, 136.	
Corn Starch Cake	1 package		6	¾ (?)	¾ (?)			Lemon	No	Roberts, 1902, 97.	
Governor Northen's White Cake	1 cup	2 cups	8 whites	1 cup white butter	2 cups	1 cup sweet	2 tablespoons		Yes	Colquitt, 1933, 134.	Has been used since 1880.

Old Cookbooks and the Kitchen

The last thing you want to do with a rare cookbook is take it into the kitchen where food flecks, water, and steam will take their toll. Even handling an old cookbook too often can hasten its demise. With my old and fragile cookbooks, I take digital pictures of each page. I can then use the recipes on an electronic device or print a copy to take into the kitchen.

Authenticity

Many readers are satisfied experimenting with old recipes. Some, however, seek authenticity. Are the ingredients the same as when the recipe was written, and can you be relatively sure the finished dish closely resembles what the cookbook author intended? And still one step further—do you want to use the same tools and cooking methods that were common when the recipe originated? To whatever degree you approach authenticity, the bibliography contains many helpful sources to help you get in step with older ways of cooking. And let me give you a little encouragement . . .

While researching *Preserving Family Recipes*, I became fascinated with hearth cooking, yet the kitchen tools were baffling. *Spiders and salamanders that aren't critters? A gridiron that isn't a football field?* And the required skills seemed near magical. *Baking without an oven or thermometer? Wrangling live coals?!* Interviewing historical reenactor cook Dennis Cotner at Colonial Williamsburg in Virginia helped. "It's just a matter of developing sensibilities," he explained.[4] He used a bathtub analogy: "You put your fingers in the tap water flowing into the tub and you understand whether it will feel warm enough for the rest of your body. You developed that sensibility." He went on to explain that the hearth is about developing cooking sensibilities concerning fire and coals added to working knowledge about ingredients, fuels, and which tools are right for the task at hand. Hearth cooks could capture and concentrate heat with a variety of implements, such as the boxlike reflecting oven or "tin kitchen" placed in front of the fire. Other tools like cranes, spits, hooks, and trammels helped cooks adjust how close the food was to the heat, while shovels, tongs, and rims on pot lids would allow a cook to place coals where they were needed. (By the way, a *spider* is a

Old Recipes and Common Sense

Old recipes are fantastic, but current food science should always be applied. For instance, unpasteurized dairy products or uncooked eggs may harbor harmful bacteria. Bitter almonds and peach pits, once used as flavorings, contain traces of substances that break down into hydrocyanic acid, a poison to humans if eaten in large enough amounts. (In 1875, dozens of guests were poisoned by peach kernels at a wedding in Dalton.)[1] Poke salat/sallet, the young greens of the American pokeweed plant, has been consumed in Georgia for centuries but must be collected and prepared properly to avoid toxins. The berries of this plant are always poisonous, yet *The Dixie Cook-Book* of 1883 calls for using them as food coloring.[2] *If an old recipe calls for an unfamiliar ingredient, research it well before you use it.*

Similarly, older food preservation methods may not be safe, potentially causing serious illness. Safe pickling and canning processes, for instance, may depend on the acidity of the produce you're working with, and some fruits and vegetables (as well as vinegars) may have a different pH level than the varieties handled by cookbook authors of yesteryear. *Use only up-to-date food preservation guidelines*. If you have questions, contact the National Center for Home Food Preservation, located at the University of Georgia in Athens.[3] Your county's Cooperative Extension office is also a helpful source.[4]

Finally, many older cookbooks contain recipes for household compounds, medicines, and "cures." Some we may laughingly dismiss, such as a recipe for "Durable Ink" I came across in the Alexander Means collection at Emory University that was so faded I could barely read it.[5] But be extremely cautious. Some could cause severe injury or poisoning.

Old kitchenware may be made of materials that react chemically with certain ingredients or that leach unhealthy substances. Or, as can be seen with this whisk, protective coatings may be wearing off. For food safety and to preserve artifacts, use old kitchenware with caution.

1. *Augusta Constitutionalist*, 8 October 1875.
2. Wilcox, *The Dixie Cook-Book*, Easter Jelly recipe, 184.
3. Contact the Center at https://nchfp.uga.edu.
4. Find your county's office at https://extension.uga.edu.
5. Manuscript, Emory, MSS 151, Box 2.

Beware Old Cookbook Remedies

Consumption [Tuberculosis]

Get the sawdust from rich pine wood, and cover with corn whisky. After forty eight hours, strain and take half a teaspoonful when the cough is troublesome. There are thousands of Georgians who have an unshaken faith in this remedy, and say it has restored to health many almost on the confines of another world.

—Tennent, *House-Keeping in the Sunny South* (1885), 219

Frost Bite

Bathe the affected parts in warm beef pickle.

—Edgeworth, *Southern Gardener and Receipt Book* (1859), 286

Gout

The best cure for the gout is to apply a leek poultice to the part affected.

—Edgeworth, *Southern Gardener and Receipt Book* (1859), 318

Gravel [Kidney Stone]

Drink strong coffee, without sugar or milk. This dissolves the gravel, and allows it to pass off, with very little pain.

—Edgeworth, *Southern Gardener and Receipt Book* (1859), 314

Nail Wound

A sure cure for a wound caused by a rusty nail, is the smoke from burning woolen rags.

—Wesleyan College Alumnae, *Macon Cook Book* (1912), 16

Nose Bleed

Two large cylinders of bacon were forced well up in the nostrils, resulting in the almost immediate relief, and an entire cessation of the hemorrhage.

—*Annie Dennis' Cook Book* (1894), 342

Scarlet Fever

Rub the patient night and morning with fat bacon, rubbing every part of the body but the head slowly and carefully.

—*Mrs. Hill's New Cook Book* (1867), 377

Snake Bite

Drink strong whisky without sugar or water. It is said that intoxication is impossible under the circumstances.

—Tennent, *House-Keeping in the Sunny South* (1885), 221

[Watering Eyes]

To prevent discomfort to the eyes from chopping raw onions, place a piece of lightbread under the upper lip, pressed close to the nose.

—Wesleyan College Alumnae, *Macon Cook Book* (1912), 12

Where a Person is Insensible from a Fall or Blow Upon the Head [Concussion]

Put a mustard plaster on the back of the neck and extremities; rub briskly; then bathe the part with hot vinegar.

—*Mrs. Hill's New Cook Book* (1867), 389

frying pan with long legs that allow it to straddle coals. A *salamander* is a metal tool that can be heated to brown food. Due to a strong resemblance, the American football field is nicknamed after the *gridiron*, a rectangular grill sometimes also used as a trivet.)

I couldn't imagine how I'd get hands-on practice to build and hone skills—until my son became a Cub Scout. On our first family campout at Rainey Mountain, I found people baking cakes in cast iron Dutch ovens and debating the merits of various types of fuel woods. A few even built backyard fire pits for practice. Indeed, camp cooking and even the common barbecue grill offer ways to build many of the same skills our ancestors used at the hearth or with woodburning stoves. Camping cookbooks abound, and many are quite good, but I've enjoyed skipping the aluminum foil tricks to instead match my skills to history. Suzanne Goldenson's *Open-Hearth Cookbook: Recapturing the Flavor of Early America* is a favorite guide.

And then there's the joy of stepping up to a historical hearth or reenactment campfire, watching an adept cook work and having a chance to ask questions. Sometimes historical reenactment societies, house museums, or homesteading groups hold events offering such chances.[5] Clarissa Clifton, author of *One Hearth, One Pot: For the Love of Food and History*, encourages simply asking to participate: "'May I volunteer to cook in your kitchen?' That is all it takes."[6] That one question launched her history-based cooking career at the Atlanta History Center and Roswell's Smith Plantation.[7]

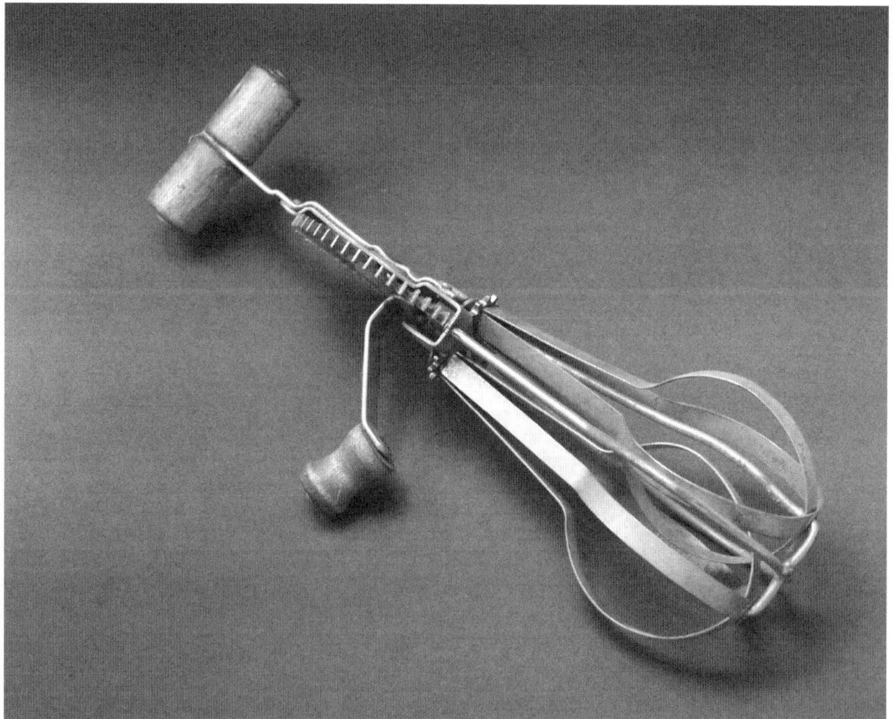

Recipes in Context II

Cookbooks as History

This section helps readers look at older cookbooks and recipe collections with a historian's eye. This can be particularly helpful if you have an old cookbook you'd like to understand better. As you skim through one, keep in mind three basic questions:

1. What ingredients and cooking tools did the author assume were available?
2. What ingredients, cooking methods, and dishes in this cookbook later fell from common use?
3. Which of today's popular ingredients and dishes don't yet appear?

These questions help us compare old cookbooks with those of contemporary times. Similar questions can be used to compare cookbooks of various time periods. For instance, we can compare Annie Dennis's end-of-the-nineteenth-century Georgia recipes with earlier ones from Mary Edgeworth (1859), Annabella Hill (1867), or Ella Tennent (1885). Or, in the other direction, we can compare Dennis's recipes with later ones by Henrietta Dull (1928), who was hired by Atlanta Gas Light to promote technical advances in the kitchen. Then-versus-now questions help build a better understanding of how Georgia foodways evolved over time.

Similarly, here-versus-there questions can help us understand Georgia foodways in relation to American foodways. Dennis was writing in the same general period as northeastern cooks Fannie Farmer, Maria Parloa, and Sarah Tyson Rorer. How are their recipes alike or different? Narrowing the geographic scope to our own region, how do the ingredients, cooking methods, and dishes in Dennis's work compare with what can be found in cookbooks from other parts of the South? Authors such as Theresa Brown (South Carolina), Marion Cabell Tyree (Virginia), Abby Fisher (Alabama), and Lafcadio Hearn (Louisiana) also shared their visions of southern cooking in the last quarter of the nineteenth century.

The here-versus-there comparisons can be focused even more tightly. For a magazine article about old desserts, I used the *Tested Recipe Cook Book* to find recipes matching the magazine's Northeast Georgia distribution area.[1] (See 1895 section.) That cookbook lists contributor name and town for the recipes, so I skimmed through nineteenth-century census and tax records. These sources once would have required hours squinting at microfilm, but now they can be found and read easily from a home computer.[2] As I learned more about the contributors, patterns began to surface about desserts offered by middle-class households as opposed to those of the well-to-do. Some types of desserts were more popular in urban areas versus rural ones. Comparing just a few recipes doesn't give enough information to draw conclusions, but it encourages us to look for forgotten trends and traditions.

One important thing to keep in mind with cookbooks is that they are ultimately prescriptive rather than descriptive.[3] In other words, they show us home life in their time and place, but it is filtered through the author or compiler. Cookbooks record what the cookbook authors thought should be done or eaten, what they thought their readers would (or should) want and use. The questions we are about to explore will help you get a grasp on the mindset behind a particular cookbook.

Creation Patterns of Historical Cookbooks

Cookbooks can be loosely grouped into five categories based on how they were created, and this helps us to better understand the recipes. Keep in mind that a cookbook may fit into more than one category:

1. **Personal Cookbooks**: Some historical cookbooks are collections of recipes gathered by a person or family simply for home use. Archivists and historians have various names for these—commonplace books, household books, manuscript cookbooks. Before it was possible to log on to the Internet or zip to the library, these volumes were a cook's way of having timely information to run a household. My rural Arkansas grandmother kept such a book,

recording previously unwritten recipes from her mother and relatives.[4] Cookbooks were available, but as a new bride living in an isolated farmhouse not yet outfitted with a phone, she wanted to remember how to make family favorites. The recipes on those pages reflected her needs, tastes, and social interactions. The notebook also reflected her learning curve as a cook: early pages held basic recipes, while later recipes were more complex as she expanded her repertoire.

Literate housekeepers collected recipes from family, friends, and neighbors for foods as well as medicines and household compounds such as cleaning products, insecticides, and dyes. Some recipes were clipped from periodicals, a practice encouraged by newspapers by the late 1800s. Early recipe collections were usually in bound notebooks or ledgers, but before the turn of the twentieth century, recipe boxes became popular, as they could be easily reorganized and edited.[5] Regardless of format, recipe collections were often passed from one generation to the next. Recipe collections can be of great research value, particularly if they hold information from minority groups.

Sadly, my grandmother's handwritten cookbook accidentally slid into the burn barrel when they were disposing of household trash, and it still pains me to think of foodways knowledge literally going up in smoke. Doubtless many personal cookbooks have been lost when too close to a burner or in the spill zone of a tipped pot. Others may have been tossed out when a cook died or the recipes seemed outdated. Some of these personal cookbooks, however, survive and have found their way into archives so that they are available for research. Some from Georgia are available in print. *The Thirteen Colonies Cookbook*, published near the national bicentennial, adapted recipes from

Preserving Your Family Foodways

If you think you may have materials of historical interest, an archival repository can preserve materials while making them safely available to family members and other researchers. (And no family fights about who inherits what; everyone will have equal access.) The Society of Georgia Archivists website (https://soga.wildapricot.org) can help put you in touch with someone to talk to about the donation process. In the meantime, store historical materials in folders and cardboard boxes that are acid-free in a climate-controlled space with no direct light. Tape and plastic lamination should never be used on historical materials.

a volume kept by the prominent Telfair family of Savannah.[6] (See 1774 section.) And the Atlanta Historical Society published a compilation of older recipes called *Tullie's Receipts* that shared transcript recipes from personal cookbooks and scrapbooks.[7]

2. **Curated Cookbooks**: The majority of cookbooks found in your local library or bookstore are curated. Here's an analogy. A museum curator works with objects in a collection, seeing that each piece is worthwhile, properly cared for, and well showcased. The curator also manages the collection as a whole—describing how the pieces work together, seeking new artifacts to fill gaps, weeding out items no longer needed, as well as defining and promoting the entire collection. This role is not unlike the role of cookbook authors with their recipes. Food historian John Van Willigen states, "Cookbooks are a distillation of what those writers know about cooking and nutrition and what they think is important."[8] We may assume that most of the recipes were created by the authors or else were adopted and then further developed by them. As we will explore later, this is sometimes not the case.

   Annie Dennis's work is a good example of a curated cookbook from Georgia. In 1904 the *Atlanta Constitution* called Annie Dennis's cookbook

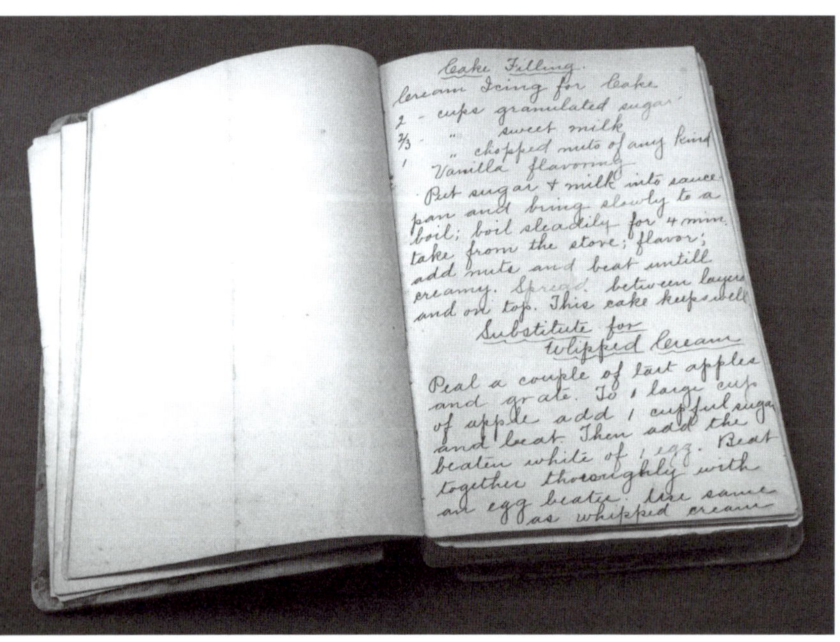

The personal cookbook pictured here (and on page ii with grape recipes) came from an Athens book sale. Unfortunately, there is no information about the creator or their location. Adding notes to family recipes helps future generations make sense of foodways.

"the only real Southern Cook Book," while the *Atlanta Journal* said, "It is the cook book of today."[9] Evolving over seven editions and almost three decades, Dennis's work outlined her vision of what southern food should be at a time when Georgia was rapidly changing.[10] Now, more than a century later, her cookbooks give us a historical glimpse into the past.

3. **Community or Compiled Cookbooks**: You might think of this type of cookbook as one of those paperback cookbooks with the plastic comb binding. The appearance and format, however, can vary a great deal. Places of worship, schools, hobby or social clubs, and other groups create such cookbooks, which can be anything from thin booklets to fancy hardcover volumes. (See 1898 section.)

   To create community cookbooks, there is a recipe-gathering and curation process, but often accomplished by a committee rather than an individual. Usually the charitable cookbook is a one-time endeavor, although some of these cookbooks become quite well known and go through many reprints or editions. Some recipes are tested before publication, but likely many are not. Recipes are often in the donor's words, although some are edited. By comparing recipes in a compiled cookbook, a reader can generally get a sense of how much editing was done from how much the writing styles or "voices" of the recipes differ—format, tone, length, et cetera. Many community cookbooks are intended for local audiences and are sold in a limited region. Some, however, become quite popular, such as *Savannah Style*, sold by the thousands by the Junior League of Savannah and well known throughout the South.

   As far as my research has uncovered, Georgia's earliest community cookbook is *Choice Recipes of Georgia Housekeepers* from Augusta in 1880. In the 1890s, additional community cookbooks appeared in Athens, Atlanta, Hapeville, and Savannah. After the turn of the century, the popularity of such cookbooks in Georgia (and elsewhere) exploded.

4. **Selective Cookbooks**: A selective cookbook is limited in some way, largely predetermining what will or won't be included—for instance, a cookbook created solely using one family's recipes or showcasing the dishes of a specific restaurant. The cookbook author or editor may simply share an existing recipe collection rather than developing one. Alice Roberts's 1902 *Drummers' Home Cook Book* offering recipes celebrating her Sparta hotel is one Georgia example.

5. **Advertising Cookbooks**: Advertising cookbooks are created with sales in mind—an ingredient (such as baking powder), kitchen equipment (such as a stove), or even the idea of "home" (such as in recipe booklets given out by a furniture store, realty office, or utility company). Some advertising cookbooks are curated by food professionals, yet many of them are uncredited. Some are reproduced for many clients, and thus a cookbook may be a giveaway for a real estate company in Georgia while it is offered with an altered cover by another company in another state. Trying to ascertain where the recipes originated can be difficult. One Georgia example, *The Way to a Man's Heart*, offered by the Savannah Gas Company, was introduced in 1938. Similarly, sometime before World War II the Dixie Canner Company of Athens released the undated cookbook *Home Canning and Cooking the Dixie Way*, which went through at least eight editions. By the 1940s another prolific producer of cookbooklets was Life Insurance Company of Georgia, started in Atlanta in 1891. Alabama cooking expert Winifred Rothermel (1901–1987) edited various editions of the *Life of Georgia Cook Book*. (See also 1916 section.)

   The lines between types of cookbooks are often blurred. A curated cookbook may be created by more than one author and, like Dennis's work, contain recipes from others. Community cookbooks may have a lead editor, such as the *Tested Recipe Cook Book* by Mary Wilson for the Cotton States and International Exposition of 1895. The point is not to force a cookbook into one category but to use these patterns to think about recipe origins, how a cookbook developed, and what you can learn.

Helpful Questions about Historical Cookbooks

Author

- Who wrote this cookbook? How might their gender, age, religious affiliation, race, education level, and social status have affected their expertise and writing?
- What does the author reveal about their perspectives on foodways and domestic life?
- Where and how did the author build their cooking expertise?

- Do the recipes reflect the author's life at the time of publication, or do they represent an earlier period in their life?

Audience

- Who is the intended audience?
- How does the author approach their audience; do they simply share recipes, or do they seek to teach and guarantee kitchen success?[11]
- Are there themes found in the cookbook? Examples might be sharing heritage, capturing regional foodways, promoting specific ingredients, or encouraging thrift.
- Are the recipes primarily for everyday foods or for dishes meant to impress with skill, effort, presentation, innovation, rarity, or the cost of ingredients?

Recipes

- Where did the recipes come from? How were they compiled and adjusted?
- Were the recipes fine-tuned over multiple editions? How?
- How do the ingredients, methods, or language of this cookbook differ from others of the same time or location?
- How do the ingredients, methods, or language of this cookbook differ from cookbooks of other times or places?
- Do the recipes reflect industrialization and globalization? In other words, are many of the ingredients ready-made from a factory or called for by brand name? Would the ingredients require shipping from another region?

In the words of folklorist Janet Theophano,

> For some, cookbooks are utilitarian references; for others, they are art objects especially if they are rare documents. Yet the allure of the cookbook is both its mystery and its concreteness. It requires of us, its readers, an imaginative leap. We must cross divides of time, space, and self. For many of us, reading a cookbook is like following a sensate trail to another world remote in space and time.[12]

A Few Details about This Book

Names

The authors of Georgia's oldest cookbooks would find it shockingly informal that at times I discuss them using their first names, but sometimes it is necessary. Several of them changed surnames multiple times, plus discussing their lives involves referring to spouses or other relatives with the same last name. I hope my readers will excuse this liberty.

When discussing racial or ethnic groups, it can be difficult to identify the most respectful words to use. Preferred terms change over time, and even individuals within a group may disagree. I hope all readers will find consideration and equality on these pages.

Sections

Each section is assigned a date so that our discussion of Georgia foodways can move forward in a chronological fashion. Please note, however, that supplementary images and recipes were chosen not by date but to support the topics discussed.

Recipes

The recipes are unedited, allowing readers to interpret spellings, punctuation, and other details for themselves. With very old recipes, I rarely note unusual spellings with the Latin "[*sic*]," as it would clutter them. I do use this indicator with later recipes where an unconventional spelling may be jarring. Manuscript recipes appear transcribed line-by-line, as this is standard archival practice and recipe writers sometimes relied on a fresh line to stand in for punctuation.

It was difficult to narrow down recipes to include. Although some are for classic southern fare, I tried to pick recipes that seem unusual in some way to interest modern readers. Admittedly, there are many sauce recipes, as I have found these can be easy, versatile, and stretch nicely to allow many people to have a taste. (Plum Pudding turned up as the oldest legible recipe in several collections, which at least gives us a chance to compare them.) If you don't find a variety of recipes to please you in the text, know that this book will help you find thousands of others.

I have tried many but certainly not all the recipes included.

Recipes for the Teaching

There are many recipes in this book that would work well in a classroom or at a historical venue. Wafers in particular are fascinating, as they are different from most modern cookies and each person can take a turn cooking one. (See 1864 and 1895 sections.) If you need a quick group cooking activity that doesn't require a heat source and is safe for all ages, try making butter (1783 section), some of the picnic recipes (1840 section), or the Orange Drops recipe (1898 section). Please avoid the Chatham Artillery Punch.

Missing Recipes

Of all the tasks associated with writing this book, securing copyright permissions was the most difficult. Descendants of cooks and authors are difficult to find. Companies change names, are bought out, or vanish. With manuscripts, even archival institutions holding the originals may be unsure who holds the copyright. Cookbooks and recipes not yet legally in the public domain are sometimes "orphans" with no one left to make copyright decisions on their behalf, thus some of the recipes I discuss could not be reprinted. I recommend searching the Internet to see if you can find a copy for personal use.

Availability of Older Cookbooks

OCLC's WorldCat is a helpful online tool for finding a library or archives with a print copy of a cookbook you'd like to see.[1] (ArchiveGrid helps with documents.)[2] The Atlanta History Center, the Georgia Historical Society (Savannah), and the University of Georgia (Athens) have particularly strong collections of older cookbooks. In Georgia, we're lucky to have the PINES system from the Georgia Public Library Service connecting 300 libraries in 146 counties, and their online catalog can help you locate materials.[3] Some old Georgia cookbooks in the public domain (copyright-free) have been scanned and are available online. Search for these using title, author, and the words "full text." Print-on-demand companies are quick to offer reprinted versions for sale through online booksellers. Regular booksellers can order recent reprints from mainstream publishers for you. A bookseller specializing in used and rare books, however, will likely be needed for significantly older titles. For general information about cookbooks and historical foodways, two helpful online tools are *The Sifter* and *The Food Timeline*.[4]

Images

Unless otherwise noted, all images were taken by the author even if permission to print them came from an institution. The kitchen objects pictured are from the collection of the author except where indicated. The majority were purchased in Georgia. It should not be assumed, however, that all the items originated in Georgia.

1733

What Ingredients Did the Georgia Colonists Have?

"Chocolate."
"A book."
"Playing cards."

During my days working at the Georgia Historical Society in Savannah, some local high school students came to visit our research library. It was the week of the annual Georgia Day celebration marking the arrival on 12 February 1733 of colony founder James Oglethorpe's group of 114 men, women, and children brought from England on the ship *Anne*.[1] The students' field trip began just outside in Forsyth Park where their teacher helped them mark off an area roughly the size of the *Anne*. Now, as they filed through the library door, the students were making jokes about so many people living in one tight space. Once settled in chairs, the group continued their discussion. The Trustees in England funding the new colony, as well as the colonists themselves, had to prepare carefully for the journey and the new settlement, the teacher explained. The colonists needed construction tools, farming implements, and household goods.

The teacher then asked the students what they would bring if they were colonists with a little room left in their travel chests. What would help them feel more comfortable in a small village amid the relative wilderness? After a few students answered, the teacher suddenly turned to me. "You work with Georgia history. What would you have brought?" I surprised myself by barely having to think before I answered, "A cookbook." I added something along the lines of "Adapting European recipes to local ingredients would have been tricky, and the hearth setup would have been crude, but imagine being able to re-create the tastes of home!" Had I indeed been a colonist squeezing a cookbook into my sea chest, it likely would have been Eliza Smith's *Compleat Housewife*. This was a relatively new release, published in London in 1727. However, literacy rates at the time were much lower (especially for women), books were relatively expensive, and religious volumes were more common than household guides. The European cooking knowledge that arrived on Georgia's shores in 1733 was likely "written" only in the colonists' heads.

Converging Cultures

Cookbooks aside, although the *Anne* represented the official beginning of the colony, its arrival was by no means the beginning of Georgia foodways, since there were people already here when the ship landed. Called "Indians" by the colonists, indigenous peoples had complex foodways, even if their know-how and customs were based in oral tradition and therefore unwritten. Across centuries, they gathered location-specific information about plants, effective agricultural practices, hunting, and weather patterns of the Southeast including the lands falling within the modern borders of Georgia. These are the deepest roots of Georgia foodways, yet trying to build even a basic understanding is sometimes more a matter of archaeology than recipes. (See 1736, 1773, and 1838 sections.)

Indigenous Foodways

Although they cannot provide a well-rounded understanding by themselves, some period accounts of interactions with Georgia's early peoples survive, such as those by the party of early Spanish explorer Hernando de Soto (ca. 1500–1542), trader and author James Adair (ca. 1709–1783), naturalist William Bartram (1739–1823), and Indian agent Benjamin Hawkins (1754–1816). Some nineteenth-century scholarly accounts exist from historian Charles C. Jones Jr. (1831–1893) and ethnographer James Mooney (1861–1921). Modern archaeological researchers such as Charles Hudson (1932–2013) and Max E. White have also expanded our understanding of Georgia's original peoples and their foodways.

Could Colonial Georgia's foodways be described as a blend of Native American and English? It isn't that simple. Georgia was created in part as a buffer between the English colony of South Carolina (founded in 1663) and the Spanish, who had been in Florida since 1513 and had at times set up outposts or missions on what is now Georgia soil. In the 1500s the French also tried settling the coastal Southeast (Florida and South Carolina). In 1619 enslaved Africans began arriving in what would become the United States. Trappers and traders of various national origins moved through Georgia lands. By 1733 it is likely that when Georgia's English colonizers arrived, foodways here were already somewhat affected by contact between these groups. This influenced the supplies and advice Georgia's colonists received in Charleston on the way to their own settlement and how their foodways developed thereafter.

The influences only increased. A few months after the *Anne*, a group of forty-two more people arrived from England, this time Jews bringing food traditions related to their faith as well as from earlier places they'd lived, such as Portugal and Spain.[2] In the second year of the colony, Lutherans from Salzburg arrived, bringing Central European food traditions with them. In the mid-1700s the original ban on slavery in the colony was overturned, beginning an influx of Africans or those of African descent. From various records, we know that people from Germany, Ireland, Italy, Moravia (now the Czech Republic), and Scotland were in Georgia during its early years. A manuscript cookbook survives from the late 1700s with recipes attributed to the Schmidt family who moved from Stuttgart to the Georgia coast.[3] Part of the recipes were written in German and part in English as the Schmidts acclimated to their new life. Did they share their foodways with their neighbors? With Savannah becoming an important port and more people arriving in Georgia along early trading trails and wagon roads eager for land and other resources, Georgia foodways became an interesting blend of traditions.

The Colonial Larder

And what did the colonists have to cook with? During my time as Education Coordinator for the Georgia Archives, I found that wills from early Georgia fascinated many students. We would read the inventories and try to piece together what the household might have been like. In a time and place where people owned far less, every item mattered, so wills often list each piece of clothing, each farming tool—and each kitchen utensil. Comparing many wills, looking at what

> "Cookbooks from the eighteenth and nineteenth centuries are rare sources of information on everyday life in America, at a time when few people recorded what the middle-class woman was doing with her days. To read a cookbook from any era is to discover the varying philosophies that affected daily life: the trends, the fads, the development of scientific rules for healthy diets, even the religious beliefs that found their way into the story of American food . . . a cookbook is one key to discovering how people ate, thought, behaved, and aspired."
>
> —Cookbook historian Mary Barile, in *Cookbooks Worth Collecting*, 7

people from various socioeconomic groups owned, can help form a picture of what kitchen spaces were like in early Georgia.

As far as ingredients go, letters, journals, and government papers record various foods gathered or grown in Georgia as well as some imported foods mentioned by early residents and visitors.[4] Although undoubtedly an incomplete list, the following foods were mentioned in period documents: Meats and related products included beef, cheese/butter, fowl/eggs, mutton, and pork, although in the first years colonists were hesitant to rob valuable calves by taking milk, and they would leave most eggs in the nest, hoping they were fertilized and would increase the flock.[5] Fish and oysters featured prominently. Wild game included doves, partridges, rabbits, squirrels, venison, turkeys, and water fowl, as well as some animals we no longer have in Georgia—or that most of us would no longer consider for the dinner table—such as bear, buffalo, eagles, and wild goats. (If you just paused over the word "buffalo," there are indeed accounts of these Wild West creatures in colonial Georgia. Although now largely obscured, Georgia land still holds traces of old buffalo licks, places where these animals licked the ground for minerals.)[6]

Colonial era grains included barley, corn, oats, rice, rye, and wheat, while produce included cabbage, calavances (beans), cucumbers, "garden greens" (types unknown), melons, peas, potatoes, pumpkins, turnips, and wild grapes. The Trustees ordered a garden be laid out to cultivate a variety of useful plants familiar to Europeans or ones collected by explorers in warmer climates that the Trustees hoped would thrive in Georgia. Fruiting trees and vines would have taken a while to establish, and some took to the climate better than others. These included apples, coconuts, figs, domestic grapes, olives, oranges, peaches, and pomegranates.

Foodstuffs mentioned in old documents also include brandy, beer, bread, sea biscuit (hardtack), cider, honey, molasses, spice (types unknown), sugar, tea, and vinegar. Many will be relieved to know at least some early colonists had access to coffee and chocolate. Rum was popular—even though it was banned by the Trustees.

Colonial and Antebellum Foodways

No cookbooks have been found that were published in Georgia before 1859. So where did literate early Georgians turn when they were interested in new recipes or needed a kitchen guide? Cookbooks popular in the Thirteen Colonies tended to be British, including *The Art of Cookery Made Plain and Easy* (1747) by Hannah Glasse and the aforementioned *Compleat Housewife*. After the Revolution and even past the War of 1812, English cookbooks remained surprisingly popular in American households that could afford them. Immigrants may also have brought non-English cookbooks from authors such as Denmark's Anne Marie Mangor or Sweden's Cajsa Warg.

If Georgia had produced an array of cookbooks beginning in the eighteenth century, we would likely find the same trends seen in cookbooks from up the Eastern Seaboard. In the colonies, rich and fatty foods were preferred.[7] Leaner breeds of animals at the time as well as wide use of wild game meant that cooks often needed to liberally add fat to dishes. Other noticeable trends involved new ingredients. Recipes began to include more indigenous foods learned from the Native

For many decades, sugar was sold in a dense cone or loaf. Cooks used "nippers" to cut pieces off. Once the chunks were pulverized, this was sometimes called "powdered sugar" in recipes, but what we now call powdered or confectioner's sugar is much finer and usually contains cornstarch. In the days of sugarloaves, cooks might be instructed to clarify the sugar of impurities by boiling it in water with or without egg whites, skimming off any scum.

Americans, such as corn and pumpkin. Another difference noted by many food historians is that sugar became more popular, a result of greater international trade. During the time between Georgia's founding and the Civil War, a wider variety of spices and exotic fruits also began arriving in Savannah. Archaeologist Anne Yentsch explored nineteenth-century American cookbooks in chronological order, graphing the decline of plums and citron in recipes along with the rise of bananas, dates, and pineapples.[8] Pineapples in particular came to be regarded as an exotic, guest-worthy treat, becoming a symbol of welcome in Savannah as well as other port cities. New ingredients were usually expensive at first, and therefore embraced primarily by the upper classes. As improved transportation made the ingredient more common, prices dropped, and the ingredient would then be embraced by those with smaller incomes. These "prestige ingredients" are likely to turn up in cookbooks, as fewer people had experience with them and therefore needed recipes for guidance.

Plumb Pudding

Shred a pound and half suet very fine,
add a pound & half of good Raisins stoned
6 spoonfull of flowr & as many of Sugar,
the yolks of eight Eggs, and half the whites,
a little Nutmeg and Mace with a little
Salt, all beat together, and boil for 4 or
5 hours.

—Recipe book of Dorothea Christina Schmitt/Schmidt (Liberty County), Alexander and Hillhouse Family Papers, 1758–1998, University of North Carolina[9]

1734

Reverend Boltzius and Salzburger Beer

Older recipes tend to be vague, sometimes a mere list of ingredients without even giving the reader clues about quantities. With that in mind, the distinction of recording the first Georgia recipe may go, on the twentieth of April in 1734, to the Reverend Johann Martin Boltzius/Bolzius (1703–1765) of the Salzburg immigrants.[1] In his journal, he penned:

> Because there is not yet any Malt made here, the Salzburgers have learnt of the English people, to Brew a sort of beer of Molasses, with Sassafras and the tops of Firr-Tree, instead of Hops, which they boil in a Kettle with Water; some add Indian Corn: The Inhabitants here reckon this Liquor to be wholesome, and the drinking of Water unwholesome; but we prefer the drinking of the Water to this Mixture, and find ourselves well after it; sometimes we mix it with a little Wine.[2]

If this adapted beer is the first Georgia recipe, it is for a concoction that received mixed reviews. More than two and a quarter centuries after the arrival of their ancestors, the Georgia Salzburger Society put out a cookbook (ca. 1963), *Ye Olde Time Salzburger Cook Book: A Book of Recipes and Remedies Used by the Early Salzburgers*.[3] Some of the recipes show a blend of "Old World" and "New World," including the two below reproduced courtesy of the Georgia Salzburger Society.

This husking peg is an example of a homemade tool to save time and tired hands. The leather loop around one or two middle fingers secured the four-inch peg across the palm, and the pointed end stripped corn husks from the cob.

Corn Beer

Boil a quart of corn until the grains crack. Put into a jug and pour in 2 gallons of boiling water. Add a quart of molasses, a handful of dried apples and a tablespoonful of ginger. It will be ready to use in 2 or 3 days.

—Mrs. Alice Rhoda Gnann Ferrel, *Ye Olde Time Salzburger Cook Book*, 30

Collard Sourkraut

Clean and wash collards. Place leaves one leaf at the time on top of the other, until you have enough to roll lengthwise (jelly roll fashion) which can be held easily in the hand. Place on a wooden board and slice as fine as possible with a sharp knife. When there is enough sliced collards to make three inches in keg, place in keg and sprinkle with one tablespoon salt, then pestle until tightly packed. Continue this procedure until you have used all the collards. If there is not enough liquid on the collards packed in the keg, to cover greens, add water to cover. Taste this liquid to be sure it is real salty. Cover top with 4 or 5 collard leaves. Place clean boards on top of the leaves and weight down with heavy stone. Cover keg with clean cloth. Leave to set for a week then remove the stone, boards and top leaves, clean rinsing in cold water to remove accumulated mold, replace top leaves, board and stone. Continue this until the kraut is sour to your taste.

—Cecil B. Gnann Jr., *Ye Olde Time Salzburger Cook Book*, 34

Tomochichi's Oyster Roast

Although we have only scant early accounts of the foodways of Georgia's indigenous peoples, these can be fascinating. For instance, Philip Thicknesse (1719–1792) visited from England in 1736. While on this trip, he met the Yamacraw, indigenous people living near Savannah. Tomochichi (ca. 1644–1739) was the Yamacraw leader, and the English considered him royalty along with his wife, Senauki, and nephew/heir, Toonahowi. Thicknesse wrote, "The first visit I made the court of Yamacra, their Majesties were just returned in their Canoes, from an Oystering party, and I had the honor of partaking with them, a repas [*sic*], to which they sat down with as good an appetite, as ever European princes did." His account added, "The Indians, who dwell within the reach of the salt water Creeks, make fires at low water on the Islands of oysters, which are then left high and dry, and roast the greatest part of an island at once."[1] Please note that resources were more abundant then; environmentalists would beg you not to try this now. This method, however, was a clever way to feed a crowd.

Oysters are such an integral part of Georgia foodways that there is not a single Georgia cookbook published during the state's first two centuries that doesn't contain at least one oyster recipe—baked, roasted, fried, pickled, and stewed as well as turned into patties or as a main ingredient in such dishes as pilafs, omelets, and soups.

[Untitled; nowadays called Angels on Horseback]

Cut fat English bacon in
thin strips & wrap a large
oyster in each. Fasten with
a fresh toothpick. Heat a
frying pan & fry just
long enough to heat the bacon.

—Owens and Thomas Family Papers, 1837–1954, Georgia Historical Society, Savannah[2]

Oyster Pie

Take seventy-five oysters, one by one, to see that there are no shells on them; put them into a bowl in their own liquor to warm. Boil four eggs hard; take the yolks and as much bread, and three tablespoonfuls of butter; rub them up together. Put this with the oysters, and let them simmer a little; season with mace, pepper, and salt. When cool put them in patties with paste [crust] at the bottom and top.

—Mrs. Spalding's Collection, in *Choice Recipes of Georgia Housekeepers* (1880), 7–8

Exploring Further

As for oyster roasts, these are still popular along Georgia's coast. Two modern cookbooks are particularly good sources for instructions—Martha Giddens Nesbit's *Savannah Entertains* and Damon Lee Fowler's *The Savannah Cookbook*. In my Georgia childhood, the oyster roast always went hand in hand with Low Country boils (shrimp, onions, potatoes, corn, and sausage) or a fish fry. Sides like slaw and hush puppies were the norm, along with various sauces. Fowler and Nesbit offer the key recipes needed. (I also call upon cookbooks discussed in the 1863 section.)

Exotic Ingredients in the Backcountry

Pour syrup into the corner of a cake pan and it will slowly spread, filling the center and then reaching the edges. While serving as Education Coordinator at the Georgia Archives, I realized that many students think England poured people into Savannah and gradually those settlers spread evenly to the modern-day borders of our state. The reality was more complex. The original boundaries of Georgia remained the same from the founding of the colony until the 1763 Treaty of Paris at the end of the French and Indian War. (Thus the date for this section.) After the treaty, the Mississippi River was our western boundary, although much of this was the land of the Cherokee, Muscogee, and other indigenous peoples. Euro-American settlement patterns often embraced Native American ones, following old paths and trade routes, with surges in the settler population each time there were pressured cessions of tribal lands. Navigable rivers were the superhighways of the past, making it much easier to move people and goods than overland by horse and wagon, so successful early settlements often were the ones located along waterways. Later, the same was true for the railways. Farms and settlements thrived where there was fertile, relatively level, well-drained land as well as good water for drinking or, in many places, for powering mills to grind grain and process lumber.

New immigrants did arrive from other countries, but those settling new farms and towns in Georgia also came from such locations as Virginia and the Carolinas, coming down the Great Wagon Road through Augusta or along other routes. Some even came from already-settled locations in Georgia. Georgia planter James Rowe Coombs explained, "In those days, whole settlements moved off together, believing the best places were a long way off, to the south or west, considering the older settlements crowded beyond comfortable endurance. And when a neighbor would make a trip to the 'New Country' and return to tell of the sights he had seen, the cheapness and fertility of the soil and the openings for energy, industry and capital, the immense advantages that lay in that direction, a panic or moving fever would soon break out and thin the ranks."[1] Georgia's first three cookbook authors—Mary Edgeworth, Ellen Verstille, and Annabella Hill—were from families who left the settled areas of Georgia and South Carolina for newly opened land, carrying their food traditions with them.

Bounty-land grants to soldiers (and certain others) after the Revolutionary War encouraged some to move to the Georgia interior, what was then the frontier or backcountry. Eight land lotteries from 1805 to 1832 did, too. Still, surprisingly large segments of the state were fairly unchanged deep into the nineteenth century. In Sam Bowers Hilliard's *Hog Meat and Hoecake: Food Supply in the Old South, 1840–1860*, the chapter on cattle describes vast open-range grazing lands in South Georgia with roving herders and periodic roundups.[2] Earlier, in the 1733 section, we learned that Georgia used to be home to buffalo. Now from Hilliard we learn Georgia had cowboys. And the areas far away from towns often had all the rustic and untamed elements we associate with the American Wild West. Firsthand accounts of early Georgia, such as those gathered by historian Edward J. Cashin in *A Wilderness Still the Cradle of Nature* or by historian Alan Gallay in *Voices of the Old South*, paint a vivid and often primitive picture of the backcountry.

With Georgia's "wild element" in mind, it is puzzling that Georgia's first cookbook, in 1859, hails from the center of the state and yet sometimes calls for ingredients such as citrus fruits, cinnamon, coconut, coffee, cranberries, Iceland moss (a thickener from an Arctic lichen), lobster, nutmeg, oysters, salmon, and pineapples—items certainly not native to the fields or waters of inland Georgia.[3] Old Georgia newspaper advertisements show that stores in sizeable towns sold a wide array of foods shipped by boat or, later, by rail. But what about rural locations? Lewis E. Atherton's *The Southern Country Store, 1800–1860* explains a great deal. Large plantations depended on middlemen called factors, located in the port cities, to sell their cotton and also send them tools, raw materials, and exotic luxuries that arrived in Georgia by ship. For people with small farms or modest working positions, the country store filled some of the same needs. Stores bought harvests, offered banking services, and sold any items they could find demand for. Depending on distance and logistics, they sometimes offered passably fresh seafood and nonlocal produce. In addition, those in the deep countryside who had cause to travel to town likely ran shopping errands for their neighbors, and itinerant peddlers also carried goods from place to place. Georgia's earliest cookbooks coincide with the golden age of clipper ships capable of securing exotics originating halfway around the world faster than ever before, and the recipes reflect that improvements in shipping and transportation were steadily expanding the array of ingredients found in Georgia kitchens.

Lemon Catsup

Roll well half a dozen lemons to increase their juice; grate off the peel; squeeze out the juice; remove the seed; add a tablespoon of grated horseradish, the same of ground ginger, half as much mace and cinnamon, one grated nutmeg. Pour over a pint of vinegar; scald five minutes. When cold, strain and bottle. Use to flavor piquant sauces.

—Hill, *Mrs. Hill's New Cook Book* (1867), 205

RICH SMALL CAKES.

Three eggs, three tablespoonsful of butter, three of sugar, three cups of flour, one teaspoonful of essence of lemon, and half a nutmeg; work all together; roll thin; cut into small cakes, and bake.

Edgeworth, *Southern Gardener and Receipt Book* (1859), 196

COCOANUT PUDDING, NO. I.

After peeling the cocoanut, grate it, and to a pound of cocoanut add half a pound of butter, six tablespoonsful of white sugar, and the whites of a dozen eggs, well beaten. Flavor with lemon and nutmeg. Bake on a rich pastry-crust, in a slow oven.

Edgeworth, *Southern Gardener and Receipt Book* (1859), 214

Indigenous Nut Milk and the Expeditions of Naturalist William Bartram

In recent years, milk substitutes such as almond milk have skyrocketed in popularity. But nut milk isn't new. In the spring of 1773, naturalist William Bartram (1739–1823) of Philadelphia began a trek through parts of South Carolina, Georgia, and Florida. In our region, he recorded that Georgia's indigenous peoples prized hickory nuts. "They pound them to pieces, and then cast them into boiling water, which, after passing through fine strainers, preserves the most oily part of the liquid: this they call by a name which signifies Hiccory milk; it is as sweet and rich as fresh cream, and is an ingredient in most of their cookery, especially homony and corn cakes."[1]

I found no instructions for nut milk among Georgia's older recipes. Many, however, are rooted in Native American expertise. Up and down the Eastern Seaboard, corn meal was long referred to as "Indian meal." In addition, a knowledge of indigenous plants useful in the kitchen reflects sharing of information and foodways.

[Walnut Catsup]
From Old Mrs. Longstreet
1828
Beat 100 walnuts in a
mortar, boil in a Gallon
vinegar 20 minutes strain
it & add one oz cinnamon,
2 nutmegs, 1/2 oz mace, 2 table

spoons pepper, 2 of spice
6 large onions boil 30 min
utes strain & bottle & cork
close.

—Recipe book of Anna Edgar (Augusta), Stephen D. Heard Papers, 1758–1889, University of North Carolina[2]

Indian Flapjack

Mix one pint of Indian Meal, 4 spoonsful of flour in one quart of milk, add 4 eggs and salt. Bake them on a griddle as buckwheat cakes
and butter them hot.

—Anna Matthews White Composition Notebook, 1828–1832, Georgia Historical Society, Savannah[3]

Hickory Nut Macaroons

One pt. granulated sugar, 4 eggs, 1 pt. flour, 1 pt. of kernels, stir together and drop on a buttered flat tin; bake slowly for 20 minutes.

—Mrs. W. W. Rawlings, in First Baptist Church (Albany), *Baptist Cook Book* (1907), 96

The yaupon bush and some of its leaves dried for use.

Exploring Further

In *The Flower Hunter and the People*, editor Matthew Jennings distills Bartram's writings about his time among Native Americans into a compact volume. In addition, Charles Hudson's *Black Drink: A Native American Tea* is interesting reading about cassina, a caffeinated beverage from the leaves of yaupon holly that was used by indigenous peoples for social and spiritual purposes. The scientific name for the plant is the unflattering *Ilex vomitoria* because colonists observed Native American ceremonies where a strong brew was used for ritual purification. Or was the scientific name a plot to discourage yaupon use from spreading, allowing shipping magnates to continue to dominate markets with coffee and traditional tea?[4] Regardless, yaupon tea is available to modern drinkers and can be purchased online. I find it smells like moss and offers a flavor like chamomile with a smoke-and-lime aftertaste.

Telfair Biskets on the Rise

American Cookery, a 1796 cookbook by Amelia Simmons published in Connecticut, is widely considered the first American cookbook. Other popular cookbooks before the Civil War included those by Massachusetts authors Lydia Maria Child and Sarah Josepha Hale as well as Philadelphia author Eliza Leslie. New York's Catharine Beecher, sister to *Uncle Tom's Cabin* author Harriet Beecher Stowe, was also a popular cookbook author. Meanwhile, the "housewife books" were particularly beloved in the South: *The Virginia House-Wife* (1824) by Mary Randolph, *The Kentucky Housewife* (1839) by Lettice Bryan, and *The Carolina Housewife* (1847) by Charleston author Sarah Rutledge.[1] Although Georgia cookbook authors Mary Edgeworth, Ellen Verstille, and Annabella Hill were busy housekeepers building knowledge and gathering recipes during this time, their cookbooks wouldn't come out until just before and just after the Civil War.

There are, however, surviving Georgia recipes from the Early Republic and Antebellum periods in personal or manuscript cookbooks. Such volumes can be found in archives as well as in private hands. The most well-known collection is likely that of the Telfairs. Sarah Gibbons (1758–1827) was born into a prominent Georgia family.[2] In 1774 she married Edward Telfair (1735–1807), a merchant and planter who eventually served twice as governor (1786 and 1789–1793). The Telfair mansion in Savannah, designed by celebrated architect William Jay, was completed in 1819. Widowed Sarah lived there for eight years with several of her grown children. Upon the death of the last of those children, Mary Telfair (1791–1875), the home became the start of the Telfair Museums, now the oldest public art museum complex in the South.[3] Thankfully, even though the building was adapted in many ways for its museum role, the old Telfair kitchen remains with its cooking hearth and brick oven. Papers from the Telfair family, which include recipes from multiple generations, are now a deposit collection at the Georgia Historical Society in Savannah. Some of the Telfair recipes made it into print in Harriet Colquitt's *Savannah Cook Book* of 1933 (explored in a later section) and the bicentennial-era *Thirteen Colonies Cookbook*.[4] The latter cookbook briefly explores Sarah's life and times as well as giving twenty-seven period-inspired recipes. Six of these recipes are adaptations from the Telfair manuscript cookbooks that includes "lists of nostrums suitable for fashionable entertainments, decorative hints, and useful remedies for common illnesses."[5]

The Telfair recipe below is for what the English still call a biscuit but Americans now call a cookie. "Biskets" and "carraway" prove that this recipe is from a time when spelling was less standardized. This point is helpful to keep in mind when searching for specific old recipes. For instance, if you're searching for old cookie recipes, keywords like "biscuit," "bisquet," "bisket," and, eventually, "cooky" may be useful. And "recipes" were often called "receipts" in the past, while "cooking" was more commonly known as "cookery."

To Make Biskets

To a quart of flour take quarter of a pound
of butter and a quarter of a pound of sugar
one egg and what carraway seeds you please
wet it with milk as stiff as you can then roll
them out very thin cut them with a small
glass bake them on tin plates your oven
must be slack prick them very well
just as you set them in & keep them dry
when baked.

—Telfair Family Papers, 1751–1875, 1909, Georgia Historical Society, Savannah[6]

Did you notice that the Telfair Biskets are lacking an ingredient that appears in almost all modern cookie recipes? For centuries, there were three methods of adding a light texture to baked goods—yeast, frothed egg, or beaten/folded dough. Each method meant extra time for the cook to nurture the yeast, whip the egg, or manipulate the dough. Then came a baking breakthrough. In your mixing bowl, blending an alkali with an acid in the presence of moisture and warmth creates carbon dioxide bubbles capable of giving dough or batter a springy texture.[7] There were many acidic cooking ingredients at the ready, such as buttermilk, vinegar,

Modern all-purpose flour is more finely ground than what early Georgians used. Steel rollers replaced stones for processing in most mills in the last quarter of the nineteenth century. For a more authentic texture in recipes older than that, replace two or three tablespoons per cup of the all-purpose flour with whole wheat flour.

or lemon juice. The alkali part of the equation was soon provided with pearlash—sometimes written as "pearl ash," also called potash (potassium carbonate)—and could be created at home with wood ashes.[8] Pearlash appeared in European recipes as early as the 1750s and in the United States by the 1790s.[9] Similar alkali leavening agents were saleratus (aerated salt potassium carbonate), soda (sodium bicarbonate), and hartshorn (ammonium carbonate)—the latter startling to modern readers when they come across recipes for "Ammonia Cakes" that call to mind the modern noxious cleaning fluid. The names of these ingredients were sometimes confused or interchanged, but for home cooks these alkali products were increasingly commercial products they purchased rather than made at home; the Industrial Revolution was creeping into recipes and cookbooks. Balancing alkali and acid in the mixing bowl, however, could be tricky. For a time, powdered alkali could be purchased in tandem with cream of tartar, a powdered acid first derived from grapes as a byproduct of winemaking.[10] By the 1850s, commercial baking powder—alkali and acid combined in a single powder—was available in American markets. These leavening products became increasingly popular in nineteenth-century recipes.

The Telfair Academy Building, as the Telfair mansion is now called, allows visitors into the original hearth kitchen. On the wall is an image of Juddy Telfair Jackson, the enslaved cook who served there for many years.[11] Despite around four decades having passed between her work life and the first Georgia cookbook in 1859, Jackson would likely have been familiar with most of the ingredients and processes called for in that volume. Although cooking over a metal stove likely started in the 1740s, Priscilla J. Brewer, author of *From Fireplace to Cookstove: Technology and the Domestic Ideal in America*, reveals that this "revolution" in cooking technology was more like a slow evolution, especially in the South. As we will soon see in the 1859 section, Georgia's first cookbook had hearth cooks in mind.

Exploring Further

In 1933 the Telfair Academy of Arts and Sciences published a pamphlet titled "Early American Kitchens."[12] Although only nine pages, it gives a helpful understanding of how the Telfair kitchen was restored. Another source from the Academy is *Nostrums for Fashionable Entertainments: Dining in Georgia, 1800–1850* by Feay Shellman Coleman. This book explains social customs and offers a catalog of dining furniture and accessories from the Telfair and Richardson-Owens-Thomas House collections.

This undated postcard showing the Telfair hearth kitchen is shared courtesy of the Telfair Museum.

This Britannia ware plated pewter tea caddy (5″ × 4″), the gift of Dale Couch and Greg Jarrell, was made in England circa 1830–1860. Old newspaper advertisements are a good way to explore the variety of kitchen utensils and serving pieces available to Georgians in the past.

Springer Vinegar and Labor-Intensive Ingredients

When leaving her North Caroline [*sic*] home as an immigrant to Georgia, among the effects that were stored away in the great lumbering wagons, was a forty gallon blue painted barrel, full of apple cider vinegar of the best quality, also a one gallon earthenware jug. As soon as the household machinery was set in motion in the new home in Georgia, a gallon of the vinegar was drawn out of the blue barrel into the jug. Immediately the barrel was refilled with a gallon of water sweetened with molasses. For forty years that process went on, the barrel never having but the one gallon less in it. So that when, after her death at an advanced age, her effects were sold for distribution of her estate, the blue barrel was sold, still full of apple cider vinegar as good as when it came from the orchard in old North Carolina.

— "Ann Springer's Vinegar," Smith and Carnes, *History of Hancock County*, 1:56

An article about vinegar in the *Cherokee Phoenix* (New Echota) of 8 October 1828 revealed much about nineteenth-century kitchens when it noted, "The method of making this liquid out of cider, wine, etc. is too generally known to need any description." It then outlined additional possibilities such as whey, tree sap (black birch or maple), or juice from elderberries, beets, carrots, turnips, or potatoes.

Meanwhile, in my twenty-first-century Georgia kitchen, adding an acidic splash to my cooking doesn't require foraging, orchards, or gardens but instead is a matter of unscrewing a bottle cap. Vinegar periodically appears on my grocery list—and so does yeast. A careful cook never ran out of yeast, just as Ann Springer

In 1783, Ann Green (ca. 1761–ca. 1838) married Revolutionary War veteran John Springer (1744–1798).[1] (Thus the date for this section.) They moved, lock, stock, and vinegar barrel,[2] to Washington, Georgia. There, in 1790, John stood in an outdoor ceremony under a "magnificent forest giant" poplar and became the first Presbyterian minister ordained in Georgia.[3] Although now gone, for years the Presbyterian Tree was a local landmark. Today roadside historical markers show where the Springers are buried and where Reverend Springer founded the well-known Walnut Hill Academy. Their son, William, purchased the old Eagle Tavern in Sparta in 1815, and we'll take up the history of that establishment in the 1902 section.[4]

1. North Carolina Index to Marriage Bonds, 1741–1868; *Daughters of the American Revolution Lineage Book*, 165:8–9; Alabama Society of the Sons of the American Revolution, application for David George Henderson Jr., approved 31 August 1950. All via Ancestry.com.

2. This saying refers to a rifle barrel, but I couldn't resist the pun.

3. Knight, *Georgia's Landmarks*, 1:1051; Presbyterian Poplar Tree, Vanishing Georgia Collection, Georgia Archives, WLK-63, https://dlg.usg.edu/record/dlg_vang_wlk063; Nevin, *Encyclopaedia*, 851.

4. *FM*, 1 September 1815; Rozier, *Houses of Hancock*, 56.

never ran out of vinegar, and many old cookbooks offer methods for using a starch such as flour, cornmeal, cooked potato, or even (as in the recipe below) peas to help yeast multiply. Sometimes the addition of hops or peach leaves supported the process and warded off mold.[1] The volume of yeast now increased, it could be kept for a time in liquid form or dried into cakes. Starches were also used to capture and nurture wild yeast:

Cheap Vinegar.

Who would have it cheaper than this? Boil a pint of corn till about half done, for three gallons. Put it into jars or jugs and fill them with hot water, sweetened with a pint of syrup to the gallon. Set them in the sun, and in two or three weeks it will be good vinegar. Less syrup will do, but the quantity named is better.

Corn vinegar recipe from the *Southern Farmer's Monthly* (Savannah) 2.11 (November 1879): 346.

To Make Yeast

Take a tea cup full of pease
mash them a little then pour
½ pint boiling water on them and
let it stand over night in a warm
place but in cold seasons it should stand
longer to ferment, perhaps twenty-four or forty-eight
hours it will then have a froth on its top and
will be good yeast.

—Recipe book of Dorothea Christina Schmitt/Schmidt (Liberty County), Alexander and Hillhouse Family Papers, 1758–1998, University of North Carolina[2]

Modern readers of Georgia's old cookbooks can't help but notice that some recipes are for things we now think of as *ingredients* or at least as single items on our grocery list—not only vinegar and yeast but also alcoholic beverages, baking powder, catsup, noodles, and mayonnaise, to name a few. Years ago, Georgians routinely turned meat from living animals into preserved products such as ham or sausage, and turned milk into butter and cheese. Grains were grown in nearby fields and then processed locally into cornmeal or flour. Homegrown or foraged produce that wasn't eaten right away was dried or otherwise preserved. How rural a household was as well as its income affected what went on in the kitchen, but on the whole Georgians in the past purchased far fewer ready-made ingredients.

It's not hard to guess why some recipes slowly faded from cookbooks in favor of store-bought alternatives. For example, although cornstarch was commercially available by the 1840s, in an 1869 issue of the *Southern Cultivator* (Athens) a gentleman described his wife's "simple process" for making a year's supply.[3] He didn't mention planting, tending, or harvesting the fifty ears of corn. Those tasks aside, I counted eleven steps and calculated that the job with all its required soaking and settling times took her four days—as long as the starch wasn't ruined by rain, wind, or a passing bird during the final step when she spread it on a cloth to dry in the sun. She had to pour heavy tubs of liquid eight times. (I hope he was not

Make Your Own Butter

In educational programs at the Georgia Archives, butter making quickly became a favorite with kids and adults alike. Here are directions for making eight small servings with a group of people: Start with a pint of room-temperature heavy whipping cream. For flavor, you may wish to stir in 1/4 teaspoon salt and/or a sprinkling of dried herbs. Take eight small plastic containers with tight-fitting lids and fill them halfway with cream—about four tablespoons in each. (The four-ounce takeout cups that restaurants use for small side dishes work well.) To speed the process, wash glass marbles with dish soap, rinse well, and then add one to each container before closing securely. Wrap each container in a cloth to catch leaks, and pass them around for folks to shake for five to ten minutes. When the marbles no longer "thunk" the side of the container, this is because they are mired in thick cream. Shake a few minutes longer until you hear a sloshing, which means the liquid whey has separated from the butter. Drain off the whey. Wash the butter in very cold water, and then spread it on a hot scratch-made biscuit.

Fig. 4.

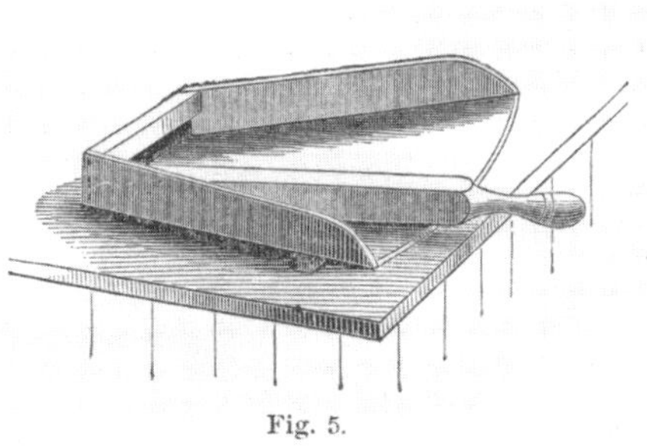

Fig. 5.

BUTTER WORKERS.

For many Georgians in the past, home processing was necessary for dairy products. This six-inch-tall butter churn was likely intended for a small household purchasing fresh milk rather than working with a large quantity from their own cow. In recent years it was used by students attending history programs at the Georgia Archives and handles just one pint. The large-scale butter workers pictured here in the USDA *Report of the Commissioner of Agriculture 1870* (Plate XXXIV) reflect the hands-on experience of larger households or businesses.

HOW TO TEST EGGS.

The best way to test eggs is to take them into a partially dark room and hold them between the eye and a candle or lamp, as represented in the accompanying cut. If the egg be good—that is, if the albumen be still unaffected—the light will shine through a reddish glow; while, if affected, the egg will be opaque or dark. The egg should be held so that the hand will exclude all direct rays of light.

This 1869 guide for testing eggs, from *Southern Farm and Home* (Macon) 1: 71, shows that even ingredients we now think of as straightforward required extra work in days gone by.

just sitting on the porch reading the *Southern Cultivator* while all this work was going on.)

Cornstarch was an early commercial product, and so was gelatin. In 2009 a team led by food writer Chris Kimball orchestrated an authentically cooked dinner from the 1896 *Boston Cooking-School Cook Book* by Fannie Farmer.[4] Reading Kimball's account of the event makes it abundantly clear why cooks would be willing to embrace time-saving kitchen products. The glittering fruit jellies the Kimball team created were appealing, but the complicated process of extracting gelatin from a calf's foot was definitely not.

On the other hand, jam, soup noodles, salad dressing, and catsup were fun and successful projects in my kitchen. And homemade rather than store-bought pie crust makes the difference between "No, thanks" and "Is there a piece left?" It depends on your tastes and perseverance, but making an ingredient at home can be a culinary adventure that builds skills and is worth the effort.

To Stone Raisins

Pour boiling water over them and let them stand in it five or ten minutes. Drain and rub each raisin between the thumb and finger till the seeds come out clean, then cut or tear apart, or chip, if wanted very fine. Some housekeepers prefer to remove seeds with a pointed knife.

—St. John's Episcopal Church (Savannah), *Ever Ready Cook Book* (1910), 53

Raisin Sandwiches

Cut raisins with scissors and extract the seeds. Moisten with sherry. Lay them between buttered bread and serve with lemonade.

—Mrs. W. M. Jones, in First Presbyterian Church, *Dalton Cook Book* (1923), 67

When I was a kid in the 1970s, boxes of raisins were still labeled "seedless." Raisins dehydrated from seedless grapes are now the norm, but have we lost something? Decades ago, if somebody made you oatmeal raisin cookies, willingly performing surgery on each and every raisin, that was showing love.

Chatham Artillery Punch, the Legendary Drink

Famous Chatham Artillery Punch
Savannah, Ga.

1½ gallons Catawba [wine]
½ gallon St. Croix rum
1 quart Gordon gin
1 quart Hennessy brandy
½ pint Benedictine
1½ quarts Rye Whisky
1½ gallons strong tea
2½ pounds of Brown sugar
1½ doz oranges juice only
1½ doz lemons
1 bottle maraschino cherries

Make stock thirty six to
forty eight hours before time for serving.

Add one case of champagne
when ready to serve.[1]

When I was a newly minted archivist working at the Georgia Historical Society in Savannah, I quickly learned that this beverage was a favorite punchline (bad pun intended) for local jokes. If Georgia Day speeches went on a little too long or the crowd was eager for the St. Patrick's Day parade to begin, someone would whisper that a swig of Chatham Artillery Punch was needed. Why is that? Alcohol has long been known to lubricate social situations and the punch has been described as "the most innocent and also the most insidious beverage that ever cooled and also thrilled the inner regions of men."[2] Jokes about this concoction have been going on since the days when Savannah's waterfront was lined with sailing ships.

The Chatham Artillery, a local militia group, began in 1786. (Thus the date for this section.) Among past civic services, the Artillery paid tribute to George Washington when he visited in 1791. The pleased president then gifted Savannah with two cannons captured at Yorktown a decade before, now on display near the river. Two hundred years after the Artillery's founding, a monument to the group was placed in Emmet Park noting famous members and heroic deeds. The punch is not mentioned, but its fame seems assured. Granted, I likely own more Georgia cookbooks than the average person, but as I wrote this section in my home office, I discovered I had seven print recipes for the punch within arm's reach, and a web search for it brings up thousands of hits. Some of these sources note that they offer the authentic recipe. *Hmmm.* In actuality, the "facts" about this recipe—as with other famed Georgia recipes—are often contradictory.

How old is the recipe? In the 1960s, the Savannah Area Chamber of Commerce enticed newspaper readers up the Eastern Seaboard to write in for the recipe for the "200-year-old drink" that "tastes as mild as tea, but it hits like a howitzer!"[3] Other sources report it was first brewed in 1786.[4] Herb Traub (1917–2008), owner of Savannah's famed Pirates' House restaurant, stated for a newspaper article that the punch was served to George Washington during his 1791 visit and that "after a few glasses the usually reserved president took off his cravat and coat and danced the night away."[5] Georgia journalist Ralph McGill wrote a humorous piece about the recipe originating on high: "It was the drink called nectar which the gods on Olympus sipped and which mortals never knew. . . . It is popularly reported that one of the gods, who could, it will be remembered, visit on earth, fell in love with an Irish girl and she got from him the recipe and it passed on down through the ages until it was brought to Savannah in 1812 by an Irishman."[6] Respected New York food writer Clementine Paddleford included a recipe for the punch in her landmark cookbook *How America Eats* and reported that the drink was created for President James Monroe when he visited Savannah in 1819.[7] This was echoed by Savannah cookbook author and journalist Harriet Ross Colquitt, who stated that the punch was served to the president on that visit when he took a brief excursion on the SS *Savannah* just before it became the first steamship to cross the Atlantic.[8]

And then there's the "how" of the creation rather than just the "when." Newspaper articles marking the death of Commodore William Hone (1819–1893) noted that after Hone moved to Savannah in 1850, he served in the Chatham Artillery running blockades during the Civil War and was the inventor of the famous punch.[9] Other accounts state that Sergeant Alonzo B. Luce (1815–1879) of the Chatham Artillery, a local restaurateur and onetime proprietor of the well-known Marshall House hotel, proposed creating the brew in a horse bucket just before the Civil War as a salute to a rival military company, the Republican Blues.[10] (An 1885 newspaper story mentioning Luce includes a description of the recipe listing finely crushed ice and just six other ingredients.)[11] But was it one man's careful concoction? Or was it, as cookbook author and local historian Margaret Wayt DeBolt suggested, a drink that "started out as an innocent punch served at social gatherings, with various members slipping in a bit of alcoholic beverage when no one was looking"?[12]

Whatever its origins, documentation on the notoriety of the punch can be found as early as 1870. An Atlanta newspaper reported that during a Savannah meeting of press associations, the group took a boat trip down to Fort Pulaski that involved band music and Chatham Artillery Punch. The response was enthusiastic, and the "merits" of the drink were "discussed upon half the night."[13] A few years later, Georgia journalists at the *Columbus Daily Enquirer* pleaded that no issue of the newspaper could be satisfactorily cobbled together to appear on Christmas Day because they anticipated the punch would figure into the holiday.[14]

In 1883 the first felling of a statesman by the punch entered public legend. President Chester A. Arthur visited Savannah and enjoyed shipboard refreshments on the Savannah River until he was brought low by a "congestive chill." This was officially blamed on overindulgence in shrimp salad, but rumors would continue for years about Chatham Artillery Punch.[15] Although Arthur lived several years after the punch incident, newspapers would later hint that the punch was connected with his 1886 death, and the death of Georgia governor Alexander Stephens (1812–1883) as well.[16] A few years later, in March of 1900, it is said that the punch laid low another statesman, although he lived long afterwards. Admiral George Dewey (1837–1917), a hero of the Spanish-American War and a presidential hopeful, visited the town to enjoy a parade in his honor. He was taken on a boat ride down the Savannah River for an oyster roast but had to be hurried back to the city due to "acute indigestion," this time blamed on chicken salad.[17] It was widely muttered, however, that shortly before his illness Dewey was seen with a glass of the punch in hand. In October of 1909, newspapers reported that stock for the punch was already being brewed weeks ahead in anticipation of the visit of President Taft (1857–1930), but this public figure decided not to partake of anything stronger than "a helping or two of Savannah's justly celebrated stewed terrapin."[18] (See 1890 section.) One Florida newspaper reported, "Nothing so thoroughly demonstrated the magnificent solidity of President Taft as the fact that he 'got by' Savannah's artillery punch bombardment thoroughly sober."[19] With a nudge and a wink, newspapers continued to suggest dignitaries were lured to Savannah by the promise of the punch to render them "dazed and dreamy"—or else left town with their heads hung low after sobering up again.[20]

In 1890, Captain James Armstrong, harbormaster of Charleston, publicly joked that the punch was so strong that pouring it into a cannon was the best way to serve it.[21] Punch recipes and stories are often linked with cannons in general or the Washington guns in particular. Sometimes one of the ingredients is an optional pinch of gunpowder![22] Although Armstrong further quipped that the drink was surely endorsed by the clergy as a "canonical," in 1892, renowned Augusta preacher Reverend W. W. Wadsworth specifically denounced the punch in a temperance speech delivered with "fiery eloquence."[23]

When stories behind a recipe have multiple versions, you can be sure that the recipe itself will have multiple versions as well. One newspaper article from 1909 suggested the real recipe wasn't to be found in any cookbook: "Like fraternity secrets the real formula served to so many visitors with the expected effect in Savannah has never been written. There is always in the Chatham Artillery a man with the secret of the brew wrapped up on his breast."[24] A couple of years later, the *Washington Post* reported that the oldest member of the Chatham Artillery was the keeper of the recipe. "When he dies, the great secret, sir, is imparted to the next oldest member, and it has thus proceeded for many generations and will continue to the end of time."[25] During World War II, Ralph McGill reported: "For many years now, many of the best minds of Savannah have been devoted to research and to combing old books, diaries and ledgers" in search of the recipe for the famous punch that "reacts like a salvo of 12-inch guns."[26] McGill gleefully proclaimed that the recipe had just been located. The version reprinted in McGill's article is much like the one above, only near double the ingredient amounts and without the gin and Benedictine. As for the seven print recipes in my cookbook collection, they range from 1933 to 2008 and vary from eight ingredients to thirteen. Colquitt's 1933 recipe includes most of the popular ingredients save for pineapple chunks, an addition that as far as I can tell only appears in more modern versions. Food historian Damon Lee Fowler notes that gin and cherries are also modern.[27]

When it comes to preparation methods, most recipe versions have the reader create a "stock" that will be mixed with champagne when it is ready to be served. Recipe users are discouraged from using the stock right away but instead are advised to let it sit for as little as eight hours or up to six weeks, either in a stone crock or in a cedar horse-watering tub. (Concerning the latter, Fowler observes, "If that offends your modern ideas about sanitation, well, all I can say is you've never experienced Chatham Artillery Punch first hand: no self-respecting germ would live through a dose of this stuff.")[28] Savannah's famed drink is usually served from a punch bowl, and it is often dictated that the punch must be poured over a cake of ice rather than served chilled or with ice cubes. Other traditions dictate that no woman or servant is allowed to serve the punch—only an officer of the Chatham Artillery or a gentleman.[29]

As for my research, the punch turned out to be the trickiest recipe in this entire book. I wanted to publish the oldest recipe possible. Despite scouring archives and tracking down old Savannah cookbooks, I could not find a detailed one before Colquitt's 1933 publication. In the early spring of 2020, I was excited to find Ralph McGill's 1944 newspaper announcement about the discovery of an old recipe, but instead of telling where the recipe was found, he merely alluded to another newspaper article. It was then that the Covid-19 virus shut down libraries, putting the microfilm I needed out of reach. Months later, sitting down at a microfilm reader at last, I found the newspaper article referenced by McGill, but it didn't tell where the recipe was located!

Next, I found that the punch recipe in Gene Nichols's 1973 *Geechee Cook Book* cited it as "From the papers of Thomas Purse—1840."[30] The likely candidate is Thomas Pilkington Purse Sr. (1802–1872), a railroad superintendent and one of Savannah's mayors during the Civil War. When I could find no papers beyond a few municipal documents, I called in favors from archivist friends. We tried all our tricks. If any of Purse's papers are held by an institution, we could not find them.[31] To make matters more baffling, I discovered the Purse family was connected to the Chatham Artillery rivals, the Republican Blues![32]

The kicker, though, was years into the search, when I found a beautifully handwritten and detailed recipe on the inside cover of a copy of *The Flowing Bowl: When and What to Drink*, written by William Schmidt in 1892. The battered old copy in my hands was donated to the University of Georgia by a Savannah matron in honor of her late husband.[33] The donor information was printed on a bookplate—*firmly pasted across the middle of the recipe*. Dear reader, picture me standing crestfallen in a canyon of tall bookshelves, unsure whether to laugh or to cry out to Ralph McGill's Olympus drinkers for help. But this part of the story has a happy ending. The good folks at the University of Georgia Libraries' preservation unit were able to safely remove the bookplate, revealing the recipe at the top of this section.

Chatham Artillery Punch is something of a cautionary tale when it comes to recipe authenticity. The more famous a dish or recipe is, the more stories and versions there will likely be. Perhaps the only solid fact about the punch is an observance by McGill: "The city knows a hundred amazing stories about things that have happened at parties in the old days when the punch was served."[34] That goes for modern days too; the punch continues to be brewed and may be more popular than ever. In 2019, Chatham Artillery Punch was added to the classic American cookbook *The Joy of Cooking*.[35]

PUNCH.

To make two quarts of punch, take three fresh lemons; rub the outsides of them over with lumps of loaf-sugar, until they become quite yellow; throw the lumps into the bowl; roll the lemons well; cut them in half, and squeeze them with a proper instrument over the sugar; bruise the sugar, and continue to add fresh portions of it, mixing the lemon-pulp and juice well with it. Much of the quality of the punch depends on this. The quantity of sugar to be added should be great enough to render the mixture, without water, quite mild and palatable. Then add, gradually, a small quantity of hot water, just enough to render the syrup sufficiently thin to pass through the strainer. Mix all well together; strain it and try it; if at all sour, add more sugar. When cold, put in a little cold water, and the best French brandy and old Jamaica rum, equal quantities, adapted to the taste.

Edgeworth, *Southern Gardener and Receipt Book* (1859), 499

Parsnip Wine and Newspaper Recipes

Personal recipe collections often contain recipes copied or clipped from newspapers. When the nineteenth century began, Georgia had five newspapers—two in Savannah, two in Augusta, and one in Louisville, the state capital at the time.[1] These sources were usually just a few pages per issue and contained relatively few images or advertisements. Recipes appeared occasionally but were not placed in their own section, as we expect today, but rather used as filler between articles. Few are labeled as recipes (or the old term, *receipts*), which means that even now, when many of our state's oldest newspapers are digitized and can be searched by keyword, finding recipes in them often requires looking page by page. (Searching for ingredients and kitchen terms is another strategy.)

The first recipes in Georgia newspapers tended to be for household compounds. The earliest I found was a 1799 pipe cleaning solution made with raw egg whites, eggshells, sand, milk, and gin.[2] One 1803 recipe calls for butter and salt, but you were to add tar and spread it on your sheep to keep the ticks away.[3] Other early recipes are for medicines promising to cure ills from rheumatism to dysentery. Finally, seventy-three years after the colonists stepped ashore, we come to what I believe is Georgia's earliest written food recipe from a newspaper—although admittedly shared from an overseas source:

Parsnip Wine

A late English publication gives the following receipt for making cheap and excellent wine, superior to that made of raisins, out of the vegetable PARSNIP—

Wash the Parsnips clean, take off the rind, boil four gallons so cut, in ten gallons of water, till they are perfectly soft; squeeze the liquor well out of them and run it through a hair sieve, and to every gallon of liquor add three pounds of sugar, and boil it three quarters of an hour: when it is cool put to it a little new yeast let it stand ten days in an open vessel, stir it frequently, put it in a cask, and when it is done fermenting bung it up for use.

—*Georgia Republican* (Savannah), 18 July 1806

As the nineteenth century progressed, technological advances meant more efficient printing processes, cheaper paper, and easier distribution of printed materials. In addition, especially after the Civil War, literacy rates and middle-class consumerism were on the rise.[4] By the last years of the nineteenth century, Georgians could choose from almost three hundred newspapers, recipes a regular feature in many of them.[5]

Getting a handle on Georgia's older periodicals is fascinating but not straightforward. Quite frequently periodicals changed names, moved publishing

Women's Pages

Sarah Hillhouse (1763–1831) was a forty-year-old widow and mother in 1803 when she took over her husband's role as publisher of the *Monitor*, a newspaper in the Northeast Georgia town of Washington.[1] Recipes were not featured. Kimberly Wilmot Voss, author of *The Food Section: Newspaper Women and the Culinary Community*, notes that Joseph Pulitzer is usually credited with starting women's newspaper pages in 1891, but that other newspapers had them near the same time or even sooner.[2] Atlanta's *Sunny South* newspaper had both a "Ladies' Department" and a "Domestic Department"—the latter edited by Georgia's cookbook author Annabella Hill—as early as 1875.[3]

1. Marzolf, *Up from the Footnote*, 10–11; Eberhard, "Sarah Porter Hillhouse."
2. Voss, *The Food Section*, 21.
3. *SS*, 6 March 1875.

locations, changed publishers, merged, or ceased publication. The Georgia Historic Newspapers database, available through the Digital Library of Georgia, makes many periodicals available online and offers publication information about them. During the span of this book's coverage (1733–1945), Georgia had specialty newspapers such as the *Atlanta Daily World* (a Black publication, 1931–2003), *Cherokee Phoenix* (New Echota, 1829–1834), and the *Jewish Tribune* (Atlanta, 1890s). Specialty newspapers tended to be smaller, focused on specific issues, and offered fewer cooking articles than mainstream papers.

Flip

The following recipe must recommend itself at once to the palate of every one who is fond of something comfortable at going to bed.

Flip.—Keep grated Ginger and Nutmeg with a little fine dried Lemon Peel rubed [*sic*] together in a mortar. To make a quart of Flip:—put the Ale on the fire to warm, and beat up three or four eggs with four ounces of moist sugar, a tea-spoonful of grated Nutmeg or Ginger, and a quartern [1/4 pint, or 4 ounces] of good old Rum, or Brandy. When the Ale is near to boil, put it into one pitcher, and the Rum and Eggs, &c. into another; turn it from one pitcher to another till it is as smooth as Cream.

—*Darien Gazette*, 28 November 1822

Yeast Corn Bread

Take one quart of corn flour, one half spoonful of lard, half a spoonful of salt, two spoonfuls of yest [*sic*], and warm water sufficient to make a batter that will drop freely out of the spoon. Set it in a pitcher or other vessel by the fire to keep moderately warm. It will become very light in eight or ten hours, and should be baked in a Dutch oven or spider, at the same time greasing the oven well. A cooking stove will answer equally well. The bread will be soft and spongy if properly managed, and greatly superior to what is termed *pone*. It should be served *hot* for breakfast or supper.

In order to have good bread it is very necessary to have good meal. It should not be ground too fine, for that will make the bread clammy and unwholesome. There is also great choice in the kind of corn. The best I have ever seen for family use, is what we call in Virginia *hominy* corn. The grain is white, very flinty and clear, sometimes almost transparent. It makes a richer bread than the softer varieties of the species.

—*Georgia Constitutionalist* (Augusta), 21 March 1834

[A Nice Cake]

A nice cake is made as follows: three eggs beaten separately, one cup white sugar, one cup flour; lemon to taste. Bake very thin in pie pans, sifting fine white sugar over each before putting it in the stove. Cook quickly and pile in a plate. The sifted sugar makes them crisp. When all are done, cut through the entire heap into quarters. This is easily and quickly made, and is sure to please.

[This is one of my favorite recipes from old Georgia newspapers. Usually it is called Jelly Cake and calls for jelly or fruit between the layers. Its sweetness makes it a good partner for tart berries.]

—*Sunny South* (Atlanta), 26 November 1881

Fig. 97.—THE SCUPPERNONG.

Image from White's 1856 *Gardening for the South*, page 374.

871. *Muscadine Cordial.*—Pulp the muscadines. A few of the hulls left will give the liquor a beautiful color. Let it stand twenty-four hours. Strain it, and to every three quarts add a quart of good brandy. Sweeten to taste with loaf sugar. Bottle, cork well, and keep in a cool place.

Hill, *Mrs. Hill's New Cook Book* (1867), 338

Marble Cake, a Duel, and Recipe Names

While sifting through stacks of books at a charity sale, I uncovered a copy of *Old Capitol Cook Book* from the Georgia Military College in Milledgeville. It is from 1973, so this vintage community cookbook is understandably a little creased and worn. The front drawing of the Old Capitol Gate, a reminder of when the city served as the state capital from 1804 to 1868, has a few food flecks on it. Inside, however, the recipes are all legible, and one in particular, on page 38, caught my attention. It is reproduced here courtesy of the Georgia Military College.

Born and raised in Scotland, David Brydie Mitchell (1766–1837) immigrated to become a Georgia lawyer with a fiery reputation.[1] His eye soon fixed on a political career, and he became mayor of Savannah in his mid-thirties. During the sultry summer days of 1802, Mayor Mitchell exchanged angry words in the courtroom with lawyer William Hunter, and later attacked him on the street "with a large bludgeon."[2] The unarmed Hunter withdrew and challenged Mitchell to a duel. Both men were wounded in the exchange, but Mitchell's bullet hit Hunter in the chest. Hunter staggered aside to request a drink of wine before dying on the spot, while Mitchell went on to serve twice as Georgia's governor (1809–1813 and 1815–1817). Mitchell holds the distinction of being our last foreign-born governor and is remembered for nurturing banking and transportation in the young state.[3] Under his watch, duels were outlawed.

Mitchell's wife and two-time Georgia First Lady was Jane Mills Mitchell (1774–1847). She and her husband eventually made a home at Mount Nebo Plantation six miles northeast of Milledgeville.[4] If you're serving up cake at a dinner party, one made from a recipe connected with a duel might add a little spice (pun intended) to the table conversation. That this is from the household of Governor Mitchell is as clear as the black and white ink on the cookbook page, right? Similar to what we learned from exploring Chatham Artillery Punch, however, recipes benefit from a little background research. This time, exploring ingredient history can help.

MRS. GOV. MITCHELL'S MARBLE CAKE

½ c. butter	1-4 c. sweet milk
3-4 c. sugar	1 ts. Baking powder
2 c. flour	1 ts. Vanilla
4 egg whites	Mix as any cake.

DARK OR 2nd PART:

½ c. butter	1 ts. baking powder
1 c. sugar	1 ts. all spice
2 c. flour	1 ts. cloves
4 egg yolks	1 ts. cinnamon
½ c. sweet milk	1 ts. nutmeg

Mix as for any cake and bake for 1 hr. in a loaf or tube cake pan, dropping a spoonful of batter here and there, white and dark until your pan is half full. This is a very pretty cake when cut.

MRS. J. F. BELL.

The first lesson this cookbook has to teach is that the copyright date tells when the volume in your hand was current, but it doesn't mean that this is when the recipes were developed or even written down. When I looked through the *Old Capitol Cook Book* at the other twenty recipes contributed by the same person as the marble cake, all are fairly old-fashioned. I then spent a few minutes with online census and cemetery records, learning that the recipe's contributor, Willie Wall Bell, wife of Milledgeville merchant Julius Furman Bell Jr., was older than I first assumed. She was born in 1892. In fact, when I looked at the contributors for other recipes I'd used from the cookbook, they were all born in the 1890s. WorldCat, the online free library database, then helped me discover that the second edition of the cookbook was quite a bit earlier—1948.[5] It is not known when the first edition was printed or if a copy still exists, but the recipes in my copy are at least a quarter century older than they seemed at first glance.

The next step is to examine the elements of the recipe itself. The more we know about old kitchens and foodways, the better we can place a recipe in time. Looking at the marble cake with the eye of a foodways sleuth, the recipe contains details that are somewhat contradictory in terms of baking history. First, are the ingredients suitable for Mrs. Mitchell's time, keeping in mind that she died in 1847?

Sugar was expensive and sold in a hard cone in Mrs. Mitchell's day, but it was certainly available. Calling for "sweet milk" distinguishes whole milk from buttermilk, which may be a sign that a recipe is from the days when households owned the cow and worked with the resulting dairy products. The term "sweet milk" is common in older recipes, including those from city folk who would have purchased specific milk products. (Soured milk was also sometimes used in recipes.) Vanilla was not widespread in Mrs. Mitchell's time because it was an expensive

A way to turn whole nutmegs into powdered spice was important for Georgia's early cooks. This four-inch grater has a hinged compartment in the top just the right size to store a nutmeg. (Cooking hint: Many modern readers still find grating nutmeg for each use is worth the bother.)

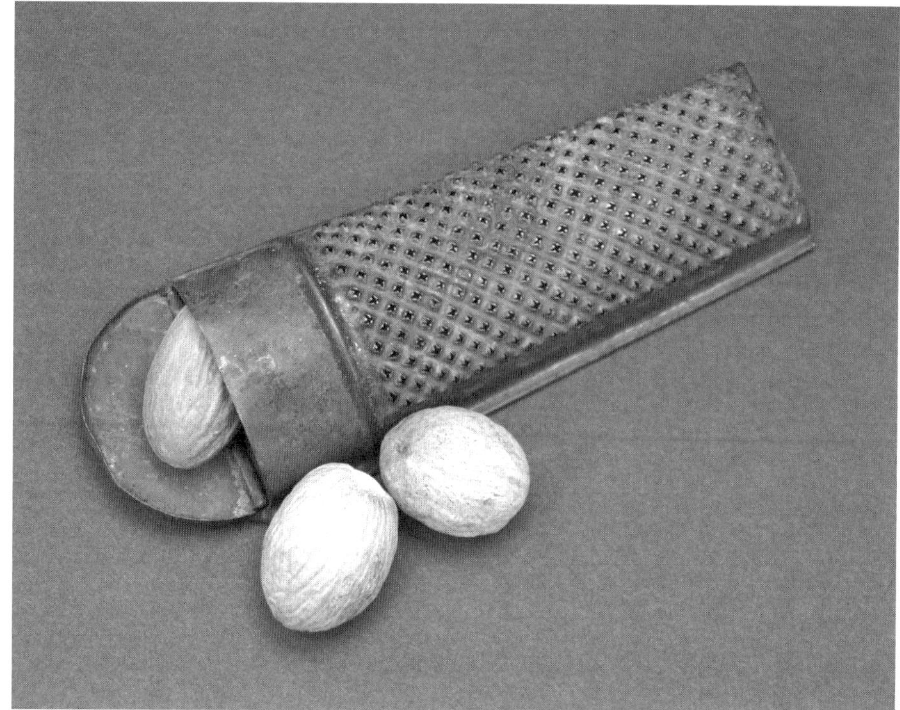

import, but she did come from a well-to-do household. The large amount of spice in the recipe is in part to darken the batter, and also aligns flavor-wise with older recipes. Spiced desserts and sauces sometimes had levels of pungent flavorings like clove and mace that can seem extreme to modern tastes. It isn't unusual to find nineteenth-century recipes for standard-sized spice cakes, for instance, calling for one or two grated nutmegs. Depending on the size of the nutmeg, that was two to six teaspoons' worth of ground spice.

The most problematic ingredient is baking powder. It was not commercially available in the United States until the 1850s.[6] Did Mrs. Mitchell have early access to the new chemical leavening due to her wealth and prominence? Through her husband, she did have family connections in the British Isles, where this ingredient was available in the early 1840s.[7] Regardless of when baking powder first arrived in Georgia kitchens, it is not uncommon for old cake recipes to be modified by later bakers who add a small amount of chemical leavening for "insurance."

Moving past the ingredients list, the latter part of the recipe doesn't give us much additional historical evidence; the instructions are quite vague. One aspect that makes this recipe seem older, however, is that the eggs are divided. This is primarily to affect the batter color. Still, the instructions are simply "mix as for any cake," so whoever wrote the recipe may have assumed a baker would beat the whites until stiff and gently fold them into the pale batter at the end. Before chemical leavenings, bakers making cakes without yeast depended upon whipping whites and yolks separately to give cake batters enough tiny air bubbles for a light texture when baked.

The two-tone cake batter itself is a clue. Early American cookbooks gave many recipes for cakes of various shades. "White" or "silver" cakes (as well as "bride" or "lady" cakes) depended upon using just egg whites so the batter would be pale. "Gold" cakes used egg yolks. "Black" cakes had batter colored with spices and molasses, while later "mahogany" cakes were darkened by chocolate or cocoa. (The "dark part" of the Mitchell batter is colored with yolks and spice alone, so it bakes into a pale brown.)

Despite having recipes for different shades of batters, home bakers in America didn't seem to combine them for a marbled effect until the mid-1800s.[8] Georgia's Mrs. Verstille included a Marble Pound Cake recipe in her 1866 cookbook, but it was one flavor of batter with swirls of pink cochineal coloring added just before

What Is Cochineal?

Most food colorings in early Georgia recipes came from the juices of fruit or leaves. Cochineal, also called carmine, however, is a bright pink natural dye imported from desert regions. It is from an insect, usually in dried and powdered form. Although many are repulsed by the idea of eating a bug, this dye still turns up in foods today as Natural Red 4. Ellen Verstille's 1866 Georgia cookbook notes that the cochineal is prepared for cakes and icing with the addition of soda, alum, and cream of tartar, but food historian Kay Moss suggests that in the past it was used more as a textile dye.[1] If natural dyes are of interest, several recipes were recorded by Milledgeville's Martha Goode Tucker (1805–1873) and published in pamphlet form as *Housekeeping Diary of an Antebellum Lady*.[2]

1. Verstille, *Verstille's Southern Cookery*, 129; Moss and Hoffman, *The Backcountry Housewife*, 116.
2. Obituary, *UR*, 17 September 1873; tombstone, Memory Hill Cemetery, Milledgeville.

baking.[9] Multiflavored cake recipes don't begin to show up regularly in southern cookbooks until the 1870s. Perhaps Mrs. Mitchell was on the culinary cutting edge, serving a marbled cake that so delighted guests that it has been long remembered?

All in all, the evidence points both for and against this being an antebellum recipe.[10] Yet even if we could be satisfied about the age of the recipe, we can't be sure it came from the Mitchell household. Now that the recipe contributor is no longer around to ask, we're left to wonder whether it may be a recipe similar to a cake Mrs. Mitchell once served or one simply named in her honor. When I was just discovering old cookbooks, I was disappointed to learn that some recipes with interesting titles don't live up to their names. Of cookbook author Mrs. A. P. Hill's "Georgia Sponge Cake," food historian Damon Lee Fowler noted that it was actually "Georgia" in name only, that when placed in context it varied little from recipes found in other regions and therefore wasn't distinctive to our state. He added, "The same is mostly true for the recipes which have been patriotically renamed for (mostly Georgia) war heroes."[11] Not knowing the origins of a recipe or how well it represents its attention-grabbing name doesn't mean it isn't valuable or can't stir up interesting conversation when it is served. Just don't jump to conclusions before doing some research.

Indigenous Foodways

Aggie Lossiah lived a quiet life on a rural farm in the Great Smoky Mountains. When she died in 1966 at the age of eighty-five, however, newspapers scattered across the country reported her death. Over eight hundred miles away, a headline from Iowa read, "Cherokee Woman Saved Old Recipes from Extinction."[1]

Looking for written antebellum recipes from Georgia is already tricky due to yesteryear's lower literacy rates, the ravages of time, and the fact that documents related to home life weren't always valued. When it comes to indigenous foodways of the past, there are additional challenges. First, our state's modern political boundaries little reflect the relationship between the region's earliest peoples and the land; we must search for historical foodways from the Cherokee, Muskogee (Creek), Seminole, and Uchee peoples across multiple states.[2] Second, traditions were often passed orally, resulting in fewer written documents.[3] Third, often what we know—or think we know—comes from period accounts from those outside the culture, and foodways were not the focus of these accounts. Fourth, there was much loss. Beginning in the sixteenth century, vast numbers of indigenous people died of diseases first brought by explorers. In the years that followed, colonists and settlers took over ancestral lands in waves of cessions. Following the discovery of gold, 1838 marked the year that the government forced indigenous people west on the Trail of Tears. (Thus the date for this section.) In later years, boarding schools for Native American youth attempted to strip away students' mother languages and cultural ties.

Today's Native American communities are sources of inspiration, preserving rich culture in ways that weave together history and modern life. And foodways can serve as cultural reconnection points. Robin Wall Kimmerer—a scientist, educator, and a member of the Citizen Potawatomi Nation—wrote of needing to "walk back along the red road of our ancestors' path and to gather up all the fragments that lay scattered along the trail," of looking for "fragments of land, tatters of language, bits of songs, stories, sacred teachings—all that was dropped along the way."[4] Foodways are also valuable traditions to be collected. There are modern Native American recipes that can be celebrated and studied for traces of the past. Tribal historians, foodways specialists, anthropologists, and archaeologists can help us understand how forced migration, new landscapes, and the passage of time impacted these recipes.

Thankfully there are two sources about traditional indigenous foodways connected to Georgia. The first is a seventy-one-page cookbook from 1951 called *Cherokee Cooklore: To Make My Bread* supported by what is now the Museum of the Cherokee People in Cherokee, North Carolina.[5] It contains photographs and recipes of the aforementioned local foodways teacher Aggie Ross Lossiah (1880–1966), the granddaughter of Georgia's Chief John Ross (1790–1866).[6] Ross became principal chief of the Cherokees in 1827 and fought for the right of his people to stay on ancestral lands. When public sentiment and government policy could not be swayed, he mitigated preparations for the forced journey. According to family legend, one of Ross's sons was part of a group that escaped, walking up a creek all night to avoid being tracked.[7] Lossiah, "a child of her father's middle age," was born fourteen years after her grandfather Ross died.[8] In the public record there are several articles describing Lossiah's youth in the mountains where she was raised by her maternal grandparents as well as her mature days sharing foodways as "Bread-Maker of the Cherokees" at Oconaluftee Indian Village, a 1760s living history site supported by the Cherokee Historical Association.[9]

The first forty pages of the cookbook contain photographs of Lossiah preparing food and cooking outdoors. Along with preparation methods for meat and corn, she shared thirty recipes, including many using indigenous ingredients such as chestnuts, possum grapes, field apricots (maypops), sassafras roots, and wild greens. The cookbook contains sixty-one more recipes from other members of the community. The matrilineal nature of Cherokee society as well as the fact that Lossiah never met her grandfather means that her ties to modern Georgia were marginal. Still, her keen interest in older ways of cooking preserved the type of foodways knowledge that was once common at Georgia cookfires. These two Lossiah recipes are reprinted courtesy of the Museum of the Cherokee People, which asked that readers using foraged ingredients follow sustainable harvesting practices, leaving enough behind to allow plants to reproduce and thrive.

Ash Cake

Make a stiff dough of cornmeal and warm water. Rake ashes back, spread hot stone of bottom of fireplace or outdoor cooking place with oak leaves, put pone of bread on the leaves, cover with more leaves and pile on red-hot ashes. Remove pone when done. Eat in any manner that bread is eaten.

—Ulmer and Beck, *Cherokee Cooklore* (1951), 50

Sassafras Tea

Gather and wash the roots of the red sassafras. Do this in the early spring before the sap rises. Store for future use. When ready to make tea, boil a few pieces of the roots, serve hot. Sweeten if desired. [Please handle the sassafras tree gently, so it survives harvesting.]

—Ulmer and Beck, *Cherokee Cooklore* (1951), 47

Although *Cherokee Cooklore* is out of print, it sold so well as a memento from the Smoky Mountains that used copies are abundant. The second source of Cherokee recipes connected to Georgia is more recent, yet harder to find. *Cherokee Cooking from the Mountains and Gardens to the Table* was self-published in 2000.[10] It shares recipes and commentary from Tony (1924–2010) and Nancy (1942–2023) Plemmons, former residents of Fort Oglethorpe and owners of a Young Harris business called the Brasstown Valley American Indian Gallery.

I first read about the latter source through the work of foodways writers Erin Byers Murray and Jed Portman. Both described the cookbook process—patiently writing down foraging, gardening, and cooking knowledge and then explaining how it weaves into Cherokee culture.[11] Even though the Plemmons book is a modern source, it focuses on an important part of Georgia's older foodways. Unfortunately, the only two copies available during my research were at libraries in West Virginia and Washington, D.C. After waiting out the travel limitations of the Covid-19 pandemic, I was able to visit the Library of Congress. There, in the old Jefferson Building's main reading room, I finally had *Cherokee Cooking* in my hands. I settled at a table and the bustle of Capitol Hill faded away for a couple of hours. When at last I leaned back from the cookbook, I reached for my laptop computer. Journaling is a longtime helpful habit, so I wrote an entry about my experience. We've looked at many recipe sources with an academic coolness, but sometimes it is good to remember what they can mean to individuals.

This place has a scholarly hush—just the occasional flutter of pages or the rumbling wheels of a book cart. And this vaulted space is certainly beautiful with its dark polished wood, brass fittings, and marble details. Up, up, up above me in the dome, twelve civilizations are celebrated with paintings of classical figures. The tall Corinthian columns are topped with labels naming fields of study—Science, Law, Poetry, Philosophy, Art, History, Commerce, and Religion. This grand and formal reading room celebrates the heights of civilization. And yet I am here to read a self-published, small-print-run work that represents a natural relationship between people and the familiar land of North Georgia. My researcher's appointment is short, so I must gulp down these pages rather than sip them. But even just leafing through this cookbook has already taught me much about foraged ingredients and old foodways. I thought this book should be a part of my project to help other people, yet it speaks to *me*. How odd that I've come six hundred miles only to find a fresh view of home, glimpsing things that are recognizable yet more complex than I ever realized. All those childhood days foraging berries and roaming for wild plums with my buddies, thinking we knew the basics of the woods. So many hikes in my grownup years with a plant identification guide in my back pocket. It's humbling to realize how much there is to learn. There's a very old and very new Georgia within this quiet book.

Several months later, a copy finally turned up with a used bookseller, so I've been able to slowly peruse recipes for sumac lemonade, hickory nut soup, bean bread, and more. Tony Plemmons's memories of his childhood and what he learned from elders reaches back almost a century, yet much of the knowledge is far older. The book is designed more for readers than for cooks making a quick meal, so some recipes are tucked within descriptions of native plants or childhood stories. In the 224 pages, I counted eighty-eight recipes. It is one of my favorite cookbooks from the entirety of my research, and I must admit that I hope sharing information about it here may lead to it being republished. If not, I've promised my copy to the Museum of the Cherokee People to make it available to others.

Exploring Further

Several Georgia locations offer educational displays and occasional programs that touch on indigenous foodways. The National Park Service supports the Ocmulgee Mounds (Macon) and the Trail of Tears National Historic Trail. The Georgia Department of Natural Resources cares for historic sites such as the Chief Vann

The log home of Chief John Ross stands on a grassy slope above the modern buildings of Rossville, Georgia, just south of Chattanooga.

House (Chatsworth), Etowah Indian Mounds (Cartersville), Kolomoki Mounds (Blakely), and New Echota (Calhoun). In addition, there are professional chefs celebrating indigenous foodways through restaurants and cookbooks—Nico Albert (Cherokee), Taelor Barton (Cherokee), Freddie Bitsoie (Navajo), Richard Hetzler (Smithsonian National Museum of the American Indian, Washington, D.C.), Sherry Pocknett (Mashpee Wampanoag), Sean Sherman (Oglala Lakota Sioux), Kristina Stanley (Chippewa/Ojibwe), and Anthony Warrior (Muscogee/Creek), to name a few. And I-Collective is a group dedicated to indigenous foodways.[12]

Frolic Foods

> If the sun were not boiling, and the sand didn't get into the salad, and the rocks were soft and smooth, and there were no hornets, and one hadn't to go three-quarters of a mile for water, what a tame affair a picnic would be.
>
> —*Milledgeville Union and Recorder*, 16 March 1880

"FOMO" on social media stands for Fear Of Missing Out, the worry that others are having fun without you. I suffer from the past tense version, "DOMO" or Disappointment Over Missing Out, due to being born after air conditioning and electronic screens began tempting Georgians to curl up at home alone. Because I value the advances in social justice and medicine, I would never wish to go backwards in time, yet there's a part of me that longs for the neighborly connections that I perceive were more common in the past—as well as more chances to sample homemade desserts. One remedy is to re-embrace the *frolic*. I came across this term in an old Georgia newspaper while helping an archives researcher. Later, a rainy Saturday afternoon offered time to explore the term via the Georgia Historic Newspapers database. (The earliest use of the word I could find in a Georgia newspaper was 1840, thus the date of this section.)[1]

To many of us in the twenty-first century, "frolic" sounds decidedly outdated. Perhaps you even picture someone skipping about in an undignified fashion while waving their hands in the air? The word sometimes carried a disapproving tone in state newspapers a century or more ago; yesteryear's journalists loved to chide unwise "frolics" due to youth or moonshine. Usually, however, a frolic was a gathering intent on good clean fun. A frolic could consist of neighbors and friends, or the participants could be from a shared place of worship, social club, hobby group, or the community at large. Frolics took place in homes but also in farmyards, barns, woodlands, and parks. They happened on the sandy edges of ponds, lakes, and rivers as well as the barrier island beaches. As I used keyword searches to skim through decades of newspapers, it became clear that although frolics were sometimes carefully planned by a host or committee, most had a casual air: "Y'all come on out and bring a basket of good food to share!"

The picnic or "dinner on the grounds" was by far the most popular frolic I found in old newspapers, and of course this type of gathering is still common now. Sometimes old-time picnics were serious, a way to feed a crowd for a political rally or religious meeting. Most picnics described in old Georgia accounts, however, could be dubbed frolics and filled my head with borrowed nostalgia. I glimpsed May Days fluttering with ribbon dances, lemonade-squeezing competitions, and town-wide picnics to the countryside with transportation provided by wagon caravans or special excursion trains. Charmingly, sunshine wasn't always desired. Night picnics by the full moon or on tables set up under trees draped with lanterns were not uncommon during hot weather. When nights turned cold, the warmth of bonfires allowed picnics out of season. Whether by day or night, newspapers noted many people brought musical instruments to picnics, and sometimes a dance floor was arranged.

I was not surprised to find picnics were popular "back in the day," nor to read about events like the fish fry, oyster roast, or ice cream social. Some of the frolics, however, were creative gatherings that may have required an old-fashioned mindset to dream up—bullfrog hunts, fishing parties, maypop wars (similar to a snowball fight, only with the spongy fruit of the wild passionflower), peanut boilings, pounding parties (bestowing those in need with a pound or so of a food item you could spare), tacky parties (ugly attire required), tally ho parties (singing carriage rides), and shivarees (rowdy gatherings outside the lodgings of newlyweds), to name a few. Another old-fashioned aspect to frolics is that some were attached to labor and agriculture. Many hands made light work, so friends and neighbors came together to ease a sense of overwhelm—a quilting bee to aid a new bride's household as winter approached, a corn shucking to stow provisions before the rains, or a watermelon cutting to avoid a bumper crop lost to rot. Berrying parties in the summer and nutting parties in autumn meant pleasant company while provisioning the family larder. Some frolics such as boxed supper auctions, cake lotteries, or homespun carnivals raised money for a community cause. Regardless of the organizer's intent for the frolic, these gatherings were a time to build or nurture friendships. In addition, unattached members of the community could "court" in a setting that was safe and elder-approved.

> There will be a picnic at A. B. Allen's spring, next Saturday. The old folks are invited to meet there, and talk about their crops, quilts, etc., not forgetting to bring something to eat. The young ladies will please turn out in full force, looking as sweet as the hot weather will permit: we know they will draw in the young men, like sheep to the slaughter, or eagles to the carcass.
>
> —*Summerville Gazette*, 14 July 1881

For our purposes, the key question is: What did Georgians eat at frolics? The food often had to be portable and stand up to a delay in eating, yet likely consisted of favorites to share proudly. Unfortunately, many of the newspaper accounts were disappointingly sparse. For instance, a Dalton paper reported in 1885: "The palate of any epicure would have been tickled to gaze on the sumptuous dinner. The rude tables, constructed of boards beneath the shadow of a huge oak, fairly groaned with the weight of good things spread upon them."[2] *Humph. List some of the foods! Give me recipes!* Whenever I found more detailed articles, I took note of the specific frolic provisions mentioned: barbecued meat, beer, bread, buttermilk, cake/poundcake, candy, chicken (fried, in a pie, or in salad form), cider, coffee, cookies, cornbread, eggs (deviled, hard boiled, or pickled), fish (caught on location), ginger ale, gingerbread, ham (often described as "cold boiled"), ice cream, ices, jelly, johnny/ash cakes, lemonade, milk, nuts, pie, pickles, popcorn, roast beef, rolls filled with chopped meat, salad, canned salmon salad, sandwiches, sweet potatoes, tarts, tea (cold), tongue, and watermelon.[3] In case you're in doubt about who was usually in charge of the food, the *Early County News* from Blakeley noted on 20 June 1879 that for a local picnic, "Bachelors are not expected to contribute anything, except what 'varments' they catch the day previously."[4]

Some of the frolics mentioned above, like peanut boilings and fishing parties, had a specific food built into the event. One popular food-based event grew out of the South's notorious sweet tooth.[5] Autumn is the time for harvesting the two primary plants Georgians have traditionally grown for sweeteners—sugarcane and sorghum. Both are large grasses that contain sweet juice in the stalk or "cane," yet there are differences. Sugarcane is grown in warmer climate zones, is typically harvested later in the season, and results in a paler, milder juice. With both plants, the canes are squeezed to extract the sweet liquid. In days gone by, a horse or mule was attached to the juicing mechanism, walking in an endless circle to press the cane. Once the liquid is obtained, it then undergoes a long process of heating and skimming off impurities, carefully monitored for temperature and evaporation appropriate for the type of cane. Sugarcane juice can result in various products—cane syrup, white or brown sugar (varying by crystal size and how much of the plant flavor remains), and molasses. With sorghum, processing turns it into sorghum syrup, sometimes called sorghum molasses.

Nowadays factories handle the steps described above, but it often used to be an annual hours-long outdoor process, and all that sweetness lured the neighbors like bees to honey. (The children's picture book *Molasses Man,* by Kathy May, is a helpful source if you'd like to see the steps.) Chewing on a stalk of sugarcane and sipping fresh juice were seasonal treats. Those waiting for finished syrup might pitch in for the stirring and skimming—or just hang out to watch and chat.

And then there was the candy pull. Homemade candy can be made by boiling sugars or syrups, so it is a natural treat for celebrating when the cane harvest is done. Regardless of whether the pulled candy is made with fresh syrup or sweetener from the pantry, repeatedly stretching this type of confection as it begins to cool adds air bubbles for a lighter texture, yet many recipes are frustratingly vague when it comes to the how-tos. I'm hoping modern-day science-loving Georgia cookbook author Alton Brown will take on some recipes. In the meantime, Georgia journalist Clara Hooks Eschmann (1917–2002) shared a particularly rich description of candy pulls from her Americus childhood in her book *Remember When—?*[6] Her account is too long to share here, but having hosted a couple of candy pulls myself, I can tell you that it is beneficial to compare vague, old-fashioned recipes to modern ones and then use a candy thermometer to know when the cooking is done—usually at soft crack stage (270°F–290°F). You'll set the cooked candy aside on a heat-safe surface and poke it every few minutes until you think you can bear to pick it up with buttered fingertips. (Some recipes advise you to flour your hands as well.) You can pull a small glob of candy between your own two hands, but a partner is helpful for handling more at once. In fact, it will likely take many sets of work partners to effectively manage a whole batch of candy. Partners step backwards so that the hot candy stretches out between the two of you, and then you can "double" the candy by folding it as you step back closer together. Each person takes a new grip on the candy and starts over. The stretch-and-fold pattern should continue as long as the candy is warm enough to be pliable or until it turns very pale. A 1947 newspaper article about cane syrup noted, "It's easy to guess where the jitterbug [dance] steps originated—at a South Georgia candy-pullin.'"[7]

This early postcard shows a cane grinding setup, while the photograph courtesy of the Georgia Salzburger Society (Rincon) gives a closer view of the rollers that squeeze cane stalks.

Unless you add flavorings, the taste of the finished candy is determined by the type of sugar or syrup used. During my time at the Georgia Archives, I created a program called Down Home Days so kids could learn about yesteryear's games, pastimes, and childhood chores.[8] The refreshment station was a place to taste old-fashioned treats including a "syrup bar" where they could taste various sweeteners once popular across Georgia. Their reactions reveal a sweetness scale. Twenty-first-century kids usually like amber-colored cane syrup with its caramel aftertaste. Sorghum syrup causes a wrinkled brow. It is a new flavor for many, but likable. Molasses? Even though I served a mild brand, the complex flavor blend of sweet, sour, and bitter caused most kids to immediately make a comical face. Thankfully, a follow-up taste of gingerbread usually redeemed molasses for most of my pint-sized taste testers.

Picnic Delicacies No. 1

Boil a number of eggs hard and when cold cut each in two lengthwise. Take out the yelks [*sic*], mash them with a fork, mix butter and add minced potted ham and French mustard. The hollowed whites of the eggs should be filled with mixture, the two halves pressed together and wrapped in white tissue paper.

—*Barnesville Gazette*, 24 September 1896

Picnic Delicacies No. 2

Cut brown bread into very thin slices, buttering lightly. Lay between two of these slices, sanwich [*sic*] fashion, a filling made of cream cheese in which has been mixed, chopped olives, new and delicious.

—*Barnesville Gazette*, 24 September 1896

"Gentle reader, were you ever at a 'Candy Pulling'—(some call them 'Candy *Stretchings*,') one of the old-time sort, when there was a most delightfully incongruous mixture of love and laughter, boys and butter, lasses and *mo*lasses? Did you ever 'pull candy' with a rosy-lipped, bright-eyed little girl, you at one end and she at the other of a piece of 'sweetness long drawn out,' and when you had drawn it out as long as you could without breaking, she with a significant smile and glance, proposed to 'double?' Eh? . . . These Candy Pullings are dangerous things sometimes."

—*Temperance Banner* (Penfield), 13 October 1855

Traveling Lunch

Sardines chopped fine, also a little ham, a small quantity of chopped pickles. Mix with mustard, pepper, salt and a tiny bit of catsup and a squeeze of lemon. Spread between bread nicely buttered.

—A. Roberts, *Drummers' Home Cook Book* (1902), 39

Five Minute Candy

½ cup molasses
½ teaspoon soda
Put it on a hot spider
well buttered just till
it boils for five minutes.

—1870s Receipt Book of Mrs. Godkin, Anderson Family Papers, 1869–1923, Georgia Historical Society, Savannah[9]

Georgia Taffy

Bring two cups Georgia syrup to a boil, add one tablespoonful of butter, continue to boil; when tested in cold water candy is brittle. Just before taking from fire stir in a pinch of soda. Pull as any molasses candy.

—Miss Hattie Oliver, in Westminster Presbyterian Church, *Savannah Cook Book* (1909), 125

PULLED SUGAR CANDY

2 cups granulated sugar
1 cup boiling water
1 level teaspoonful of Cream Tartar
1 teaspoonful butter
1 teaspoonful of vanilla
1-2 teaspoonful soda

Add sugar to boiling water also Cream of Tartar and boil until it threads and breaks. Then pour on marble and sprinkle over this one half teaspoonful of soda. Begin to pull at once. The butter has been added as soon as the sugar and water have come to a boil.

Miss Lena Kendall.

St. Paul's Church (Albany), *Southwest Georgia Cook Book* (1924), 111

Elise's Tea Cakes

This is the recipe just as it was written:

Mammy Elise
Tea Cakes

3 Eggs 2 cups of sugar
4 of flour a large spoon
—full of Lard a Teaspoon
full of Soda in a Teacup
of Claber or thick Butter
milk beat the white & yolks
of the eggs separately
good

To many twenty-first century readers, the recipe above is vague enough to be a cooking puzzle. How much is "a large spoonful" of lard? Clabber is a term for curdled sour milk that few cooks use anymore. And we're used to seeing mixing method plus baking time and temperature in recipes, but this one doesn't give those details.

In addition, this recipe is also a history puzzle. Where did it come from? How does it fit into Georgia foodways?

Solving these puzzles involves seeking clues. Our initial clues can be found with the manuscript recipe. To see it handwritten on a blank page inside an 1858 copy of *Miss Beecher's Domestic Receipt Book*,[1] one must go north of downtown

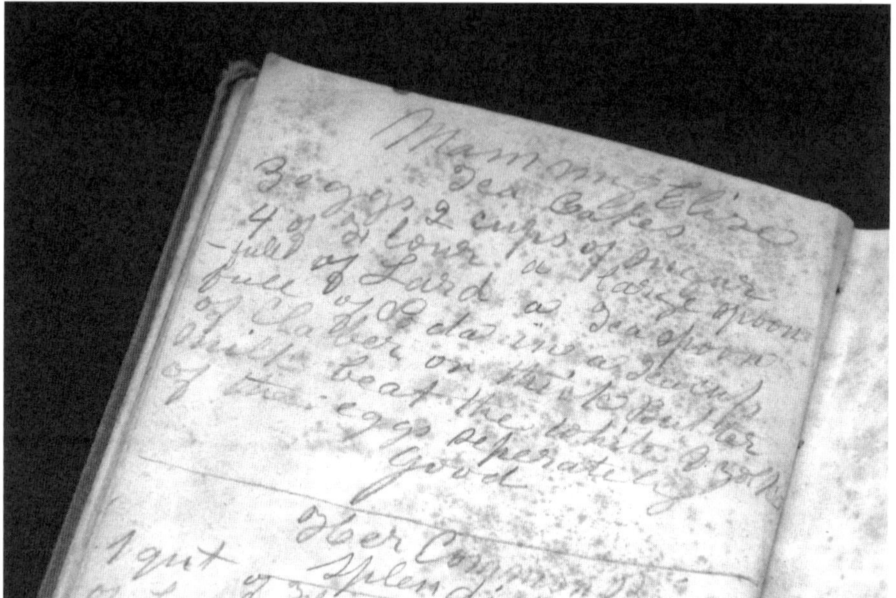

Permission to include the transcription and photo of the recipe is courtesy of the Kenan Research Center, Atlanta History Center.

Atlanta. Between the neighborhood that includes the governor's mansion and the Buckhead commercial district, you'll come to the Atlanta History Center. There you'll search for the cookbook using their online catalog dubbed Terminus. The online catalog shares the name originally chosen by the Western & Atlantic Railroad in the late 1830s for the settlement that would become Atlanta. In its early days, Terminus was merely a few wooden buildings and dirt roads clustered around the end of the tracks. By 1843, both the railroad and Terminus were growing nicely, so it was decided to rename the village Marthasville in honor of the young daughter of Governor Wilson Lumpkin (1783–1870). This daughter, Martha Lumpkin Compton (1827–1917), came to be considered "the Godmother of Atlanta" even though the town was renamed once again only two years later.[2] And it just so happens that Martha was the owner of the cookbook with the tea cake recipe penciled inside.

Yet there's more to the history of this recipe.

The cook credited with the tea cakes was named Elise. No surname is given. As for "mammy," this is such an outdated and culturally burdened word from slavery times that many Americans wince or immediately shortcut to a stereotype, assuming what Elise looked like, her demeanor, and her role in the household.[3]

Historical foodways researchers such as Jessica B. Harris, Toni Tipton-Martin, and Michael W. Twitty, however, are breaking down unhelpful stereotypes, expanding our understanding. Kimberly Wallace-Sanders's *Mammy: A Century of Race, Gender, and Southern Memory* and Rafia Zafar's *Recipes for Respect: African American Meals and Meaning* as well as other books listed in the bibliography explain much about cooks and recipes of the past.

Background knowledge about the substantial ways Black cooks and researchers contributed—and continue to contribute—to the nation's collective foodways is important. At the same time, we also want to uncover more about this specific recipe, so the next clue-gathering step focuses on the cook through primary documents. Unfortunately, the politics, social norms, and prejudices of the past affected what was written down and preserved. There are generally fewer sources available to learn about women in past centuries than about men. African American genealogy often holds extra challenges. There were free persons of color in antebellum Georgia, but they were relatively few, and the source that genealogists rely heavily on—the federal census—did not record names for individuals held as slaves.[4] Other primary sources such as deeds of sale often referred to them by description or first name only, and such documents were sometimes thrown away once they became legally useless. In addition, learning to read was largely forbidden for people who were enslaved and often strongly discouraged for decades after Emancipation, resulting in fewer useful items like manuscript recipe collections, letters, and diaries. Since many factors surrounding an individual's life affect what personal documents were created and saved, it is worth the search. Genealogists and other researchers do find helpful records as well as fascinating personal documents for women and people of color from the past. Thus, with a mindset that was realistic yet hopeful, I began to search for supporting materials.

In terms of the tea cakes, the Lumpkin connection is significant, as this family was prominent enough that some of their records are preserved in archives.[5] There are journals, scrapbooks, and correspondence—hundreds of pages, in fact, of looped, handwritten cursive recording political and business dealings as well as personal thoughts on religion and society. When trying to understand the household's daily life and foodways, however, the details are actually quite sparse. If there is information about Elise here, it is the proverbial needle in the haystack and wasn't found by skim reading.

Martha Lumpkin Compton's footnote in Georgia history meant a smattering of newspaper articles just before and after the turn of the twentieth century—more than would usually exist about a woman of her era even from a prominent family. In an 1893 newspaper piece, Martha was living with a Black woman named Judy at Cedar Hill, Governor Lumpkin's former house.[6] In 1902 there was an article reproduced in several Georgia newspapers praising Caroline Holt (1839–1902), a lifelong companion a dozen years younger than Martha who had just died at the age of sixty-three.[7] The newspaper reported that Caroline had been the fifth generation of her family to be owned by the Lumpkins, and that at the age of two she was given to fourteen-year-old Martha. Over a decade later, in 1917, Martha died at the age of ninety. A newspaper article reported that she left an unusual will, bequeathing a large sum of money and most of her home furnishings to "the daughter of the old negro mammy, now dead, who nursed her as a baby."[8] The actual will does not mention a "mammy" or Elise but does leave money to the daughter of "my devoted servant Caroline."[9]

Elise? Judy? Caroline? The names multiplied, but the history of the recipe did not become clearer. When complex history and sparse documents made the life of Elise feel impossibly remote, I was glad for the cooking portion of the puzzle. Despite all the years and cultural changes, Elise was a fellow home baker. The beauty of foodways is that they allow us to try the motions of another's hands and taste a creative endeavor that they spent time and energy on. Foodways scholar Marion Bishop noted of her grandmother, "When she is gone, her recipes will give many of us access to her, through aroma, taste, and texture."[10] Although what we are reaching for with the tea cakes is not recalled memories but rather a shared sensory experience, can foodways grant us an introduction, an opportunity to connect with a long-dead stranger?

I shut down my computer and went to the kitchen. I measured out a "teacup" of buttermilk, approximately two-thirds of a standard cup. When I decided I

On 13 August 1943 the Scottish diarist William Soutar (1898–1943) wrote:

> Why do we wish to be remembered, even when none remain who looked upon our face? Surely, though it must retain an element of self-consideration, it is a last acknowledgement that we need to be loved; and, having gone from all touch, we trust that memory may, as it were, keep our unseen presence within the borders of day.[1]

1. Mallon, *A Book of One's Own*, vii.

would try this recipe, my grocery shopping included a splurge for "the good stuff" from an artisan dairy as it pours pleasingly thick and lumpy from its glass bottle. I also sought out beautiful brown eggs from a friend with backyard chickens. Unwashed eggs (not available in most grocery stores) don't need to be chilled, and Elise would not have had a refrigerator, so I made sure my eggs were room temperature. I wanted to pay attention to the details and do the recipe justice.

Working with Elise's recipe was a different sort of research and learning. I began to sense her abilities. Even though I didn't have to chop wood, build a fire, or haul water, those tea cakes were work. I looked longingly at my stand mixer but instead soldiered on with an antique mixing bowl and a wooden spoon.[11] Incorporating all that flour ended with me working the dough with my fingers. The egg whites, however, were the real challenge. My son and I fumbled our way through the first few minutes of turning them into foam with a whisk we made from twigs bound with cotton twine, the sort of kitchen tool our foremothers likely knew well. The whites barely thickened even in a copper bowl suited for the task. We moved on to a tool that was invented before the Civil War but likely not popular in Georgia kitchens until the latter part of the century—an eggbeater.[12] That worked much better, yet made our unaccustomed hands ache. Despite working nonstop, it was almost an hour before I slid tea cakes into the oven. You can believe I was then darn grateful for the faucet, hot water heater, and dishwasher in my climate-controlled kitchen.

Martha thought Elise's recipe important enough to be worth the time, effort, and cookbook space to record it.[13] The recipe is sparse, yet nonetheless hints at expertise built of practice and thoughtfully gathered knowledge. Basic cooking can be an art—tossing in a little of this and a little of that—but baking is more akin to science, dependent on observation and care. My precise measuring spoons, electronic kitchen scale, and thermostat-controlled oven meant that I could more easily narrow down the variables for success. Elise, on the other hand, would have baked on the hearth (with a Dutch oven or a reflector), in a brick oven, or in a wood-burning stove. She would have depended on her intelligence, collected knowledge, and well-developed sensibilities about building heat and using it to her advantage.

What type of wood is on hand, and how seasoned is it? Are the coals ready, and how much air circulation do they need for optimum temperature? The "large spoonful of lard" in the recipe likely meant that Elise didn't measure in the way of modern cooks and therefore would have depended on experience to know by the look and texture of the dough that the ingredients were in the correct proportions. Soon, in the quiet of my kitchen, the scent of toasting flour and caramelizing sugar told me that the tea cakes were nearly finished baking. I thought of Elise standing in another Georgia kitchen long ago noticing the same.

I did find a connection with Elise through baking. In addition, if she was indeed a part of the Lumpkin household, she was a fellow North Georgian and likely even a fellow Athenian. Martha's cookbook now has a permanent home in Atlanta, but the recipe was probably written down in my hometown. The Lumpkin family was established here in Clarke County by the early 1820s.[14] Fifteen decades later, during my early childhood, my family also moved to Athens, as my father's career in sedimentary geology took us first to the University of Georgia's Marine Institute on Sapelo Island and then inland to the main campus. The Geography and Geology Building where my father had an office is in the shadow of the UGA football stadium and on the slope of the aforementioned Cedar Hill. The 1842 home with its thick walls of stone block is presently called Lumpkin House. It still stands near the crest of the hill, so during my growing up and college years I passed it many times, wondering why an old-fashioned stone home was tucked at an odd angle among modern glass college buildings, Cedar Street cutting precariously close to one of its side walls. In researching the tea cake recipe, I learned that eighty-one-year-old Martha left Cedar Hill and moved to Decatur around 1908, soon after the Lumpkin family legally handed property over to the university.[15] Part of the deal was that if the house is ever demolished or removed, a vital slice of campus land reverts to Lumpkin descendants.[16] This legal clause preserved a piece of architectural history likely connected to the tea cake recipe.

On the Saturday morning when my tea cakes were still warm, I packed some up and drove the half dozen miles from home to campus. Although as an adult I lived as far away as California, my husband and I chose to resettle in my hometown among family when it came time to raise our son. Now here I was on campus at the start of a sleepy weekend, the mild air carrying that autumn scent so familiar to Athenians and football fans. I found a parking space at the Science Library, this time not going inside to use the substantial cookbook collection but instead walking to Lumpkin House. The old building is currently filled with office spaces, but if there was a kitchen inside during the building's six decades as a private residence, it would have been at the back of the ground level. I walked behind the building, reaching out to run a hand over the rough stone. Then I looked over my shoulder. During the period when the house was built, kitchens were usually a separate building, to keep heat and cooking smells away from the main house and to protect it in case of a kitchen fire. If there was a kitchen building, the traces are now covered up by the wide cement walkway to the College of Agriculture's Conner Hall.

I circled to the front of Lumpkin House again. From my basket I pulled out a Blue Willow plate, its pattern so popular in the South since the late eighteenth century that Athenians today still find weathered shards of it washed up on sandbars in the Oconee River below town. I made a small pyramid of tea cakes. Then, after giving Elise a nod, I took a bite. It wasn't a fancy cookie, but it was pleasing, soft and mildly sweet.

I first used muffin tins, a helpful way to ensure an unfamiliar dough doesn't spread out of control. Once I knew the dough was thick enough, I dropped spoonfuls onto a baking sheet instead.

In that quiet moment, I realized the house indeed sits atop quite a hill. The 1893 newspaper article recalled an avenue of oaks creating a thick tunnel over an unpaved drive connecting with Lumpkin Street, an Athens artery that was once an important trading path for Native Americans.[17] Now, even on a weekend, university buses rumbled past and backpack-toting students strolled manicured sidewalks. Oconee Hill Cemetery—where Martha's father and my father are both buried—once would have been in view but is now hidden by the tall Chemistry Building. In fact, old Clarke County maps show that once upon a time Cedar Hill must have been a fine place to look out over fields to wooded hills blue in the distance. For a few minutes, a place familiar since childhood felt both historically old and interestingly new.

As I ate small bites of tea cake, my thoughts turned to what life may have been like for the people who lived and worked atop that hill, those who called it home. When visiting a historical site, it isn't unusual to have such thoughts, yet my work with Elise's recipe made a difference. I had invested time and effort to move past the surface. The tea cakes weren't easy to make when I took on even a few of the tasks of a nineteenth-century cook. All cooks had it tough before plumbing and electricity. Yet putting myself specifically in Elise's cooking apron, even briefly, meant allowing some of the realities of history to invade my contemporary life. Although we don't know life dates for Elise, the period of the recipe meant that each person connected to Cedar Hill lived in a time of great upheaval, renegotiating their role in the household and in society as a whole with regard to the roller-coaster transitions of war, Emancipation, Reconstruction, and the onset of the Jim Crow era. Before or after the Civil War, Elise as servant and cook would have shouldered many responsibilities and worries. Perhaps she was a parent as well, adding more responsibilities and worries.[18] What choices did she have, and what choices were put beyond her reach? And then there was Elise as a person with the whole range of human needs, emotions, and hopes.

I sat down for a while atop Cedar Hill and thought back on the sources from the nineteenth, twentieth, and twenty-first centuries that I read while researching this recipe. Many period writings are fraught with racist language and degrading attitudes. While this is hardly surprising, we history explorers are nonetheless sometimes still surprised by our emotional reactions.[19] While serving as Education Coordinator of the Georgia Archives, helping teachers as well as students from college age down to elementary schoolers work with primary sources, my job required that I be vigilant about the possibility of old documents causing fresh pain. Many of the more recent secondary sources I read to understand Elise's

Augustus Baldwin Longstreet (1790–1870) published a collection of stories called *Georgia Scenes* back in 1835. In one tale called "The 'Charming Creature' as a Wife," he spends the better part of two pages praising his sister-in-law's housekeeping. The size of the biscuits on her table is consistent, and she knows exactly how much ham it takes to feed a crowd. Yet he isn't praising her cooking. He's praising her ability to manage pantry supplies and household workers, describing the skill set required to be a successful household mistress. Foodways historian Karen Hess wrote, "In the antebellum South, any house of pretension had skilled slaves in the kitchen. I have so often written that the near mythic quality of Southern cookery is to be attributed to the presence of African American women cooks. They did the cooking; it's as simple as that."[1]

Comparing southern cookbooks over time, we can see a growing pride in hands-on cooking abilities. By the third quarter of the nineteenth century, most well-off women respected personal cooking skills even if they still hired cooks (who were almost always Black). Unfortunately, many of the recipes shared by upper-class women in various cookbooks were likely developed not by the recipe contributors but by uncredited cooks in their kitchens—who may not have been consulted about sharing their work. Due to gender, race, religion, or other factors, many of our past food experts were not given a voice. Toni Tipton-Martin's *The Jemima Code* and Rebecca Sharpless's *Cooking in Other Women's Kitchens* are good places to begin exploring this concept.[2]

One thing to keep in mind, however, is reflected in the Hess quotation above—"house of pretension." Kitchen duties were a matter of gender and race but also of socioeconomics. In diaries that middle-class Magnolia Le Guin (1869–1947) of Henry County kept from 1901 to 1913, she recorded kitchen work as a constant burden.[3] She periodically hired local women to help in the kitchen, but her financial resources wavered with the economy and the harvest year. Her ability to find a lasting kitchen partnership that worked well also wavered, so usually she cooked on her own. As we will see in the 1867 section, the Civil War changed social norms but also the assets of many Georgians. Lower-class women had been cooking all along, as had many of the middle class. Introductions to the cookbooks of Georgia authors Annabella Hill (1867), Ella Tennent (1885), and Annie Dennis (1921 edition) all discuss that the war affected women's roles, requiring middle- and upper-class women to expand their hands-on skills. Literate middle-class women were arguably the primary audience for cookbooks and the ones most likely to keep manuscript collections of recipes. Thus the answer to "Who did the cooking?" depends on many factors and changed over time.

1. Hess, in A. Fisher, *What Mrs. Fisher Knows*, 78–79.
2. For those exploring race and foodways, Georgia cookbooks of interest for their imagery may include those in sections 1912, 1916, 1933, and 1943. Additional sources to consider include McRee's *The Kitchen and the Cotton Patch* and Bethlehem Methodist's *Bethlehem's Kitchen Secrets*.
3. Le Guin, *A Home-Concealed Woman*.

recipe also held painful stories, even if the overall story of Black history is one of perseverance, resilience, and accomplishment. To add to the emotional mix with the tea cake recipe, learning more about the Lumpkin family uncovers Governor Lumpkin's key role in the 1838 Trail of Tears, the forced removal of the indigenous peoples who once used a path within sight of where I was now sitting.[20]

As society shifts and evolves, individuals within it may look back at history with anger or acceptance as well as guilt, denial, or personal disconnect. Often we experience a mixture of these depending on our own background and what's going on in our lives. It's far easier to look at the tea cakes recipe with colorblind eyes and take it at face value—an appealing old-fashioned cookie. But I believe it is Georgia's oldest known written recipe from a Black cook and has much to offer beyond creating a pleasing treat.

After all my research, reading, and baking, it would be nice to be able to say that I have a good understanding of this recipe and its gifts, but I must admit that I'm still learning. More than facts, this recipe taught me a great deal about slowing down, seeking, and reconsidering history. For that I am grateful.

Research did not uncover who Elise was—a few clues but barely a trace of the million-and-one traits and memories that make a soul unique. Time erases many things. But look back at the beginning of this section. There's the tea cake recipe if you'd also like to connect with Elise's legacy. Read. Bake. Taste. Listen.

Exploring Further

Athenian Nicole A. Taylor wrote *Watermelon & Red Birds: A Cookbook for Juneteenth and Black Celebrations*. Other foodways writers connected with Georgia who explore Black foodways from various angles include Curtis G. Aikens, Mashama Bailey, Erica Barrett, Jennifer Hill Booker, Dora Charles, Clarissa Clifton, Erika Council, Cheryl Day, Sharon Kaye Hunt, Flora Mae Hunter, Ruth Jackson, Sonya Jones, Edna Lewis, Matthew Raiford, Todd Richards, Sallie Ann Robinson, Stephen Satterfield (film), Deborah VanTrece, and Dexter Weaver.

Mrs. Edgeworth's Antebellum Homestead

The Southern Gardener and Receipt-Book, 1859
Mary Lewis Rowland Michal Edgeworth (1818–ca. 1872)
478 pages. 505 food recipes with 531 additional recipes or advice segments for farm and household needs.

"A final glimpse at the plantation-era dinner table" and "extensive" is how southern foodways expert John Egerton described Georgia's oldest known published cookbook.[1] History buffs might describe it as "a window in time," allowing the reader to better picture farms and kitchens on the eve of the Civil War. Here you'll find early recipes for classics such as "barbacue," biscuits, corn bread, "purlow," sweet potatoes, and even mac 'n' cheese, which Edgeworth calls A Dish of Maccaroni. Some recipes reflect yesteryear's favorites rarely appearing in today's cookbooks, such as Syllabub, Rusks, and Marguerites.

Despite being in old-fashioned paragraph format, most of the food recipes seem familiar enough, although they may instruct how the coals of the cooking fire should look or advise capping a storage jar with leather. Measurements are sometimes old-fashioned (gill or wineglassful) and at other times according to life experience—"butter the size of the hen's egg" or heating a liquid until "blood warm." A little research will help the reader locate now-unusual ingredients, decide upon necessary substitutions, and define confusing terms. For instance, an Internet search for Edgeworth's recommended "bell metal kettle" reveals it

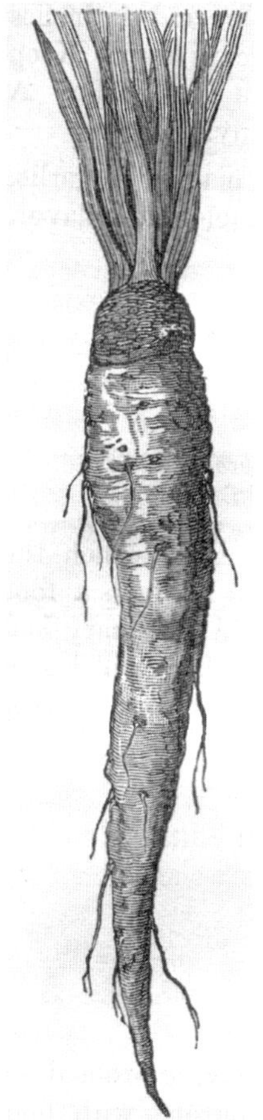
Fig. 74.—SALSIFY.

This image from page 295 of the Georgia book *Gardening for the South* by William N. White (see 1876 section) shows salsify, a root we rarely see anymore that Edgeworth called "vegetable oyster." She gave directions for boiling, frying, or turning this ingredient into patties.

was a pot made of bronze or brass. Similarly, modern muffin tins can usually serve as "patty pans." But cooking experience alone often works fine; reading through Edgeworth's recipe for Bread Fritters reveals that this dish is simply a multistep French toast. And today's readers exploring the Edgeworth cookbook may thank their lucky stars for modern-day kitchen conveniences, as the batter for Pound Cake No. III requires the cook to "beat it all well together for an hour with your hands."[2]

Over a century and a quarter passed between the founding of Georgia and the publication of its first cookbook.[3] Still, at the time of its writing, the elders in Mary Edgeworth's community may have started their lives as colonists rather than U.S. citizens, and you'll find recipes with roots in the British Isles, such as Bannock and Yorkshire Pudding. Baking enthusiasts may find it interesting that mace and rosewater are more popular in the cookbook than cinnamon and vanilla. And there are dishes and ingredient combinations that seem novel today—Apple Molasses, Red Sugar Beet Pie, alcoholic Milk Lemonade, and more.

A key question for any cookbook is to determine the audience. Who was Edgeworth writing for? There are recipes for fancy meals that reflect the famed tradition of southern hospitality and ingredients that would have been expensive for rural Georgians in the 1850s.[4] Yet there are many simple recipes as well as gardening instructions for basic vegetables. Overall, the book was designed help those living in remote areas, both well-to-do and not, in the days before quick information. If you lived in "the backcountry" and needed advice before plunging in to cure your horse of heaves, dye cloth, kill bedbugs, or estimate the weight of cattle, this was the go-to book for you. And you could also use it to bake an impressive cake when the circuit-riding preacher came through.

As was typical for many cookbooks of the day, a large portion of the recipes are dedicated to making sure food would not go to waste, since small-scale home canning was just beginning to take hold.[5] Some recipes for preserving food before home refrigeration seem dubious to modern readers. Edgeworth recommends floating eggs in lime-water or packing them in sand with the small end of the shell pointing down. Her method to preserve milk was to slowly heat it in corked bottles that, when cooled, were stored in sawdust, and she recommended adding lumps of charcoal to salvage meat "in a putrescent state." Soup, pudding, and hash recipes often include information for adding leftovers or making the recipe stretch to more servings. Her recipes contain many uses for stale bread or leftover potatoes. Some recipes helped save the abundance of harvest for months when food choices would have been slimmer. For instance, there are recipes for making typical pickled cucumbers, but also pickled beans, beets, cabbage, grapes, lemons, melons, onions, oysters, peaches, radishes, tomatoes (ripe and green), and walnuts.

For the modern reader used to packaged medications, the non-cooking sections of the book may be baffling and amusing. Onions tied to the armpits and stomach are likely not an effective antidote for poison. Breastfeeding mothers with inflammation were encouraged to slather on polecat oil—skunk musk. Perhaps they felt some relief, but they were undoubtedly unpopular at social gatherings. Edgeworth's full ingredient list for various cures would require a modern botanist and chemist to sort out the harmful from the benign or helpful, but it is fascinating reading.

The Early Life of Mary Edgeworth and Rowland Springs

We find many clues about antebellum life in the cookbook, but little about its author. At the time that foodways scholar John Egerton was writing in the early 1990s, he noted that Edgeworth was "a Georgia lady about whom little is recorded."[6] Thanks to scanning and database projects, there are now more research avenues available for the history behind the cookbook. A published family history reveals that author Mary Lewis Rowland was born in Spartanburg, South Carolina, in 1818.[7] She lived before government birth and death certificates, and no obituary or tombstone have been found, so her life dates are a challenge to verify.[8] It seemed that with each census record or online family tree uncovered by research, her birthday slipped back a few years until she was listed as being ten years younger.[9] This may simply be a series of errors, but perhaps she was "fudging it" to ease social pressure; it is likely that she was at least half a decade older than her second husband.[10]

Mary was the granddaughter of Revolutionary War veteran Thomas Rowland (1750–1836) and the daughter of War of 1812 veteran, merchant, and planter John Sharpe Rowland (1795–1863).[11] Her mother, Frances Machen Lewis Rowland (1799–1869), was well known for her weaving and a frequent winner at fairs for her handiwork.[12] Mary was the oldest of eleven Rowland offspring, six of whom lived to adulthood.[13]

In 1836, likely at age eighteen, Mary married merchant Joseph Michal (born 1806).[14] It is not known how Mary met her husband, although her father and husband appear on the same page of the tenth volume of *Appointments of U.S.*

Postmasters.[15] (During that time, store owners often served as postmasters, allowing their establishment to become a communications and social hub for the sake of increased business.) The next year the newlywed couple had a daughter, but the child died just past her first birthday.[16] A few months after this loss, in 1839, Mary and her husband moved two hundred miles southwest with her parents, establishing a new life in Georgia's hilly Cass County (now Bartow County) on land that the Trail of Tears had recently made available.[17] In their new home, Mary and her mother both gave birth to sons that year, and the 1840 census shows the two families settling into a life of agriculture. Patriarch John Rowland engaged in trading and a 2,500-acre plantation called Etowah Valley less than three miles from the famed Etowah Indian Mounds. This plantation was praised in the era's *Portraits of Eminent Americans Now Living* and is documented in modern local histories.[18] Mary Rowland Michal's family kept a separate household in the same census district until Joseph died in the autumn of 1840 of bilious fever, leaving her a young widow with a year-old baby.[19] At some point Mary and her son moved in with her parents.[20] A few years went by and then, in April of 1844, Mary's son and her youngest brother both died.[21] The boys were buried on a high hill near the house, where Mary would continue to live for the better part of a decade.

In addition to the Etowah Valley home, in 1843 the Rowlands had purchased property ten miles to the northeast and turned a natural spring once frequented by Native Americans into a spa named Rowland Springs. The property became known as "a resort for the fashionable."[22] George White's 1849 *Statistics of the State of Georgia* stated that the Springs were "too well known to need a particular description. They are becoming every season the centre of fashion. Multitudes from every part of the State resort here to partake of the excellent water, as well as the liberal fare of the worthy proprietor."[23] A historical marker erected by the Etowah Valley Historical Society states that the 1849 rate was $1.25 per day, which included four meals.[24] The hotel accommodated six hundred guests.[25] Rowland managed this property until 1851, when it was leased out to new proprietors.[26]

The same year that patriarch John Rowland stepped back from the Springs, Mary married Salathiel Carpenter Edgeworth (ca. 1823–1888), a recent graduate of the Medical Department of the University of Pennsylvania who dabbled briefly in politics.[27] He was the son of Achilles Edgeworth (ca. 1792–1858) and Elizabeth Keziah Carpenter Edgeworth (ca. 1797–ca. 1855).[28] Mary and Salathiel, likely distant cousins, lived for a time in the nearby county seat, Cassville.[29] Mary's

The Imaginative Leap in Rowland Cemetery

Every historical researcher hopes that the facts will come together to make sense of the past, and credible sources add up to a reliable if hazy picture of Mary's life. In addition, most researchers also hope for moments described by historian Janet Theophano as "an imaginative leap" crossing "divides of time, space, and self."[1] There are times when empathy breathes into the facts, bringing history alive. Careful researchers don't let such an encounter trick them into making assumptions, yet it is a gift that stirs our intrigue and helps keep us on the long research trail. During my journey into the world of Georgia's early cookbooks, such a moment came the morning I baked Elise's Tea Cakes and ate them at Cedar Hill. (See 1858 section.) It also happened after finding the Rowland Cemetery. From my April 2018 journal:

> I crept through the far reaches of Metro Atlanta's rush hour traffic to get to Cartersville. The Rowland Cemetery was supposed to be on the edge of Highway 113/61 near the Cartersville Airport. I drove up and down the divided road a couple of times before a flag fluttering atop a steep hill caught my eye. Sure enough, I then also saw the jagged "teeth" of tombstones below the flagpole. . . .
>
> I hiked up through masses of dandelions and clover to reach the small cemetery surrounded by a black metal fence. It appears some of the eight gravestones were repaired or replaced not long ago. The first graves laid out in this cemetery were for two four-year-old boys, the son and younger brother of cookbook author Mary Edgeworth. Neither grave tells the exact day of death, just that for both children it was this same month—April—only 174 years ago.
>
> It was windy and cool in the cemetery high above the roadway. Peaceful. After all those hours of research, it was the first time I felt fairly sure I'd intersected in a physical place with Mary. There wouldn't have been cars rushing over the pavement below in her day. No gas station or airport runway would have been in view. As lovely as I found the spot, it must have been even more lovely back then. There have been many spring flowers, summer thunderstorms, sunny autumn days, and winter snows since then. I wondered if Mary spent time alone on that spot and, if so, what she thought about. As a gift from one mother of a boy to another, I took some time to pull rangy weeds from her child's grave. Pensive, I then headed back down the hill, ankles cold and itching from the deep grass, and drove to the Georgia Room to see if there were more parts of Mary's story I could uncover before the library closed.

Neither at the library that night nor during research sessions afterwards did I find a reason for the tandem deaths of the two boys—an accident or shared illness? There are currently no copies of the local paper known to exist for that month, nor have any related documents surfaced. I hope that as with time passing between John Egerton's research and mine, more may be uncovered in the future.

1. Theophano, *Eat My Words*, 6.

new in-laws, relatives of the celebrated Anglo-Irish novelist Maria Edgeworth (1768–1849), had left South Carolina for central Georgia by the 1840 census. Eventually Mary and Salathiel moved about 150 miles southeast to live near these relatives in Fort Valley. Had Mary lived in modern times, her moving van would have merged onto Interstate 75 at Exit 296 and then pulled off a few hours later at Exit 142.

A Georgia Cookbook with South Carolina Roots

It was in 1859, several years after moving to Fort Valley, that Mary published her cookbook through a Philadelphia press. It enjoyed endorsements from newspapers in Georgia, North Carolina, and Pennsylvania as well as the popular women's magazine *Godey's Lady's Book*.[30] For the next two years, positive reviews as well as booksellers' advertisements appeared in newspapers in various parts of Georgia and up the Eastern Seaboard as far north as Virginia and Maryland. One can only wonder if the book would have continued to gain momentum had the Civil War not broken out.

Mary's work was actually a heavily revised edition of a book self-published in 1840 by merchant and home gardener Phineas Thornton (born 1779) of Camden, South Carolina.[31] Thornton's second edition from 1845 was reprinted in 1984 by Oxmoor House as part of the Antique American Cookbooks collection, and the introduction by history writer Shirley Abbott calls it "a how-to manual for the independent rural Southern family of the 1840s." At first it is puzzling how the cookbook could have jumped fourteen years as well as more than 250 miles, especially when Thornton died in 1851. Mary "affectionately" dedicates her edition to Elizabeth Thornton (1784–1886), Phineas's widow, yet does not elaborate on their relationship.[32] Thankfully, a clippings folder in the Camden Archives and Museum offers clues. A short memoir written by Elizabeth in 1856 reveals that her husband's business partner was his brother-in-law, Dan Carpenter.[33] After further research, it seems that Dan was also Salathiel Carpenter Edgeworth's grandfather. In other words, Mary carried on the work of her great-uncle by marriage.[34]

From Mary's writings, we can deduce she was educated, and we know her family background offered both social connections and plentiful resources. Unlike many of her peers, during prime years of her adulthood she was no longer absorbed by caring for a husband and children. Throughout the North Georgia period of her life, if she was so inclined, she would have been able to go behind the scenes in her parents' plantation kitchen as well as the elaborate kitchen of the Rowland Springs resort. Finally, she also had access to prime avenues of information in her early years—the Rowland and Michal postmaster connections. Abbott's modern introduction to Thornton's second edition states:

> The country storekeeper knew everybody, was in an excellent position to speculate in commodities, buy and sell real estate, or go into politics. If the storekeeper was also the postmaster, like Phineas, he also knew everybody's business. . . . And in the time-honored way of country postmasters, Phineas certainly read all the newspapers and periodicals, maybe even the mail, that passed through his hands. Information was a commodity in 1840. . . . Phineas and his ilk cornered the market in it. . . . Out of such communiqués, out of his own knowledge and curiosity and good will, out of the hundreds of conversations he heard, Phineas Thornton stitched his book together.[35]

Since baskets of various shapes and sizes were used for gathering, carrying, and storing certain foods, handweaving containers like this heavy-duty basket from split oak was a food-related skill farm families once needed to know.

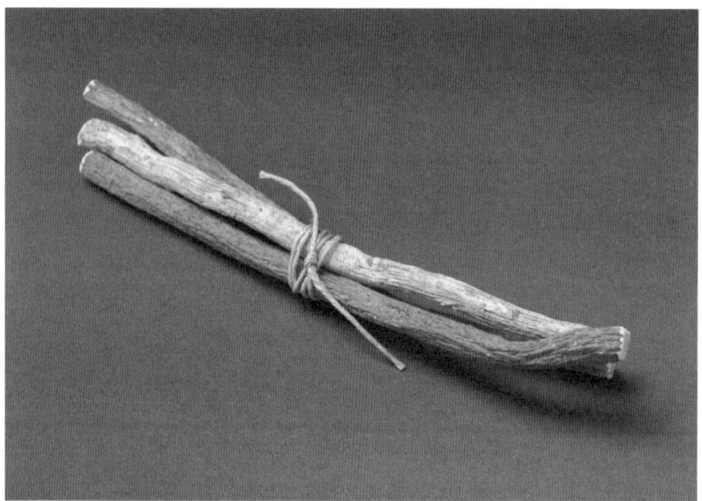

The Industrial Revolution changed the availability of many ingredients and their forms. These are dried roots of the licorice plant, which would have been used to flavor confectionery as well as for medicinal purposes.

In Camden, one of the oldest cities in South Carolina and now a draw for history lovers with its museums and Revolutionary War sites, traces of Phineas Thornton can still be found. His tall tombstone stands within the tree-lined lanes of the Quaker Burying Ground (leased by the Quakers for the term of "999 years at a yearly rental of one Pepper Corn, if lawfully demanded").[36] At the local archives, letters from his wife written with spidery lettering across cream-colored paper describe the vegetables and fruits he grew as well as the flower garden placed at the front of their home.[37] This house, built around 1823, is still standing on the western edge of the downtown area and for many years has been a funeral home.[38] What is now a wide lawn and business parking lot was once the proving ground for Thornton's gardening knowledge. Mary praised him, writing that he was "well known as one of the best gardeners of the South."[39]

Comparing Thornton's second edition with Edgeworth's third shows that Mary didn't merely put a fresh cover on an old book. Mary heavily edited many sections, especially where medicines were concerned. In her book, Mary credits Thornton with the gardening portion and her physician husband (as well as other "reliable sources") with the medical advice. As for the food recipes, some of Mary's are identical to Thornton's, but there are also altered recipes as well as completely new ones. Anyone comparing the two works might wonder if Mary had a sweet tooth or if the increasing affordability of sugar made for a wave of new recipes; she added a host of desserts as well as sweetened social beverages. Thornton's second edition offered 208 food recipes, while Mary more than doubled that, to 505.

As mentioned, the intended audience is key to understanding a cookbook more fully. Abbott's introduction states, "The recipes Phineas Thornton gives his readers are homey and practical, a long way from the sumptuous banquet tables of New York and Virginia."[40] Some of Mary's additions could be labeled similarly, foods perhaps served in the more modest household where she was a first-time bride. Other additions, however, may reflect the rich social life available through family connections and the elite world of Rowland Springs.

War and Recovery

While Mary's cookbook was still a recent release, the Civil War broke out. Back in Bartow County, newly renamed in a show of Confederate patriotism, the Rowland family continued their agricultural pursuits. Additionally, Mary's father took on the role of superintendent of the Western & Atlantic Railroad from 1861 to 1863. Thus John Rowland was officially in charge on 12 April 1862 when Union raiders commandeered the locomotive called *The General*, launching the famed Great Locomotive Chase. This event basically happened under Rowland's nose; the tracks passed within easy hiking distance of his home. No doubt Mary's father was relieved when the locomotive was recovered, but he did not live to see the outcome of the war. After a brief illness, he died the year after the Chase. By the time Union general Sherman finished his 1864 March to the Sea, Bartow County was hard hit. Cassville was destroyed and the county seat later moved to Cartersville.

Fort Valley was to the west of Sherman's March and fared better. Mary's husband, however, did take part in the conflict. A letter in the Georgia Archives from 1862 is the only known document in Mary's handwriting.[41] After asking Governor Joseph E. Brown to excuse her for "taking the liberty to write," she requested his help settling her husband in a surgeon's position. Mary's tone is distant. She did not mention her connection to the Rowland family or add her maiden name to her signature. Still, the governor had been a frequent guest at Rowland Springs, and therefore he may have known who she was.[42] Salathiel later appears in Civil War records as a sergeant in Georgia 12th Cavalry Regiment and as a Confederate surgeon.[43] He survived the war.

There are two more glimpses of Mary. In 1868 a journalist from Macon's *Georgia Weekly Telegraph* newspaper visited the Edgeworth farm in Fort Valley, about 900 acres according to county tax digests, to learn about the advantages of the "deep ploughing" technique.[44] According to the account, the Edgeworths' farm was particularly successful and well known in the area. The article discusses the crops—mainly cotton and corn—and the farming techniques used to make them flourish. Surprisingly, the writer brings the Edgeworths into personal focus, relating that he and Salathiel came upon a tree of ripe figs and stopped to graze for a while. He then praises the Edgeworths' pleasant hospitality and mentions that the doctor's "kind lady" presented him with a "useful" copy of her cookbook. Census records from two years later, 1870, show Salathiel as a forty-seven-year-old "retired physician" and Mary as a forty-two-year-old "authoress."

Mary wrote a will at the time of her second marriage that was probated in March of 1872, providing the only information currently known about her death.[45] It is likely that Mary was around fifty-four years old when she died. Widower Salathiel lived for sixteen more years, and during this time the cookbook was rereleased as *The Southern Household Companion*. We'll see what became of their farm in the upcoming section on horticulture (1876), but for now we'll leave the Edgeworths with four recipes offered in Mary's volume.[46]

To Barbacue Shoat—A Southern Dish

Shoat means a fat young hog, weighing about 24 pounds without head or feet. Make several incisions between the ribs of a fore-quarter, and stuff it with rich force-meat. Put it in a pan with a pint of water, salt, pepper, two cloves of garlick, a tumbler of good red wine, and one of mushroom catsup. Bake it, and thicken the gravy with brown flour and butter. To facilitate the carving, joint and cut the ribs before cooking. Lay the ribs up in the dish.

Green Apple Custard Pie

Peel and core your apples, stew them quickly in enough water to prevent them from burning. When done, mash and strain them, and to a quart of fruit add four eggs well beaten, one pint of sweet milk, four ounces of melted butter, a nutmeg, a teaspoonful of lemon-juice, and a half-pound of light sugar. Let your apples cool before you add the eggs, &c. Bake in rich pastry crusts.

Spiced Tomatoes

Pour boiling water over a bushel of tomatoes and skin them; then boil them well, after which add a table-spoonful each of cayenne and black pepper; a tea-spoonful of salt; half an ounce of cloves; one ounce of mace; mix well, and put the tomatoes in jars, and pour a coating of suet over them, and tie buckskin over the tops. Prepared in this way, they will keep a year.

Turnip Bread

Let the turnips be peeled, and boiled in water till soft and tender; then strongly press out the juice, mix well together, and when dry, beat or pound very fine, and mix with their weight of wheat meal; then season as you do other bread, and knead it up thin, letting the dough remain a little to ferment; make the dough into loaves, and bake it like common bread.[47]

Civil War Make-Do Coffee

In April of 1862 it rained so much that Savannah native W. W. Gordon found his wartime Virginia campsite up to six inches deep in water. In a letter to his mother now archived at the Georgia Historical Society in Savannah, he reported that the food situation was also worrisome due to poor supply lines and the fact that the soldiers brought no cooking utensils. Surely his mother's heart sank when she read "we got nothing at all but raw Beef given us to eat which we broiled in the ashes." But a few sentences later she had cause to feel encouraged. Gordon reported that they received some bacon, which they broiled in the coals and ate with hard biscuits. He then added an interesting foodways tale:

> We got some coffee & sugar yesterday and were put to it to know how to make it. But the inventive genius of soldiers overcame all difficulties. They searched the country round about until they found an old iron pot with a hole in one side. This they burned & washed out until it was passably clean & then parched the coffee in it. They then put it in a haversack and pounded it small as I used to do the ice for Milk Punch. They then borrowed the Tin Horse bucket from the Driver of our Ambulance and boiled the coffee in it. Having no cups we filled our Canteens from the Pail, hung them up to cool sufficiently for us to drink from them—having first put our sugar in—& then we supped like Princes.[1]

William Washington Gordon II (1843–1912) came from a prominent Savannah family. His father was a successful lawyer who also served in the Georgia legislature and was mayor of Savannah in the mid-1830s.[2] Our canteen-coffee drinker married Eleanor "Nellie" Kinzie (1835–1917), and the two became the parents of Girl Scouts founder Juliette Gordon Low (1860–1927). (See 1864 section.) Nellie served on the Honorary Committee of the Girl Scouts and is acknowledged in the 1913 Scout handbook, *How Girls Can Help Their Country,* which includes sections on growing food and cooking.[3] In 1960 the Girl Scouts produced a small cookbook titled *Centennial Receipt Book: Juliette Gordon Low, Hostess and Homemaker, 1860–1960*. This volume includes stories and recipes from the Gordon family, although there is no mention of coffee.

Nowadays, coffee is often a gourmet drink served up by a barista either hot or chilled, ranging from black and bitter to sweet and creamy—or even flavored with spices and syrups. Although yesteryear's coffee seems basic by comparison, Georgia's cookbooks still had much to say about the labor-intensive process of brewing a decent cup o' joe starting from raw beans. Many modern coffee drinkers will be surprised that eggs were involved. It was thought that the eggs bind up impurities in coffee much as they do in the process one uses to clarify broth. In addition, the calcium-rich eggshells were sometimes added because both the eggs and their shells are alkaline, so they can neutralize some of the acid in the brewed coffee.[4]

> Coffee is as much improved by washing before roasting, as potatoes before cooking, for those who dislike to drink dirt.
>
> —*Southern Field and Fireside* (Augusta), 23 July 1859

> Parch the coffee until a dark brown color. To every pound, when nearly cold, add the yolks and whites of three slightly beaten eggs, putting it in with the hands until every grain is well glazed. This retains the aroma. Spread on dishes to get perfectly cold and dry; then grind, but not too fine. Keep in a close box or canister. Allow one heaping tablespoonful of ground coffee to one pint of boiling water. Mix the coffee with a little cold water before pouring on the boiling water. Stir well and let boil three or four minutes. Set it by the fire ten minutes and it is ready to serve.
>
> —Second Presbyterian Church (Augusta), *Choice Recipes of Georgia Housekeepers* (1880), 145

> The coffee . . . thoroughly and evenly roasted . . . must be tender and brittle, to test which take a grain, place it on the table, press with the thumb, and if it can be crushed, it is done. Stir in a lump of butter while the coffee is hot, or wait until about half cold and then stir in a well-beaten egg. The latter plan is very economical, as coffee so preserved needs no further clarifying.
>
> —Wilcox, *The Dixie Cook-Book* (1883), 137

Ersatz coffee helped Georgians face mornings during the Civil War when supplies were short. Sometimes coffee was mixed with palatable ingredients to help it stretch farther, while sometimes coffee was impossible to get at all. An 1886 newspaper article from Cuthbert, Georgia, recalled, "Coffee had been almost the sole table beverage of the South, and no privation caused more actual discomfort among the people at large than the want of it. There was nothing for which they strove so eagerly and unceasingly to procure a substitute. Few, indeed, were the substances which did not, first and last, find their way into the coffee pot. Wheat, rye, corn, sweet potatoes, peanuts, dandelion seeds, okra seed, persimmon seed, melon seed, are but a few of the substitutes which had their turn and their day."[5]

> Take rye and parboil it over a slow fire, then wash it in two or three waters till thoroughly clean: dry in the sun, spreading it thin, when dry parch in small quantities over a slow fire, taking care to brown, but not to burn it. Grind and make as usual.
>
> —*Southern Cultivator* (Athens), July 1861

> Take one pound of coffee and one pound of dried apples, cut the apples into small pieces, and brown the coffee and apples together, and take an equal quantity of both and make coffee and drink it as usual, and you will find it equal to the real imported coffee, and one pound will go as far as two of the other.
>
> —*Augusta Washingtonian*, 24 June 1843[6]

Exploring Further

Several Georgians left first-person accounts that give us glimpses of the Civil War's impact on foodways.

Dolly Burge (1817–1891) lived in Covington and kept a diary that was later published. On the last day of 1861 she wrote, "The enemy has blockaded our coasts so that we can neither export our produce or import our needfuls. . . . Every thing is very high. Coffee 75 cents & not to be had at that. Salt 18 & 20 dollars a sack."[7] Burge didn't tell us product amounts, but according to an online inflation calculator, the modern equivalent would be $26 for the coffee and over $600 for the salt.[8]

Eliza Frances Andrews (1840–1931) of Wilkes County kept a journal at various times in her life. *The War-Time Journal of a Georgia Girl, 1864–1865* relates the challenges of the steady flows of soldiers and refugees asking for food. She recorded one quiet moment on a spring afternoon when a soldier came. "He sat on the soft grass before the door, and we fed him on sorghum cake and milk, the only things we had to offer."[9] Others did not ask. "The streets of Washington are crowded all the time with idle men and women who have no means of support. They are loitering in the shade of every hedge and tree. . . . Where they lodge, Heaven only knows, but how they are fed, the state of our orchards and cornfields can testify. Capt. Cooley hung up two by their thumbs the other day, for robbing father's orchard, but the discipline was of no avail, for we have not gathered a full-grown peach or pear this season."[10]

Susie King Taylor (1848–1912) of Liberty County wrote a memoir about serving as a nurse and educator in the camp of the 33rd United States Colored Troops. When she needed simple fare to nurture injured soldiers, she created a custard using canned condensed milk and turtle eggs![11]

Coffee Jelly

One package gelatine, cup of cold water, 2 cups white sugar, 2 cups strong coffee, 3 cups boiling water. Soak the gelatine in the cold water, have the coffee boiling, pour over the sugar and stir until dissolved. Add the boiling water to the soaked gelatine, and when thoroughly melted add the coffee mixture. Strain into a mould previously wet with cold water. Serve with whipped cream.

—Mrs. Thos. J. Charlton, in St. John's Episcopal Church, *Favorite Recipes from Savannah Homes* (1904), 87–88

"COFFEE SOUFFLE"

1½ cups coffee — 1/3 cup granulated sugar
1 tablespoon gelatine — ½ cup milk

Mix well. Heat in double boiler. Add yolks of 3 eggs slightly beaten and mix with 1/3 cup granulated sugar and ¼ teaspoon salt. Cook until it thickens. Add the whites of the eggs beaten stiff and ½ teaspoon of vanilla. Mold, chill and serve with whipped cream. —Mrs. W. R. Lipscomb.

Service Star Legion Cook Book (1927), 116

Geechee Foodways

Orienting within Recipe Collections

McIntosh County's Sapelo Island, my first home, is a place where orienting oneself comes naturally. The cardinal directions are easy to find as the sun rises east out of the ocean, arcs over the island, and slips away to the west behind the distant horizon line of the mainland. When I was a child adventuring the sandy roads on a bicycle, the sun's position as well as wind direction and the distant sound of the surf helped me figure out where I was in relation to the north-south stretch of beach. There are other ways of orienting too. My father was a scientist who studied the salt marshes and estuaries through the island's University of Georgia Marine Institute, and his explanations about how the creatures and plants in those zones interact oriented me to my place along the food chain.[1] It meant I was the crabber resignedly returning the "keeper-sized" female to the tidal creek so her mass of orange eggs would hatch into more crabs. And while many of my young friends had little idea how food reached the table, I was the pint-sized cook wrangling jimmy crabs into the boil pot and gathering pickleweed (*Salicornia virginica*) from the edge of the marsh to add to the dinner salad.

Orienting oneself on Sapelo applies to time as well. A sense of history can be difficult to find in this modern world, yet Sapelo holds obvious signs of previous lives—oyster ring middens left by indigenous peoples, remnants of centuries' worth of agricultural pursuits, and a front range lighthouse used as a watchtower for enemy submarines during World War II. On Sapelo, there were no velvet ropes separating me from the past. Nor was I separated from the historical flow of community. Building ruins made of weathered oyster shell tabby from the time of antebellum plantation owner Thomas Spalding (1774–1851) were a part of my daily world, and so were island neighbors whose ancestors handled the construction.[2]

Sapelo's Hogg Hummock is an African American community whose residents largely descend from the people brought to the island for slave labor.[3] Various communities like this along the coasts of South Carolina, Georgia, and northern Florida developed a culture rich with language, stories, arts, crafts, music, and foodways that tends to be called Gullah in South Carolina and Geechee to the south. In 1863 the Emancipation Proclamation set into motion changes for Georgians eager for liberty and the pursuit of happiness, including on the coast. Along with Hogg Hummock, sites like the Geechee Kunda Cultural Arts Center and Museum (Liberty County) and Pin Point Heritage Museum (Chatham County) are good places to learn more.[4]

Sweetgrass basket woven in 1977 by Sapelo's Allen Green (1907–1998).

My family lived a couple of miles south of Hogg Hummock in the Institute quarters. We shared the narrow backyard shaded by live oaks with the dormitory for student and research groups next door, and thus my first experience with professional cooking was the dorm kitchen where women from Hogg Hummock cooked meals for visitors. My playtime was often graced by the good cooking smells, which were more prominent in mild weather when the kitchen's back door was propped opened for ventilation. I remember pressing my nose against the rough screened door to watch the efficient workflow. Sometimes the cooks slipped me tastes and asked if the seasonings were right, even though they already knew the answer. Experience and cookbooks had taught them much. And, just as the Hogg Hummock men who handled the island boats had been taught skills by the generations before them, these women had also learned cooking from mothers, aunts, and grandmothers. Even after our family moved to Athens, return stays always involved chats at the screened door. I learned from Hogg Hummock women that the leaves of the island's bay trees improve the flavor of soup, that there are recipes to make good use of the puckery juice of the island's now-wild sour oranges, and that the bulbous fruits of the prickly pears growing along the beach road make shockingly pink jelly.[5] These women shared stories about earlier generations who cooked wondrous spreads for Sapelo's large-scale landowners and their famous guests.

Like others from the Institute, my mother swapped recipes old and new with neighbors from Hogg Hummock. As a tenderfoot to Sapelo life, I'm sure she received more than she gave. When you live on an island less than a dozen miles long and three miles wide—an island largely reclaimed by the wilderness and without a causeway to the mainland—there is no last-minute zipping to the supermarket to get a forgotten ingredient for supper. There was the tiny B J Confectionary that carried a few staples, but residents skilled in life on a barrier island kindly shared with newcomers about simple pantry-based recipes, kitchen substitutions, and fresh ingredients from the island itself. I treasure this know-how, and thus was delighted when some Sapelo residents self-published a book in 2004 with 177 recipes titled *The Foods of Georgia's Barrier Islands: A Gourmet Food Guide of Native American, Geechee and European Influences on the Golden Isles* by Yvonne J. Grovner, Cornelia Walker Bailey, and William "Doc. Bill" Thomas.[6] Many of the recipes are modern, yet the authors also discuss and share older foodways. Ingredients include ones potentially fished, hunted, and gathered on the island (including alligator and whelk). Given the area's agricultural history, there are plenty of rice recipes as well as ones perfect with island products such as Geechee red peas and purple ribbon cane syrup.[7]

Thinking of the old stories I heard in childhood, I wondered how many old Sapelo recipes were available. I searched archival records from the years that first automobile industrialist Howard J. Coffin (1873–1937) and then tobacco company businessman Richard J. Reynolds (1906–1964) owned much of the island in the twentieth century. I had no luck, yet there are older recipes. The Georgia Historical Society in Savannah preserves papers from the Spalding family, including recipes of matriarch Sarah Leake Spalding (1778–1843).

Plum Pudding Mrs. Tho' Spalding

1801

14 eggs beaten light
1 loaf of bread soaked in one qt
of milk
1 lb of suiet [suet]
1 " " Raisins
1½ lbs of Currants
½ " " Citron
3 tablespoons of Flour
1 glass of brandy
1 teaspoonful of each kind of spice
Flour your fruit and add
to the batter dip the pudding
cloth in hot water & greese & flour.
Pour mixture in Tie up but
leave space for swelling.
Put a plate in bottom of boiler
put the pudding in boiling
water.
Half of the above quantity is enough for a family of
eight.

—Spalding Family Papers, 1772–1940, Georgia Historical Society, Savannah[8]

And there's more. The Spaldings' son Charles (1808–1887) married Evelyn West Kell (1820–1898), and her manuscript recipe book from the 1870s is now preserved at Duke University.[9] After a family reunion in North Carolina, I took a detour to Durham where the castle-like David M. Rubenstein Rare Book & Manuscript Library sits atop a hill. I sat down in the archives reading room and an archivist placed an old brown notebook in front of me, the marbling on its chipped cover streaked with residue from the dried-up rubber band that once held it closed. "Sapelo Island, Ga." was inked along the spine.[10] I carefully leafed

Corn Muffins

One pint sifted meal and 3 gills milk, 1 pint sour milk, or 1 gill sour cream, 2 tablespoons boiling hot lard, 2 eggs, 1 teaspoon soda, ½ cup sugar; add the eggs, beaten separately, to meal and milk; pour on lard, boiling hot.
—Miss Sawyer, Sapelo Island, McIntosh Co., Ga.

This recipe can be found in the Atlanta cookbook created for the Cotton States and International Exposition.[1] (See 1895 section.) In the late nineteenth century, Amos Sawyer of Massachusetts purchased parts of Sapelo once belonging to Mary Spalding.[2] The 1880 census shows him with three daughters—Ellen, Mary, and Fanny.

1. Wilson, *Tested Recipe Cook Book*, 147.
2. Sullivan, *Sapelo*; Sullivan, *Thomas Spalding*.

my way through ninety yellowed pages containing 189 food recipes and another 33 for medicinal or household needs. There were recipes for shrimp, fish, and oysters as well as quite a few using coastal rice—biscuits, bread, cake, griddle and journey cakes, muffins, pie, pudding, and waffles.

Rice Journey Cake or Waffles

To ½ pint of soft boiled rice, a small
teacup of milk, ½ pint of rice flour
& 1 egg—bake quickly.[11]

Once back home, I spent time looking over the Sapelo recipes from my childhood and from my research. It dawned on me that working with the recipes was akin to another island interest. Growing up, my brother and I spent many hours combing the beach's high tide line for treasures. His collecting was straightforward, as he liked pen shells (*Atrina rigida*) with their mother-of-pearl swirls, the bigger the shell the better. He put his newest additions on his windowsill and then went off to the next adventure. My shells took longer. On the beach I had layered many small shells in cushioning sand inside my red pail. After a rinse, I'd spread them on a towel atop the kitchen table and begin sorting. I wanted to build a collection with an excellent example of each kind of shell. Rough sorting was easy, separating the spiraled snails from the two-shelled bivalves. Sometimes, though, I couldn't tell the difference between similar shells until they were placed side by side. The more I worked with the collection, the more I learned. Handling the shells taught me their similarities and differences. I came to appreciate the beauty of even those shells that seemed small and simple.

The island seashells involved a process of collecting, sorting, identifying, and organizing—and so did working with the island recipes. Comparing and contrasting recipes taught me more about the dishes and ingredients. Which recipes remind me strongly of the island as I know it? Which recipes show the flow of history? Which recipes are Geechee? I began to see connections in ingredients and flavors. I sensed the flow of time through changes in kitchen methods. I'd found a new way to experience a deeply familiar place.

Mrs. Randolph Spalding

The upcoming 1880 section explores *Choice Recipes of Georgia Housekeepers*, a cookbook written by the women of the Second Presbyterian Church in Augusta. Fifty-one of the recipes were credited to "Mrs. Randolph Spalding's Collection." I instantly thought of Sapelo Island's Randolph Spalding (1825–1862), another son of Thomas and Sarah, who died of pneumonia during the Civil War.[1] His widow, Mary Dorothy Bass Spalding (1823–1898), never remarried and in the 1880 census was a fifty-seven-year-old living in McIntosh County with her son.[2] She died on Sapelo just a month after her sister-in-law, Evelyn. My research turned up no connections between Mary Spalding and the town of Augusta almost 150 miles north of Sapelo—but neither did I find a more likely "Mrs. Randolph Spalding."[3] The recipes remain a mystery hopefully to be solved as archives continue to preserve, scan, and index historical documents. The recipes themselves are largely standard for their time and place, yet one assumes the reader will be using fresh crab.

Crabs Buttered

Pick all the meat out, mince it fine, put it into a saucepan with two or three tablespoonfuls of wine, one of lemon, pickle, or pepper-vinegar, three or four of rich gravy, or a large tablespoonful of butter rolled in flour, some nutmeg, some mixed mustard, and thicken it with the yolks of two eggs well beaten; put it into the shells, grate crumbs of bread over the top, moisten with butter, and bake a light brown.

—Mrs. Spalding's Collection, in *Choice Recipes of Georgia Housekeepers*, 9

1. *Baltimore Sun*, 9 April 1862; tombstone, Laurel Grove Cemetery, Savannah.
2. *UR*, 27 September 1898; tombstone, Saint Andrews Cemetery, Darien.
3. I found no evidence of a recipe notebook in archival collections.

Like my brother with his pen shells, many people approach recipes knowing what they like. Find a recipe and enjoy the food—straightforward and wonderful. If you feel a deeper pull, however, there's another joy to be found. The process of working with recipes as a group or collection helps us orient ourselves history-wise and knowledge-wise within foodways.

I found working with the Sapelo recipes particularly challenging because my personal history overlaps with the island's long and complicated history. I was naturally curious about the older recipes that seem unusual to a twenty-first-century reader, yet because of the stories that inspired my search, the recipes that interested me most in Evelyn's notebook were Hettie's Rusk and Julia's Pudding. The references to the cooks were informal compared to how she handled the names of other recipe contributors, so I wondered if these were the recipes of Geechee women. Granted, the names were common, but there are nineteenth-century women with these names buried on the island.[12] Even with the other recipes, I pondered who did the cooking in the kitchens of yesteryear's large-scale landowners. (See 1859 section.) There are no easy answers, but it is important to ask the question.

Hettie's Rusk

Rub together 1 good spoonful of butter
& 2 good spoonsful of brown sugar
beat 2 eggs light & add to it—
then take a small cup of milk &
stir in alternately with a pint of
patent flour a little at a time
do not make it too stiff
it must be mixed with a spoon
have the oven heated
before mixing it & bake quickly.[13]

Julia's Pudding

1 cup of butter 2 of sugar 3 of flour
1 of milk. 1 cup raisins, 1 of currants.
1 teaspoon soda, 2 cream of tartar.
Wine sauce for it.[14]

Most people appreciate Sapelo Island's wide green marshes and spreading live oaks. Beauty aside, it is a place I recognize with an inner unfurling of peace, a deep familiarity no matter how time has changed both me and the island. When I began courting with my husband and again when my son was old enough to understand, introducing Sapelo to them was fundamental. My favorite shady bike route. The perfect climbing tree I was sure no one else knew about. The old dorm, now replaced and standing empty. That good crabbing spot and the prickly pear patch still thriving along the beach road. Later, using knowledge learned from now-gone Hogg Hummock friends, I carefully removed the thorny skin of the prickly pear fruit so my son and I could puree the inside. Amused by the idea of opposites (as well as our stained fingers), we added our puree to Georgia cookbook author Alton Brown's homemade marshmallow recipe.[15] The pillowy confections were indeed quite the contrast to the barbed fruit as well as comically pink. Rooted in history and community, they were delicious.

Exploring Further

I've shared my experiences as someone who loves both Sapelo and historical recipes, yet the Hogg Hummock residents far outstrip my time on the island and have both ancestral roots and an intimate view of Gullah-Geechee culture. My writing serves best if it leads you to their work. Hogg Hummock resident Cornelia Walker Bailey (1945–2017) is an invaluable source for autobiographical pieces as well as cultural writings. (One of my favorites is *Sapelo Voices*.)[16] Her son, Maurice Bailey, along with Yvonne Grovner and others, is actively working to preserve Hogg Hummock's way of life.[17]

Modern books about Geechee-Gullah foodways explore its African roots and other influences. They range from large-press best sellers to self-published offerings. The Georgia sources I found in addition to the 2004 Sapelo volume are *Bress 'n' Nyam: Gullah Geechee Recipes from a Sixth-Generation Farmer* by Matthew Raiford of Brunswick and *"My" Official Georgia Geechee Cookbook* by Sharon Kaye Hunt.[18] Cookbook author Sallie Ann Robinson is from Daufuskie Island, South Carolina, yet lived in nearby Savannah for a time. *Dwelling Place: A Plantation Epic* by historian Erskine Clarke explores life on a Liberty County plantation, including the work of its cooks. Sixty-four of Evelyn Spalding's recipes are transcribed in the *Ashantilly Cookbook* sold by the Ashantilly Center of Darien, once the Spaldings' mainland house and now a nonprofit dedicated to educational programming.[19]

Wafers and Recipe Time Lags

During the last months of the Civil War, Union general William T. Sherman sent his troops through Georgia on a destructive March to the Sea. By December of 1864 the soldiers reached Georgia's oldest city, and Sherman telegraphed a message to President Lincoln offering up Savannah as an early Christmas gift. Young Juliette "Daisy" Gordon (1860–1927), the daughter of letter writer W. W. Gordon II from our 1862 section and the future founder of the Girl Scouts, witnessed life in Savannah at that time.[1] She later wrote about her family's experiences and included an interesting detail related to Georgia foodways. Nancy, a woman in the Gordon household who had recently been freed from slavery, "without my grandmother's knowledge, hastily made Bené cakes, molasses candy, and wafers, and took the tray of dainties into the street, where she sold them to the soldiers. Triumphantly, she brought the money to my grandmother, for we had been nearly starved during the siege."[2]

Bené or benne is sesame seed, familiar to us today sprinkled across hamburger buns. Thin wafer cookies with this seed added are a Savannah classic, with the distinctive ingredient thought to have been brought from Africa during the slave trade.[3] Savannah's Byrd Cookie Company, started by Benjamin Byrd in 1924, has long ensured that these treats are readily available.[4] The centennial cookbook for Gottlieb's, a favorite Savannah bakery for a century beginning in 1884, notes that this treat is "as Southern as you can get," and Margaret Wayt DeBolt's 1978 *Savannah Sampler Cookbook* offers nine benne recipes both sweet and savory.

Benne seed plant, the heirloom ancestor of modern sesame, in W. White, *Gardening for the South* (1857), 324. Old-fashioned benne seeds can be purchased online.

Thus when I started looking through even older Georgia cookbooks, I assumed there would be a steady trail of benne recipes back through time. Instead, the oldest recipe I found from Georgia was the 1933 *Savannah Cook Book* recipe for Benné Candy.[5] Moving my research to old newspapers, there were advertisements for small companies in Savannah, Augusta, and Columbus selling benne treats in the first half of the twentieth century.[6] In newspapers from the 1800s, however, benne was a matter for agricultural discussions on chicken feed and seed oil. As early as 1809, a Savannah newspaper discussed enslaved Georgians growing the seed and noted its usefulness for "making into cakes" but explained no further and offered no recipes.[7]

Karen Hess (1918–2007), one of America's foremost food historians, wouldn't have been surprised. She noticed a trend with historical recipes that many foodways scholars have since echoed: "The lag between practice and the printed word is one of the most frustrating aspects of work in the discipline of culinary history."[8] She gave the example of knowing colonists made hearth cakes with corn, yet not finding a written recipe until 1796, a delay of almost two centuries. Why are there lags? Hess explained that many recipes are not written down, and even when they are, few survive to become public record. She added, "Such an omission could be an oversight or result from a feeling that 'everybody' knows how to make it."[9] Consider that popcorn, a very popular snack, involves multiple ingredients—a specific type of dry flint corn, an oil with a high smoke point, salt, and possibly seasonings—as well as cooking knowledge to make it turn out well, yet we don't usually find recipes for it.[10] (Given today's microwave oven shortcuts, this probably won't change.)

Benne wafers and benne candy are recipe variations, and Georgia's historical cookbooks offer many non-benne recipes for the thin cookies and the brittle-type candy most often used with these seeds. As for wafers, this very thin cookie was quite popular in the past but is no longer a staple in today's cookbooks. Are we now a culture largely preferring big, soft cookies embedded with chunks of chocolate, nuts, or candy? One clue about yesteryear's wafer popularity may be in the directions of the Atlanta Exposition Wafers recipe you'll find in the 1895 section; wafers are a comparatively dry cookie, giving them a long shelf life. They would have been handy for long-ago housekeepers to have on hand for when company dropped by.

When wafer recipes do appear in modern sources, they almost always direct the cook to drop or pipe batter onto a sheet pan to bake many at once. In the days of hearth cooking, however, the common method was one-at-a-time using a wafer iron, allowing a cook to make cookies without an oven. A daub of batter was placed between two small yet thick pieces of metal joined by a hinge. A long handle allowed the cook to safely hold the wafer iron over coals, turning it periodically to heat both sides. One of the distinctive features of the wafer was that when it was just finished cooking, it was pliable. Hot-from-the-iron wafers were usually rolled into a tube shape that became firm and crisp as they cooled.[11] Still-warm wafers could alternatively be draped over a form such as a knife handle or the bottom of a small cup, cooling into a crunchy cookie curve or miniature bowl—forerunners to today's ice cream cones. (Another popular wafer found today is the folded-and-tucked fortune cookie at Chinese restaurants.) Although usually a specialty item now only sold online, nonelectric wafer irons have not vanished completely. Today's lightweight versions usually have nonstick coating and can be used over coals or natural gas flames—a fun way to make treats on camping trips, after barbecuing, or even in a kitchen with gas burners. Rolled or curved wafers can be filled with jam, whipped cream, or frosting.

The historic wafer recipe below comes from the Gordon family courtesy of the Juliette Gordon Low Birthplace in Savannah, a venue that offered historical wafer-baking programs during my 1970s childhood.[12] The handwritten recipe is labeled with the name Mrs. McAlpin, likely the person who gave Mrs. Gordon the recipe. We don't know for sure who Mrs. McAlpin was, but the McAlpin surname was prominent in nineteenth-century Savannah. The Harper Fowlkes House (1842) on Orleans Square, for instance, was once owned by McAlpins.[13]

Sweet Wafers

½ lb white sugar (or brown)
⅓ lb wheat flour
¼ lb butter
4, 6, or 8 eggs
4 tablespoonsful of rose water
Mix like cake
As soon as taken out of the wafer [iron] they must be rolled up.

Comparing this recipe to the Atlanta Exposition Wafers recipe in the 1895 section is helpful, as baker Jesse Koonce elaborated on the mixing process for wafers. A kitchen scale is a good tool with this recipe, which makes around four dozen wafers using my 6.5-inch modern iron. If you're measuring by volume, a little estimating will be in order.[14] The recipe's range for the number of eggs is confusing to modern cooks used to purchasing cartons with regularly sized eggs inside; folks who raise backyard chickens can attest that egg sizes can vary greatly. After comparing the Gordon recipe to other wafer recipes and experimenting, I use four large eggs so the mixture is the consistency of cake batter. As an overflowing iron is quite the mess, I use just a tablespoon of batter at a time, and this cooks in about a minute over medium heat, turning the iron over halfway through for even cooking.

As for the rosewater, before improvements in shipping increased world trade, flavorings from exotic locations such as vanilla were expensive. Rosewater could be made at home and was a popular flavoring deep into the nineteenth century. It remains popular in places like England, India, and the Middle East and can be purchased at specialty grocery stores or online. Or you could replace some of the white sugar in the wafer recipe with flavored sugar made with the old Georgia recipe below.

Extract of Rose

Gather each morning the roses that bloomed the day before. Throw the leaves into a jar with layers of powdered crush sugar. Do this while roses continue to bloom. This is nice for flavoring cakes.

—*Verstille's Southern Cookery* (1866), 222

Make sure the flowers you are going to use are indeed roses, which are edible, and have not been treated with pesticides. Put the petals (not the green leaves) in a jar with enough granulated sugar to cover them well, checking and stirring them periodically to be sure they are drying. After a few days, dry petals can be sifted out or, if a nice color, crushed for pretty flecks in the sugar.

Wafer irons and *waffle* irons look similar, but the grooves on the iron for making waffles are deeper to hold more batter. The wafer iron (irregular octagon), which belongs to the author, has a cook surface four inches by six. An eighteen-inch handle makes it easy to reach coals, yet its weight of almost six pounds makes it difficult to wield. The waffle iron (rectangle) belongs to the Root House, an antebellum house museum in Marietta supported by the Cobb Landmarks and Historical Society. Its reconstructed hearth kitchen is open for viewing and periodically hosts foodways programs. (Photograph permission courtesy of the Root House.)

Verstille's Southern Cookery and the Influence of Travel

Verstille's Southern Cookery, 1866
Ellen Jane Lockhart Verstille (11 January 1832–18 May 1871)
238 pages. 968 food recipes with 17 additional recipes for medicine and 11 for household needs.

The first edition of *Verstille's Southern Cookery*, written by "Mrs. E. J. Verstille of Louisiana," is noted as the first cookbook to include recipes for gumbo, one of that state's most celebrated dishes.[1] In fact, Verstille instructs (page 237) on how to properly prepare sassafras leaves for the dish's distinctive filé flavor. One modern foodways writer calls Verstille's work a "stepping stone that captures the cooking methods, flavors, and ingredients of Louisiana."[2] A decade after the cookbook was first published, however, it was published again, this time in Macon and credited to "the late Mrs. E. J. Verstille of Columbus, Ga."[3] How was Mrs. Verstille "of" two states almost four hundred miles apart? And what does that mean for the recipes?

So that we have a better sense of what we're discussing, let's first take a look at *Verstille's Southern Cookery*. Unlike Mary Edgeworth's cookbook published seven years before, Verstille's book is a guide for the kitchen, not the entire farm. Much of Verstille's work could be called plain. Recipe titles are utilitarian, with little beside Love Cake or Very Nice Rolls to stir the cook's imagination. (Her section titled "Promiscuous Dishes," however, may give the modern reader pause, as nowadays we don't often use the term to mean "wide-ranging.") Upon closer inspection, the recipes themselves range from primitive to sophisticated.

The Big Hominy recipe, for instance, begins by instructing the reader on how to fashion a large-scale pestle and mortar from a pine tree! On the other hand, in her cakes section she describes applying frosting "with a cornucopia made of letter paper" to mimic the professional pastry chef's piping bag and explains how to decorate with gold leaf, using a feather to apply egg white as adhesive and cotton to pat the shining edible foil into place.

Verstille's Southern Cookery is one of the least "chatty" of Georgia's early cookbooks. Only two sections—soups and meats—offer general cooking advice, and those are brief. Verstille's use of two commercial products—baking soda and isinglass, a thickener and clarifier made from collagen extracted from the swim bladders of fish—indicate that the effects of the Industrial Revolution are reaching Georgia cookbooks. Verstille even calls for a specific brand, Cooper's American Isinglass, a commercial product once sold shredded or in sheets.[4] Otherwise, aside from the occasional items such as cinnamon, cocoanut [*sic*], or vanilla, most of the ingredients are items that could easily be raised on a southern farm. As is common with cookbooks before canning jars and home refrigeration, many recipes are intent on food preservation.

BIG HOMINY, TO PREPARE FOR COOKING.

Cut a block from a large pine-tree, the thickness of the tree, and three and a half feet in length; a mortar must be made of this block in the following manner—place the block in an upright position, and put clay around the circumference of the upper surface about an inch and a half in width; apply fire, and let it burn out the upper surface until it assumes the shape of a bowl, and to the depth of about two feet. After it is burnt it must be well scraped and cleaned. A pestle may be made of any kind of oak, and three feet in length; the bottom of it should be about two inches in diameter, and it should be graduated upwards until is about as large around as a saucer; three or four nails must be driven up to their heads, and at equal distances apart, around the edge of the pestle at the bottom. Now put it into the mortar five quarts of corn, and sprinkle it with hot water; use just enough water to moisten the corn; beat with the pestle, always striking in the centre. When done the grains should be about half cracked, and the husk will readily come off. When you have done beating spread it out, let it thoroughly dry, and then fan the husk from it.

As for the intended audience, an inexperienced cook would likely have struggled with this cookbook. Many recipes are lists of ingredients with no methods or instructions. Verstille often tells readers simply to "add enough flour to make a stiff dough" or season with "a bunch of herbs." Other instructions may have been clear to readers of her time but baffle modern readers—measuring out an ingredient in a dollop "the size of a partridge egg" or instructing those making her pancakes to "Eat with liquid sauce."[5] Twenty-six of the recipes are credited to outside sources, but aside from instructions for curing ham taken from Georgia's *Southern Cultivator* agriculture magazine, the credits are mere initials, such as Mrs. C's Cake or Mrs. L's Corn Bread.[6]

Now that we can better picture Verstille's cookbook, let's take a moment to think about how recipes may be shared and dispersed, which will allow us to ask helpful questions about Verstille's book as well as other cookbooks we'll explore. To

BARBECUED PIG.

The first thing to be done, is to have a hole dug in the ground four feet long, about two and a half wide, and one and a half deep. A small pig should be selected, and one not very fat. Have it killed and cleaned late in the afternoon. Very early on the next morning make a fire of oak bark, to have a few coals to begin with. Have ready three or four small sticks of white-oak, just long enough to stretch from one side of the pig to the other. Then fasten them on the inside, at regular distances apart, making the pig perfectly flat. Then have two poles, and tie the two legs of each side to a pole. Put very few coals in the hole, and place the pig over it. Be very careful not to have too much fire. For the first three hours, it should be constantly basted with salt and water. Gash the fleshy part, as the heat will then penetrate better. Then make a very strong seasoning of vinegar, salt, red and black pepper, and three quarters of a pound of lard or butter. Baste the pig continually with this mixture, using a mop, and turn it frequently. From one half to three fourths of a day should be consumed in cooking. When done, it should be a dark rich brown.

SAUSAGE MEAT, NO. 1.

The best proportions are, to every one hundred pounds of chopped meat, three pounds of salt, ten ounces of sage, and fourteen ounces of red and black pepper mixed.

SAUSAGE MEAT, NO. 2.

Cut up hams and shoulders, and then chop the pieces finely. Season with salt, red pepper, ground ginger, and sage, to the taste.

INSTANTANEOUS GINGER BEER.

Fill a bottle with pure cold water; have a cork ready to fit it, also a string to tie it down with, and a mallet to drive the cork in, so that no time may be lost. Now put into the bottle sugar to your taste (syrup is better) and a teaspoon of good ginger. Shake it well; then add the sixth part of an ounce of soda, cork rapidly, and tie it down. Shake the bottle well, cut the string, the cork will fly out, and you may then drink the beer.

Pages 40 and 233 of *Verstille's Southern Cookery* (scans courtesy of Cynthia Graubart). The cork tying method can be found in Mary Ronald's 1895 *Century Cook Book*, page 558. For a standard wine bottle (750 ml), we used one cup of a 1:1 simple syrup and calculated the soda to be one teaspoon. We made a tasty bubbling drink, but, alas, it sent no corks flying.

give you an example, a prized inheritance from my mother is her recipe box stuffed with index cards and scraps of paper. This is where I go to re-create the familiar tastes of my childhood, yet the collection is more than that. As I began reading books about food history, I realized my mother's cache of recipes reflects the food trends of her early-1940s to early-1990s lifetime. By the time she was a teenager, she often snapped up recipes as various dishes rose to popularity—casseroles, fondue, or dump cakes. Women in my mother's life wrote recipes down for her, adding their names and sometimes even the date. Thanks to this source information, I know my mother's collection holds recipes from four generations as well as recipes showing how my parents' union connected her sprawling Oregon family with his from Arkansas. When she was a bride preparing to leave home, my mother wrote down favorite Pacific Northwest recipes she grew up with. These are tucked into the same recipe box as the carefully folded letter from my southern grandmother sharing her preferred method of cornbread with the new daughter-in-law.

My mother's recipe collection reflects not just our family's roots but also its whereabouts. In her box are recipes from the friends she made when my father's schooling took them to university towns in Montana and Indiana. After graduation, there were recipes from the Georgia locations where my father conducted scientific research—Sapelo Island, Savannah, Skidaway Island, and Athens. As my mother created a home in each new place, she collected pleasing recipes she found novel even if they were run-of-the-mill to other cooks around her. The recipe stash reflects my mother's tastes and her family's preferences as well as general trends, times, and places. While it would be a mistake to assume that another recipe collector gathered recipes the same way or for the same reasons, this gives us a starting place for asking questions about the recipes in Verstille's cookbook. What was Mrs. Verstille's background? What moves and travels might have affected her recipe stash?

Ellen Jane Lockhart was born in Georgia and buried in Georgia.[7] In her thirty-nine years, however, she ranged from the Atlantic Coast to beyond the Mighty Mississippi. She was the daughter of Dr. Henry Lockhart, a Georgia physician who also had extensive agricultural holdings, and Mary Ann Beall, originally of Maryland.[8] Census records show that before Ellen married at age nineteen, she lived with her family in several places along the fall line separating southern coastal plain and piedmont regions—Warren County (Georgia), Russell County (Alabama), and Muscogee County (Georgia).[9] She married in Columbus in 1851, yet this union took her to the coast, joining her with a Connecticut family that had lived many years in South Carolina before moving on to Savannah.[10]

Ellen's husband, Henry Verstille (1828–1897), was the grandson of noted miniaturist painter William Verstille (1757–1803) and his wife, Eliza Sheldon.[11] Two of William and Eliza's adult children, Charlotte and Tristram, left New England at separate times but by the early 1820s reunited in South Carolina to teach at the Black Swamp Academy in Robertville.[12] They soon had the care of their young nephew Sheldon, whose father had died.[13] Adding to this unusual household, Tristram married a South Carolina woman and had two sons—William Henry, who did not survive early childhood, and Henry William (1828–1897), future husband of Ellen. Although the Verstilles left Robertville for Savannah thirty-five miles to the south by the 1840s, we will soon see it is likely that associations with South Carolina families—Lawton, Grimball, and Robert—eventually led Ellen hundreds of miles west.[14]

When Ellen married Henry, he had attended both the University of Georgia and Yale.[15] An entry for UGA's *Centennial Alumni Catalog* states that he "Studied law but never practiced. Was at different times Teacher, Merchant, Civil Engineer." It further states that he "Was a man of remarkable ability in the many lines of work his fancy led him."[16] The 1850 census suggests Verstille did at least briefly try his hand at legal work, but soon multiple Savannah newspaper ads show that in the first years of his marriage he entered and exited a series of business partnerships selling dry goods or cotton.[17] Meanwhile, around 1855, Ellen gave birth to a daughter, Rosa.[18] There were more family changes around this time as well. Cousin Sheldon had also been a Savannah merchant but left to become a pioneering citizen, first merchant, and postmaster of the new town of Wardville, Texas, about fifty-five miles southwest of Dallas.[19] By the summer of 1856, Ellen's father-in-law, Tristram, was part of a company manufacturing rope in Columbus.[20] As for Ellen's immediate family, Henry dissolved his last known partnership in Savannah that year.[21] By December, multiple ads were placed in the Columbus newspaper:

> LESSONS IN MUSIC
> MRS. H. W. Verstille,
> WILL be prepared to receive pupils in MUSIC, on and after the first Monday in January next, at her residence on Jackson street, near the corner of Jackson and St. Clair streets.[22]

While ads for music lessons are not rare in Georgia's antebellum newspapers, usually they were offered through schools or by men.[23] Ellen, however, had married into a family where education and the arts were valued, and where a woman (Aunt Charlotte) was a wage earner. Regardless, the music lessons were short-lived. By the end of the year, Ellen gave birth to daughter Florence—almost eight hundred miles away in Texas.[24] It is through another newspaper ad that we learn the sojourn in Texas was also relatively short-lived. In March of 1859 the *Dallas Daily Herald* carried husband Henry's advertisement for "My Store-house and Stock of Goods at this place; also my dwelling."[25] Along with around seven acres of land and an orchard, Henry noted, "I have also a splendid Piano Forte for sale. Intending to remove from the State this Spring with my family, I will dispose of the above property low to a cash purchaser." The Verstille family left behind Cousin Sheldon, who died in Texas the following year, yet they moved toward other networks forged back in South Carolina.[26]

By the 1850s, two brothers connected to Robertville, Wilson C. and Grimball A. Robert, had moved to Avoyelles Parish, Louisiana, about 140 miles northwest of New Orleans. Wilson (born ca. 1807) was listed as a surveyor and lawyer respectively in the 1850 and 1860 censuses. His younger brother, Grimball (born 1812), was listed without an occupation in the 1850 census and did not live until the next census. Grimball was murdered near Bayou Rapides in 1854.[27] If that didn't give the Verstille family second thoughts about the area, local history holds that in 1861 Wilson was also murdered.[28] Over several months in 1862, Ellen's husband and father-in-law served as executors of Wilson's will, periodically posting legal notices in the local paper—"All persons holding claims against the above estate are notified to present the same to the Executors, Henry W. Verstille and Tristram Verstille, at Evergreen."[29] While the rural areas and swamps may have still been wild and woolly, the small town of Evergreen was home to numerous families as well as the Evergreen Home Institute (started in 1856) that, according to a historical marker in the area, "had a noteworthy influence on education in Avoyelles and Louisiana."[30]

Even if life in Evergreen was calm, the era was not. The Verstilles likely reached Louisiana not long before the Civil War broke out in 1861. Additional newspaper articles from the same year when Henry was executing Wilson's estate show that he was also serving the parish community as commander of the seventy-eight militiamen of the Avoyelles Fencibles.[31] The Fencibles and four other companies became a part of Lt. Colonel W. W. Johnson's Special Battalion pressed into service to help defend New Orleans in April of 1862. Union forces overcame nearby forts, so Johnson's men were "told to scatter, go back home 'and disappear as best they could.'"[32]

By the end of 1862, Henry Verstille had done more than retreat. Surviving records show in December that he enlisted with others from Georgia into the

60th Alabama Regiment, Company D, and would go on to serve the Confederate cause in Tennessee and Virginia. As for Ellen, her father had died in January of 1862, leaving her mother widowed at Beall Wood, their property in Columbus.[33] Was Ellen in Columbus in April of 1863 when frustrated women armed themselves, marching through the business district and raiding wartime speculators?[34] Henry was back in Columbus by 1864, as noted by a surviving $20 receipt to him from the Quartermaster of the Confederate States Army for 2,000 pounds of straw.[35] No records have been found to show whether the Verstille family were present in Columbus in April of 1865 when it became a battleground and then fell to the Union Army.

The year after the Civil War ended, Ellen's cookbook was published by "Mrs. E. J. Verstille of Louisiana." Foodways historian Shirley Abbott noted that this cookbook (as well as Mrs. Hill's cookbook that we'll explore next) used a New York publishing house: "Southern cooking, long famous in the region, was turning into an exportable commodity just at a time when the South was desperate not only for things to export but for some means of reasserting the worth of Southern culture on any level."[36] Shortly after the cookbook came out, a lengthy review "cordially recommending" the cookbook appeared in the *New Orleans Times-Democrat* and was soon shared by a newspaper in Columbus.[37] The only advertisements found for the original printing of the cookbook are from Baton Rouge.[38] Ellen's last appearance is the 1870 census, where she is "keeping house" in Columbus. A year later she died at age thirty-nine, leaving behind a husband, two teenaged daughters, and a foodways legacy.[39]

Exploring Further

If you're up for a stroll, Mrs. Verstille was laid to rest in Historic Linwood Cemetery full of impressive monuments and greenery. She was later joined by a couple of other Georgia foodways figures—Coca-Cola inventor Dr. John Pemberton (1831–1888) and Tom Huston (1889–1972) who popularized roasted peanuts as an on-the-go snack southerners still instantly know by its logo with the rounded red triangle.[40]

Mrs. Hill's New Cook Book for the Young and Inexperienced

Mrs. Hill's New Cook Book, 1867
Annabella Powell Dawson Hill (13 March 1811?–29 January 1878?)
427 pages. 961 food recipes with 196 additional household recipes or advice segments.

Sometimes learning the history behind an old, familiar object all but transforms it. I learned firsthand from Mrs. Hill that this holds true with old cookbooks. Food historian Damon Lee Fowler calls Mrs. Hill's cookbook a "seminal work, one that could almost be called the southern *Fanny Farmer* of its day," and "a critical link in the chain of southern food history."[1] A plain reproduction copy had been on my bookshelf for years, a favorite reference when working with historical recipes. The only thing I knew—or thought I knew—about its origins was that the book was published in the dark days after the Civil War and the author had more than her fair share of tragedy. After discovering Annie Dennis and seeking Georgia's early cookbook authors, I bought a 1995 reprint of Hill's cookbook with historical commentary by Fowler. His interpretation is thorough, well researched, and fascinating, covering Hill's life while also putting her cooking practices into context. Fowler's edition as well as primary sources that have become available since his early 1990s research shed more light on Mrs. Hill's life, times, and career. I no longer view Hill as a sad character.

Hill's cookbook sticks close to home—at least compared with Mary Edgeworth's *Southern Gardener and Receipt-Book* published eight years before.

This 1886 edition of *Mrs. Hill's New Cook Book*, the kind gift of JoAnn Wood, is the only 1800s Georgia cookbook I own that isn't too battered or plain to photograph. Damon Lee Fowler's *Classical Southern Cooking* helps modern cooks better understand many of Annabella Hill's recipes.

Whereas Edgeworth ranged over the whole farm or plantation, advising us not only on how to put food on the table but also how to build pig troughs, keep dogs from stealing eggs, and build a beehive, Hill is more concerned with what to do with the ham, eggs, and honey once they arrive at the house. Butchering diagrams, a guide for fattening fowl, and instructions for running the home dairy are about as much as Hill expects that a cook needs to know of the farm, and she assumes you have homegrown vegetables ready to pick by the time you reach for her book.[2] She divides the cookbook into sections by the type of food, with most introduced either by general advice or by inspirational quotations. The meat section includes drawings showing how to carve and truss. Smaller sections in the back are for other household needs—homemade medicines and cleaning solutions as well as tidbits of practical advice that today's social media users call "life hacks." Hill also took pains to add a list of recommended tools for the kitchen, dairy, and laundry, which may have been cursory then but are made interesting by the passage of time.

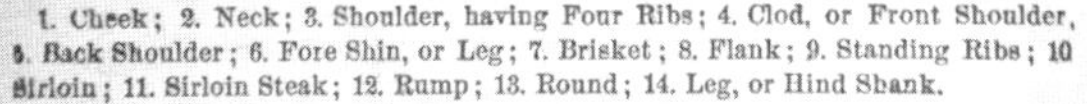
1. Cheek; 2. Neck; 3. Shoulder, having Four Ribs; 4. Clod, or Front Shoulder, 5. Back Shoulder; 6. Fore Shin, or Leg; 7. Brisket; 8. Flank; 9. Standing Ribs; 10 Sirloin; 11. Sirloin Steak; 12. Rump; 13. Round; 14. Leg, or Hind Shank.

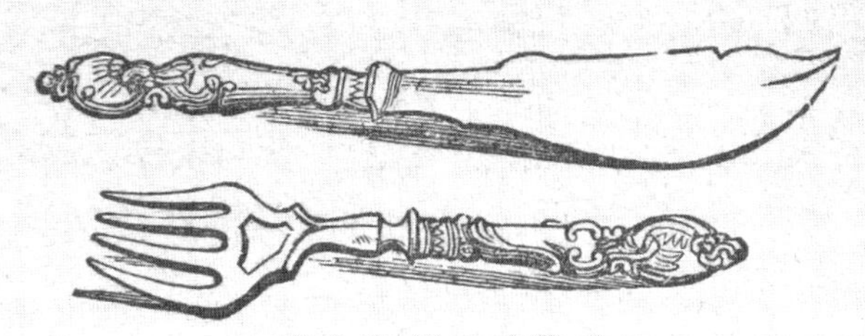
A Fish Knife and Fork.

As far as Hill's audience goes, it is as clear as her first sentence—"To the young and inexperienced Southern housekeepers I desire to dedicate this work."[3] She continues, "The rules that I give are collected from experience and other 'reliable' sources, and if faithfully and attentively practised will insure success. To experienced housekeepers, the directions may seem *tediously minute*."[4] (The emphasis is Mrs. Hill's.) Although Hill mentions her own favorite cookbooks from time to time throughout the work, she feels a new clear and detailed cookbook is necessitated by "this peculiar crisis of our domestic as well as national affairs."[5] She is speaking about the recently ended Civil War (1861–1865). Many southern women—herself included—found their assets reduced and their household duties or roles readjusted. Women who once upon a time would have dictated the menus and then swept through the kitchen periodically to keep tabs on the cook's progress suddenly found themselves in need of putting on an apron to get the work done.[6] For instance, it was written about Liberty County's 1866 bride Lydia Walker: "For a dainty girl of twenty-three who until now had never had to fetch herself a glass of water, even learning to cook and keep house with all the attendant repulsive chores was no simple task."[7] Hill knew how to teach needed skills. She came from a family often focused on education, which shone through her cookbook and elsewhere in her life.

Most sources give Annabella Powell Dawson's birth year as 1810, although one obituary listed a birthdate of 13 March 1811.[8] Whether she was born in 1810 or 1811, she is the eldest of Georgia's cookbook authors. Annabella came from Revolutionary War stock, her maternal grandfather having served in the Continental Army.[9] Her parents, Major John Edmonds Dawson (1775–1811) and Annabella Burwell Dawson (1785–1835), left Virginia as newlyweds around 1802 and came to Georgia, where they built a life of prosperity and influence that included his stint in the Georgia state legislature as well as friendships

478. *To Know when the Oven or Stove is Hot Enough for Baking.*—Sprinkle in a little flour; if it turns slowly a good brown color, the oven is right; if it burns immediately, it is too hot. Leave the door of the stove open a few minutes to allow it to cool. It will be right when you can hold your hand in to count twenty. But this is not a reliable rule, since some persons endure heat better than others. Baking may be done in the stove, in a brick or iron oven; if a brick oven is used, kindle the fire when the dough is put to rise; by the time the bread has risen, the oven will be ready; when the oven is hot enough, clean it out, and give the dust a few moments to settle before putting the bread in. When an iron oven is used, set the bottom side up before the fire until well warmed; in putting coals under, mash the larger ones with the back of the shovel, that all may be of the same size; where one or two larger coals than the rest are left under the oven, cake or bread is very apt to bake with large holes, or as cooks express it, "blow up" in holes. At first the heat should be strongest at the bottom of the oven; put the oven lid on cold, or slightly warm; cover it with hot embers; heat gradually. Baking can only be learned by experience. It is a good plan to heat the flour very hot before making it up. After sifting, I always place the flour well spread in the sun, or before the fire, taking care it does not scorch.

with governors Milledge (served 1802–1806) and Irwin (served 1806–1809).[10] The couple established themselves first in Washington County not far from Milledgeville, which became the state's capital in 1804. A few years later, the Dawsons moved north to the Indian Creek area four miles southwest of Madison (Morgan County).[11]

In 1811, shortly after the last move, John Dawson died. He left behind a widow in her mid-twenties as well as two sons and three daughters, the youngest child being the infant Annabella. One of the children's uncles, Colonel Richard A. Blount of Milledgeville, and local planter Douglas W. Porter were appointed co-guardians, managing the children's educations and assets.[12] Annabella's brothers were eventually sent to schools including Mt. Zion in Hancock County and Madison Academy, while her older sisters were sent to the Warrenton Female Academy (previously known as the Mordecai Female Seminary) in North Carolina, a school noted for its inclusion of Jewish culture and lack of pampering for its well-to-do pupils.[13] Annabella herself was sent to board in Madison as well as in Columbia, South Carolina, to attend school, possibly because the Warrenton school was sold in 1819, before she was old enough to attend.[14] Annabella's mother married guardian Douglas Porter, but he died in 1823 when Annabella was around the age of thirteen.[15] Despite early losses, Annabella wrote in a memoir focused on her oldest brother, the prominent Baptist minister Reverend John E. Dawson (1805–1860), "Our home was one of love and refinement."[16]

In 1827, around the age of seventeen, Annabella married an up-and-coming lawyer with a family background similar to her own. Edward Young Hill (1805–1860), like Annabella, had a grandfather who served in the Revolutionary War.[17] His parents were Abbeville County, South Carolina, planter Joshua Hill Sr. (1763–1855) and Nancy Wyatt Collier Hill (1769–1848).[18] Edward was a recent graduate of Franklin College (now the University of Georgia) in Athens. Soon after marriage, the couple moved southwest to Monticello in Jasper County, where they lived for almost two decades. In 1845, when Annabella was in her mid-thirties, the Hills moved again, this time ninety miles west to LaGrange in Troup County near the Alabama border. Edward's work, family ties, and agricultural interests likely influenced these moves. During his law career, Edward served as Solicitor General of the Ocmulgee Circuit and as a judge for the Coweta Circuit. Edward was also interested in politics, serving in the state legislature.[19] In 1849 the Whig Party nominated Edward for an unsuccessful bid for governor against George W. Towns.[20] In 1851 he also threw his hat in the ring for U.S. senator, losing out to Robert Toombs.[21] As an interesting side note, the newspaper reporting the outcome of the Hill-Toombs senate race also reported that S. C. Edgeworth made an unsuccessful bid that same election cycle for the office of secretary of state; of the five key state positions up for election in 1851, two were being sought by the husbands of future Georgia cookbook authors.[22]

732. *Jumbles, No.* 1.—Three eggs, half a pound of sifted flour, half a pound of butter, half a pound of loaf sugar, one tablespoonful of rose-water, one nutmeg. Stir the sugar and butter to a cream. Beat the eggs light; add all to the flour, and stir hard with a knife. Sprinkle flour upon your board; flour your hands well; take up with the knife a portion of the dough, and lay it on the board; roll lightly with the hands into long, thin rolls. Cut into equal lengths; curl into rings; lay gently into an iron or tin pan, buttered (not too close, as they spread). Bake in a quick oven five minutes. Grate sugar over the top. The top of the oven should be nearly *red hot.*

Just when my research into the lives of the Hills seemed all work and no play, I came across this tidbit. It is of no great historical import, yet it brings this family a little more in focus. In the late 1840s, one young lady had this experience:

> There was always a big ball in Decatur at the principal hotel on Friday night of Superior Court week. Our judge was Hon. Edward Young Hill, one of the handsomest men I still think I ever saw in my life. I looked forward to that big ball with delight. I was just entering my teens and several times the judge would ask me to dance with him and he was a splendid dancer.[23]

The starry-eyed girl was none other than Rebecca Latimer Felton (1835–1930), who would later become the first woman to serve in the U.S. Senate (1922).[24]

In the Hill home, there was both sunshine and sorrow. Six of Annabella and Edward's eleven children didn't live past the age of ten. (At the time of Annabella's death, only two of her children were still living.) As Annabella entered her forties, however, the 1850 census gives a glimpse of a full house. The Hill family was involved with the founding of a girls' academy, LaGrange Collegiate Seminary, and boarded students in their home.[25] Fowler states that during this time the Hills were "socially prominent and well-known in the community for their hospitality."[26] Years later, Annabella's obituary in the *Atlanta Constitution* would say of the couple, "Both young and attractive, they were the admired

396. *To Fry Ochra.*—Boil a quart; strain it well from the water; mash it smooth; season with salt and pepper. Beat in one or two eggs, and add flour (about half a tumbler of sifted flour) to make the batter stiff enough to fry as fritters. Serve on a flat dish upon a napkin. They should not be piled; send in as fast as fried.

400. *Onion Stew.*—Cut up six white onions, medium-size; slice as much Irish potatoes after peeling. Put all in a stew-pan; pour over a pint of hot water; season with salt and pepper; cover close; simmer gently; when nearly done, add a tablespoonful of butter, with a heaped teaspoonful of flour rubbed into it, and half a tumbler of sweet cream. Stir from the bottom to prevent its scorching, and when just ready to boil, pour into a hot covered dish; serve immediately. This is a fine accompaniment to boiled poultry or mutton.

centre of a social circle which at that day rivaled the best in the state."[27]

The storm of the Civil War was brewing, however, as was tragedy closer to home. While giving an anti-secession speech in November of 1860, Edward suddenly took ill with what seems to have been a stroke and died soon after, leaving Annabella a widow at age fifty. Within months, war began and claimed two of their sons. By the time it ended, Annabella's financial situation had changed enough that she needed to sell off property. Her obituary would later report that after the war she spent time in the household of one of her married daughters. Yet the same article reported, "But inactive life did not suit her temperament or satisfy her sense of duty."[28] Annabella's forays into education were not over.

In 1867, around the age of fifty-seven, Annabella published her cookbook. The dedication page voiced compassion and encouragement for the inexperienced new housekeepers of the day, and practical help followed with recipe after recipe. Annabella's work is often described as a Reconstruction Era cookbook, but Fowler makes a strong case that her "heyday" of cooking was before the Civil War, and thus her work should be compared with other antebellum southern cookbook authors such as Mary Randolph (Virginia), Lettice Bryan (Kentucky), and Sarah Rutledge (South Carolina).[29]

Closing the door on more than two decades of family life in LaGrange, Annabella moved seventy miles northeast to Atlanta, the city that in 1868 became Georgia's new and present capital. As the 1860s ended, newspapers in Atlanta and across the state frequently carried Hill's name either as a cookbook author with a two-dollar volume selling to strong reviews, a cooking expert endorsing cookstoves, or as the principal of the new Orphan's School set up in Atlanta and funded by a lottery. Over the next few years, the Hill cookbook was marketed as far away as New York City. Annabella took time to write a biography of her older brother and also took on the role of "Editress" in charge of the "Domestic Department" of the *Sunny South* newspaper. On 29 January 1878, not long after the Orphan's School closed, Annabella Hill died suddenly at her home around the age of sixty-eight.[30] Her obituary stated, "She was queen alike of the parlor and kitchen, and her book on domestic economy is among the best that has come from an American pen."[31]

Wet Devil Sauce

Receipt for Making "Wet Devil" Sauce

Chutney (Tirhoot)	1 ounce
Worcester Sauce	1 "
Mustard	1 "
Catchup	4 "
Sweet Oil	1 "
Cayenne Pepper	¼ "

William Jones's Captain's Steward. S. S. Scotia 1870. [Mem][1] Gave him 10 s. for it.

—De Renne Family Recipes and Remedies, 1860–1949, University of Georgia[2]

There is something intriguing about this recipe found on a scrap in the papers of Savannah's De Renne family. What concoction is so delicious that you must bribe the captain's man to bring the recipe home? In the culinary world, "devil" has long meant "spice"—think deviled eggs, crab, or ham—which can be accomplished through dry spice mixes or wet sauces. Easing into the recipe at hand, comparing it with recipes of a similar period helps us determine that "sweet oil" was likely olive and "mustard" the yellow powder rather than the prepared condiment. So far so good. But then half of the ingredients—chutney, "Worcester," and catsup—are already sauces with their own complex recipes. Chutneys are spiced fruit relishes that originated in India and became favorites in the West to accompany meats. Nineteenth-century newspapers show "Tirhoot Chutney" marketed by various companies, but its popularity faded in the twentieth century.

333. *Pickle Sauce.*—Into a tumblerful of melted butter stir a large tablespoonful of chopped mustard pickle, with a tablespoonful of the vinegar; stir three minutes, or until thoroughly hot.

334. *Curry Sauce.*—Add to a pint of broth or melted butter an even tablespoonful of curry powder; wet into a paste with cold water; or boil in the broth an apple or an onion cut up; when soft enough to mash fine, strain; wipe out the stew-pan; return to the stew-pan, and add the curry powder; simmer two minutes. Parboil the onion before adding it to the broth; this is more delicate than to add it raw.

335. *Sauce for Barbecues.*—Melt half a pound of butter; stir into it a large tablespoonful of mustard, half a teaspoonful of red pepper, one of black, salt to taste; add vinegar until the sauce has a strong acid taste. The quantity of vinegar will depend upon the strength of it. As soon as the meat becomes hot, begin to baste, and continue basting frequently until it is done; pour over the meat any sauce that remains.

These sauce recipes appeared on page 171 of *Mrs. Hill's New Cook Book* (1867).

I found no recipes or current products. As for Worcestershire sauce, Sue Shephard's *Pickled, Potted, and Canned* explains that it was "discovered" in an English cellar. A customer sent an Indian recipe to a chemist shop to be blended but never picked it up. "It was forgotten for many years, by which time it was well matured. Made from a well-kept secret recipe, and still bearing the chemist's name of Lea and Perrins, it has become one of the most famous and most ubiquitous of bottled sauces."[3] Last but not least, catsup likely originated in the Far East to make use of the liquids left over from pickling fish or vegetables.[4]

Between the chutney and the "catchup," there are so many variables that the Wet Devil Sauce served in 1870 on the high seas is a mystery. But is it a *complete* mystery? Arthur Payne's 1889 *Housekeeper's Guide to Preserved Meats, Fruits, Vegetables, &c.* explains that chutneys are based on "the fundamental theory of the mixture of hot, acid, and sweet forming an agreeable compound."[5] Was the magic of Wet Devil Sauce simply adding bitter (mustard) as well as salty and umami (Worcestershire) to the chutney principle? Perhaps Wet Devil Sauce can be looked on as a challenge rather than a set recipe. Using the six ingredients listed, can you come up with a blend that satisfies all your taste receptors? And can it call to mind exotic lands connected to Georgia by ships that harnessed the winds?[6]

Exploring Further

If you're a barbecued meat and barbecue sauce lover, know that in recent years several Georgians have written about old traditions. Joseph E. Dabney documented customs in the Appalachians as well as in the Low Country,[7] while Atlanta journalist Jim Auchmutey wrote *Smokelore: A Short History of Barbecue in America*. As for cookbooks, Auchmutey coauthored *The Ultimate Barbecue Sauce Cookbook* (1995) with Atlanta's Susan Puckett. From the

STANDING SAUCE. — Put in a glazed jar, with the juice of two lemons, five anchovies, some whole Jamaica pepper, sliced ginger, mace, a few cloves, a little lemon peel, horseradish sliced, some sweet herbs, six eschalots, two spoonfuls of capers and their liquor, into a linen bag, and put it into one quart of sherry; stop the vessel close; set it in a kettle of hot water for one hour, and keep it in a warm place. A spoonful or two of this liquid is good to any sauce.

This recipe for Standing Sauce comes from the Athens agriculture magazine *Farmer & Artisan* 3.10 (11 March 1871): 147.

competition circuit, the late Wiley McCrary of Atlanta and Savannah wrote *Wiley's Championship BBQ: Secrets Old Men Take to the Grave*, while Myron Mixon of Unadilla wrote *Smokin' with Myron Mixon: Recipes Made Simple from the Winningest Man in Barbecue*. From the restaurant world, Atlanta chef Kevin Gillespie shares some of his grilling and smoking expertise in *Fire in My Belly*. Also see the 1866 and 1928 sections.

Enclaves

From Congee to Flapper Food and Beyond

With ingredients and recipes, it is tempting to ask if they are typical or atypical, Georgia or not-Georgia. A more helpful approach celebrates that our complex foodways develop over time through many influences. *Ethnicity*, edited by Celeste Ray, the sixth volume in the *New Encyclopedia of Southern Culture* series, helps us understand how various groups have enriched the South. Our southern ancestors were either indigenous or immigrants, all with foodways to share. (See 1733 section.) How do we connect with the legacies of various groups, celebrating the range of our foodways past and present?

In this section, we'll use the word "enclave" to describe a group of Georgians that maintain some cultural or ethnic distinctions. Margaret DeBolt's *Savannah Sampler Cookbook* includes information and recipes about various enclaves contributing to the foodways of Georgia's first city.[1] Attending festivals and celebrations connected to these enclaves can bring such recipes alive. Thankfully, the Internet can help us keep informed of cultural happenings in our community and across the state.

Another connection point is that places of worship, community centers, or historical groups are sometimes aligned with enclaves and may create cookbooks. As discussed in the 1863 section with the Geechee enclave, modern cookbooks can be keys to understanding older foodways. In the 1734 section we discussed the Salzburgers who immigrated from what is now Austria. Two centuries after their arrival, the Georgia Salzburger Society's cookbook provided glimpses of how this enclave embraced a new place while preserving a shared identity. Another example is Georgia's Chinese-American community. Travels through China several years ago made me curious about the similarities between Chinese rice culture and the historical Georgia one glimpsed during my coastal childhood, so I was intrigued to discover *Favorite Recipes of the Augusta Chinese Community* by the Chinese Consolidated Benevolent Association (CCBA).[2] In 1873 a construction company brought around two hundred Chinese workers to widen and deepen the Augusta Canal, and some made the town their home.[3] (Thus the date for this section.) A few years later, in the early 1890s, a Chinese restaurant operated in Brunswick, and by the turn of the century there was a Chinese community in Savannah with a restaurant sharing their foodways.[4]

Augusta's CCBA began in 1927, and the latest edition of their cookbook contains 307 pages of recipes, some with ingredients you'll need an Asian grocery to find, yet some adapted to time and place and calling for familiar ingredients like White Lily flour and catsup. The cookbook has several pages explaining traditional Chinese cooking, but I was curious to know which recipes best reflected the Augusta community's history. I wrote to the CCBA, and a member of the cookbook committee kindly sent a list with comments. Here are two recipes courtesy of the CCBA.

The first, featuring rice, affords a comparison with early Georgia rice recipes, which span from sweet muffins to savory croquettes. Rice pudding, a dessert common in older Georgia cookbooks, is often similar in texture to this savory dish.

Congee or Rice Broth (Jook)

1 chicken, approximately 3 lbs (or meat of your choice)
3 quarts water
1 cup rice
2 pieces orange peel, size of a quarter
green onions, chopped
sesame oil
soy sauce

1. Using a heavy stew pot, place a chicken in the water, bring to boil, remove scum and then add rice and orange peel.
2. Cook on medium for 1.5 hours stirring twice to prevent rice from sticking.
3. Remove and debone chicken and cut into bite size pieces before returning them to broth.
4. Season to taste. Serve with green onions, sesame oil and soy sauce. Enjoy.

—Mickey Wing, in *Favorite Recipes*, 214

RICE PUDDING.—To one cup of boiled rice add half a cup of butter, five eggs, sugar to taste, and cream enough to make it liquid. Flavor with essence of lemon, and bake in rich paste in deep pudding dishes.

This recipe for Rice Pudding comes from the Athens magazine *Farmer & Artisan* 2.24 (10 December 1870): 117.

CCBA member Kathryn Rufo shared the following recipe from her mother-in-law, who came in the 1920s from the warm-climate countryside near Guangzhou. Rufo noted this recipe is an "excellent way to preserve extra eggs without refrigeration," and it calls to mind the egg-preserving methods shared by Edgeworth, Verstille, and Hill.

Salted Eggs

2 doz large eggs
½ lb salt (approx.)
1 glass jar, gallon size
6 cups water (approx.)
1 medium size raw potato

1. Bring water to a boil and add salt. Stir until dissolved.
2. Place a raw potato in salt solution. Add more salt until it floats. Remove potato and allow water to cool.
3. Place eggs in a glass jar and add cooled, salted water. Let sit for 30 days. Eggs will be ready when an egg is broken and yolk is a firm orange ball.

—Kathryn Rufo, in *Favorite Recipes*, 303

Religion also can create enclaves. Here are a few examples of how this has enriched Georgia foodways: Many Catholics follow the tradition of eating fish on Fridays, and thus some community cookbooks from Catholic churches abound with fish recipes. Georgia has several Jewish community cookbooks filled with typical southern fare but also with special recipes such as challah bread, potato latkes, and hamantaschen cookies. Speaking of Jewish foodways reminds me that sometimes individuals participate in overlapping enclaves. I visited Atlanta's William Breman Jewish Heritage Museum to look at the undated manuscript recipe book of Ernestine May Brown (1855–1920) of Albany.[5] It was everything a researcher could hope for—in good condition with beautifully clear handwriting—yet all in German! Brown brought both Jewish and Central European food traditions with her to Georgia.

In recent years the Macon County *Montezuma Amish Mennonite Cookbook* by Ruth Yoder became popular. Similarly, Greek Orthodox churches in Atlanta and Savannah support Greek festivals, and so far I have found two community cookbooks—*The Key to Greek Cooking* and *The Art of Greek Cooking*.[6] After looking through these cookbooks as well as *Modern Greek Cooking* by Georgia author Pano Karatassos, I approached the archival collection of Greek immigrant and Columbus candy store owner Alex Mitchell (1871–1940) expecting to find Mediterranean traditions. My untrained eye didn't detect any, reminding me that enclaves and the individuals within them choose how tightly to hold to traditions and the degree to which they share them. The following recipe from Mitchell's 1889–1966 candy store, shared courtesy of the Columbus State University Archives, reflects its time and place. In the 1920s, flappers were young women who embraced such racy behavior as bobbed hair and short hemlines.

Flapper Food

2 pounds chocolate or chocolate coating, cut in bits
1 pound marshmallows, large, cut in half
½ pound pecans, chopped

Melt chocolate in double boiler, making sure water does not get in the candy. Use warm water, not boiling, to melt. Stir continuously. When melted, add marshmallows and pecans, coating thoroughly with chocolate. Spread evenly in an 11-by-7-inch pan lined with wax paper. Put in refrigerator until chocolate hardens.

—Mitchell Family Papers, 1819–1930, Columbus State University[7]

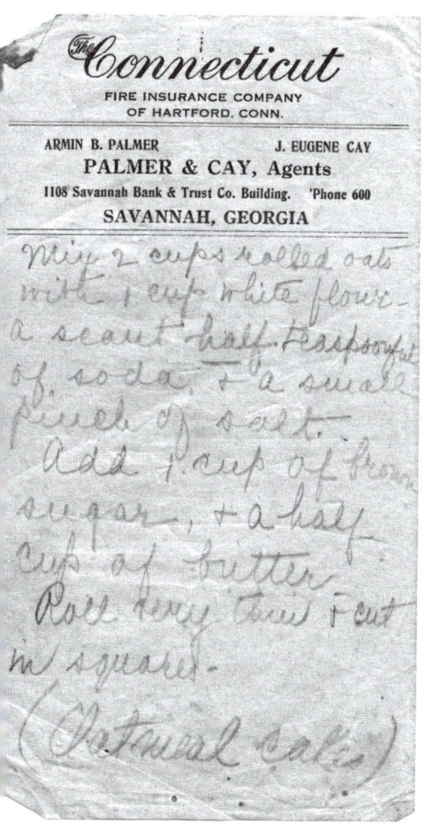

The Connecticut
FIRE INSURANCE COMPANY
OF HARTFORD, CONN.

ARMIN B. PALMER J. EUGENE CAY
PALMER & CAY, Agents
1108 Savannah Bank & Trust Co. Building. 'Phone 600
SAVANNAH, GEORGIA

Mix 2 cups rolled oats with 1 cup white flour - a scant half teaspoonful of soda, & a small pinch of salt. Add 1 cup of brown sugar, & a half cup of butter. Roll very thin & cut in squares.

(Oatmeal cakes)

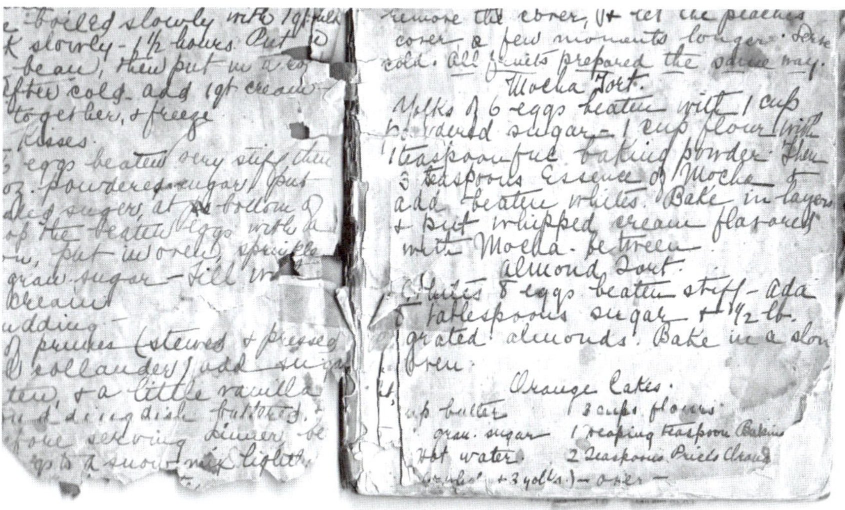

Remove the cover, & let the peaches cover a few moments longer. Serve cold. All fruits prepared the same way.

Mocha Tort.
Yolks of 6 eggs beaten with 1 cup powdered sugar - 1 cup flour with 1 teaspoonful baking powder. Then 3 teaspoons Essence of Mocha & add beaten whites. Bake in layers & put whipped cream flavored with Mocha between.

Almond Tort.
Whites 8 eggs beaten stiff - add tablespoons sugar & 1/2 lb. grated almonds. Bake in a slow oven.

Orange Cakes.

The Oatmeal Cakes recipe was found with the undated handwritten cookbook of Bertha "Bert" Kayton Rosenheim (1874–1967) of Savannah (Breman manuscript 2022.005.002). The recipes were inherited by family member Judy Byck in the condition seen here, and she donated them to help save them for future generations. Use of these images is courtesy of Judy Byck as well as the Cuba Family Archives for Southern Jewish History at the Breman Museum, which is currently the home of the Savannah Jewish Archives.

Exploring Further

We are lucky to have contemporary cookbook authors connected to Georgia who explore world cuisines and help us bring them into local kitchens. Some authors to look for include Jennifer Hill Booker (France), Von Diaz (Puerto Rico and other islands), Ford Fry (Mexico), Asha Gomez (India), Eddie Hernandez (Mexico), Suzy Karadsheh (Mediterranean), Seung Hee Lee (Korea), Judith McLoughlin (Ireland), and Deborah VanTrece (global).

Undated postcard of peach trees blossoming in Marshallville, Georgia.

Georgia Horticulture and Recipes

Does any recipe ingredient seem more representative of Georgia than the luscious peach? Mary Edgeworth's 1859 cookbook contained advice on how to manage a peach orchard and shared recipes using fruit, pit, and leaves. Had Mary lived longer, she might have felt the need to do a new edition with more peach information. Not long after they were gone, the Edgeworths' farm in Fort Valley was swept into peach production. In fact, after being divided by the new Georgia Highway 96 heading east out of town, in 1924 the Edgeworth farm was made part of the new Peach County.[1] Almost a century later, Edgeworth land still grows peaches. One morning in early spring, I stood on the roadside looking out over avenues of short, pink-petaled trees stretching into the distance. Come summer, I visited the Lane Packing Company's visitor center just down the road for peach treats from fresh fruit to jam to ice cream.

Peaches arrived in Georgia long before the colonists. In *The Georgia Peach: Culture, Agriculture, and Environment in the American South*, historian William Thomas Okie explains that peaches likely originated in Asia and spread to Europe long ago via the Silk Road. This distinctive stone fruit, with "pits that traveled easily and germinated readily," arrived in the "New World" with the Spanish explorations, Christian missionary efforts, and intercontinental trade.[2] Georgia's indigenous peoples cultivated them; naturalist William Bartram found peach orchards around their former towns in the 1770s,[3] and Indian Agent Benjamin Hawkins (1754–1816) reported the Muscogee serving him peaches.[4]

A Culinary History of Atlanta traces the history of our capital city back to Standing Peachtree, a Muskogee village and trading center by the Chattahoochee River graced by a peach tree atop a hill.[5] In antebellum Georgia, early varieties of peaches were mostly grown for alcohol and hog feed, but horticulturists came along who saw value in developing the peach and diversifying Georgia's crops.[6] In 1857, Belgian immigrant Prosper Jules Berckmans (1830–1910) began purchasing land in Augusta and was soon well known for Fruitland Nursery and helping to found the Georgia State Horticulture Society in 1876.[7] (Thus the date for this section.) After Berckmans's death, his nursery eventually became the grounds of the Augusta National Golf Club, home of the Masters Golf Tournament.[8] Samuel Henry Rumph (1851–1922) of Willow Lake Nursery in Marshallville was also vital to the rise of the Georgia peach industry, developing a celebrated peach he named the Elberta after his wife in 1875.[9]

"I was peeling nice soft peaches for dinner just to save Mrs. Arp the trouble, and get an approving smile, when suddenly she came up behind me and said, 'William, are your hands right clean?' I held them up for her to look at as I remarked, 'If they were not at first I reckon they are now.'"

—Georgia humor writer Bill Arp (1826–1903)[1]

1. C. Smith [Arp], *The Farm and the Fireside*, 70.

As transportation improved in Georgia with advances in road surfaces as well as railroad efficiency, faraway markets were easier to reach. In 1895 the Georgia Department of Agriculture noted an "enormous increase" in peach growing in the state.[10] The next year, an Atlanta newspaper reported that the Georgia fruit industry was booming in Mary Edgeworth's part of Southwest Georgia: "Three or four years ago, hundreds of farmers of this section became interested in the industry, and many of them planted large orchards."[11] It continued, "Leaving Fort Valley in a buggy one can go in a southerly direction for forty miles and hardly get out of sight of peach orchards." In 1901 a Pennsylvania newspaper reported on "Georgia's Peach Belt":

> Perhaps the largest peach-growing district in the globe is that around Fort Valley and extending to Albany, Ga. The peach orchards cover more than 14,000 acres within a radius of ten miles of Fort Valley, and in this area there are something like 1,900,000 peach trees. . . . It is impossible for one who has never visited this region to realize what immense proportions the fruit-growing industry has reached. The railroads are taxed at the height of the season to get the crops to markets. Each fruit car carries an average of about 400 cases, and this year's crop will require not fewer than 2,000 cars to move it.[12]

By the 1930s, the nine million trees in the area could produce 10,000 to 15,000 carloads.[13] Why all the bother over peaches? Georgia-born novelist Pat Conroy wrote, “A ripe peach is a thing perfect unto itself, and the fruit is a tree’s way of expressing devotion to sunshine.”[14]

An image of a peach from the U.S. Department of Agriculture’s *Report of the Commissioner of Agriculture 1887.*

Many Georgians grew peaches in home gardens and on subsistence farms. Three years before Mary Edgeworth put out her cookbook, horticulturist William N. White (1820–1867) of Athens published *Gardening for the South, or the Kitchen and Fruit Garden.* For those wishing to better picture kitchen gardens in the 1800s, it is a wonderful source complete with illustrations. For example, White explains the proper planting, fertilizing, pruning, and pest control for peach trees as well as giving directions for drying peaches in a brick oven. His descriptive list of peach varieties reads like poetry: Late Red Rareripe, Lemon Cling, Pride of Autumn . . . He owned White’s University Bookstore in downtown Athens across Broad Street from UGA’s main landmark, the Arch, and served as one of the editors of the *Southern Cultivator* (Augusta/Athens).[15]

William was married to Rebecca Benedict White (ca. 1822–1885), who served as the editor for the Household Department in *Southern Farm and Home* (Macon) soon after she became a widow.[16] Three of her recipes using fresh produce follow:

Squash Biscuit

One cupful of strained squash; two tablespoonfuls of sugar; one tablespoon of melted butter; a little salt; one teaspoonful of soda; one cup of sour milk; flour to roll out. Serve hot for tea.[17]

Tomato Corn Cakes

Take a dozen ears of green corn; grate off the kernels fine; scald a dozen medium-sized tomatoes and remove the skins; beat three eggs well, and mix the whole with a pint of milk, and flour enough to make a batter; add salt, pepper, and allspice to the taste. Fry on a griddle, avoiding excess of grease.[18]

Spiced Strawberries

Five pounds strawberries, four pounds of sugar, two tablespoonfuls of ground cloves, the same of mace; after cooking twenty minutes add one pint of good cider vinegar, and boil as preserves. Red currants, cherries, raspberries and peaches are all very nice put up in this manner.[19]

[My twenty-first-century palate found this stunningly over-spiced. Made with just a fraction of the spices, however, it has a unique flavor profile for a pleasing dessert sauce.]

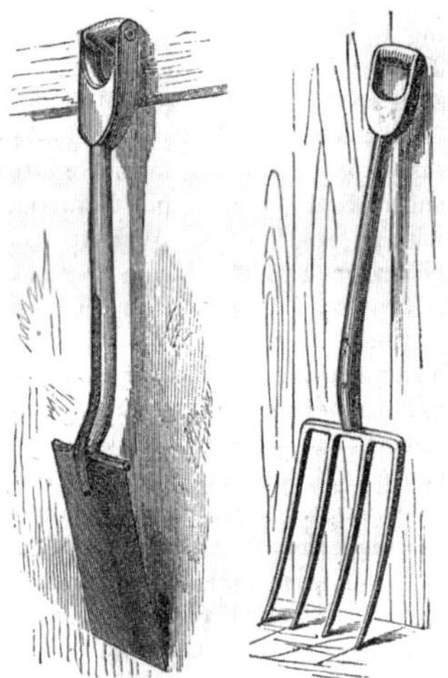

Images from White's 1856 *Gardening for the South*, pages 75 and 213.

The work of the Whites highlights the role of agriculture periodicals. Sometimes linked to agriculture clubs, these periodicals provided a way for scattered rural farmers to share information, ask questions, and do business with each other. Most of them acknowledged the important role of the farm wife, providing household information and recipes. We'll learn more about Marietta's *Phoenix Agriculturist* in the 1885 section and Atlanta's *Southern Ruralist* in the 1912 section. Other agriculture periodicals included *Farmer & Artisan* (Athens), *Georgia Farm Journal* (Madison), *Georgia Grange* (Atlanta), *Southern Farmer's Monthly* (Savannah), *Southern Field and Fireside* (Augusta), *Southern Cultivator* (Augusta/Athens), and *Southern Planter* (Macon). As with the newspapers, tracking these periodicals is tricky, as they sometimes changed publication locations, merged, or went extinct in short order. Staff managing the Georgia Historic Newspapers database do a valiant job sorting out various sources and providing online access.[20]

" Fruit in Georgia ;" Simon Thomas, of Washington county, " Mechanism on the Farm ;" J. Norcross, of Fulton county, " Fruit and Vines."
D. W. Lewis, Secretary.

Water-Proofing for Boots and Shoes.—Linseed oil, one pint; oil of turpentine or camphene, a quarter of a pint; yellow wax, a quarter of a pound; Burgundy pitch, a quarter of a pound. Melt together with a gentle heat, and when required for use to be warmed and well rubbed in the leather before the fire or in a hot sun.

Delicious Dish of Apples.—Take two pounds of apples, pare and core them, slice them into a pan, add one pound of loaf sugar, the juice of three lemons, and the grated rind of one. Let these boil about two hours. Turn it into a mould, and serve with thick custard or cream.

Gen. Beauregard it is said intends to reside permanently in Paris.

Recipes like this one from *Farmer & Artisan* 2.24 (10 December 1870): 106 were sometimes used as page filler in old periodicals.

Once we start looking at the early twentieth century, the Georgia Department of Agriculture has long been a provider of recipes. In 1917 it began publishing the *Farmers and Consumers Market Bulletin* for classified advertisements as well as news.[21] As my mother's file box can attest, the publication is a source of easy-to-clip recipes. Some of these recipes can now be found in *The Best of Georgia Farms Cookbook and Tour Book*, a GDA publication with a good deal of history woven in.[22] Recipes also came from government sources due to the Smith-Lever Act of 1914. Through land-grant universities offering Cooperative Extension, local instruction became available relating to gardens, cooking, and food preservation. Some agents have also written newspaper recipe columns and community cookbooks. Although it is an independent organization, the Georgia Farm Bureau should also be remembered for its work advocating for Georgia agriculture since 1937 and for *A Legacy of Georgia Cooking*, a cookbook that offers modern favorites yet also takes an interest in older foodways.

Exploring Further

There are a couple of modern theme cookbooks not to miss. *Peaches* is by Atlanta cookbook author Kelly Alexander. *The Peach Truck Cookbook* was inspired by coauthor Stephen Rose's childhood summers spent in Fort Valley.

Peach Salad

Use Elberta peach, or any large clear seed peach not too ripe; peel and split in half, removing seed. Fill cavity with chopped nuts. Arrange both slices on lettuce leaf; tip with mayonnaise.

—Loula Harris, in Alumnae of Shorter College (Rome), *Sweets and Savouries* (1915), 10

When it comes to famed Georgia ingredients, there are three *P*s—peaches, but also peanuts and pecans. And, really, we should add in an *O* for the Vidalia onion too. The search was tricky, though. I certainly don't mean to slight the other ingredients in terms of their importance, but unlike the meteoric rise of peaches, there isn't nearly as much information about these other three ingredients during our 1733–1945 period. As with our research on recipes from enclaves (see 1838, 1863, and 1873 sections), sometimes exploring a specific ingredient means finding modern sources and researching your way back in time.

Our second *P*—pecans—have enjoyed steady popularity. One Georgia cookbook of note for this ingredient is *The Pecan Cookbook*, edited by Farrel J. Zehr and published by Koinonia Farm, a community near Americus that gained much attention during the Civil Rights Movement for its support of desegregation. This farm still exists and has a thriving mail order pecan business. Another book, *Pecans: Recipes & History of an American Nut*, includes recipes by Athens author Rebecca Lang.[23] If you're looking for a recipe for a superlative pecan pie, prominent food journalist Clementine Paddleford (1898–1967) claimed that the best was by Atlanta's Callie Williams (born ca. 1892), who baked for the Magnolia Tea Room in Rich's Department Store.[24] Her recipe can be found in *The Great American Cookbook*, a revised version of Paddleford's 1960 classic *How America Eats*.[25]

"CARAMEL NUT DELIGHT"

1 cup of brown sugar — 1 cup of pecans
1 cup of cold water — 2 tablespoons of corn starch

Make into a paste with cold water. Method: Boil sugar and water until it thickens to the constituency of thick custard. Stir in corn starch and whip until cold. Sprinkle nuts on top and serve with whipped cream or boiled custard.

—Mrs. Samuel Hale Sibley, President Marietta, Ga., Chapter.

This pecan recipe is from the *Service Star Legion Cook Book* (1927), 116.

The other nuts we're briefly discussing, peanuts, are actually a legume. They have long been a southern favorite but rocketed in social popularity with the

Pecan groves gracing land near Eatonton.

1977–1981 presidency of Plains peanut farmer and former governor Jimmy Carter (1924–2024). As far as I could ascertain, his home county of Sumter boasted just four cookbooks before 1977. By the time he left the White House, there were eleven, including one by his mother (1898–1983), *Miss Lillian and Friends: The Plains, Georgia Family Philosophy and Recipe Book*. One not to miss is *Ruth Jackson's Soulfood Cookbook* from 1978, which taught me the joy of mixing peanut butter with finely chopped raisins.[26]

Peanut Candy

1 cup of raw shelled peanuts, beaten, 1 cup sugar. Dry out sugar perfectly; have vessel that you cook in very dry; then pour sugar in the vessel, and stir constantly while it is melting. As soon as melted, pour in peanuts and take it off the fire immediately. Pour on buttered dish.

—Mrs. Estes, in *Hapeville Presbyterian Cook Book* (1898), 21

Peanuts are grown commercially in South Georgia, including in Sumter County where President Jimmy Carter grew up. The Boyhood Home & Farm near the town of Plains, owned by the Carters from 1928 until 1949, is now a part of the Jimmy Carter National Historical Park, and the kitchen has been restored to its 1937 appearance. (Photo courtesy of the National Parks Service.)

As for the *O*, the vegetable of the group, until the 1940s, Georgia newspapers have little to say about the Vidalia onion. There is some evidence that the lauded onion before then was the Goshen onion of Elbert County.[27] My research uncovered six twentieth-century cookbooks dedicated to the Vidalia onion, beginning in 1981 with *The Original Vidalia Onion Cookbook*, compiled by Pam McIntyre for the Vidalia Chamber of Commerce.

Onion Pickle

Use small white onions; scald in salt and water for four mornings; the fifth morning lay them in cold milk and let them stand all day. Wipe dry and put in small jars; cover with vinegar, spiced with red pepper and stick-cinnamon.

—Mrs. James Wallace, in Second Presbyterian Church (Augusta), *Choice Recipes of Georgia Housekeepers* (1880), 166

The Recipes and Three Pillars of Tunis Campbell

Hotel Keepers, Head Waiters, and Housekeepers' Guide, 1848
Tunis Gulic Campbell (1 April 1812–4 December 1891)
192 pages. 104 recipes.

When Annabella Hill took up life in Atlanta after the Civil War, she wasn't the only cookbook author pulled toward Georgia's new capital. Tunis Campbell, author of the 1848 *Hotel Keepers, Head Waiters, and Housekeepers' Guide*, had been living on the Georgia coast for several years until his career drew him first to Milledgeville and then to Atlanta. The recipes Campbell recorded are grounded in northeastern foodways and published before he arrived in Georgia around 1865. (As though to prove this, his cornbread recipe was sweet.) The recipes are, however, examples of the different cooking traditions that flowed into the South in the wake of the Civil War and Reconstruction, brought by soldiers, federal government workers, social reformers, investors, and opportunists. And Campbell influenced far more than foodways in Georgia. An article in the *New Georgia Encyclopedia* calls him "the highest-ranking and most influential African American politician in nineteenth-century Georgia."[1]

Born in New Jersey in 1812, Campbell worked at various bakeries and hotels as a young man. Around the age of thirty-six, he published his guide for the food service business. The first half of the book outlines everything food servers should know and presents a military-like system allowing staff to follow signals and act as a well-oiled machine. Cookbook scholar Toni Tipton-Martin observes that Campbell's guide went beyond rules and regulations: "He instead sought to educate his people, instilling in them a desire to achieve the highest degree of professionalism and pure moral character."[2] The second half of the book contains recipes—18 soups, 15 savory sauces, and 27 recipes for cooking proteins such as beef, mutton, and fowl as well as cod, eel, and lark. There are 39 dessert recipes, mostly tarts, puddings, and custards.

In addition to his food service career, Campbell was also a minister, missionary, lecturer, and political figure. At first Campbell focused on anti-colonization, the abolition of slavery, and temperance.[3] He helped to establish schools and churches in New Jersey. Then Campbell came south at the end of the Civil War with the Freedmen's Bureau, intent on improving living conditions for the formerly enslaved population along the Georgia coast. Promoting the "Three Pillars of Self-Sufficiency"—education, religion, and farming—he rose to prominence during a time of social chaos and economic hardship across Georgia and the South.[4] The assassination of Abraham Lincoln and his succession by Andrew Johnson changed Reconstruction policies, and Campbell was let go from the Freedman's Bureau. He continued as a community leader and Justice of the Peace in McIntosh County and, in 1867, was elected to the Georgia General Assembly as senator for the Second District (Liberty, Tattnall, and McIntosh Counties). His grown son, Tunis Campbell Jr., was elected to the Georgia House.

Campbell's chosen path in Georgia was one of difficulty and controversy. Local newspapers from the time reported many clashes between Campbell's followers and other residents. Campbell's home was burned, and his family lived in fear.[5] In 1868, thirty-three Black legislators including Campbell and his son were expelled from the Georgia Assembly. Meanwhile, political adversaries pushed to have Campbell arrested on charges associated with his former service as Justice of the Peace. His eventual conviction caused what the newspapers called a riot in McIntosh County.[6] In 1876, at the age of sixty-four and despite support from the national government, he was convicted and served time in a labor camp in Washington County. Upon his release in 1877, Campbell moved permanently to Boston with his family. Subsequent city directories show his occupation as a clergyman, while his son was a shoemaker.[7] He died in 1891 at the age of seventy-nine.[8]

The year that Campbell returned to the North, he published *Sufferings of Rev. T. G. Campbell and His Family in Georgia*. (Thus the date for this section.) This short book focuses on his career as a social reformer, so the personal details he shares are largely dry and objective. When his narrative touches on the fine points, however, it reflects his past life connected to food. He describes dismal prison meals as well as family support through care packages, taking time to name items that arrived in monthly boxes of "nourishments" from his wife, Harriet—pickled eggs, strawberry preserves, and treats such as sugar-cakes and pound cakes. These foods are not found among his published recipes, reflecting home instead of the food service world.

The following marmalade recipe is based on quinces, which look much like pears, yet are tart and hard until cooked. They were a popular ingredient in nineteenth-century American cookbooks but gradually fell from favor.[9]

To Make Marmalade

To two pounds of quinces, add three quarters of a pound of sugar, and a pint of spring water; put them over the fire, and boil them till they are tender; drain off the liquor, and bruise them; then put them into it again, let it boil three quarters of an hour, and put it in to your pots or saucers.

—Campbell, *Hotel Keepers, Head Waiters, and Housekeepers' Guide*, 186

Choice Recipes of Georgia Housekeepers

Choice Recipes of Georgia Housekeepers, 1880
Second Presbyterian Church, Augusta
180 pages. 694 food recipes with 1 additional recipe for medicine and 14 for household needs.

The preface for *Choice Recipes of Georgia Housekeepers* begins thus:

> Almost every housekeeper has a little hoard of recipes of her own—some handed down in her family for generations, some the results of her own experience or experiment, some obtained from the [manuscript] collections of her friends. Of the last-named class, perhaps, many have a certain private celebrity, and have found their way into the individual collection of every notable housekeeper in the circle or community.[1]

The Editorial Committee laments that personal recipes are treasures vulnerable to loss and that "the circle of exchange is comparatively small." They claim first and foremost that their red hardbound cookbook is designed to preserve and share recipes, assuring the reader that "the price of the book will not be money expended in charity, but will receive a valuable equivalent." Their full mission isn't clear in the cookbook itself, but a review from a Georgia newspaper noted that it was written by the ladies "to pay the balance due on their church."[2]

The committee described their book in plain terms. "This is a book of home cookery—the savory dishes of our infancy." An unnamed reviewer in the *Atlanta Constitution* in 1894 echoed this: "In turning these pages one catches the aroma of the old-time southern kitchen. To one surfeited with the fancy dishes of modern cuisine it will be a relief to try these old Georgia dishes."[3]

The editing process also seems to have been basic. The committee "simply arranged the recipes sent to us." Certainly, the recipes vary enough in length and tone that individual writing styles and voices shine through whatever editing was done. One recipe tells us to make a batter "thick enough to hold a silver spoon upright," while another calls for a "dust of pepper."[4] Because the editors didn't standardize the contributions, this is Georgia's first cookbook where the recipes aren't all in block or paragraph form; some include modern-style lists of ingredients. Editing of the whole was also limited. The Editorial Committee conclude their preface by explaining about the cookbook's twenty-three sections or departments: "We have endeavored, as far as possible, to make each department complete, but where material was not furnished us, unless there seemed an urgent necessity for it, the deficiency has remained unsupplied." Whereas Annabella Hill (and, later, Annie Dennis) tried to curate a well-rounded collection of recipes, this cookbook offers something more like "1880 Augusta's greatest hits." There's everything from entrees to side dishes, yet almost half of the recipes fall into the dessert category. (As a home baker, I am not complaining.)

The Editorial Committee did not claim to be innovators, admitting in the preface that "several benevolent or denominational societies like our own, throughout the country, have published similar books for various causes." Historians generally credit Union supporters during the Civil War at Philadelphia's Great Sanitary Fair of 1864 for introducing America's first community charity cookbook, while others point to earlier temperance cookbooks.[5] *Choice Recipes* is Georgia's earliest known cookbook of this type. In our modern times, scholars embrace these cookbooks that historian Anne Bower calls "distinctively American cultural artifacts, capable of telling us much about their authors and their communities." Bower explores how women used these books to raise money but also for "personal development, friendship, cultural stimulation, and opportunities for public life through their participation in volunteer causes."[6] Bower edited a book called *Recipes for Reading: Community Cookbooks, Stories, Histories*, with the work of over a dozen scholars exploring what these cookbooks can reveal about their time and place of creation.

Because it was a community effort, *Choice Recipes* is the first of Georgia's cookbooks to credit recipe contributors by name. By contrast, both Verstille and Hill credited a few of their recipes to others but used only initials, as in "Mrs. C's Cake." While the anonymity of the earlier cookbooks may seem odd today, know that

back in 1847 southern cookbook author Sarah Rutledge published *The Carolina Housewife* simply as "by a lady of Charleston" because it was thought unbecoming for a woman to have her name in print.[7] Barely thirty years after Rutledge, more than half the recipes in this Georgia cookbook are credited to a particular person—454 recipes out of 709. There are over sixty contributors, mostly married women listed under their husband's name or initials such as "Mrs. C. S. Arnall." Eight females have the title "Miss." One recipe, Mustard or Chow Chow Pickle (see below), is credited to a man.[8] There are also four recipes credited in the title, yet without surnames—Aunt Betsey's Cookies, Vallie's Cake, Annie's Ginger Bread, and Eve's Pudding[9]—possibly indicating by period tradition that these are the recipes of women of color. As for the church, the 1877 *Shole's Augusta City Directory* lists First Church (founded in 1804) and Riverside Chapel for Presbyterian worshipers. Local newspapers noted that Second Presbyterian was organized in the spring of 1879 and by July installed its first pastor.[10] Not surprisingly, the newspaper list of new Second Presbyterian members includes many of the cookbook contributors.

Genealogy buffs are always looking for sources that list the names of their ancestors, but how do recipe credits help us if we're simply interested in

foodways? Names give additional avenues of research. Now that so many information sources such as census records, city directories, and newspapers are available online, contributor names show us that *Choice Recipes* came together from the households of middle- or upper-class merchants, doctors, insurance salesmen, and manufacturers. A few of the contributors were the wives of farmers, but most lived urban lives. By the time of the cookbook, Augusta had a population of close to 24,000 people, and the Second Presbyterian Church at 1253 Greene Street was located near the heart of the city.[11] Our pickle contributor, for instance, was a cotton factor who lived in the nearby Summerville historical district west of downtown.[12] Contributor by contributor, fact by fact, we begin to be able to picture the community behind the cookbook, glimpsing a time and place that generated its own take on foodways.

Vallie's Cake

5 eggs.
5 cupfuls flour.
2½ cupfuls sugar.
2 cupfuls sour milk.
1½ cupful butter.
2 teaspoonfuls mace.
2 teaspoonfuls cinnamon.
2 cupfuls raisins.
1 teaspoon soda dissolved in water.
1 gill wine.
Put in soda last thing.

—Mrs. C. A. Rowland, in *Choice Recipes*, 80

Mustard or Chow Chow Pickle

1 lb. mustard.
Vinegar to thin.
1 teaspoonful black pepper.
1 teaspoonful cinnamon.
1 teaspoonful cloves.
1 gallon mixed vegetables.
1 cupful sugar.
1 teaspoonful allspice.
1 teaspoon celery-seed.
2 teaspoonfuls turmeric.
A little mace.
A little olive oil.
1 teaspoonful mustard-seed.
1 teaspoonful cayenne pepper.

Cut fine different kinds of vegetables, spread on a dish, sprinkle a little salt over them, place them in the sun for six hours. Drain the water off constantly. Mix the mustard into a paste with sweet or olive oil; mix with the vegetables and add vinegar until they will pour out thick; then add the spices. Put all into a stone jar, place it in a kettle of water on the fire until the pickles boil up. Add the sugar and put away the jars for use.

—Mr. Robt. P. Sibley, in *Choice Recipes*, 163–164

A Friar's Omelette

Boil and mash a dozen apples as for sauce; stir in one-quarter pound of butter and the same of sugar; when cold, add four eggs well beaten. Sprinkle a baking-dish well with bread-crumbs, pour in the mixture, strew breadcrumbs over the top, and bake. When cooked, turn out, and grate loaf sugar over it.

[This uncommon dish gets attention at brunch. Prepared applesauce speeds the recipe along.]

—Mrs. N. B. Moore, in *Choice Recipes*, 33

Syllabub

1 qt. cream.
1 tumblerful good wine.
½ pound sugar.
Churn or whip to a stiff froth.
[Many old Georgia recipes include egg whites.]

—Unattributed, in *Choice Recipes*, 138

Sans Souci Catsup and Georgia Restaurants

Deep in the summer of 1882, the Albany newspaper reported an "unprecedented" bumper crop of tomatoes. "All of this year's tomato lusciousness cannot be utilized with ordinary table use," it mourned. Yet it offered a solution. "The '*San Souci*' restaurant is famed for its catsup, and all the catsup used there is of home manufacture. Through the cleverness of Mr. John Mock, one of the proprietors, we are enabled to publish his formula, which may be of service to housewives."[1] For many summers afterwards, the newspaper republished the recipe and it was shared through other publications. The result was that "Mr. John Mock's tomato catsup recipe is going 'like hot cakes' all over the State."[2]

In 1891 Mock retired from his "first-class and popular resort"—a billiards saloon with a restaurant located above and a "famous cool, shady and delightful retreat" seasonal ice cream garden on the side—but thanks to the preservation and digitization of old newspapers, his catsup can still delight.[3] If you've never made homemade tomato catsup before, I promise it is worth the effort, even if it takes a while to "cook down" into a thick sauce. Each bite of Mock's condiment is more fragrant than anything store-bought, offering a spicy first impression, a tomato-tang middle, and a citrus finish. We shared our batch with friends, neighbors, and my son's whole school class. While some felt it was more like cocktail sauce or even barbecue sauce, it got rave reviews and all agreed it worked well anywhere you'd normally use catsup. (As a reminder that historical research sometimes is affected by typographical errors, a recipe with the same ingredients but under the name "John Mack" appeared almost four decades later on page 97 of the *Atlanta Woman's Club Cook Book*.)

A Recipe for Tomato Catsup [by John Mock]

Wash and mash your tomatoes; put them in a preserving kettle and boil one hour; strain the mass through a sifter; then to four quarts of liquid, add one quart of vinegar; two tablespoonfuls of salt; two tablespoonfuls of ground mustard; two tablespoonfuls of black pepper; one tablespoonful of whole allspice; one teaspoonful of cloves; one teaspoonful of ground cinnamon; one teaspoonful of mace; two lemons sliced; two large onions cut fine; six pods of green pepper unbroken. Boil down to one-half; strain off the spices; bottle when cool and use new corks.

To the above may be added one cup of brown sugar.[4]

Nowadays, catsup or ketchup means a tomato product. This wasn't always the case. For additional catsup recipes, see sections for 1763 (lemon), 1773 (walnut), and 1885 (baked tomato) and well as these:

Pepper Catsup

Take 12 bell peppers (ripe) & three onions
cut them up fine into a quart of
vinegar, a tablespoonful of mace one
of cloves one of spice & three sticks
of cinnamon add some salt, boil down
to about half & when cold bottle it.

—Murrell Family Papers, 1832–1977, University of Georgia[5]

Grape Catsup

Five pounds grapes boiled and strained. Take two and a half pints of sugar to one pint of vinegar, one tablespoon cinnamon, one teaspoon cloves, one tablespoon each allspice and white pepper and two tablespoons salt. Boil until catsup is thick. Bottle and seal.

—A. Roberts, *Drummers' Home Cook Book* (1902), 101

Cucumber Catsup

Lay twelve fine full grown cucumbers for one hour in cold water; peel and grate. Mix with cucumbers six small onions grated; season to taste with white pepper, salt and vinegar, making it thick as a rich marmalade. Bottle and seal. Keep in a cool place.

—A. Roberts, *Drummers' Home Cook Book* (1902), 101

Employees at Mock's ice cream garden may have been familiar with this type of scoop (7½ inches long). Twisting the "key" atop the scoop moves a metal piece around the inside to dislodge the ice cream.

Exploring Further

If you are intrigued by reading about Albany's Sans Souci, *The Lost Southern Chefs* by Robert Moss contains information about Lexius Henson's notable nineteenth-century restaurant in Augusta as well as some others in Georgia. Professional food establishments are discussed in the sections for 1887, 1897, 1902, and 1935. And Georgia eateries during our book's 1733–1945 period that later became the subject of a cookbook include these:[6]

Bedingfield Inn (Stewart County)
Frances Virginia Tea Room (Fulton County)
Glen-Ella Springs (Habersham County)
Gottlieb's Bakery (Chatham County)
Johnny Harris Restaurant (Chatham County)
Mary Mac's Tea Room (Fulton County)

The Chameleon *Dixie Cook-Book*

The Dixie Cook-Book, 1883
Estelle Woods Wilcox (1849–29 May 1943)[1]
689 pages. 1,218 food recipes including 135 in the "Popular Dixie Dishes" section.

The Dixie Cook-Book of 1883 and its revised 1889 version, *The New Dixie Cook-Book*, are encyclopedic housekeeping guides full of interesting recipes. If I ever am put in charge of a late nineteenth-century house museum (or find myself in an apocalypse desperate for homesteading know-how), I'll want them close at hand. But despite being published in Atlanta, these aren't Georgia cookbooks.[2]

Estelle Wilcox helped with the production of the *Centennial Buckeye Cook Book*, a charity volume published in 1876 to benefit a church in her hometown of Marysville, Ohio. Once the project was complete, she and her husband, journalist Alfred Gould Wilcox (1841–1900), now living in Minnesota, purchased the copyright as the heart of a complex publishing and marketing plan. Over the course of almost thirty years, Estelle collected additional recipes as well as revising and renaming the cookbook; chameleonlike, it changed to suit various locations and audiences. There was even a popular supporting magazine called *The Housekeeper*.[3] The Wilcoxes created offices in various cities, hiring agents to help sell both cookbooks and magazines by subscription.[4] The Atlanta office manager and publisher was a Kentucky native named Lucy A. Clarkson, who was lauded in her day as a woman business leader.[5] By the time of Alfred's death in 1900, the Wilcoxes had sold more than a million books.[6]

482 *KITCHEN LUXURIES.*

CAKE SPOON.—This is a peculiar form of spoon, the spaces through the bowl of which double the amount of work done by it in beating cakes, eggs, etc.

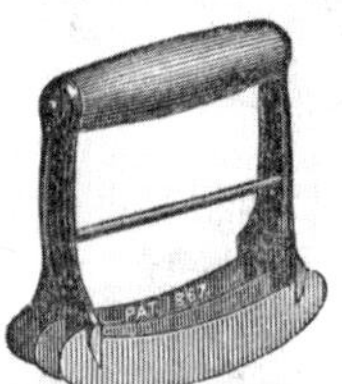

TENSION CHOPPING KNIFE.—In this knife the blades are made of fine steel, wrought very thin, and are kept firm by the tension of the frame in which they are set. It does very rapid work, and is an excellent knife for family use. Most people consider hash a very delicious breakfast dish, in spite of all the hits newspaper paragraphers have made on it, and a good implement for making it is indispensable in every well ordered kitchen. The chopping knife is a great saver of butchers' bills, and ought to be respected accordingly.

IRON SINK.—The best sink for service and convenience is made of cast-iron in one solid piece. There are several sizes manufactured, and the largest size that can be afforded should be selected. The iron sink never leaks, is easily cleaned, does not need painting, does not get foul like wood, or wear out like zinc. The waste-pipe is easily and firmly attached, and in short it has all the merits and none of the faults of other sinks.

FLUTED CAKE PAN.—The cake pan represented by the cut is of a peculiar and desirable form for many purposes. It is kept in most kitchen furnishing stores, and does not exceed the ordinary form in cost. This, like many other articles which we name here, is not a necessity, but a luxury, which those whose purses are not too short will find it convenient to have in the house.

The Dixie Cook-Book's drawings covered meat carving instructions and helped readers learn about kitchen utensils, set elegant tables, and decorate desserts.

In the "Publisher's Notice" at the front of *The Dixie Cook-Book* (1883), Wilcox states that it includes "choice treasures from the garners of many a Southern household, handed down from generation to generation, besides many other recipes, contributed by the ladies of the South, for the more modern Southern dishes." Many of the recipes in this edition are credited to specific individuals by name and town. At a time when there were thirty-eight states in the Union, all but five were represented in Wilcox's cookbook.[7] Despite the fact that the cookbook carried testimonials from former Georgia first lady Mrs. Joseph E. Brown, leaders of Athens's Lucy Cobb Institute, and the wife of *Atlanta Constitution* journalist Henry W. Grady, only eighteen recipes, less than 2 percent, are credited to Georgia. Six years later, the "new" version of the cookbook swelled from 689 pages to 1,288 pages, covering additional recipes, ingredients, and techniques. (For instance, it helpfully clarifies for the reader, "Spaghetti is macaroni in another form, a solid cord instead of a tube.")[8] Regrettably, all contributor information was removed from the 1889 version, as were all but one of the recipes previously credited to Georgia.[9]

Wilcox is arguably the most well-known and successful of nineteenth-century American cookbook authors who transformed a body of recipes into a series of books marketed outside traditional booksellers, but she was not alone. Several nineteenth-century cookbooks were published in Atlanta but have roots elsewhere. Dr. Alvin Wood Chase (1817–1885) of Michigan was a traveling doctor who published various books in various locations.[10] *Dr. Chase's Third, Last and Complete Receipt Book and Household Physician; or, Practical Knowledge for the People* was published in 1888. Virginia E. James (1833–1922) of Texas published a variety of cookbooks including the 1890 title *Arnold & McCord's Key to Good Cooking* "published for Arnold & McCord, Wholesale Grocers, Atlanta, Ga."[11] This book later turns up from other publishers as *Mother James' Key to Good Cooking*. A third example is Annie R. Gregory (1847–1917) of Illinois, whose *New Dixie Receipt Book* came out in 1902. She was another prolific author who widely sold cookbooks by subscription, many of which were identical aside from title

Self-Publishing

Foodways scholars examining an old cookbook will wish to know how widespread or popular it was. This can be tricky because Georgia had private printing companies as far back as the colonial period.[1] In modern times, the style of binding and other clues usually help us identify a privately printed cookbook, but nineteenth-century "vanity press" cookbooks often look quite similar to major cookbooks of the period. The twelve-page cookbooklet pictured here was found at Darien's Ashantilly Center in the book collection of William G. Haynes (1908–2001) and marked as belonging to his mother, Laura Lee Grant Haynes (1871–1951). *Kitchen Lore: Being a Few Choice Recipes*, by Mrs. M. F. Stevens, was printed by Foote & Davis Company of Atlanta, the same publisher as the well-known *Tested Recipe Cook Book* of 1895, but it was likely a small, privately printed project. Unfortunately, this cookbooklet is undated, and my research turned up little about it. Although *Kitchen Lore* probably didn't have a big impact on Georgia foodways, it is still useful. The section called "Soup Garnishings," for example, included multiple recipes for croquettes. Thanks to Stevens's soup-and-croquette pairing, our family has now branched out from tomato-with-grilled-cheese. On the page following those pictured, Stevens added: "The formation of all croquettes is a white sauce made in the following proportions: one tablespoon butter, two tablespoons flour, one cup milk or stock. Cook butter and flour together and add milk last."

1. McMurtrie, "Pioneer Printing."

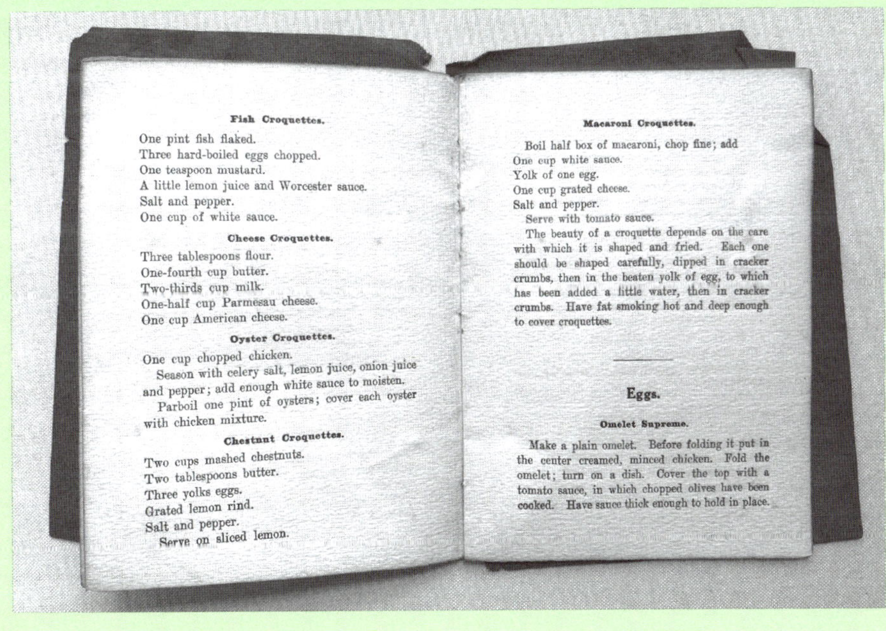

Fish Croquettes.

One pint fish flaked.
Three hard-boiled eggs chopped.
One teaspoon mustard.
A little lemon juice and Worcester sauce.
Salt and pepper.
One cup of white sauce.

Cheese Croquettes.

Three tablespoons flour.
One-fourth cup butter.
Two-thirds cup milk.
One-half cup Parmesan cheese.
One cup American cheese.

Oyster Croquettes.

One cup chopped chicken.
Season with celery salt, lemon juice, onion juice and pepper; add enough white sauce to moisten.
Parboil one pint of oysters; cover each oyster with chicken mixture.

Chestnut Croquettes.

Two cups mashed chestnuts.
Two tablespoons butter.
Three yolks eggs.
Grated lemon rind.
Salt and pepper.
Serve on sliced lemon.

Macaroni Croquettes.

Boil half box of macaroni, chop fine; add
One cup white sauce.
Yolk of one egg.
One cup grated cheese.
Salt and pepper.
Serve with tomato sauce.

The beauty of a croquette depends on the care with which it is shaped and fried. Each one should be shaped carefully, dipped in cracker crumbs, then in the beaten yolk of egg, to which has been added a little water, then in cracker crumbs. Have fat smoking hot and deep enough to cover croquettes.

Eggs.

Omelet Supreme.

Make a plain omelet. Before folding it put in the center creamed, minced chicken. Fold the omelet; turn on a dish. Cover the top with a tomato sauce, in which chopped olives have been cooked. Have sauce thick enough to hold in place.

Recipes for cordials appeared in the "Popular Dixie Dishes" section, page 10.

MINT CORDIAL.—While dew is on pick mint without bruising, put two handfuls in a pitcher with quart French brandy, cover and let stand twenty-four hours; remove mint and add same quantity fresh mint for two succeeding mornings, then add one pound loaf sugar, bottle and cork well. Some prefer to add three quarts water.—*Mrs. E., Atlanta, Ga.*

PEACH CORDIAL.—Pare and cut one pound fruit, sprinkle with one pound white sugar, let stand for two hours, boil until they become a thick syrup, strain, add brandy to taste and bottle.

and publication place.[12] A variant on the chameleon cookbook doesn't change publication place or the title page but merely the book's cover. *Modernistic Recipe-Menu Book* by Jessie Marie DeBoth (1890–1959) was published in Chicago in 1929 yet was offered as a mail order item through a Georgia newspaper with a special cover that added "*The Atlanta Constitution's*" above the title.[13]

From Wilcox to Gregory, "chameleon cookbooks" that depend primarily on a core of recipes from elsewhere preserve little of Georgia's foodways existing at the time of publication. They were, however, sources of new recipes and information that flowed into the state and left their mark on our cooking.

Fig Sauce

Figs are very fine for dessert, stewed slowly until very soft. Season with two ounces loaf-sugar to a pound of fruit; cook two hours; add a glass port or other wine, also lemon-juice if liked. Can be seasoned with a few bitter almonds or orange-peel. [Please note that bitter almonds now carry a health warning.]

—A Georgia housekeeper, in Wilcox, *The Dixie Cook-Book*, 166

House-Keeping in the Sunny South in a Time of Transition

House-Keeping in the Sunny South, 1885[1]
Ella Ruth Offutt Ogden Tennent (11 August 1855–1 February 1909)
285 pages. 797 food recipes, 43 medicine recipes, and 31 household recipes or advice segments. In addition, there are information sections for the home dairy, raising poultry, canning, and flower gardening as well as advice for furnishing and decorating various rooms.

If you're looking for recipes with a quaint southern feel, *House-Keeping in the Sunny South* doesn't disappoint. There's a recipe on page 84 using that cool, crisp ingredient known as the cucumber, but instead of cutting it into coins for salad, you're instructed to slice it lengthwise and let those slices "lay in salt water awhile" before rolling them in cornmeal and frying them in lard. If that doesn't intrigue you, how about recipes for Lemon Ice Foam (page 207), Persimmon Beer (203), or cinnamon-and-sugared Tomato Pie (148)? There's Watermelon Cake (122) with white and pink layers to resemble a real slice complete with raisin "seeds"—and you can add a "rind" of green using a recipe on the previous page that mentions tinting cake batter with spinach.

Tennent's recommendations for handling traditional southern ingredients such as okra, squash, and corn help expand our understanding of Georgia's tables in the late Victorian Era. There are ten recipes for ham (92–94) that span from hog-killing day to the dinner table. Bake with mustard and pepper? Boil in cider? Glaze with egg yolk, cream, and cracker dust? In addition to the recipes we may consider making, for many of us there's a bit of modern revulsion reading through recipes such as Backbone Pie or Stewed Brains (97–98). Tennent's cookbook sometimes calls for ingredients that most of us are not used to anymore, such as guinea fowl and mutton. In the late 1800s backyard farmsteads, hunting, and foraging were more common, and this cookbook came from a time when people handled most household needs as do-it-yourself projects, such as this one (226):

> **A Cheap Fly Trap**
> Fill a large tumbler with soapsuds; take a crust of corn bread and punch a hole in the middle (a small one), then spread thickly with honey or molasses, placing the side thus treated to the water. Many will get in, but not one in fifty will get out.

Cooking Becoming More Modern

We hear the echo of Annabella Hill's postwar cookbook when Ella Tennent promises in her preface that the recipes will be "tasty and inexpensive" to "meet the pressure of the times." When *House-Keeping in the Sunny South* was published, the nation was still rebounding from an economic depression. In addition, the Civil War was just a couple of decades in the past, and Reconstruction had ended only eight years before. In many ways, the South was still recovering. In fact, this cookbook hails from Marietta, now considered a bedroom community of Atlanta, an area hit hard by the conflict. Many of the recipes in Tennent's book are credited to southern cooks, and census records reveal most were old enough to have learned cooking in antebellum kitchens. Ella Tennent, however, was twenty-nine when she published her cookbook, meaning that she was still a child when the war ended and that she came of age in a somewhat different world than the Georgia cookbook authors before her. Despite the antiquated feel for modern readers, comparing Tennent's work to earlier Georgia cookbooks by Edgeworth, Verstille, and Hill shows the Gilded Age with its abundant technological advances and social changes glittering through the recipes.

Refrigeration is one example of expanding technology affecting Georgia's cookbooks. Mary Edgeworth's 1859 cookbook included instructions on how to build an icehouse, but no recipes expressly called for ice. Annabella Hill's 1867 cookbook gave instructions titled "To Make an Ice Vault in a Cellar" and explained how to rig up a pair of buckets to make ice cream. Hill also implied ice use by using the word "refrigerator," in that era an insulated wood cabinet or "icebox" for storing perishables. In the antebellum South where natural ice was not abundant, it had to be shipped at great expense from the frozen lakes of colder climates. As first canals and then railroad lines decreased shipping time and prices, ice became more affordable.[2] Because she was forty-five years younger than Annabella Hill, Ella Tennent had her cooking heyday in an era when ice became regularly available for middle-class homes in urban and suburban areas. She offers a whole section of recipes for ice cream, sherbets, and ices as well as our state's earliest known written instructions for iced tea (23).

Experiments in artificial refrigeration, using evaporation or compression to lower temperature, began in the seventeenth century, and by the 1870s were being put to commercial use. In Ella's lifetime, the ever-growing railroad network and refrigerated freight cars allowed perishable foods to be shipped far and wide to those who could afford them. In Tennent's cookbook and those that came after it, out-of-season or out-of-region fresh ingredients were becoming more common, as were recipes for foods served chilled, like this one (207).[3]

Lemon Ice Foam

Make a strong lemonade, fill a tumbler half full; put in three tablespoonsful of finely crushed ice, and fill with thick sweet cream. Have a tin cup which fits tightly over the tumbler; shake back and forth rapidly till the whole is in a foaming state.

—Jack, Ward & Co.

[An Atlanta bakery, confectionery, soda fountain, and "Headquarters of Toys and Fancy Goods," Jack, Ward & Co. was in business from the beginning of the Civil War until the year the cookbook came out. The *Atlanta Constitution* included it in

This picture from an undated brochure by the Bohn Refrigerator Company of St. Paul, Minnesota, shows what a large icebox looked like inside. The ice chamber capacity of this model was 100 pounds.

an 1885 list of places where "an Atlanta man can wet his whistle." The article encouraged men to cut the list out and paste in their hat for quick reference.][4]

Factory-produced ingredients are another example of technological changes in Georgia kitchens seen through its cookbooks. Verstille's 1866 cookbook and Hill's 1867 one each called for a single brand-name product—Cooper's isinglass and Cox's gelatin, respectively. *House-Keeping in the Sunny South* shows a marked increase in brand names such as Baker's chocolate, Cox's gelatin, Durkee's salad dressing, Fleischmann's yeast, Patapsco baking powder, Price's cake coloring, and Royal baking powder. Ella or her recipe contributors may have been calling for a brand name they preferred. On the other hand, as paper and printing prices decreased beginning in the middle of the nineteenth century, there was a corresponding increase in magazine advertisements and commercial cookbooklets sharing recipes calling for specific brands. Some of these recipes were simply copied into home recipe collections and found their way into published cookbooks.

Heating methods were yet another way that advances in technology affected Georgia cookbooks. The cookbooks of Edgeworth, Verstille, and Hill were likely developed for hearth cooking. Hill's list of suggested "articles for the kitchen" begins with a stove or range "if preferred."[5] The back of Tennent's cookbook includes a list headed "Utensils Necessary in the Kitchen of a Small Family," and an iron range is a requirement. At the same time, Tennent took advantage of the flexibility of this newer cooking method: the woodburning stove provided a clean, hot surface for pots, yet it could be also opened for access to flame, coals, or ashes if they were more useful for the cooking task at hand. Tennent's recipe for Roasted Eggs (72), for instance, calls for cooking in hot ashes, and her Milk Toast (18) for live coals:

Roasted Eggs

Wet brown paper with water and wrap around the eggs. Place them in hot ashes. When they pop they are done, serve with butter, pepper and salt.

Milk Toast

It is ruinous to toast bread inside the stove. Have a long toasting-fork and hold the bread near a steady fire; a bed of live coals is best. When all is well browned lay in a deep dish and pour boiling milk over, previously salted, with a little melted butter added.

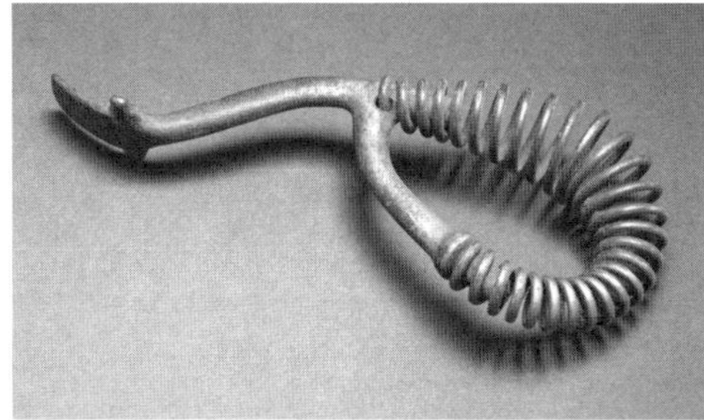

A spiral-handled lifter (a type also used with laundry flatirons) fit into a groove in the round "burners" or eyes on the surface of a woodburning stove, allowing cooks top access to the firebox below. The stove, pictured here with permission, is located in the Tift House on the grounds of Tifton's Georgia Museum of Agriculture & Historic Village (a part of the Abraham Baldwin Agricultural College formerly known as Agrirama).

Ella Tennent and the Phoenix

As we've just explored, Tennent's recipes show many advances in technology. There are also many social changes seen in her cookbook. To understand this better, let's get to know the author.

Ella Ruth Offutt was a "honeymoon baby," born in Scott County, Kentucky, in 1855, nine months after the marriage of Benjamin Offutt and Ruth Downing.[6] While Ella was still a toddler, her mother died of typhoid fever, and she was raised in large part by her well-to-do paternal aunt and uncle, Emaline and James Scott, in neighboring Bourbon County.[7] In 1874, eighteen-year-old Ella married thirty-year-old Virgil M. Ogden, from a family of merchants.[8] The following year, Ella gave birth to a son, but he lived only nine months.[9] After this rocky start, tragedy seemed to be behind the couple. By the 1880 census, the Ogdens had moved to Marietta, Georgia. Virgil was listed as a farmer, and a daughter, Virgie, had joined the family during a sojourn in Ohio.[10] The family's exodus from Kentucky, however, may have been for medical reasons. Virgil was suffering from consumption (probably tuberculosis), and by the 1880s Marietta was known for its clean water and "pure atmosphere" in a region claimed to be "the healthiest in America."[11] Regardless of the climate, in March of 1882, Ella became a widow at age twenty-six.[12]

At the time that the Ogdens moved to Marietta, one of the town's leading physicians was Dr. Gilbert Tennent Jr.[13] Descended from the Presbyterian family that helped start Princeton University, Tennent grew up in Edgefield, South Carolina, until his late teenaged years, when he moved with his family to Marietta in 1850.[14] While he was in his early twenties, both of his parents died, leaving him the senior family member with seven younger siblings ranging from ages twenty to seven.[15] He followed in his father's footsteps to become a physician, despite Civil War service interrupting his early career path, and then settled close to home.[16] In census records he is always listed as living with younger siblings, apparently remaining a bachelor until a few days after Christmas in 1882. Just months shy of his fiftieth birthday, Gilbert married the Ogden widow. She was twenty-two years younger and brought a five-year-old daughter to create an instant family.[17] Little is known about the marriage, yet Ella seemed to enjoy remarkable freedoms. At a time when few women were known outside their own neighborhood, for the next twenty-seven years newspapers in Marietta and Atlanta reported on Ella's array of creative pursuits, beginning with *House-Keeping in the Sunny South*.

In August of 1883, while the Tennents were settling into marriage, the Cobb County Agricultural Association welcomed the formation of its twelfth agriculture club.[18] The usual meeting spot was three and a half miles southwest of Marietta at Union Chapel, a rural gathering place for ecumenical worship as well as educational and social events.[19] Because the chapel was built "over the ashes of an antebellum structure," the Phoenix Agricultural Club was chosen as the name, recalling the ancient mythical symbol of rebirth.[20] Members met to share farming ideas as well to create a monthly journal called the *Phoenix Agriculturalist*—"The only Farmer's Magazine in the world printed and published literally in the field itself, by farmers and for farmers."[21] They organized an annual fair with premiums (prizes) awarded for the best livestock, handiwork, and cooking.[22] It was here that Ella's talents began to publicly shine.[23] In her preface, she wrote about the early days of the club: "It has ever fostered the interests of the housekeeper as well as those of the farmer. Each month a special premium has been offered for some specimen of cookery. The premium exhibit has always been the best of its kind, with scarcely the possibility of improvement. It was these triumphs of Cobb County women that suggested the idea of a New Cook Book; but we are not indebted alone to Cobb County, or the South. Many noted housekeepers, all over the land, have contributed their tried and valuable receipts."

Stabilization efforts are currently under way on the former meeting place of the Phoenix Agriculture Club. A roadside historical marker calling it Nesbitt-Union Chapel Ruins states that in 1886, Mr. and Mrs. R. T. Nesbitt sold the chapel to the church's trustees, and that it was supported for many years by donations and fundraisers. Although nothing in Tennent's cookbook or its advertising alludes to the volume being created to raise funds, *House-Keeping in the Sunny South* almost certainly promoted the club's reputation and membership.

A Sense of Place behind the Recipes

Tennent's cookbook gives individuals credit for many of the recipes—over half, in fact. Because Ella specifically credits herself for fourteen recipes, we're left wondering where the uncredited recipes came from. Most of the uncredited recipes are short and basic, so perhaps Tennent wrote down her methods for certain dishes but did not consider them crafted recipes worth specifically claiming. We'll likely never know. Still, the contributors' names are research trails we can follow to learn more about the foodways recorded in Tennent's cookbook. Unfortunately, it is a messy process. There is a list of 287 contributors and their towns at the front of the cookbook, but the alphabetical order is flawed and the list is incomplete. There is no index to help sort out individual recipes. Last but not least, Tennent's crediting system is, shall we say, informal. Because I was familiar with previous Georgia cookbooks, I recognized that some of the recipes in *House-Keeping in the Sunny South* were reprinted. Annabella Hill's recipes are sometimes credited to "Mrs. E. Y. Hill" and at other times simply to "Mrs. Hill," her cookbook is never mentioned, and none of her recipes appear verbatim. (This is also true for some famous non-Georgia cookbook authors such as Eliza Acton, Marian Harland, and Marion Cabell Tyree.) Similarly, Tennent includes recipes from *Choice Recipes of Georgia Housekeepers*. (See 1880 section.) The original Augusta contributors are not consistently credited, nor is their cookbook, which Tennent calls "Augusta Cook Book." But even if imperfect, the recipe credits in *House-Keeping in the Sunny South* help us connect to culinary traditions and social networks.

Tennent's cookbook leans more toward social diversity than many others of its time. Since it is community-oriented, yet isn't connected with a specific place of worship, we find the recipe of a Protestant minister a few pages away from one gleaned from the *Catholic Herald*, as well as a few contributor surnames that are traditionally Jewish. More than a dozen recipes are from males. There are also four recipes that may be from Black cooks, guessing by the fact that their credits are handled differently—the title "aunt" is given to three of the four, and their names appear in quotation marks.[24]

Geography is part of sorting the origins of *House-Keeping in the Sunny South*'s recipes, so let's start at Tennent's kitchen and move outward. We know many of the recipes are ones she received praise for. Nine are from her relatives. Eighty-two recipes are from Marietta cooks. Although contributor identities are sometimes difficult to verify, a trip to the Georgia Room of the town's Switzer Library showed that many of the surnames match those found in local history books.[25] For instance, Tennent shares close to a dozen recipes that won premiums including some from the Phoenix Agriculture Club and from Mrs. R. T. Nesbitt, an original landowner of Union Chapel.[26] Recipes from Marietta sometimes shed light on celebrated local foodways. "This is the cake that attracted so much attention at Dr. Buttolph's silver wedding anniversary a few years since," Tennent tells us of the Silver or White Cake (130). Of the Lemon Biscuits

(134–135) she writes: “These small cakes are the ones that have been so popular at the festivals in Marietta.” The contributors for this cookbook come from the families of locally prominent doctors, pastors, judges, and military men. But the collection didn't end there. Several recipes from bakeries, confectioneries, and hotels around Atlanta are included, as well as ones from Georgia hotels as far as Dalton to the north and Thomasville to the south. (See 1887 section.) Tennent included recipes from the wives of former governors Joseph E. Brown (1821–1894) and Charles J. Jenkins (1805–1883) as well as politician Robert Toombs (1810–1895).

Tennent's “all over the land” statement was accurate. At the time when our country had thirty-eight states, twenty-three were represented in the cookbook, as well as “Indian Territory,” Mexico, and Canada. Now that we know something about Tennent's life, it is not surprising that the top three states in terms of number of recipes are Georgia (133), Kentucky (69), and Ohio (13). And Tennent dipped into publications as well, sharing recipes from over twenty cookbooks and thirteen periodicals. Although Ella was Episcopalian until late in life, she knew about the popular 1875 cookbook *Housekeeping in the Blue Grass* by the ladies of the Presbyterian church in Paris, Kentucky (Bourbon County), and shared over two dozen of their recipes.[27]

Housekeeping and Women's Earnings

Back in 1867, Annabella Hill sprinkled housekeeping advice through her cookbook. “Never leave things lying about,” she tells her readers. “Rise early in the morning, or you will not get a fair start with your business.”[28] But for the sheer number of housekeeping opinions from an early Georgia cookbook, Ella Tennent wins the premium. She penned housekeeping advice sections for most rooms of the house. In “Vestibule and Hall” she tells us, “The hall is the key-note to the whole house,

> “Never feed the chickens about the doors. Have a place remote from the house, and they will never come nearer. If you are troubled with chickens making a pleasure park of the house, walking into the parlor and viewing your mirrors and statuary, it is your own fault.”
>
> —Tennent, *House-Keeping in the Sunny South*, 256

therefore everything about it should be dark and solid. Light colors are frivolous and gilding is out of place" (page 231). In "The Family Dining Room" she notes, "It has been the custom to have pictures of still life in the dining-room—of game and fish; but this is hardly a cheerful view, to see representations of the game and fish that one is soon to eat—in all the agonies of death" (242). About carpeting in this room, she adds, "remember that green, drab and red are the least desirable colors" (241). Reading one's way through the house, it is sometimes difficult to refrain from muttering, "Well, that's *your* opinion." Still, the writing offers a fascinating tour through a middle-class Victorian home. As she prescribes frugal decorating using repurposed scarves, painted pickle jars, or a handful of oat stems, one wonders what Tennent would have thought of contemporary lifestyle blogs and vast craft stores.

ADVICE TO YOUNG WIVES.

DON'T EXPECT TO BEGIN WHERE THE OLD FOLKS LEAVE OFF, but rather be willing to begin where they did, and gradually increase your comforts and luxuries. Many a young wife is rendered unhappy because she is unable to keep up the grandeur of her girlhood's home. If she marries a wealthy man, it is not unreasonable to expect it, but if her husband is poor, she should gracefully yield to the inevitable, and not allow the sacrifices she is compelled to make to cloud her young life. There is a poor prospect indeed ahead of the couple who commence housekeeping without having resolved to live within their means. Never buy a handsome carpet, curtains, or anything of the kind without you have the money to pay for them. The merchant will add a third to the cost because they are bought on credit, and perhaps when he grows impatient for collection you will be obliged to borrow the money and pay interest. You had better be compelled to look at your patched carpet and bare windows than to see the sheriff coming up the walk. Many persons are willing to economize, but they do not know how; they are brought to want and cannot see the cause of it; they cannot recall any great losses; nobody has cheated them; they have not been burnt out, yet here they are penniless. They do not recollect that it is "the LITTLE foxes that gnaw the vines." Bottles not corked, towels lost, soap left to melt in the water, crockery broken, pins and hair-pins scattered broadcast, bonnets left in the rain, as little as you may think of it, each helps to swell the wave which finally engulfs you.

Most of Tennent's household guidance as well as her section "Advice to Young Wives" (281) boiled down to tidiness and economy, but her social views likely stretched further than those of her mother or grandmother. One Georgia history book exploring antebellum times explained cultural norms this way: "No greater humiliation could befall a family than to have one of its girls go to work to earn money."[29] In contrast, Ella wrote in her 1885 cookbook, "Every woman in good health, no matter where she lives, can make money. If on a farm, there are her garden, fowls, dairy, etc. all to bring in a revenue. If she lives in a city, she will find no limit to the demand for sewing, embroidery, and crocheting. If she is talented and well educated, her chances are still better. No honorable work is degrading" (282).

House-Keeping in the Sunny South was not the end of work for Ella Tennent. The same year that the cookbook came out, a newspaper reported that Ella replaced nationally-known writer Julia Ward Howe as superintendent of the Women's Department at the World's Industrial and Cotton Centennial Exposition in New Orleans.[30] In Marietta, the local newspaper promoted Ella's efforts selling homemade ink and chutney as well as giving quilting lessons.[31] It also reported that, beginning in the early 1890s, Ella was an award-winning employee of N. W. Ayer & Sons, "the largest advertising agency in the United States."[32] And Tennent did not stop writing or editing. In 1887 the periodical *Southern Cultivator* (its offices now in Atlanta) hired her to "take charge" of their Household Department, while later that same year Athens publisher T. L. Mitchell hired Tennent to edit a housekeeping journal called *Women's Work*.[33] The latter publication, a monthly, sixteen-page journal with a cost of fifty cents per year, was advertised as far away as Louisiana, Virginia, and Kansas.[34] In 1888 Ella began editing *Tennent's Home Magazine* at the subscription price of one dollar per year.[35] It is not known how long either publication lasted, but in 1891 the *Marietta Journal* quoted Ella as saying of *Tennent's*, "Its fame has spread like a prairie fire."[36] As late as 1903, Ella also wrote articles for Atlanta publications such as the *Old Homestead* and the *Sunny South*.[37]

In 1908 Ella was still going strong. She received a prize from a private cooking club in Philadelphia for a chocolate cake with a filling made of chocolate, coconut, raisins, figs, and pecans.[38] Yet less than a year later, early in 1909, she was suddenly gone.

> Mrs. E. R. Tennent, wife of Dr. Gilbert Tennent, died at the family residence, on Atlanta Street, on Monday afternoon last, after a brief illness.[39] This occurrence carried sadness and sorrow to hundreds of people and friends who knew this remarkably brilliant and talented woman who possessed an intellect and culture of a high order. Gifted as a writer, she was the author of that famous

cook book, "Housekeeping in the Sunny South." Mrs. Tennent was formerly of Paris, Ky., and of a distinguished family. She was kind-hearted, generous, noble impulses, and was always ready and eager to be of service, or do others a kindness or favor.[40]

Ella's fifty-three-year life was marked by staggering losses but also by great successes—especially for her gender. Through her writing, middle-class domestic life in North Georgia in the late nineteenth century becomes a little more vivid. And it is evident that Ella thrived in the kitchen, yet she wasn't stuck there with a wooden spoon in her hand. There was a wide world outside her door, and she connected with it.

Corn Hoe Cake (15)

Mix into a stiff dough one pint of corn meal with cold water; add a teaspoonful of salt. Dust the gridiron with meal and lay on in thin cakes.

—"Aunt Polly"

Lemon Biscuits (134–135)

Ten ounces of sugar, fourteen ounces of flour, five ounces of butter, three eggs, a little soda and cream of tartar, fifteen drops of oil of lemon, and water to make a stiff dough. Cut them and bake in a hot oven.

—Mrs. J. A. Massey[41]

[These turn out looking like a sugar cookie but have a soft crumb like a madeleine. Be sure to use food grade lemon oil.]

W. P. Stevens' Sausage (95)

To twelve and a half pounds of meat put three large tablespoonsful of salt, two of black pepper, a half teaspoonful of red pepper, two of thyme powdered and sifted, two of sage, and a teaspoonful of salt petre.

—W. P. Stevens

[W. P. Stevens was an executive in a lumber company and built the Marietta Inn, now called Stanley House, as a summer residence for the favorite uncle of President Woodrow Wilson.[42]]

CATSUPS.

To one half bushel of skinned tomatoes, add one quart of good vinegar, one pound of salt, one-fourth of a pound of black pepper, one ounce of African cayenne, one-fourth of a pound of allspice, one ounce of cloves, three boxes of mustard, twenty cloves of garlic, six onions, two pounds of brown sugar, and one handful of peach leaves. Boil this mass constantly stirring for three hours to prevent burning. When cool, strain through a sieve and bottle. It will improve by age and create and give zest to appetite almost under the ribs of death.—*Dr. Gunn.*

BAKED TOMATO CATSUP.

Bake the tomatoes by putting them in a stove pan with enough water to keep from burning; then press them through a sieve. To every six quarts of juice add the same quantity of vinegar. Put on a slow fire and let it boil until it thickens; then add a half ounce each of cloves, allspice, and pepper, one-fourth ounce of cinnamon, two grated nutmegs. When almost as thick as mush, add a large tablespoonful of salt. Cool and bottle. The flavor of this catsup, though unlike all others, is decidedly superior. Baking the tomatoes renders a thin and watery catsup impossible.—"*Auntie Barnes.*"

These tomato catsup recipes from page 70 can be compared with those in the 1882 section—and I also want to help any readers that may be "almost under the ribs of death."

PEPPER SAUCE.

Take one hundred ripe fresh red peppers, and to one gallon of vinegar put two tablespoonsful of mustard, two of salt, one of black pepper. Boil until the skin can be slipped from the pulp of the pepper, then strain and bottle. It is better to boil the pepper in water till soft, then strain, put in the other ingredients and boil.—*Whitlock House.*

CUCUMBER SAUCE.

Grate the cucumbers and season with salt to suit your taste. Let them stand four hours, then squeeze out every particle of water with the hands. To one cup of cucumber put four cupsful of best vinegar, four tablespoonsful of black pepper. Stir up, and if not salt enough add a little more.—*Mrs. James Pitner.*

The M. G. Whitlock House resort, source of the pepper sauce recipe on page 51, burned in the 1890s, but Marietta's present-day Whitlock Inn stands on some of the same land.

Orange Jelly Baskets (168)

Take six oranges, cut with skin in such a manner as to form a round basket with a handle; cut notches in edge of basket for ornaments, carefully remove the pulp. For jelly, take a half a box of gelatine, two cups of sugar, one cup of orange juice. Pour over this one and a half pints boiling water, boil till thoroughly dissolved, and fill baskets when cool. Set on ice.

—Capital City Club Restaurant

[This Atlanta social club, chartered in 1883, is now located on West Brookhaven Drive.[43]]

Golden Cup Cake (119)

Half a cup of butter, one of sugar, two of flour, six eggs. Flavor with essence of nutmeg.

—"Bossy"

QUEEN'S CAKE.

One pound of butter, one pound of sugar, one pound of flour, one gill of cream, one gill of wine, one gill of brandy, one pound of fruit, eight eggs, and one nutmeg.—*Mrs. Martha Berrien Duncan.*

LOAF CAKE.

Nine pounds of flour, five pints of sugar, four pints of butter, five pints of fruit, fifteen eggs, half a pint of wine, half a pint of brandy, two quarts of milk, and a pint of yeast; spices to taste.—*Mrs. Martha Berrien Duncan.*

While census records indicate that Mrs. Duncan and her husband, a farm laborer, had only five children, the batter for her Loaf Cake (page 125) called for almost two bags of flour and sixteen sticks of butter, and would weigh over twenty-four pounds! The recipe may follow older traditions. First Lady Martha Washington had a recipe for Great Cake that called for forty eggs (see V. Williams, "Great Cake").

Phoenix Club Pound Cake (117)

Premium.

Eight eggs, one pound of flour, three-fourths of a pound of sugar, half a pound of butter, two teaspoonsful of Royal baking powder. Flavor with French brandy, essence of nutmeg and essence of lemon.

—Miss Ruby Lofton

Tomato Pie (148)

Slice very thin tomatoes which have just begun to turn. Lay them evenly in the paste [pastry crust] and cover with sugar. Add a little lemon juice and grated peel and cinnamon. Cover with strips of paste and bake one hour.

Lost Famous Baking Recipes

1886, The Famous Cakes of Laura McCray

I grew up in Athens without ever hearing the name Laura McCray—also known as Aunt Laura Billups—so it was a little startling to read, "Any one who has not heard of her, has never heard of Athens."[1] Granted, the writer was Professor Sylvanus Morris (1855–1929), who wrote his historical (and often humorous) account *Strolls About Athens During the Early Seventies* more than a century ago.[2] About McCray he added, "One who has not eaten her cakes don't know how a cake ought to taste. For many a longer year no bridal table was complete without Aunt Laura's cake. She has filled orders from Paris to Watkinsville." Although Morris gave no details, he noted that when he attended the university as a student in the 1870s, she furnished his meals.[3] Another account of Athens from 1913 recalls the same "cateress," noting that she was "dear to many homes of the city, not only on account of the fineness of her confection, but also by reason of the fact that many people cannot pass her house without remembering that it was she who baked their wedding cake."[4]

I first learned about McCray through an article about her written by Eve B. Mayes for the *Athens Historian* titled "The Finest Cook in All the South." I had no idea anyone from my hometown had ever been thus lauded, or had graced the advertisements of a national brand of flour (Gold Leaf).[5] Laura McCray (1818–1913) was born into slavery on the Wilkes County homeplace of politician Robert

Toombs, moved to Athens around 1846, and was freed by the Emancipation Proclamation when she was forty-five.[6] By the 1880 census, her occupation was "Confectionery Baking" and it was said her cakes were of "unparalleled lightness and delicacy."[7] Unfortunately for us, the same source added, "the famous recipe for them is still known only to her and her children. Time and again she has been offered large amounts for the recipe, but she has always refused, and the secret of her wonderful cakes will be handed down to her children after her." As far as research could ascertain, however, the recipes are lost to time. But are those cakes *completely* lost?

Various articles about McCray noted that her cakes were sent "across the ocean" as far away as Europe, North Africa, and Asia.[8] It is likely that the shipped cakes were not sponge cakes but rather dense fruitcakes able to survive shipping and long waits. For many years, fruitcakes were in fashion for celebrations including weddings.[9] Whether they were sponge cakes or fruitcakes, McCray reportedly baked for noteworthy occasions from the wedding of Georgia journalist Henry W. Grady to a visit from president-elect William Howard Taft to the coronation of England's King George V.[10] A newspaper article reprinted from the *Savannah Press* a few days after McCray's death noted, "the pinnacle of her fame was reached when the delectable product of her art graced the wedding feast of President Grover Cleveland in the White House."[11] That wedding took place in 1886 (thus the date of this section). It just so happens that a slice of the Clevelands' wedding cake, a "25-pound nut-laden fruitcake," still exists. Although surely not something of "unparalleled lightness and delicacy" after almost fourteen decades, a slice is preserved in the Grover Cleveland Birthplace Museum in Caldwell, New Jersey—intact save for a nibble off one corner by a daring Cub Scout in the 1950s.[12] There were multiple public celebrations of the Cleveland wedding and only one newspaper article about Laura McCray mentioned the Cleveland connection, but could this be a slice of Laura's cake?

Knowing that McCray was born on the homeplace of Georgia planter and politician Robert Toombs (1810–1885), my interest also sparked when I came across a short and vague cake recipe posthumously credited to his wife, Julia Dubose Toombs (1813–1883).[13] Prominent women of the past commonly received credit for any product of their kitchens even if they didn't cook it themselves, so the recipe is relevant in a discussion about Laura McCray. I wouldn't bet money on McCray connections to the museum fruit cake or the Toombs recipe, yet they are possibilities and serve as reminders that even after much time has passed, there may still be clues and research avenues for lost recipes.[14]

McCray's home and bakery was located on the south side of Prince Avenue between Franklin Street and Milledge Avenue. This undated postcard image looks much as it did in her time.

Sponge Cake

Ten eggs, leaving out six yolks; half a pound of flour, three-fourths of a pound of sugar.

[Despite being brief, the recipe works rather well. Because the only fat comes from the egg yolks, it is very light and dries out quickly.]

—Mrs. Robt. Toombs, in Tennent, *House-Keeping in the Sunny South* (1885), 116

1913, President Wilson's Fruitcake

Perhaps famed Athens baker Laura McCray passed the torch? In the same month that McCray died, the confection of another Georgia baker fed Washington, D.C., dignitaries. Margaret "Maggie" Walker Dodds (1869–1936), a twice-widowed mother of five from Cedartown who was "famous among her friends in Georgia as a cake baker," used "a very rare and much sought after recipe" to make the official presidential Christmas fruitcake in 1913.[15] How did the confection of a Georgia home baker end up in the White House?

President Woodrow Wilson (1856–1924) was born in Staunton, Virginia, but had deep Georgia connections. He spent most of his childhood in Augusta while his father served as a Presbyterian minister there from 1858 to 1870.[16] During that time he met his future wife, Ellen Louise Axson (1860–1914), whose father was a Presbyterian minister in Floyd County.[17] It was through the Axson family that home baker Maggie Dodds found herself suddenly connected to the White House. Maggie had been a young congregant of Reverend Axson and knew his family well. With a couple of nudges from Dodds, First Lady Ellen Axson Wilson extended a request for the fruitcake during her first year in the White House. On Christmas Eve, one newspaper reported of the dessert, "It has been made in Georgia by a Georgia woman, following that same Georgia recipe that Mrs. Woodrow Wilson used when she was a Georgia girl."[18]

Sadly, the First Lady's first Christmas in the White House was her last. She died a few months later, and it seems this recipe is now lost. All we know is that the Axson/Dodds fruitcake was "large" and "very rich."[19] Interestingly, however, the president's mother, Janet "Jessie" Woodrow (1830–1888) kept a manuscript recipe notebook that was later shared in *The Economy Administration Cook Book* dedicated to First Lady Wilson in the inaugural year. That published cookbook includes a recipe that might very well have been used in Augusta at what is now known as the Boyhood Home of Woodrow Wilson. If those walls could talk, they might tell stories of Christmas celebrations using the recipe below.[20]

Fruit Cake

One pound sugar.
One pound butter.
One and one-fourth pounds flour.
One dozen eggs.
Large tumbler molasses.
Two pounds raisins.
Two pounds currants.
One pound citron.
One nutmeg.
Three tablespoons cinnamon.
Two tablespoons cloves.
Two tablespoons allspice.
One-half teaspoon mace.
One-half cup hot water.
One teaspoon soda.

Dissolve soda in hot water, beat the eggs very light—yolks and whites separately; cream butter and sugar together. Sift the flour several times. Seed raisins, wash and dry currants; slice citron thin. Flour all the fruit. Grate nutmeg and mix all the spices with a little flour to prevent them lumping. Beat all together very thoroughly, adding a little of the flour at a time and bake in a slow oven four hours. This will keep for years. It is better in two months than when fresh. When wanted for use overlay with icing.

White House Menus

Breakfast, March 5, 1913

Oranges.

Cereal with Cream. Bacon and Eggs.

Steak. Hot Cakes.

Toast.

Tea. Coffee.

First Wilson family breakfast in the White House.

Luncheon, March 5, 1913

Fruit.

Fried Oysters. Cold Slaw.

Tartare Sauce.

Broiled Chicken. Creamed Potatoes.

Green Peas.

Apple Fritters. Hard Sauce.

Coffee.

Served to President Wilson's Woodrow relatives—twenty-five in number—brought together in Washington, D. C., for the inauguration.

Dinner, March 5, 1913

Cream of Celery Soup.

Baked Fillet of Halibut. White Sauce.

Roast Capon.

Cauliflower. Mashed Potatoes.

Fruit Salad. Charlotte Russe.

Coffee.

Dinner served in the state dining room, White House, to the Wilsons—thirty-three in number—assembled for the inauguration of their kinsman, twenty-eighth President of the United States.

Menus from Woodrow Wilson's inauguration printed in Rhodes and Hopkins, *The Economy Administration Cook Book*, 42.

1916, Jeannette Rankin's Lemon Pie

During the presidency of Woodrow Wilson, something new happened—a woman was elected to the U.S. House of Representatives. This turn of events was startling to many. Those who opposed the election of Jeannette Rankin (1880–1973) were vocal in the newspapers, but so were Rankin's supporters. One New York reporter was determined to prove that Rankin wasn't damaged by the manly world of politics: "Miss Rankin is a very feminine woman. She dances well and makes her own hats, and sews, and has won genuine fame among her friends with the wonderful lemon meringue pie that she makes."[21] The article was repeated by newspapers across the nation. Before long, one newspaper observed that Rankin's pie "has a fame all its own."[22] Even eighty-four years later, a children's book by Kathleen Krull spotlighting Rankin's lifelong campaign for world peace made sure to mention the pie.[23] Although Jeannette Rankin hailed from Missoula, Montana, she purchased a farm in Bogart just west of Athens in 1923 and then later moved to Watkinsville.[24] Krull states, "Famous for her lemon meringue pie, she befriended children from the neighborhood, seeking their opinions, sharing stories of her life."

As luck would have it, I knew one of those children. When I was growing up on the outskirts of Athens, a lady named Mavis Nunnally Allgood (1922–2018) on Barnett Shoals Road had towering magnolia trees in her yard with plenty of shade for bike-riding kids on a hot summer day.[25] On her front porch, now-grown Miss Mavis shared stories about growing up near Jeannette Rankin and being welcomed into her life. The image that has stayed with me is of young Mavis chatting while Rankin readied herself for bed, the elder holding one hair curler at a time over a lamp flame, warming it so that it would work its magic on her tresses overnight. Alas, I learned of the lemon meringue pie too late to ask Miss Mavis if she ever tasted it. But I am still left feeling that I touched history.

The following undated recipe is not connected to Jeannette Rankin but instead hails from the Varner family of Butts County. Using one bit of Georgia foodways history as a surrogate for another may hit the spot if reading this section leaves you craving a cool, tart slice of pie.

Lemon Pie

To one pie 1 lemon grated, yolks of 3 eggs
1 cup sugar, 1 cup water, 1½ tablespoonfuls
flour. Whites of eggs with a little sugar
for meringue after the above is baked
and put in the oven to brown for a moment.[26]

—Edward Varner Family Papers, 1730–1965, Georgia Historical Society, Savannah

Jessup Whitehead and Fine Dining

Lithia Springs. Warm Springs. Radium Springs. When names flash past on road signs, sometimes it is difficult to think past urban sprawl to the origins of a place. Early Georgians may have fulfilled their water needs using rivers, creeks, or wells, but water flowing obligingly from the ground was also a possibility. Settlements sometimes formed around springs, which were first appreciated by Georgia's indigenous peoples. Some springs came to be particularly valued for their mineral content as well as their temperature—soothingly warm or refreshingly cold.[1] As we saw from the family of cookbook author Mary Edgeworth (1859 section), profits could be made by offering hospitality to those wanting to "take the waters."

Lithia Springs in Douglas County west of Atlanta was once called Salt Springs. There, in 1887, the "mammoth" Sweetwater Park Hotel opened where "the health-giving properties of the water are already gaining a national reputation."[2] Surely guests long remembered the elegant rooms, gardens, and spa waters, but there was also the food. "The Sweetwater Park hotel guests, we have abundant grounds for saying, have gone to their homes in all parts of the country remembering in a special manner that hotel's superlatively fine French rolls and bread. There are other things too, but these first and above the rest."[3] This claim came from Jessup Whitehead, chef de cuisine of the Sweetwater Park kitchen.[4]

Jessup Whitehead, born in London in 1833, came to the United States before the Civil War.[5] He lived southwest of Kansas City but left to serve in the Union Army.[6] In the ensuing decades, Whitehead followed seasonal kitchen work in

Colorado, Illinois, North Carolina, and Virginia, according to numerous census records, city directories, and newspapers. He worked his way up in the kitchens of passenger ships, riverboats, and hotels.[7] Not willing to leave his cooking to chance, Whitehead developed reliable written recipes that by the late 1870s he crafted into articles for periodicals such as the *Chicago Herald*.[8] In turn, he reworked these writings into cookbooks.[9] His recipes were often repeated from book to book, and the cookbooks sometimes changed name with various editions or publishers, but some titles to look for include *Whitehead's Family Cook Book*, *Cooking for Profit*, and *The Hotel Book of Breads and Cakes*. In the mid-1880s Whitehead came to Georgia, bringing his recipes and expertise to Sweetwater Park as well as to Atlanta's Markham House.[10] At the same time, his cookbooks were marketed through Atlanta newspapers, sometimes with the tagline "If you must cook, be a good cook."[11]

By 1889 Whitehead had moved on to the Hotel Monte Sano in Huntsville, Alabama.[12] There, after a brief illness, he died and was buried at the age of fifty-five. "HE WAS A GREAT COOK," proclaimed the front page of the Atlanta paper announcing Whitehead's demise.[13] Hours before his death Whitehead wrote a will, leaving his publishing business in the hands of his two young adult sons and a friend.[14] Thus Whitehead's cookbooks continued to be published posthumously as late as 1921.

So how about that roll recipe? A list of ingredients appears on page 8 of *Whitehead's Family Cook Book*:

1 coffeecupful of milk or water.
½ cupful of potato yeast.
1 egg or the yolk only.
3 tablespoonsful of melted butter.
1 tablespoonful of sugar.
1 teaspoonful of salt.
1½ pounds of flour—6 cupfuls.

Baking instructions proceeded through five paragraphs—and I still had questions. Since many of Whitehead's cookbooks are available online, I then checked *The Hotel Book of Breads and Cakes*, where Whitehead's discussion of yeast on page 124 aims to help the reader past "all ignorant imaginings of luck, chance, water-witchery, mystery, hidden knowledge, moon's age, and the like having to do with fermentation."

Dear reader, the French Rolls bring good news, bad news, and yet more good news. If you are determined to master baking them, it is good that Whitehead's string of cookbooks are repetitive enough that the recipe is in several volumes with varied notes. The bad news is that it will take time to sort out the baking process. Thankfully, the second helping of good news is that Whitehead wrote not just for cooks but for readers; stories, quotes, and jokes are tucked among the cooking instructions. Cooking tips are sprinkled here and there, too. For instance, I learned that a brick can be a helpful cooking tool, placed wet in an oven to give off steam or placed hot atop a grilling steak to add heat from above. There are also fascinating glimpses of what Sweetwater Park may have been like. Although this historical structure was lost to fire during the off-season in 1912 and its grounds are now covered by suburbia, the Gilded Age lives on in recipes for dishes that may have been served there.[15] In *The American Pastry Cook* (2–3), Whitehead recommended individual servings of Charlotte Russe made in ornamented paper cases so that ladies with gloved fingers could eat them at "ball suppers." This cookbook also offers recipes for Wild Plum Ice (31) that could be ornamented with botanical designs cut out of his Gelatine Paste

SOME ARTICLES FOR THE SHOW CASE.

2—Angel Food or White Sponge Cake

WHITEST AND FINEST CAKE MADE.

5 whites of eggs—or six if small.
5 ounces fine granulated sugar—½ cup large.
2½ ounces flour—½ cup large.
1 rounded teaspoon cream tartar.
1 teaspoon vanilla or lemon extract.

Mix the cream tartar in the flour by sifting them together. Whip the whites firm, put in the sugar and beat a few seconds, add the flavoring, then stir in the flour lightly without beating. As soon as mixed put the cake in the oven. It needs careful baking like a meringue, in a slack oven and should stay in from 20 to 30 minutes. A small, deep, smooth mold is the best and should not be greased. When the cake is done turn it upside down and leave it to get cold in the mold before trying to take it out.

When you have pure cream tartar from a drug store use only half as much as of the common lest the cake taste of it.

3—Plain Glaze or Icing for the Above.

4 tablespoons powdered sugar.
1 white of an egg.

Put the sugar in a cup and mix it with the white of egg. As soon as the sugar is fairly wetted it is ready. It dries pearl white; takes but a minute to make. Spread it all over the bottom and sides of "angel food."

COST of material 15c., size 1 quart; weight 15 oz.

A few months after the opening of the Sweetwater Park Hotel, an ad in the 30 October 1887 issue of the *Atlanta Constitution* for Whitehead's cookbooks noted two "Salt Springs specialties," rolls and angel cake. Whitehead includes the cake recipe in *Cooking for Profit*, 4.

Cake Decoration in White Icing.

BY JESSUP WHITEHEAD.

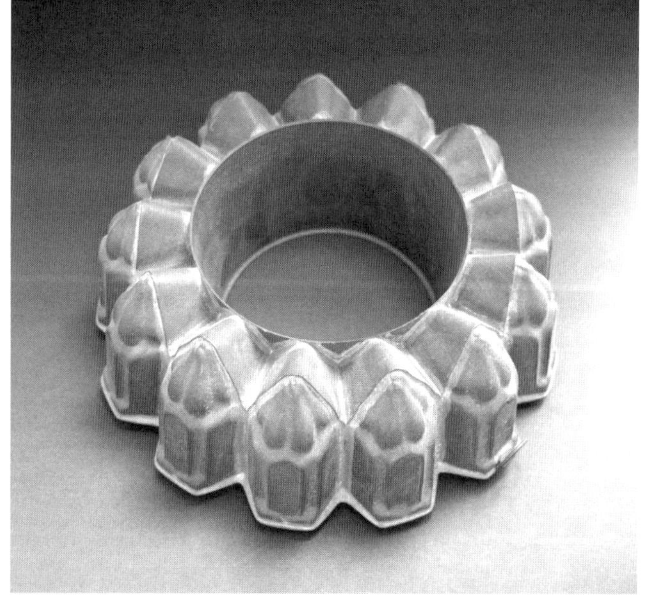

Whitehead's cookbooks (here *Cooking for Profit*, 193) show how to decorate elaborate desserts. Some would have been created using molds akin to those shown (copper dome molds each just under 6 inches; tin border mold 9½ inches in diameter).

(35), ice cream molded into egg shapes using real eggshells (32), Champagne Jelly (49), and Rose Cream Candy (53), as well as meringue Kisses (36) promised to be "soft, tender, sweet, fragile, round, plump, smooth, delicate, nice, light." I can almost hear violins playing by candlelight.

Exploring Further

Please see 1897, 1902, and 1935 sections for more information about foodways connected to Georgia lodging establishments. The recipes from Georgia hotels below were preserved in Ella Tennent's 1885 cookbook *House-Keeping in the Sunny South*. Later hotel recipes can be found in *The New Perry Hotel: A Century of Southern Hospitality* by Bobbe Nelson and Nanette Green.

Corn Meal Muffins (14)

Into one pint of buttermilk stir half a teaspoonful of soda. Beat the whites and yolks of two eggs separately, and then together, and stir it into the buttermilk. Add a tablespoonful of lard, a teaspoonful of salt and enough corn meal to make a thick batter. Pour into muffin irons hot and well greased.

—Mrs. Ples. Shellman, National Hotel, Dalton, Ga.

[It is a shame that the Sweetwater Park Hotel did not have a cat. In 1885, National Hotel was saved from fire by a feline "which raised a peculiar and unusual alarm."[16]]

A Showy Fruit Piece (174)

Take a watermelon and cut a slice off one end, so it will sit firmly on a waiter; then cut the other end in points; from each point suspend a large bunch of grapes; on top place a large ripe pear with the leaves; around the melon place small red apples, oranges, pears, plums, or any other fruit in season.

—Mitchell House, Thomasville

Sherbet (198)

Five quarts of water, five dozen lemons, add sugar till very sweet. When it begins to freeze, add the whites of twelve eggs beaten to a stiff froth and slightly sweetened.

—Kimball House, Atlanta[17]

Sectional View of Lobby, Kimball House, Atlanta, Ga.

The original 1870 Kimball House hotel burned in 1883. These postcards are from the second building, which opened the same year as the publication of Tennent's cookbook.

Barbee's Terrapins and Prestige Ingredients

You're inviting your _____ over to dinner. (Fill in the blank with something like "new bosses," "potential clients," or "future in-laws.") You want to impress these people and make them feel special, so what will you serve? Pricy steak or lobster? A classic French dish worthy of Julia Child? If you were living in the first few years after Georgia's founding as a colony, you would have chosen something fatty. Kay Moss, an expert in eighteenth-century southern foodways, explained, "If one wishes to accurately reproduce an upper class meal for guests, copious butter, suet, and bacon will enter the dishes."[1] Sugar as well as spices shipped from around the world would also have been expensive and therefore suitable for making a good impression.[2] As shipping improved, tropical produce like coconuts, bananas, and pineapples finally could reach markets before spoiling and were striking additions to Georgia tables.[3] In the Gilded Age at the end of the 1800s, a fancy footed celery vase showed off leafy stalks at the center of the table.[4] Newfangled refrigerated boxcars meant celery could reach your local market without wilting even though the price reflected the effort. A few years later? Choose a chilled salad or frozen dessert to show that you could afford reliable home refrigeration. Food historian John Van Willigen notes that recipes and ingredients considered to be "prestige markers" change over time. "What was either high or low prestige at some point in the past can have a different meaning years later."[5]

Beginning in the early 1890s, Georgia cornered the market on one prestige ingredient that today many wouldn't even consider edible—the terrapin. Yes, a reptile. In fact, the very reptile that now causes road signs to be placed near Georgia marshes warning motorists to slow down lest the animals be turned into roadkill. But terrapin was a prestige ingredient throughout the Victorian Era, and a staple in many old cookbooks. (See 1927 section about Savannah's Mrs. Habersham and her famed terrapin stew.)

Alexander Barbee (1858–1929) was a Savannah streetcar conductor who went into the "pavilion business."[6] In the early summer of 1890, the local newspaper announced a new rail line to Isle of Hope a handful of miles southeast of the city. It was run by Barbee and investor George Willis, who used the occasion to entertain rail guests at the conductor's "pretty two-story cottage" constructed on the Isle.[7] Soon Barbee went into business with local postmaster Joseph Bandy on an establishment that combined mail service with selling newspapers and terrapin stew.[8] Raising terrapins became a hobby. "For years Mr. Barbee ate terrapin, talked terrapin, thought terrapin," learning their habits and needs, until after eight years he knew enough to raise the animals for profit.[9] Terrapins grow about an inch a year and were graded by size, ready for eating when over 5.5 inches.[10] By 1913 there were enough market-ready terrapins in Barbee's 150-by-60-foot plot of tidal land to net $24,000 a year.[11] (According to one online inflation calculator, that would be almost $740,000 today.)[12] A few years later, Barbee's marshy outdoor pen expanded to fourteen acres.[13] When news got out about his successes, there were some doubters about his ability to raise the animals in captivity, but he stunned government authorities by hatching more than twelve dozen in a hotel room.[14]

Barbee had found a marketable niche. "The demand for diamond-back terrapin is not a large one; but it is larger than the supply," noted one newspaper in 1916.[15] And savvy Barbee offered not just a recipe ingredient or a meal but an experience. Savannah matrons could enjoy fresh air and the beauty of the marsh on an outing to Isle of Hope, treating their children to a streetcar ride as well as fifteen cents' worth of fun in the petting-zoo-like atmosphere.[16] For an additional fifty cents, the kids could bring home a tiny terrapin as a pet while Mother splurged on the protein for a fancy dinner.[17] One local terrapin supper story involves Girl Scouts founder Juliette Gordon Low, whose invited guests were surprised when they arrived to find her napping. "They could see their hostess stretched out on a chaise longue in the drawing room, a newspaper over her face, asleep. No one dared to wake her, although they were very hungry. Finally, Bella, her English maid, came in and touched her. She awoke immediately and told her guests that supper was ready." Later it was revealed that the terrapin was found to be spoiled, so Bella had been sent on a seven-mile trek to Barbee's for more. "The hostess wasn't asleep at all—she just wanted to avoid being asked why supper was not served!"[18]

It wasn't long before Barbee's market expanded far beyond Savannah. Live terrapins were "sent up in barrels" since they were considered "much more easily transported than watermelons."[19] It was said that Barbee terrapins were as well known in fine hotels in Egypt as they were in New York.[20] In 1903 Barbee anticipated that he would get $35 per dozen the next winter over his usual $28, it being an election year. "There is more entertaining done. . . . The demand increases and the price advances."[21] Whether or not Theodore Roosevelt's second term indeed ratcheted up profits is not known. Eventually both canned terrapin meat and ready-made stew were popular Barbee products.[22]

Terrapins, Barbee learned, could also do things most recipe ingredients can't. Around 1910, Barbee's pet terrapin Toby was born, by one account hatching in the hand of famed orator William Jennings Bryan (1860–1925).[23] The terrapin soon followed Barbee around and ate out of his fingers. In later years Toby lived in the household bathtub and was best buddies with Duke, the family dog (who was trained to fetch terrapins from the pen upon command). Dog and terrapin slept curled up together.[24] Eventually Toby learned to "shake hands," wink, wave, and even play the piano on command, although he was sometimes guilty of "causing havoc," insisting on crawling up someone's pant leg.[25]

Dining and ingredient-shopping were just part of the Barbee Pavilion experience. Across the years it offered various tourist enticements such as an ice cream parlor, a venue for dances and plays, and a "strangely assorted zoo" that at one time included a sloth, a tiger, a monkey, and a dog born with only two legs.[26] Famed boxer Jack Dempsey once made an appearance at the pavilion.[27]

All this fuss for terrapins. So, what is it like to cook and eat these creatures? According to one prominent antebellum caterer, James Prosser (1782–1861) of Philadelphia, terrapin was best eaten in cold weather. Regardless of the season, it wasn't a process for the squeamish. It was thought best to boil terrapin alive, and Prosser recommended high heat "so that he shan't languish." As for the finished dish, "It wants to be a quiet thing, a suave thing, just pervaded with a most beautiful and natural terrapin aroma," and eating it was a "divine satisfaction."[28] Accolades aside, the days of terrapin popularity were numbered. One Barbee's diners in the 1920s said it "tastes like the dark meat of chicken," yet the meal brought concern. The small, dark legs and flippers appearing whole in his soup "didn't strike me as

RECIPE

BARBEE'S SOUTHERN STYLE DIAMOND BACK TERRAPIN SOUP

FOR 10 PEOPLE: Use 5 cans Barbee's pure Diamond Back Terrapin meat;
Work 15 yolks of hard boiled eggs through sieve, then add 1 lb. butter, and work eggs and butter together until mixture is very smooth. Add to above mixture 2 fresh raw yolks of eggs, mix raw yolk of eggs thoroughly into above mixture. Add ½ lb. sifted flour. Stir thoroughly into mixture.

Have 3 pints of fresh cream (over fire). Add butter and egg mixture; salt and a little nutmeg to 3 pints of cream on the fire. Keep stirring until cream and contents come to a boil; then add entire contents of 5 cans of Barbee's Pure Diamond Back Terrapin Meat, liquid as well as meat ,and allow to remain and boil 3 minutes.

Put into heated serving bowl one tablespoon of good Sherry Wine just before adding the hot soup. Great care should be taken to stir gently and not too hard so that the pieces of meat remain firm.

(In case Soup is desired for more than 10 people use one additional can for each two additional people, and other articles in proportion.)

RECIPE

ANOTHER DELICIOUS WAY OF PREPARING AND SERVING BARBEE'S FAMOUS CANNED DIAMOND BACK TERRAPIN MEAT "ISLE OF HOPE STYLE"

Put 5 cans of terrapin meat in a sauce pan. Heat and pour off liquid into top of a double boiler; add 8 ozs. good sherry wine; take 5 ozs. of butter, ¼ lb. sifted flour, a good dash of grated nutmeg, pepper and salt to taste, then work together until smooth. Stir into liquid in double boiler and heat until it thickens. Stir in 2 cups thick cream. (If mixture is too thick add more sherry wine). Add terrapin meat, heat thoroughly but do not stir. Serve on toast.

RECIPE

HOW TO PREPARE BARBEE'S FAMOUS LIVE DIAMOND BACK TERRAPIN

Put 2 live terrapin into boiling water and leave for 2 minutes. Then remove the outer skin from feet, neck and head with a towel. Put the terrapin in a kettle with 2 qts. of cold water, an onion, carrot, bay leaf, 1 clove and boil until the feet are soft. When done open the shell; take out all the meat and the liver, removing the gall from the latter with a scissors—remove the tail, claws and head. Cut up the legs in inch long pieces. Reduce the broth by boiling down to a cupful and put into a jar with the meat, adding 2 ozs. of sherry wine. The terrapin is then ready to prepare in any style desired.

REASONS WHY BARBEE'S PURE DIAMOND BACK TERRAPIN MEAT IS AN OUTSTANDING DELICACY

HANDY FOR EMERGENCY AND YACHTING PARTIES.

OUR CANNED TERRAPIN MEAT CAN BE KEPT FOR YEARS AND BE USED WITH PERFECT SAFETY.

ABSOLUTELY NO REFRIGERATION REQUIRED TO KEEP SAME.

WITH CANNED TERRAPIN MEAT, SOUP CAN BE SERVED IN SUMMER AS WELL AS WINTER MONTHS.

THERE IS CANNED WITH THIS MEAT THE HEART, LIVER, STOCK FROM THE TERRAPIN, ETC., THAT BELONG WITH TERRAPIN.

OUR MEAT CANNOT BE DISTINGUISHED FROM FRESH KILLED TERRAPIN.

Another foodways trend of the 1890s was the chafing dish, a stand holding a bowl over a flame to keep foods warm. Annie Dennis offered a special section of chafing dish recipes in her 1894 cookbook, where she wrote: "This is something that has been resuscitated; something our grandmothers prided themselves on managing with dexterity. We are finding that it is something that cannot be improved upon, hence it grows more popular every day" (318). The cartoon image is from the title page of Owen, *Chafing Dish Delicacies*.

anything that could be delicious."[29] Was the flavor partially due to the terrapins' marsh crab diet? One antebellum Georgia newspaper shared that terrapins could be set loose in the house to gobble up pests. "Put a terrapin where it can feed upon roaches, and you may make it as fat as you please; and as for the flavor imparted to it by the roaches, nothing can be finer."[30] Even in 1916 a newspaper article noted, "The heyday of the terrapin's fame was before the war, when these toothsome reptiles were abundant all over the South. Today they are chiefly appreciated by persons who learned to eat them long ago. Very conservative clubs, where elderly Colonels and Majors foregather, and very expensive hotels, which must have the most expensive goods on their menus, are Mr. Barbee's best customers."[31] (That said, the most recent cookbook we'll look at in this book is by the Junior League of Augusta in 1943, and it contains a recipe for terrapin.)[32]

The Barbee family continued the Pavilion after Alexander's death in 1929, once even saving all the "stock" during a hurricane by piling 3,000 crawling terrapins in the restaurant's main dining room.[33] Eventually, however, streetcar service ended, ending easy transportation to and from the city. The pavilion finally closed in 1968 after three-quarters of a century.[34]

Recipes and Kitchen Innovation

This section aims to stop for a moment to reflect on devices that saved labor and time, allowing Georgia cooks to reach new creative heights.

Bread

Four quarts of flour, one large tablespoonful of lard, four tablespoonfuls sugar, one yeast cake, one teaspoonful salt. Make a stiff dough with warm water, knead thoroughly; set to rise about six hours, then knead lightly with a little flour; make into rolls or loaves; set to rise again, when risen, bake.

—Independent Presbyterian Church (Savannah), *Hints from Southern Epicures* (1892), 36

Making homemade baked goods with yeast means ensuring the dough rises at an even, ideal temperature—quite the challenge in the days before central heat and air. Mary Scott Mapp (1848–1917), a forty-three-year-old Milledgeville mother of three, pondered the problem.[1] She wanted a dough-rising chamber that shut out dust and drafts, yet with wide doors for easy access. She needed reliable heat distribution and a thermometer for accuracy. The source of the warmth had to be dependable but also shielded, so that the long-burning flame would not be a fire hazard.[2] Mary indeed figured out how to make a "bread raiser" that fit the bill. On 8 October 1891 the local *Union & Recorder* newspaper announced:

A Gem for Housekeepers.

The perfect Bread Raiser, patented by one of Georgia's fair daughters. A thing that supplies a long felt want. No failure in bread with this. Write for prices, or call at J. W. Domingos' China store and see it.

For months, advertisements in the Milledgeville newspaper showed a drawing of the five-dollar cabinet-like device "so simple a child can use it." The ad included eight testimonials from local housekeepers as well as professionals at the nearby Normal and Industrial College. On 26 January 1892 the invention earned U.S. Patent No. 467,820. It also earned Mapp a gold medal from the Inventive Society of Paris, space in the Inventions Room at the World's Columbian Exposition in Chicago in 1893, and an exhibit at Atlanta's Cotton States and International Exposition in 1895.[3] As part of the latter opportunity, Mapp shared a pair of recipes, for Ginger Wafers and for Egg Sauce, in the cookbook put out by the Women's Building. (See 1895 section.) Oddly, neither involved yeast. The latter recipe, however, presented another kitchen problem:

Egg Sauce

One-half cup sugar, ½ cup water. Cook without stirring until it ropes, turn slowly into the beaten white of one egg, juice of ½ lemon, tablespoon of jelly; beat well.

—Mrs. F. B. Mapp, Milledgeville, Ga., in Wilson, *Tested Recipe Cook Book* (1895), 141

When made with quality jelly (our favorite is Concord grape), Mapp's egg sauce is so good that my family slathers it on everything from pound cake to vanilla wafers. My electric mixer makes it easy to literally whip up this treat—beating the egg white, then incorporating the ropelike filaments that sugar creates when dropped in water once it reaches the hard ball stage, around 250°F—but Mapp

"Well I don't get to do much more but cook and see after the wants of babies. . . . I nearly live in the cook room." Thirty-five-year-old Magnolia Wynn Le Guin (1869–1947) wrote this in her journal on 7 March 1905, echoing the domestic misery of many. By the end of the century there would be microwaves, slow cookers, and dishwashers, but labor-saving devices were few during the time that she was raising five children while also taking care of elderly parents in Henry County. Several of Magnolia's volumes were later published as *A Home-Concealed Woman: The Diaries of Magnolia Wynn Le Guin, 1901–1913*, a book that includes twenty-one of her recipes.

Cake Cutters.—These two engravings show a few of the many designs in cake cutters, made of tin, to give fancy forms to cakes. They may be had of all house furnishing stores, and are among the luxuries of the kitchen—very nice where they can be afforded, and they are not very costly. The effect is very pretty when different or even a single fancy form is used.

The Dover Egg Beater is generally regarded as the best in the market, and we know of no rival that has all its excellencies. It is not costly, and is very durable. By an ingenious contrivance the inner circle revolves in a contrary direction to the outer circle. With this the egg beating is a very simple matter.

Lb. cake
1 lb. flour
1 lb. butter
1 lb. sugar
10 large or 12 eggs

Cream butter + sugar till arm breaks. Add egg yolks - Beat thoroly
Beat whites stiff
Sift flour 3 times
Add alternately.
Bake slowly
Do not open stove.

Estelle Woods Wilcox's 1883 *Dixie Cook-Book* promoted helpful kitchen products such as cookie cutters and the Dover Egg Beater pictured on page 488.

I found this Georgia recipe between the pages of an old cookbook given to me by my friend Janet Wright. The pound cake instructions from her mother, Meta Johnson Wright (1908–1983) of Isle of Hope (Savannah) begin: "Cream butter & sugar till arm breaks." Georgia cookbook author Henrietta Dull (see 1928 section) confessed to the *Atlanta Constitution*'s Doris Lockerman on 29 April 1948 that there were times her signature angel food cakes caused insomnia due to "painful nervous prostration of the arms from beating 25 dozen eggs in one afternoon."

didn't have that advantage. She would, however, probably have had a Dover eggbeater, patented in 1857 during her childhood.[4] I've tried the older methods of beating egg white, from whips to eggbeaters, and it is amazingly difficult to form stiff egg white peaks with these tools. (See 1858 section.)

Almost all of Georgia's early cookbooks included a recipe for the popular dessert Charlotte Russe, at its most basic a custard poured into a pan or mold lined with sponge cake.[5] Here is an 1880 version offered by Augusta's Second Presbyterian Church:

Charlotte Russe

6 eggs.
1 qt. milk.
1 box gelatine.
1 pt. cream.
Sugar.
Vanilla.

Make the yolks of the eggs, one pint of the milk, and sugar to taste, a custard: dissolve the gelatine in the other pint of milk. Whip the whites of the eggs lightly with the cream, previously sweetened and flavored. Add all together, stirring it until cool. Take a sponge-cake, cut out the centre, leaving the outside crust or shell; pour in the above mixture to congeal, replace the top crust, and ice it.

—Mrs. Spalding's Collection, in *Choice Recipes of Georgia Housekeepers* (1880), 130

Anyone who's ever tried to hollow out a cake or line a mold with slices of it knows that it can be a tedious business. Sometimes it goes well, and sometimes you're left trying to hold together a pile of crumbs. In the autumn of 1921, newspapers nationwide held advertisements for the new Mary Ann Cake Shell Pan that "bakes a cake with a center lower than the edge, making a place for delicious filling."[6] Although the finished dessert wasn't a Charlotte Russe, later Mary Ann pan ads suggested various flavors of sponge cake and custard (possibly with a few spoonfuls of liqueur) as well as fillings of meringue and fresh fruit—the same sorts of evolutions that were happening with Charlotte Russe recipes.[7] The desserts were culinary "sisters," often using the same ingredients and satisfying the same need, yet one dessert required a lot less preparation time. A century later, Mary Ann pans are still available, while early versions pop up in Georgia antique shops. Meanwhile, Charlotte Russe recipes have made it to the modern era, but they almost always call for lining the pan or mold with prebaked sponge cookies called ladyfingers, which are much easier to work with.

Preserving the Past

As innovations come and kitchens change, there are those who take care to preserve older traditions. Beginning in the early 1980s, frequent Columbus newspaper articles celebrated Alfonso Biggs (1904–2003). Biggs died just short of the century milestone, but he had already made his mark. His obituary recalled him as "an encyclopedia of local culture" and "a keeper of black history."[1] In his later years, Biggs donated large amounts of family and collected artifacts to Georgia institutions.[2] In 1997 the ninety-three-year-old even won a Governor's Award for the Arts & Humanities.[3] But earlier in his life, the Talbot County native had also built a sixty-five-year catering career that including cooking for five Fort Benning generals as well as presidents Roosevelt, Truman, and Eisenhower.[4] His love of cooking and history came together in his "retirement" years when he demonstrated older cooking techniques for various groups and gatherings.[5] Thankfully, the Alfonso Biggs Collection at Columbus State University includes recipes. Nine of Biggs's family recipes were included in a cookbook put out by the Columbus Museum in 2015, *Chattahoochee Cookin': The Cookbook*, a supplement to an exhibit they put together the same year.[6]

4 cups meal
1 teaspoon salt
Boiling water
Mix meal and salt, add boiling water to make a stiff batter.

Take a tablespoon of batter in your hand and press it into a thin round cake.

If you have an open fire, have before it an oak plank well heated and greased. Place the cakes on the plank in front of the fire, bake on one side and turn and bake on the other until thoroughly done, about 45 minutes. These can also be baked on a griddle on top of the fire.

When done pull apart butter and send to the table hot.

—Reprint courtesy of Columbus State University Archives, Columbus State University, Columbus, Georgia

1. Kaffie Sledge, "Local Chef, Historian Alfonso Biggs Dies," *LE*, 31 December 2003.
2. Mick Walsh, "Georgia Man Gives to College Generations of Artifacts, Antiques," *Tallahassee Democrat*, 31 August 1991; "Columbus Man's Gift to University Allows Visitors to Step Back in Time, *LE*, 27 February 1999.
3. *LE*, 3 February 1997.
4. Ibid.
5. Pat Quinley, "A Taste for Things Past," *LE*, 4 September 1983.
6. Bush, *Chattahoochee Cookin'*, recipe on page 21. Manuscript, Columbus State University, MC 97. Publication permission courtesy of the Columbus State University Archives.

The Mary Ann pan reflects another trend. Occasionally old recipes instructed cooks to visit their local tinsmith to request a pan of a certain size or shape.[8] The 1852 advertisement for J. B. Hicks's "Copper and Sheet Iron and Tin Manufactory" in Columbus offered many ready-made kitchen items for sale, including ornamental cake and jelly molds. The proprietor also offered custom work.[9] It is difficult to know when factory workers and hobbyists became the only tinsmiths left, but by the 1920s there are very few newspaper ads or city directory listings for the simple tinsmith shop. At the same time, mail order catalogs rose to popularity, giving home bakers and cooks access to a greater variety of kitchenware. Still, coming up with an idea and having kitchenware made to the creative cook's specifications became much more difficult.

This Mary Ann Shell Pan—turned upside down so readers can better see what the finished cake shape would be—made multiple small cakes, each with a depression to hold custard, fruit, or other toppings.

For Woman's Work.

In the Kitchen.

HAVE a tinner make a long pan with a partition in the middle, for baking cake. Fill one-half of the pan with the plain cake dough, add spices, raisins, etc., to the other half, and put it in the other end of the pan. This plan enables one to have two kinds of cake with very little more time and labor than is required for one. Two small square pans will do.

From *Woman's Work* magazine (Athens) 14.2 (December 1901): 11.

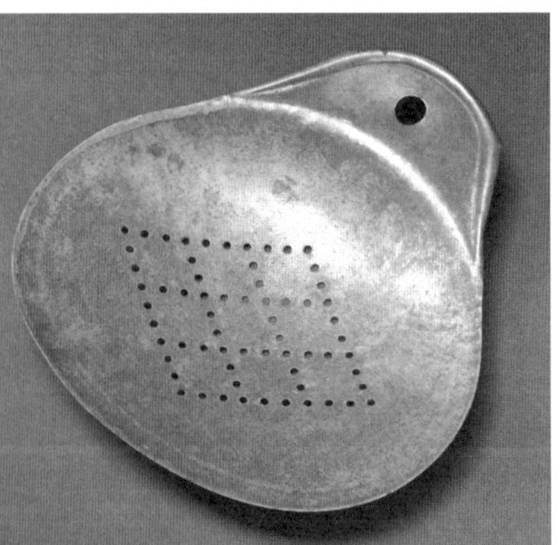

Tinsmiths created kitchenware to fill many needs, such as straining wet foods, baking fluted cakes, molding miniature desserts, and skimming cream floating atop milk.

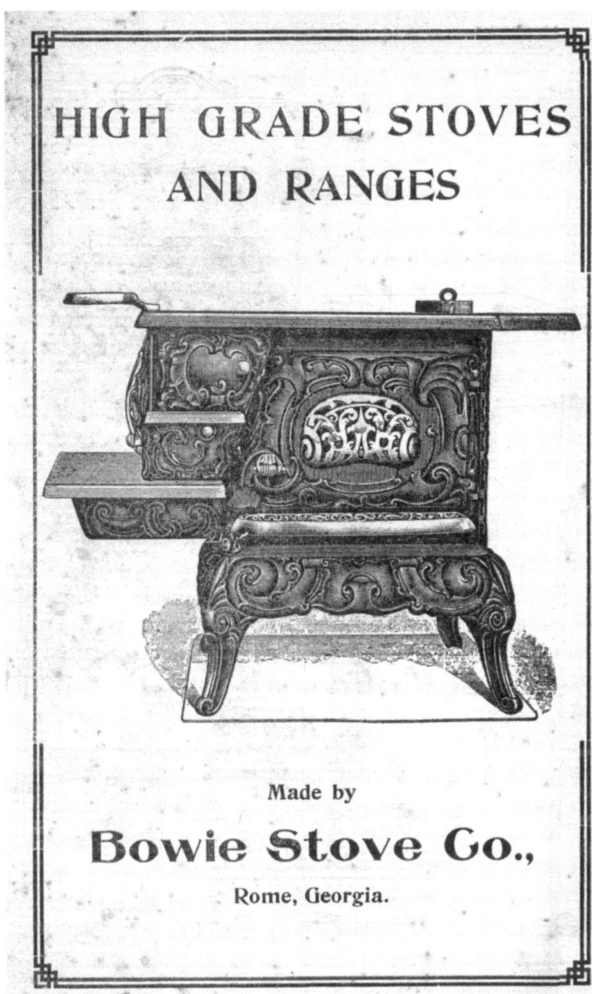

These advertisements are from *The New South Cook Book* of 1905 from the First Presbyterian Church of Rome, Georgia (from the collection of Cynthia Graubart). Transitioning from hearth to woodburning stove must have been challenging, yet both meant managing flame and coals. Moving on to a range fueled by oil, gas, or electricity must have been strange indeed, even if it was liberation from chopping wood, stoking fires, shoveling ashes, and "blacking" to prevent rust. As late as 1945 the front cover of the *Delicious Foods* cookbook for the Westinghouse Electric range encouraged cooks to think "fuel by wire is modern."

Hints from Southern Epicures and Foraged Ingredients

Hints from Southern Epicures, 1892
Independent Presbyterian Church (Savannah), Flower Committee
67 pages (with advertisements). 209 recipes.

Georgia's second church-affiliated community cookbook came a dozen years after the first (see 1880 section), both from Presbyterian congregations. With this cookbook, they weren't kidding about "hints" in the title; most of the recipes are undetailed as though simply suggestions from one experienced cook to another. Most are for common dishes, although there are a few surprises. On page 38 of the "Drinks" section, Pousse Cafe is an alcoholic cocktail with equal quantities of curacoa [curaçao], chartreuse, maraschino, anisette, and brandy. The liquids separate into layers because of their differing densities, "affording the illusion of a draught of liquid rainbow."[1] What really caught my attention with this cookbook, however, is that there were native plant ingredients that, despite a coastal childhood, I'd never heard of before.

From Rice Bird Pie to Blackberry Wine, I counted thirty-eight recipes in this cookbook where an intrepid cook could forage, hunt, or fish for the main ingredient. While modern cookbooks tend to assume the reader is going to purchase all the ingredients at a store, older cookbooks weren't shy about including things gathered locally, indicating that Georgians generally used to have a much better understanding of useful wild foods. I turned to old Georgia newspapers to see if I could get a better feel for plant foraging, learning that "fighting General Green" meant keeping the woods from growing back over cleared areas. Many foraged foods came from the edges of fields, ditches, abandoned gardens, and other places where General Green was trying to reclaim territory.

Newspapers often reported the first cotton blossom of the season as well as the first sightings of various foraged foods and whether they were sparse or abundant that year. On 18 August 1870, for example, the *Daily Sun* of Columbus reported, "For two weeks, may-pops, muscadines, summer (wild) grapes, have been ripe and are still ripening. Folks, white and black, all ages, are gathering them—mostly for own use; some few are sold. Pretty soon our market will be flooded with wild grapes and muscadines. May-pops are dull sale." During tough economic times, foraged foods could be a godsend. Atlanta journalist Celestine Sibley once interviewed an old-timer who wryly recalled "when things was so tight you prayed every fall the persimmons would hold out till the poke sallet come up in the spring."[2]

What did Georgians gather? I found older recipes and newspaper mentions of crab apples, wild grapes of various types, hawthorn, honey locust, mayhaw, maypops, persimmons, wild plums, prickly pear, watercress, and wild black

Mangoes.

The proper cucumbers to be used for this purpose are those of the largest sort, which must be taken from the vines before they are too ripe or yellow, the young mushmellon is better. Put them in strong salt and water, three or four days. Stir well every day, then put them in a kettle with same salt and water, with vine leaves over and under, and a little rock alum; set them over a very slow fire for five hours. When very green take them out and drain them well, then boil some vinegar and pour over them hot. The next day drain them well again. Cut a piece out of side and take out seeds with a teaspoon or apple scraper; dry them well with a towel, and put in the following stuffing: Horseradish, mustard-seed, garlic, pepper-corns, mace, cloves, allspice, some cabbage, cut up fine. When full take the piece that was cut out and sew it on; boil a sufficient quantity of fresh vinegar, and pour on the mangoes hot; tie them down close.

Swamp Plum Preserves.

One-and-a-half pounds of sugar to one pound of plums, one-half pint of water to every pound of sugar. Thoroughly scald the plums, until they begin to burst, then take them out of the kettle, and put them in a bucket of cold water. Let them remain until cold, then put them back into the kettle. Use the water that they were scalded in for making the syrup, as it has already so much acid.

The "mango" in the top recipe (33) was popular in many cookbooks of the 1800s but later faded away. It is a pickled cucumber or melon stuffed with spices and pickled pieces of vegetables or fruits. Some recipes called for simply fitting the melon or cucumber back together once filled. Other recipes, like this one, called for needle and thread!

As for swamp plums, despite reaching out to coastal gardeners and scientists, I was unable to determine a specific type of plum for this recipe. Most require well-drained soil. Perhaps these were wild plums growing on the edges of swamps?

Quince Preserves.

Pare and core quinces the same as peaches, put them in cold water and boil until they begin to look clear, then make your syrup with one half pint of water to every pound of sugar, preserve as peaches.

Ogeechee Limes Preserves.

Cut off the ends, par-boil in two waters, in the first put a small piece of alum. To one pound of limes add one and one-fourth pounds of sugar, boil together over a slow fire, until they are clear and tender; take them out, boil the syrup until thick. Put the limes back and let them warm through again.

Revolutionary-era naturalist William Bartram discovered the Ogeechee tupelo tree along the Ogeechee River in Georgia (see Gilman and Watson, "*Nyssa ogeche*"). Female trees produce small, sour red fruits, up to an inch long, that ripen in autumn. According to Eugenia Cox in *Low Country Cooking* (iv), Georgia diarist Emma LeConte Furman (1847–1932), born into a family of famed naturalists, wrote about enjoying Ogeechee lime preserves in Liberty County before the Civil War. Around that time and just into the twentieth century, Savannah newspapers sometimes announced when this foraged fruit arrived at local markets. I posted a question about Ogeechee limes to an online coastal gardening group, learning that some Georgians still grow this fruit and cook with it.

cherries. Some were eaten fresh, while others went into preserves, alcoholic beverages, or baked goods. Wild berries included blackberries, dewberries, elderberries, mulberries, and strawberries. It seemed that "nutting parties" focused on chestnuts, chinquapins, and hickory nuts.

Exploring Further

The two Cherokee cookbooks explored in the 1838 section contain an array of foods that are foraged, hunted, or fished. Marie Mellinger's *Out of Old Fields: A Wild Edibles Cookbook* from Rabun Gap is an interesting read from 1975, while the recent *Southeast Foraging* by Chris Bennett lists 120 wild foods complete with photographs. Should you decide to partake of wild foods, do careful research first to ensure they are safe to eat. And please keep sustainability in mind, not damaging the collecting area and leaving enough behind that the plant or animal can reproduce well.

Annie Dennis and New Freedoms

Annie Dennis' Cook Book, 1894
Annie Elizabeth Dennis (6 September 1856–18 May 1920) and
Augusta Amelia "Daisy" Wright Mell (5 November 1869–22 November 1944)
388 pages. 952 food recipes, 23 medicine recipes, and 2 household recipes.
154 are credited to 69 contributors, mostly from Georgia.

If I were a new cook in the mid-1890s, this is the cookbook I would have wanted. The average Annie Dennis recipe is longer and more thorough than those in many cookbooks of the time. The basics are here, such as biscuits, fried chicken, and iced tea. Dennis even explains how to slice a pineapple, scramble eggs, and make toast. Yet she offers dishes to impress as well. Recipes for fruits and vegetables are in sections (for instance, the scuppernong recipes are grouped together), which is particularly helpful if you find yourself with a bumper crop. She also includes recipes for locally gathered foods including crab apples, wild grapes, 'possum, frog legs, and, on page 58, this one.

Maypop Jelly

Use the seed of ripe maypops. Boil them fifteen minutes and strain; add one pint of sugar to one of juice and boil twenty-five or thirty minutes, or until it is a firm jelly.

There are many chilled salads and desserts that were modern for their time. On the other hand, Dennis seemed to be cooking on a wood-burning stove at a time when this technology was beginning to give way. Several recipes call for using fire or coals. For instance, her preferred method of broiling bacon (164) was to take one of the circular eyes off the stove to reveal the coals below and cook one strip at a time on a fork. Her roasted corn (225) was wrapped in brown paper and placed in ashes. She describes the "old-fashioned way of preserving" tender fruits by leaving them in the sun for several hours, thereby avoiding a cooking process that may destroy delicate flavors (25). She explains how to select a chicken (177) by looking for smooth skin on its toes. Many of the recipes give brief explanations about older ways of cooking.

Annie Dennis, born in Talbotton in 1856 to Peter Early Dennis and Caroline Spain Dennis, was the only surviving girl in a houseful of brothers.[1] Her grandfather had been one of first European-American settlers in Talbot County, building a mill and a substantial farm.[2] The publisher's preface to the 1921 seventh, final, posthumous edition of Dennis's cookbook puts it this way: "Born of pioneer Georgia stock, just before the war between the States, she arrived at the age of maturity at that epochal time in the history of the South when it required every energy of her people to maintain the traditional hospitality of the old South with the attenuated revenues of the new South." At one time, the trajectory of the Dennis family meant that Annie should have had a life of privilege and luxury. Judging from writings of the time, the hope most likely would have been a successful marriage, raising children, and settling more deeply into upper-crust

Talbotton was home to the Collinsworth Institute for men as well as the Le Vert Female College where Annie Dennis was educated.[1] The schools drew many to the town. As noted on one of the city's historic markers, immigrant Lazarus Straus wanted a place where his children could be educated and opened a store in Talbotton.[2] The Straus family would later resettle in New York, where they eventually became the owners of Macy's department store. One county history book noted that a friendship with the Dennis family continued even after the Straus family moved north.[3] Eldest son Isidor Straus (1845–1912) and his wife, Ida, perished on the *Titanic* in 1912. Ida was to have taken a lifeboat but made the decision to instead stay with her husband, a romantic act that has since been immortalized in memorials and on film.

1. *GWTGJM*, 6 July 1874.
2. W. Davidson, *A Rockaway in Talbot*, 1:168.
3. Ibid., 1:171.

plantation life.[3] By the time she wrote her cookbook, however, Annie's role in the family farm was far more hands-on. She was also able to make choices and have freedoms her grandmothers could scarcely have imagined.

Annie may have had chances early on to see high-level kitchen skills in action. Her father, a judge for the Inferior Court, owned a hotel on the main square during her early childhood.[4] In 1860 a local newspaper reported on a public exhibition for the local militia: "At night the young and old, gay and handsome, imaginative and matter of fact, regaled themselves with a 'flow of soul' at a 'military and civic' party, tastefully and sumptuously prepared by Judge Dennis and lady."[5] The Civil War, however, interrupted the lives of the Dennis family. Peter and his oldest son, William, joined the fight. Both survived, and Talbotton was spared the worst destruction seen by some other towns.[6]

A Career Begins

In the late 1870s, as Georgia was recovering from war, area newspapers began to report travels by "Miss Annie Dennis."[7] A passenger rail line finally established in Talbotton made these ventures easier, although the *Travelers' Official Railway Guide* reported the speed was a time-dragging fourteen miles per hour.[8] The 1883 obituary for Annie's father holds a clue to some of these journeys, noting that "he had as much as any man to do with the inauguration of our County Fairs, in which he always took great pride."[9] The preface for the final edition of Annie's cookbook notes, "In the early eighties, with the encouragement of her father, she was induced to prove her excellence in domestic science, by displays of her handiwork at the State fairs at Macon and the expositions at Atlanta, Augusta and Columbus. So great was her success that the premiums awarded to her for excellence amounted in the aggregate to nearly ten thousand dollars." This was a considerable sum at the time, especially for a single woman. By the time Annie was twenty-two, she was sometimes leaving the state to participate in fairs and bring home top premiums (cash prizes).[10]

Cookoff, a book about American cooking competitions, explores the beginnings of the agricultural fair movement. In 1813, Massachusetts farmer and fair organizer Elkanah Watson added competitions for domestic products, needlework, jams, and baked goods to his local fair. "These contests not only lured women to the fair but also, by besting their peers, gave the undervalued farmwives some much-deserved recognition. . . . Thanks to Watson their prowess in their private kitchens could lead them to public accolades. American farm women responded, and by midcentury female competition was a mainstay of the fair, as was female attendance. Consequently, many generations of American women have grown up thinking of cooking and baking as not just an end in itself but as a path to blue ribbons and personal glory."[11]

Industrialization and travel improvements gave rise to large-scale, international fair exhibitions such as those in New York (1853), Philadelphia (1876), and Chicago (1893). On a somewhat smaller scale, Atlanta hosted three expositions. (See 1895 section.) At Atlanta's 1887 Piedmont Exposition, an event drawing nearly 20,000 visitors on opening day, thirty-one-year-old Annie earned $255 in premiums. The Atlanta newspaper noted, "One especially beautiful and interesting exhibit was made by Miss Annie Dennis, of Talbot County, in which I am sure our lady readers could not fail to be interested. This lady has a space all to herself, and everything on exhibition was the work of her hands. There were over four hundred articles on exhibition, three hundred specimens of jellies, preserves, canned vegetables, candied fruits and fruit syrups, candied figs, pears, crabapples and citron and green tomatoes, and all as nice as ever bought from the confectioner's at a dollar a pound, the fruit and vegetables all raised on her farm; very nice sugar made from the cane of her own raising."[12]

The exposition turned out to be good publicity—and a nudge to pen a cookbook. In November of 1893 Annie wrote a preface to the first edition in which she credits her father's interest in the Talbot County fairs for her initial success. She adds, "These several exhibits, with the kindly newspaper mention that has been given them, have induced a large number of ladies to write to me at various times for my way of making this, that or the other thing. My correspondence became so voluminous as to suggest a book of recipes to meet the universal demand." And the cookbook's preface hinted that Dennis's work showed a level of systematic thoughtfulness not seen in a Georgia cookbook since Annabella Hill a generation before:

> Now, what I know about cooking would not make a book, so I have associated with me Miss Daisy A. Wright, and for nearly a year we have been engaged in compiling this work. The task has been sometimes difficult, but always pleasant, and the names that are attached to some of the gems that add so much of worth to its pages, show how finely we have been assisted by ladies whose hospitality is as noted as their liege lords are famous. When what we knew and what they knew was not up to our idea of the requirements of a model cook book, we have gone to the newspaper for help. The best things we could get have been used, sometimes

without change and sometimes so changed that their own mother would not recognize them, but none except after a fair test to prove their merit.

For the cookbook to come into existence, Annie was required to navigate quite a few obstacles. She was educated at a time when many women were not. Her family supported her work. She had access to a proper kitchen along with the supplies needed to test the recipes—no longer something to take for granted in the South after the Civil War. At the same time, the war swept away an antebellum way of life that might have led to Annie becoming the "mistress" over the kitchen rather than an actual cook.[13] The cookbook took considerable time for compiling, writing, testing, and editing. Annie, however, was single and thus may have had fewer daily obligations than her married peers, especially those with children. Annie needed help compiling additional recipes, and her family's social standing made it possible for her to include recipes from reputable sources. The Panic of 1893 led to a serious economic depression that endangered the financial survival of many creative and business pursuits, yet Dennis had personal income. Finally, establishing a good working relationship with a printer would have been a challenge to a woman living in a small town in that day and age. But Annie had an "in" to the printing industry.

An Atlanta Connection

Joseph Dennis was Annie's elder brother by four years. His attempts at publishing a newspaper in Talbotton were short-lived, and at the age of thirty-nine he appears in the Atlanta city directory as a printer. By 1893 he is with the American Publishing and Engraving Company—the same company that published the first edition of *Annie Dennis' Cook Book*. In 1898 the directory lists Joseph as the president of a new venture called the Mutual Printing Company, which would become Annie's press for the remainder of her cookbook editions.

In the mid-1890s Annie was a new author, and her star was rising in part because she could partake in the wonders of Georgia's capital. In the spring of 1894, even as newspapers carried articles and advertisements for her cookbook,[14] thirty-seven-year-old Dennis served on the Women's Department for the planning of the upcoming Cotton States and International Exposition.[15] Her recipe for My Premium Crackers appears in the *Tested Recipe Cook Book*, a souvenir for exposition visitors. (See 1895 section.) While the exposition was in full swing, a lengthy article about Annie Dennis appeared in the *Atlanta Constitution*, calling her "a most remarkable woman, a true southern woman who has done as much, if not more, to develop the resources of her section and state, and to teach other women the capabilities with which they are all endowed than any one we know." It describes Dennis's work as she and her brother managed the 2,000-acre family farm in Talbotton that included growing grain, raising hogs, a forty-cow dairy, and vegetable gardens "with up to twenty acres in tomatoes alone."[16]

Annie seemed entrenched in rural life, yet according to the 1900 census she moved to Atlanta. City directories between 1900 and 1908 show her running a series of boardinghouses. (See 1897 section.) Journalist Evelyn Hanna wrote almost twenty-five years after Annie's death: "Now Miss Annie at one time conducted a boarding house in Atlanta and a list of the guests reads like the social register. Young men who brought their best girls to her famous Sunday night suppers came only by invitation."[17] Meanwhile, ads for her cookbook were a common feature in newspapers statewide, and "agents" were recruited to help promote it.[18] Articles and advertisements contained endorsements from the likes of novelist Maude Andrews-Ohl as well as Mrs. William King, who served as editor for the Women's Kingdom page in the *Atlanta Constitution*. (Following a Women's Press Club meeting, Mrs. King even brought members and guests for a special reception at Annie's home.)[19] In 1913 the cookbook became a promotional gift for shoppers at King Hardware Store.[20] Annie Dennis was becoming a Georgia household name.

The Close of the Day

In the 1910 census, Dennis was living in Vineville, a historic section outside of Macon, in the household of her brother. Under "Trade or Profession," Annie is listed as "Authoress." A decade later, at the age of sixty-three, she died unexpectedly of a stroke in Macon.[21] The *Atlanta Constitution* called her "one of Atlanta's well known women" and reported that she was only visiting for a wedding.[22] It added, "She had apparently been in good health, and passed away in her sleep." She was buried in Macon's historic Riverside Cemetery above the Ocmulgee River and near grassy earthworks once dug by hand to defend the city during the Civil War.[23]

At the time of her death, Dennis was working on the seventh edition of her cookbook. Mutual Publishing Company published it posthumously, noting that almost 100,000 copies of her work had been sold thus far. Annie's legacy continued for many years, if mentions of her work in the *Atlanta Constitution* are any indication. One of the more interesting articles appeared the year after her death, noting that when her family went through her belongings, they found "an astounding number of proposals of marriage . . . some of these from men she knew and others from men she had never seen."[24] Despite the patterns of life a southern woman of her time and socioeconomic status was expected to follow, Dennis made her own choices.

JOLLY BOYS.

Scald one cup of meal. Beat to a cream, one quarter of a cup of butter, add well beaten three eggs, then one pint of warm milk, that has been scalded and cooled. Beat; add meal, one yeast cake dissolved in two tablespoonfuls of warm water, half a teacup of sugar and sufficient flour to make a soft dough. Cover and stand into a warm place until very light, over night is better. In the morning make out into balls size of English walnuts, place on floured cloth and when light, (about one hour), fry in smoking hot fat. Dust with sugar and serve.—*Mrs. Clifford Williams, Macon, Ga.*

SWEET POTATO JOHNNY CAKE.

Take one pint of best corn meal, salt to taste (half a teaspoonful is the ordinary seasoning). Rub into the meal a large tablespoonful of lard, next add to it one pint of smoothly mashed sweet potatoes. If the potatoes are not very sweet add a tablespoonful of sugar. Mix thoroughly to a rather soft dough, but not too soft to handle. Have the middle stave of a barrel head (oak wood) washed clean, rinse it, leaving it wet and on this evenly spread the dough not quite out to the edges of the board. Dip a knife blade in cold water and with it smooth over the surface of the Johnny-cake, and stick with a fork as you would biscuit. Set it before the fire with a brick or flat iron to support it. Let it brown nicely, then loosen it from the board by means of a coarse thread passed between the Johnny-cake and the board, close to the latter. Turn the board over and lay the brown side of the Johnny-cake down on it, again setting it before the fire to brown the other side. When that is done, cut it in three inch wide pieces—there will be about five of them. Send to the table hot from the board, butter well and eat immediately. This is a delicious bread for a winter supper or breakfast. But it must be cooked by the reflection of the fire to have the genuine Johnny-cake taste. In the stove? No! Before the fire!—*Selected.*

SAVOY CAKES OF OLDEN TIMES.

Beat eight eggs to a froth separately; then mix together, add a pound of powdered white sugar stirred in gradually. Beat the whole ten minutes, add the grated rind of a fresh lemon and half the juice, a pound of sifted flour and a couple of tablespoonfuls of coriander seed. Drop this mixture by the large spoonful, on buttered baking plates several inches apart, sift white sugar over them and bake immediately in a quick, hot oven. These cakes make a delicious addition to the afternoon tea table.

BAKED TOMATOES.

Remove the meat from whole tomatoes; season crumbs of light bread with butter, onion, pepper and salt; fill tomatoes and bake.—*Mrs. Laura Wimberly Warren, Kirkwood, Ga.*

SCALLOPED TOMATOES.

Scalloped tomatoes make a delicious dinner dish. To prepare it, peel large ripe tomatoes, slice, and sprinkle with salt. Cover the bottom of a baking dish with a layer of stale bread crumbs, then slices of tomatoes, more bread crumbs, with bits of butter, salt and pepper; continue to arrange the tomatoes and seasoning in this way until the dish is full; spread the top with butter, and set in a hot oven to bake an hour. Add sugar if desired.

Assistant Daisy Wright

Daisy was the project underling and was not listed as an author after the first edition, yet research reveals that many of the recipe contributors were her relatives. In addition, those interested in old Georgia cookbooks from a women's studies standpoint will find Daisy a fascinating historical figure in her own right. In her journey from orphan to civic leader, she stretched the boundaries of women's roles.

In 1869, while Annie was a thirteen-year-old schoolgirl, Augusta Amelia "Daisy" Wright was born in Augusta to Reverend Arminius Wright and Sarah Amelia Bardwell Taft Wright.[25] It was a second marriage for Daisy's parents, who had both experienced the death of their first spouse. Daisy had three full siblings and five older half-siblings, a large family that became sources for many of the cookbook's recipes. Reverend Wright was later affiliated with the Methodist Church in Columbus, and it was here that Daisy spent most of her early years. Wright family papers archived in Columbus and Athens reveal the daily patterns of a quiet life for a post–Civil War minister's family.[26] Church and domestic activities absorbed their time, including those related to foodways such as raising chickens, fishing, and tending an extensive garden. Many of these patterns fell apart when Daisy's parents died, Reverend Wright when she was ten and her mother when she was fifteen.

According to the preface of the cookbook's first edition, in 1893 twenty-four-year-old Daisy was in Talbotton helping with the cookbook. As for the connection between Dennis and Wright, Daisy's father spent time in Talbotton before his death and may have served on the faculty at the town's Le Vert Female College. Both families were active in the Methodist Church. In addition, Daisy was close to her uncle, Dr. Edward L. Bardwell of Talbotton. Dr. Bardwell lived within walking distance of the Dennis family and was their physician, attending Annie's father hours before his death back in 1883.[27]

By the turn of the century, Daisy reappears with regularity in various records. According to the 1900 census, she lived with Annie Dennis in one Atlanta boardinghouse. It is the last joint record of the cookbook duo. The following year, at the age of thirty-one, Daisy married banker, civic leader, and two-time widower George Anderson Mell (1852–1931) of Athens. The couple never had children, but family letters showed they lavished time and attention on his daughter as well as Daisy's nieces and nephews.[28] Daisy also supported the local

Methodist church, genealogical organizations, and the YMCA. When World War I broke out, she put substantial energy behind several organizations including the American Red Cross and United States War Savings Stamps. When the soldiers returned home, she then concentrated on suffrage, helping to organize the League of Women Voters in Athens. Once the Nineteenth Amendment was ratified, giving women the right to vote in the summer of 1920, Daisy was among the first to register. In 1928, Daisy was one of seventy-four women featured in the book *Prominent Women of Georgia*.[29] Once widowed, Daisy moved to DeKalb County and died there in 1944 at the age of seventy-five. In her papers archived at the University of Georgia, one finds photographs of Daisy with millinery projects, sheet music for an anthem she wrote in honor of America's soldiers, her poem that was published in the *New York Times*, and information for three patents—the Right Window Wedge (stopping rattling panes), the Right Baby Shirt (description unknown), and a combination of warm and lightweight fabrics designed to help soldiers during World War I.[30]

The Cotton States and International Exposition

A Tale of Two Cookbooks

The Atlanta Exposition Souvenir Cook Book: A Safe Guide to Ordering and Cooking
Ida Dean Graves Jones Bailey (13 August 1864–18 February 1908), editor
67 pages (with advertisements). 162 food recipes.

Tested Recipe Cook Book
Mary Elizabeth Monk Wilson (7 November 1842–1 April 1915), editor
161 pages (with advertisements). 502 food recipes, 4 medicine/household recipes. 417 contributors listed.

It was a wonderland. The Cotton States and International Exposition, held on land that is now Atlanta's Piedmont Park, opened for fifteen weeks in the autumn of 1895. Thousands of visitors poured through, lured by Buffalo Bill Cody's Wild West Show, the real Liberty Bell on loan, international villages, exotic animals, and The Chutes, boats allowing riders to careen down a tall ramp and splash into the lake. At nighttime, newfangled electric lights lit up the grounds, turning the lake's fountain into a colorful show. The organizers, of course, hoped the visitors would also be impressed by exhibited innovations in agriculture and technology. The Expo was designed to show how far Atlanta and the South had come in the three decades since the Civil War, courting new trade and industry.

When President Cleveland visited in October, his favorite Expo buildings were the Woman's Building and the Negro Building, perhaps a hint that the Progressive Era was beginning.[1] If he wanted to purchase souvenirs for the First

Lady, he could have brought home a cookbook from both buildings. Over a century later, however, only one cookbook is remembered. Hopefully that will now change.

This four-inch silver spoon decorated with a cotton boll was a souvenir from the Exposition.

The collection of recipes that Mrs. Wilson compiled in her role as leader of the Committee on Agriculture and Horticulture for the Board of Women Managers was reprinted in the 1980s and is still cited by foodways scholars today, so we will start with this cookbook, moving from the familiar to the unfamiliar. While the original cookbook was a green hardcover,[2] with a silvery sketch of the Women's Building on the front, the cover photograph chosen for the 1984 reprint known to today's readers is a period photograph of four ladies in lace quietly enjoying tea. It isn't exactly a misleading image, as the cookbook is full of dainty treats and foods that would impress company. Like the Women's Building itself, the cookbook was to show the sophisticated side of Georgia. In the introduction to the 1984 reprint, Atlanta historian Darleen Roth states: "It should be pointed out that the food described in these pages represents aspiring kitchen efforts and not simple southern fare. There are Sally Lunns and corn breads, but no grits; chicken dishes and ham, but no pork; pickled vegetables, but no greens; fancy gravies and sauces, but no pan juices."

Roth also observes that the cookbook "constitutes a veritable roster of the Atlanta feminine elite and their friends" who are "the arbiters of society, the guardians of the social register, the models for decorum."[3] Still, the Wilson cookbook is not fluff. Roth adds, "We take their efforts for granted today, but the women within these pages were the founders of the first women's organizations in Atlanta, the first activists, the first lobbyists." For example, the editor was born Mary E. Monk in Alabama but moved to Atlanta upon her 1860 marriage to Dr. Henry Wilson (1839–1917).[4] Her husband served as a surgeon during the Civil War and was later mentioned frequently in Atlanta newspapers as a physician, business owner, real estate investor, city councilman, and railroad supporter. Both Mary and Henry were active in various causes that publicly linked them to many of the individuals mentioned in the cookbook, including community leaders Nellie Peters Black and Emma Hemphill, who shared the recipes below.[5]

Recipes in the cookbook come from 417 contributors. Locations are given for most, helping us know that over half of the recipes came from Atlanta.

Twenty-three Georgia counties are represented, as well as sixteen other states. Well over a century after its creation, *Tested Recipe Cook Book* remains a source of useful and inspiring old recipes as well as a window on a segment of Georgia society in the Gilded Age.

A sherbet recipe on page 128 was contributed by Mrs. Henry L. Wilson, the book's editor.

Punch Sherbet

Take a quart can of fine peaches; rub through a sieve. Add 1 pint of water, 1 cup of sugar and 1 cup of orange juice. Freeze like a punch and serve in glasses, adding a tablespoon of champagne to each glass when the sherbet is served.

Credit for a jam cake on page 50 went to the equally estimable Mrs. N. P. Black. Mary Ellen "Nellie" Peters Black (1851–1919) is remembered as "Georgia's Pioneer Club Woman."[6]

Jam Cake

(One of my favorite recipes)

Yolks of 8 eggs, 1 cup butter, 2 cups sugar, 3 cups flour, 1 cup jam, 1 cup wine, 2 heaping teaspoons baking powder, 1 teaspoon each of cloves, cinnamon, and mace. Sift baking powder in flour, beat eggs and sugar together until light, add butter well creamed, then the flour, spices, jam, and lastly the wine. Bake in layer pans, put together with icing. A fine substitute for fruit cake.

A stewed chicken dish on page 14 came from the formidable Mrs. W. A. Hemphill. Civil War widow Emma Batts Sanders Luckie (1844–1900) married William Arnold Hemphill (1842–1902), who owned the *Atlanta Constitution* for a time and served as mayor of Atlanta.[7] Emma Hemphill was one of Atlanta's suffrage forerunners, holding a controversial reception for the National Woman's Suffrage Association in 1895 when Susan B. Anthony visited Atlanta.[8]

Creole Stew

Put into the stewpan one-half onion cut fine, one teaspoon of flour, one can of tomatoes, pepper and salt to taste, one and one-half cups water. Into this put one chicken, cut up as for frying. Sift flour lightly over the chicken, and let the whole remain for one hour (do not let it boil). Then it is ready for use, to be served with rice, which has been boiled until each grain stands alone. Serve the rice first on the plate and put the stew over it. Dinner dish.

In terms of the Cotton States Exposition, however, the cookbook Wilson edited is only half the story. In 1928, State Librarian Ella May Thornton put out *Finding-List of Books and Pamphlets Relating to Georgia and Georgians*. It was here that I first came across mention of another Exposition cookbook. I thought it an error, a mix-up between Wilson's cookbook and the works of popular American cookbook author Ida Bailey Allen.[9] (See the 1932 section.) Digitized newspapers, however, revealed a research trail. Unfortunately, there are no known copies of the cookbook in Georgia, and access to the two known copies, both in Washington, D.C., was temporarily forbidden due to shutdowns over the Covid-19 virus. Finally, after many months, I found myself sitting down at a Library of Congress table to look at the small cookbook now rebound in dark red buckram.

In the interim, I learned much about the lead editor, Ida Bailey. Just months before the end of the Civil War, she was born in Roxboro, North Carolina, but at a young age moved across the border to Danville, Virginia.[10] Listed in various census records as either "mulatto" or "black," she studied at Scotia Seminary and Shaw University, North Carolina schools now known as Historically Black Colleges and Universities (HBCUs).[11] For a time she lived in Boston, attending the Blish School and the New England Conservatory of Music. The result of all these studies was that Ida became an educator herself. And in 1891, after divorcing a previous husband, she married Henry Lewis Bailey (1866–1933), a teacher and physician who held degrees from Harvard and Howard University.[12] Beginning in the late 1880s, Black newspapers from Washington, D.C., were sprinkled with news of Ida's charity work as well as her public talks in support of education and racial equality. A decade after the cookbook, Ida and Henry aided civil rights leader W. E. B. Du Bois in founding the Niagara Movement against racial discrimination. Then, in her mid-forties, Ida became unexpectedly ill. Calling for paper, she penned some last words on faith and social equality that included "Be brave men; be brave women."[13] At the time of her 1908 death, she was president of the Dunbar Circle, an intellectual group intent on equality.[14] Du Bois wrote a eulogy praising her dedication and leadership.[15]

My hope when I began turning cookbook pages was that I would find another window on a past segment of Georgia society, this time a reflection of the arts, industry, and intellectual activities celebrated by the Negro Building as well as traces of the women's clubs from Atlanta's Black community.[16] I was hopeful because while Bailey wasn't from Georgia, one newspaper article indicated she had spent time in the state.[17] By the time of the Expo, Atlanta's Sweet Auburn was already a vibrant neighborhood and Georgia was home to at least eight colleges for Black students.[18] Ida and her husband moved in the same social circles as Georgia's

John Hope (1868–1936, president of both Morehouse College and Clark Atlanta University), W. E. B. Du Bois (1868–1963, faculty at Clark Atlanta University), and well-known Atlanta businessman Alonzo Herndon (1858–1927).[19] My desire for this to be a Georgia cookbook, however, wasn't realized. *The Atlanta Exposition Souvenir Cook Book* is essentially a Washington, D.C., cookbook.

Two-thirds of the recipes are credited. Because contributors' locations are not given and the forty-five contributors are sometimes listed by partial names ("Miss Matthews"), it is difficult to fully research the community behind the cookbook. The twenty-eight advertisements in the back helped, as sometimes contributors and advertisers were from the same households. Some of the contributors and advertisers were also found in newspaper articles about Bailey's community work. (Bailey herself contributed no recipes.)

There are some recipes in Bailey's cookbook that would make fine offerings for company, yet this is a cookbook more intent on the basics. There are advice sections called "The Kitchen," "The Table," "Domestic Economy," and "Hints to Young Cooks." And the cookbook has a modern slant. The women putting together the cookbook called themselves the Domestic Science Committee, and a beginning essay calls the kitchen "the great laboratory of the household." There are many seafood recipes, perhaps reflecting Washington's location near the Chesapeake. Beef and chicken are the primary proteins, and no wild game is represented. Unlike in many Georgia cookbooks of the era, corn isn't a major ingredient. The recipe contributors who could be traced came from all over the country, and this seems to be reflected in the recipes themselves.

Although this cookbook doesn't help to preserve Georgia foodways, we know it was created for sale in Atlanta. It is an example of recipes flowing into our state, and this cookbook is particularly important because it focused on an underserved community. Furthermore, this cookbook was put together by people who were activists and lobbyists. Even if it requires research to make connections between those behind the Bailey cookbook and leading Georgians like John Hope and Alonzo Herndon, *The Atlanta Exposition Souvenir Cook Book* is a valuable source.

A wafer recipe (page 41) was credited to Jesse Smith Koonce, who was born in 1873 in Alabama and grew up on the Georgia-Alabama border. He later became a confectioner and caterer in Washington, D.C.[20] His "biscuit bags" instruction likely means to portion the dough using a pastry bag. (For more information about wafers, see 1864 section. This recipe is close to the Gordon wafer recipe, yet double in amount, and creates a slightly thicker batter.)

These measuring utensils represent the precise and orderly future glimpsed by the Domestic Science Committee putting together *The Atlanta Exposition Souvenir Cook Book.*

Atlanta Exposition Wafers

(Mr. Koonce)
1 pound of flour.
9 eggs.
11 ounces of butter.
1 pound of sugar.
Flavor with vanilla.
Cream butter and sugar until very light. Add eggs whipped to a light froth (white and yolks together); then the flour very gently; use biscuit bags for this purpose as you would for jumbles. Put in tin cannisters in a dry place. These cakes will keep for months if properly handled.

A recipe for Bird's Nest (page 34) came from Dr. Laura E. Joiner (1873–1954), who was born in Iowa. Her father, Reverend E. C. Joiner, was one of the pioneers of the African Methodist Episcopal (A.M.E.) Church.[21] Laura was a 1903 graduate of Howard University Medical School.[22] She was also one of the members of the Domestic Science Committee for the cookbook and wrote the sections "Domestic Economy" and "Bill of Fare."

Bird's Nest

(Miss L. E. Joiner)

Hard boiled eggs; surround each egg with thin slice of bacon or hashed meat finely chopped; place in well greased tin and brown in a quick oven; cut each, half in two, and put a bit of butter on each. Serve hot.

This tomato recipe (20) was offered by public school teacher Mary Louise Meriwether. At the first convention of the National League of Colored Women in 1896, Meriwether shared the speaker's platform with Ida Bailey and spoke on "Woman's Work Among Men."[23] Born in Illinois in 1848, she married Washington, D.C., lawyer James Henry Meriwether.[24] Their daughter, Edith, married the son of civil rights leader Booker T. Washington.[25]

How To Prepare Sliced Tomatoes

(Mrs. M. L. Meriwether)

Let the tomatoes be cold and crisp, slice into a deep dish. Make the following dressing and pour over them: Into a saucepan put one teaspoonful of mustard, one of salt, one egg and a tablespoonful of brown sugar; stir well together, add two tablespoonfuls of sweet milk, one-half cup of vinegar. Put on the stove and stir constantly till it comes to a boil. If you like you can add a little sweet oil while the dressing is cooking. This dressing is nice for lettuce or any other salad.

Exploring Further

Recipe lovers intrigued by the social, educational, and political circles of Ida Bailey may also be interested in *Southern Homecoming Traditions: Recipes and Remembrances*. In this 2006 work, author Carolyn Quick Tillery explores the food traditions of Atlanta's HBCUs.[26] Cooking traditions from the Sweet Auburn area of Atlanta can be found in the 1986 Ebenezer Baptist Church's *Edibles from Ebenezer*, and recipes from the family of Martin Luther King Jr. (1929–1968) can be found in *GG's Home for the Holidays Cookbook* by Alveda King.[27] The National Council of Negro Women put out two cookbooks containing a few recipes connected to prominent Georgians: *The Historical Cookbook of the American Negro* (1958) and *The Black Family Reunion Cookbook* (1991).

The Georgia Mystery Cookbooks File and Mrs. Bell

One Hundred Choice Dishes for One Hundred Cents, 1897
Mrs. Emma Bell
37 pages. 105 recipes.

"MRS. BELL'S COOK BOOK, the best on the market,
for sale by Geo. M. Downs, 12½ N. Broad street.
Lady agents wanted."

One of my keyword searches through digitized newspapers turned up the above advertisement in the back pages of the 20 March 1898 edition of the *Atlanta Constitution*. Excited about another nineteenth-century cookbook from Atlanta, I fired up my computer connecting me to a world of online search engines, catalogs, and databases. Nothing. I added it to my archives search list and tried all my best research tricks. Still nothing. With a sigh, I finally consigned Mrs. Bell to my "Georgia Mystery Cookbooks" file. Little did I know that a few years later the snippet advertisement would point toward a widowed mother with dozens of "boys," a baseball game presided over by a whip-wielding Atlanta mayor, and the nostalgia of one of our capital's last original antebellum lampposts.

Sometimes help doesn't come from a screen or page, but from a person. I came across a note on the webpage of Georgia cookbook author Cynthia Graubart that she was working on a history of the state's community cookbooks. A kindred spirit! I was a little awed by Cynthia's impressive bio, but I reached out and soon found myself navigating my car through a spring downpour to her Atlanta area home. Umbrella left dripping by the door, I was welcomed into a living room fragrant with hot tea and zucchini bread. (Tip: Should you find yourself seeking to compare research notes with a cookbook author, meet up at a time when they are testing recipes.) Before long, Cynthia offered not just baking samples but a chance to look at some of her collected treasures. "Have you ever seen this one?" she asked. And there in my hands was a cookbook by a Mrs. Bell.

This cookbook was not intended to be a kitchen workhorse. Published at a time when most cookbooks were small hardcovers, *One Hundred Dishes for One Hundred Cents* is an oversized softcover thin enough to be called a pamphlet. The title is in gold lettering across gray-blue cardstock, and holes for a ribbon on the side reminded me of a fancy restaurant menu. As for the title, I checked cookbook prices in newspaper advertisements in 1897, finding a range from 75¢ to $2.50, so perhaps Mrs. Bell's cookbook sold for a dollar. The dishes inside could be called "middle of the road"—most neither too elaborate nor too plain. There are Escalloped Oysters, Chicken Coquille, and Charlotte Russe but also muffins, hash, and vegetable soup. The paragraph-style recipes are somewhat minimal and thus best suited for experienced cooks. The Roast Turkey recipe on page 15, for example, simply instructs the reader to add gravy made "the usual way." Instructions in other recipes are also vague at times: "thicken with a little flour," "bake slowly," or add "a little butter." Unlike most of the cookbooks we've looked at so far, it offers no general cooking tips or commentary. Despite a publication date near the turn of the twentieth century, there are elements recalling older cooking traditions—referring to baking powder as "yeast powder" or recommending storing food in stone crocks.

Cynthia graciously encouraged me to use my cell phone's camera to capture each page of the cookbook, so I had ample time to examine the text for clues once back in my home office. First I wanted to see if "Mrs. Bell's Cook Book" from the advertisement and *One Hundred Choice Dishes* were one and the same. The cookbook shared by Cynthia was printed by Franklin Printing and Publishing, an Atlanta company established near the start of the Civil War that later specialized in publications for the state government as well as several periodicals such as the *Southern Cultivator* agricultural journal.[1] The George Downs mentioned in the ad was indeed an employee of Franklin Printing and Publishing.[2] Furthermore, the advertisement came out just a few months after the publication of *One Hundred Choice Dishes*. Although I found no evidence that the company tried any further to promote the cookbook either as "Mrs. Bell's" or under its official title, an advertisement at that time made sense. I even realized that I'd already come across the cookbook's recipe for fruit cake, credited to Mrs. Bell but shared by a Mrs. Lida Drane Hall in the 1909 *Macon Cook Book*.[3]

There was another part to the mystery. Who was Emma Bell? "Emma" was a popular name for the period, and "Bell" isn't uncommon, so the census as well as old newspapers offered many leads to follow. Emma Bell Miles (1879–1919), for instance, was an Appalachian naturalist and writer who lived not far from Chattanooga.[4] But there was one Emma Bell mentioned with far greater regularity than the rest. She ran a boardinghouse often lauded for its good food, and she retired in 1897, the same year as the publication of *One Hundred Choice Dishes*.[5]

Intrigued by glimpses of an institution that was famed for its cuisine a century ago but now largely forgotten, I continued along this avenue of research. Some accounts of boardinghouse manager Emma Bell made her several years younger than the dates eventually carved into her Westview Cemetery tombstone: 3 August 1843 to 3 March 1914.[6] Both the *Atlanta Journal* and the *Atlanta Constitution* covered her death with substantial obituaries, giving her age as sixty-six instead of seventy.[7] The rest of the facts seemed to line up with what can be found in census records, city directories, and other sources.[8] Mrs. Bell began life as Emma Edwards in Vicksburg, Mississippi.[9] She married a Confederate veteran and cotton broker named John Bell before giving birth to a daughter in Selma, Alabama, in 1867.[10] In her mid-twenties she gave birth to a son and became a widow.[11] Her *Atlanta Journal* obituary reported that in her early widowhood she was "penniless" and had no means of support. "Only a few days before her husband's death she had transferred a $10,000 paid up life insurance policy to pay his debts."[12] By 1872 she was taking in a few renters, and by 1874 she was running a boarding establishment soon well known in Atlanta as Bell House.[13]

As the years went by, Bell House moved to various locations including buildings on Walton Street and Pryor Street.[14] The heyday of the establishment, however, was when it was located on Peachtree Street. Bell House moved several times along Atlanta's "main street," including many years in the stately antebellum Leyden House with its tall white columns, which survived the destruction of the Civil War by being commandeered as Union headquarters.[15] On the grounds was one of Atlanta's original gas lampposts that first lit up Atlanta on Christmas night of 1855.[16] Mrs. Bell called this beacon "a sentinel angel over my boys."[17] Around fifty men at a time lived at Bell House, and their ranks included bankers, doctors, businessmen, at least one professor, and more than one judge.[18] Despite their distinguished careers, they were referred to as Bell House Boys, and many of them may have indeed been immature at their arrival. One newspaper article listed some of the men "who had been with Mrs. Bell ever since they left their mothers."[19] In a tribute several years after Bell's death, one former boarder stated, "I have seen young men come there as green as gourds. I have seen them eat with their knives and say, 'Have you saw Jim Smith?' I have seen them stay there less than five years, and Mrs. Bell made polished gentlemen and successful business men out of them. . . . Mrs. Bell has been a most powerful influence in the building of Atlanta, and the city owes her much for the men she has made."[20]

Lest it seem that Bell House was something of a finishing school for those with stiff upper lips, for many years Atlanta newspapers were sprinkled with appealing accounts of the goings-on at Bell House. There were seemingly endless evenings spent chatting on the veranda, mild pranks (including pokes at the apparently good-natured Mrs. Bell), reunion barbecues, charity projects, summer concerts by moonlight, and even an annual fundraising baseball game against the members of the Capital City Club.[21] In 1907, then-current Atlanta mayor and one of the first Bell House Boys, Walthall "Cap" Joyner (1854–1925), was pressed into umpire service.[22] He brought a buggy whip onto the field to help with the task, but still the Bell House Boys lost.[23]

And then there was the food. Former Bell House Boy I. S. Jonas reflected in an 1893 newspaper piece, "After all, the kitchen is the foundation of social structure in our highest and best civilization, and Mrs. Bell's has been famous for nearly two decades. Such steaks—thick, juicy, red and tender. Salads perfumed with just the faintest conceivable whiff of onions, with dressing that diffuses its rare aroma throughout the senses. Coffee black as night and bitter as sorrow. She controls the flavor of the pudding and the amount of salt in the soup, and we boys have grown to love the taste of her custards and waffles as we the love the faces and voices of one another."[24] Fourteen years later, Jonas continued his newspaper reveries: "Her table was the first to be supplied with the season's earliest strawberries, peaches, asparagus and spring chickens. The Peachtree street millionaires couldn't coerce the dealers to sell them their choicest products until Mrs. Bell saw fit to voluntarily break her monopoly. And, O, ye dyspeptic consumers of hot bread! Can ye not remember the snowy color, and flaky texture, and feathery lightness of those wonderful buttermilk biscuits and billowy, yeasty rolls imprisoning the melting flavor of Getty's golden butter! Mrs. Emma Bell—a goddess, who all her life has given what was good. She understands the art of making life happy by making the best of everything."[25]

Yes, *One Hundred Choice Dishes* does cover the foods listed by Jonas, which might be another clue connecting the cookbook to the boardinghouse. If they are indeed connected, then another name should be introduced. Some of the culinary magic of Bell House surely also rested with its head cook, Malinda Fuller. Records are sparse for Fuller, but both the *Atlanta Constitution* and the *Atlanta Journal* announced her death one week after Emma Bell's in March of 1914, noting she was "a great favorite" with the Bell House Boys who called her Aunt Malinda.[26] According to census records, Fuller was a Black mother of two. She and her husband, brick mason Osborn Fuller, had been living with Bell since at least 1900.[27] Upon her death at age fifty-seven, Malinda had been working for Bell House for seventeen years, and thus even though she was listed in the census as illiterate, she was instrumental in the Bell House kitchen during the time *One Hundred Choice Dishes* was published.[28]

Is there enough evidence to link the advertisement, *One Hundred Choice Dishes*, and Bell House? The publication date coinciding with the year Emma Bell officially retired is compelling. I then compiled a list of Bell House Boys

The Georgia Mystery Cookbooks File

There are still three cookbook mysteries. If anyone knows about these authors or works, please contact me through the University of Georgia Press.

- On 18 June 1876 the *Columbus Daily Enquirer* stated, "Mrs. M. J. Jourdan, of Atlanta, is publishing 'A New Cook Book with Original Recipes.'"
- On 9 September 1881 the *Columbus Daily Enquirer* reported, "We have received a cook book which is compiled by Mrs. A. E. Radcliff, of this city. Mrs. Radcliff is as thoroughly posted on culinary affairs as any lady in the land, and her book will be of much value to young housekeepers as well as others."
- On 17 February 1894 Atlanta's *Sunny South* newspaper contained an advertisement for *Woman's Work* magazine (Athens) that listed various books that would be serialized in that periodical including *Leaves from My Cookbook* by Hannah Hughes. "These are old reliable Georgia and Virginia Recipes, interspersed with many quotations from history and fiction concerning the art of cooking. It has been pronounced by well-known writers and housekeepers the most valuable collection of culinary matter yet to be found."

What Became of Bell House?

Emma Bell's 1897 retirement didn't seem to be a strict one.[1] She simply moved across the street, and there are many early twentieth-century articles linking her to Bell House. Her obituary added, "Those of her 'boys' who left the house from year to year never were sick or weary but Mrs. Bell knows where to find them and help them with the smooth touch of her hand or the gentle words from her wise and tender heart."[2]

Upon the deaths of Bell and Fuller, life at Bell House wavered and changed, but the "Boys" took it upon themselves to organize as a club, install leaders, and incorporate.[3] At some point Georgia cookbook author Annie Dennis (see 1894 section) was even brought in to cook.[4] In 1917 the Bell House Boys dug up their lamppost and moved to another location on Peachtree Street. The previous building had been bought by Coca-Cola entrepreneur Asa Candler, who soon discovered the extent of Bell's easygoing management style. Usually sale of a property means turning over the keys, but Bell House had gone unlocked for at least twenty years, and no keys could be found.[5] Several more moves occurred before the end of Bell House in 1951 when the club was down to just eight members.[6] The lamppost was then donated to the Atlanta Historical Society, which has become the Atlanta History Center.[7] I contacted the staff and was assured the post is preserved as part of the city's history. Bell House's culinary excellence is part of the city's history as well. Even after Bell House was no more, famed Georgia journalist Celestine Sibley reminded readers, "there were boardinghouses that were famous for their cuisine. Bell House in Atlanta was such a place."[8]

1. *AC*, 17 June 1897.
2. *AJ*, 3 March 1914.
3. *AJ*, 9 March and 22 April 1914.
4. Frank Daniel, "Bell House to Close after Long Tradition," *AJ*, 24 December 1950.
5. *AC*, 10 April 1917.
6. *AC*, 22 November 1951.
7. *AC*, 16 November 1951.
8. Celestine Sibley, "Boarding House Is Mourned," *AC*, 23 February 1956.

from newspaper articles and hoped to find one of them connected with either the publishing house or the reprinted fruit cake recipe. No such luck. This is the way of history research. Sometimes we must leave something as "probable yet inconclusive," hoping more evidence surfaces as time marches on. In the meantime, we can enjoy reviving the recipes!

Soda Biscuit (3)

One quart flour, one kitchen-spoonful of lard worked into the flour. Sift one even teaspoonful of soda and a little salt into flour. Mix with buttermilk into a soft dough. Knead well, roll, cut out with biscuit ring, and bake in hot oven.

Beefsteak and Onions (10)

Dip into flour one pound thick, tender steak. Sprinkle on it a little salt. Put into a skillet a kitchen-spoonful of lard. Let it get hot. Have ready one pint of chopped onions. Stew in a little water until tender. Drop steak into hot lard. Brown on both sides and take up. Drop stewed onions into same lard. After they are pretty brown, sprinkle a little flour in the pan. Pour in a little water to make gravy. When ready, pour over steak and serve.

Exploring Further

The 1894 section gives brief information about Atlanta boardinghouses run by Annie Dennis. There are several Georgia cookbooks that share recipes of restaurants that began as early twentieth-century boardinghouses: Mrs. Wilkes' (Savannah), Smith House (Dahlonega), and Dillard House (Dillard).[29]

Georgia's Turn-of-the-Century Community Cookbooks

The Hapeville Presbyterian Cook Book, 1898
Hapeville Presbyterian Church
76 pages (with advertisements). 250 food recipes and 24 household recipes.
Contributors not listed.

The Home Cook Book, 1898
Emmanuel [Episcopal] Church, Athens
158 pages (with advertisements). 347 food recipes and 8 household recipes.
Contributors listed.

The Southern Housekeeper: A Book of Tested Recipes, 1898
Central Presbyterian Church, Atlanta
144 pages (with advertisements). 489 food recipes and 36 household recipes.
Contributors not listed.

There isn't a hard definition for what makes a cookbook a "community cookbook." *The Dixie Cook-Book* (1883 section) and *House-Keeping in the Sunny South* (1885) are a little tangled in terms of who did the compiling, how wide the recipe-collecting field was, and who benefited from the sale of the cookbook. The 1880 *Choice Recipes* (Augusta) and 1892 *Hints from Southern Epicures* (Savannah), created by committees and filled with recipes from locals, are a little more comfortable to call community cookbooks. I don't know what was going on in 1898—maybe something in the biscuit flour? Georgia saw three more church cookbooks published in a single year.

The first time I picked up *The Home Cook Book,* it was an odd sensation. I'm used to the nudge of history in my hometown of Athens through old buildings and monuments, but southern foodways expert John T. Edge was right when he observed that "fund-raising cookbooks can be read as community histories."[1] Here was a fragile book more than a century old that swirled up personal memories, strengthening my sense of community. Emmanuel Episcopal's Gothic granite building on Prince Avenue is a steadfast fixture for every living Athenian. When I was a middle-schooler, a teacher coaxed me into serving as a junior docent for Emmanuel's Christmastime building tour. Although the cookbook doesn't say so, it was likely written to raise funds for that very building; the cookbook came out between the 1895 laying of the cornerstone and the 1899 completion.[2] The cookbook's advertisement for McGregor stationers suddenly brought up memories of my mother purchasing typewriter ribbons there. Despite the passage of a century and a quarter, my life intersected with the history preserved in the cookbook.

Similar thoughts come about when I pick up *Choice Recipes*, a 1910 cookbook from the First Presbyterian Church just five blocks to the east. This cookbook, too, was supported by McGregor's. In the dozen years between the two cookbooks, the business got a telephone—and there were so few phones in Athens that the number was just two digits. There's a Shredded Wheat advertisement boasting a lady in a leg-o'-mutton-sleeved shirtwaist blouse, her hair swept up Gibson Girl style, as well as one for Costa's, a pre–World War II confectionery and soda fountain so wonderful that old ladies (once girls in leg-o'-mutton sleeves with upswept hair) still reminisced about it when I was a child. Some of the surnames of the cookbook contributors are familiar from street signs and the names of university buildings—including the route to my father's office (Soule, Rutherford, Snelling) and my college dorm (Mell Hall) as well as dorms around it (Lipscomb and Brumby).

Early community cookbooks serve as connection points, allowing us to relate to history in a personal, grassroots way. They can also help us learn about regional and national foodways. Historian Frank Boles noted that community cookbooks focus on favorite local recipes. "Because of this narrow focus, fundraising cookbooks became, quite unintentionally, the first American 'regional' cookbooks and also provide a record of how recipes moved from region to region."[3]

My research turned up forty-six Georgia community cookbooks from sixteen counties before 1945. As much as I would love to touch on all of them here, there are simply too many. What is most important to the discussion, however, is that community cookbooks are often particularly hard to find and vulnerable to loss. In many archives, until they are at least a century old, they aren't treated as rare books or pamphlets but instead left uncataloged in clippings files. Small historical societies that collect local materials often pass them by. Even when it comes to recent community cookbooks, you'll rarely find a copy at the local library. There are reasons for this. Community cookbooks are usually sold only by the organizations that created them, and print runs are small. The bindings can be fragile. But the main reason is that, traditionally, they don't garner much respect. Despite their historical and cultural value, they have long been dismissed for reflecting home life and "women's stuff." (The cover of one recent Georgia community cookbook shows a row of dancing teddy bears in chef hats, so sometimes the lack of respect is easy to understand. But remember that old truth about not judging a book by its cover?)

The Athens Regional Library System is one institution working to solve the problem. Their Archives & Special Collections is gathering community cookbooks both old and new from the five northeast counties the system serves.[4] Volunteers do most of the legwork to collect the cookbooks, keeping track of the collection by database while the new additions are being cataloged. Related displays and programs help promote the effort, which has been named the Laura Billups McCray Community Cookbook Collection after the famed Athens cook discussed in the 1886 section. In time, hopefully more libraries and historical societies will begin to collect local cookbooks as well.

Cold Slaw

Shred the cabbage fine enough to fill a quart dish. Dressing: Boil one-half cup of vinegar, pour it over 2 well-beaten eggs, dessertspoonful of sugar, teaspoonful of mustard, one-fourth cup of cream, teaspoonful butter, then return to the fire and cook until it is the consistency of thick cream. When cold, pour over the slaw, salt and pepper to taste.

Hot Slaw

As cold slaw, except pour the dressing over the cabbage while it is hot, and cover dish closely for 15 minutes on the back of the stove.

—*The Hapeville Presbyterian Cook Book*, 56

Georgia Chicken Pie

Cut up and boil well one or two chickens, according to size. Line the sides of a deep dish with rich pastry [crust]; then put in a layer of chicken, with pepper, salt and butter, a few slices of hard boiled egg and very thin strips of biscuit dough. Continue the layers until the dish is filled, then add the liquor the fowls were boiled in; dredge with a little flour, and cover with pastry. Make a hole in the center large enough to permit adding more liquor should the pie become too dry while baking. Slices of Irish potatoes may be added, if desired. Bake quickly.

—Mrs. Josiah Sibley, *The Home Cook Book*, Athens, 34

Peanut Sandwiches

Stale bread, thinly sliced and well buttered. Roasted peanuts, chopped up into a fine paste, and well mixed with mayonnaise, or thick cream. Salt to taste, and spread thickly between the slices of bread. Fashionable hostesses, when setting them on a plate, tie them up with narrow brown ribbon, having the same tint as the paste.

— Unattributed, *The Home Cook Book*, Athens, 125

Larded Potatoes

Pare and punch a hole through the potato lengthwise, roll a thin piece of seasoned bacon and put it in the potato; bake until done; serve hot.

—*The Southern Housekeeper*, Atlanta, 23

Orange Drops

Grate the rind of 1 orange and squeeze out the juice, taking care to remove the seeds. Add to this a pinch of tartaric acid; stir in confectioner's sugar until it is stiff enough to form into balls. This is a delicious candy.

—*The Southern Housekeeper*, Atlanta, 134

[An average orange yields four to five tablespoons of juice. For each tablespoon of juice, you'll need at least one cup of powdered sugar. Granulated citric acid derived from citrus fruits can be used in place of grape-derived tartaric acid, but be sure it is labeled "food grade." Because tart candy is a cultural norm for modern kids, I use up to a teaspoon of acid. Admittedly, an electric stand mixer is the fast tool for this recipe, but hands or a potato masher is the old-fashioned way.]

Drummers' Home Cook Book and the Town Hotel

Drummers' Home Cook Book, 1902
Alice Eleanor Gobert Roberts Britt (17 June 1853?–15 May 1921)
120 pages. 356 recipes.

When you're a kid stuck in the backseat on a road trip your family repeats multiple times a year, you soon have favorite landmarks. On our way to the coast, the small town of Sparta had a regal courthouse that loomed above the highway. Beside it there was a huge building with a broad porch and tall white columns, its historical marker too hard to read as we whizzed past. If we had stopped to read that marker at 12664 W. Broad Street, I would have been fascinated that our family station wagon was bisecting the old Augusta-to-Macon stagecoach line and that the big building stood on the spot of the 1700s Eagle Tavern. (See 1783 section.) It was there in 1825 that local citizens treated the Revolutionary War hero Marquis de Lafayette (1757–1834) to a ball during his grand tour of the United States (1824–1825). The celebration menu is now lost to time, but more Georgia foodways would flourish on that spot. After the tavern burned sometime in the 1830s, the columned Edwards' House hotel took its place. Traveler James Buckingham wrote that his lodging conditions in Sparta in 1839 were "the most revolting we had yet witnessed."[1] (We don't know where he stayed.) By the 1890s the situation was vastly improved, and Edwards House had become Drummers' Home, a hotel marketed to "drummers" or traveling salesmen.[2] Run by Alice Roberts, "universally known as Miss Alice," Drummers' Home rose to

Mollie's Place

On Jordan's Stormy Banks: Personal Accounts of Slavery in Georgia shares narratives recorded by the Federal Writer's Project including one by Mollie Kinsey, who was born around 1855 in Washington, Georgia, and later moved to Sparta.[1] "Mr. Britt, a businessman there in Sparta, and for whose wife I'd nursed, would tell people to go down to eat at Mollie's Place. I fed white and colored. I had a place in the front where I served the white, and they liked my vittles too. Soldiers, railroad men, and drummers come to eat at my place." Sadly, none of Kinsey's recipes are known to survive, but even her brief narrative helps us better picture foodways in her time and place.

1. Andrew Waters, *On Jordan's Stormy Banks*, 19–24; quote at 22.

prominence.[3] "Miss Alice was a superb cook and the hotel was so pleasant that traveling salesmen would bring their families there for the 'winter season,'" recalled one former guest.[4] An elaborate garden provided fresh produce for the kitchen.[5] In 1900 it was voted the most popular hotel in Georgia and awarded a silver wine dispenser by the Georgia Hotel Association.

Within two years of her triumph, Roberts released a cookbook, sold by area merchants and newspaper offices for seventy-five cents.[6] Foodways historian Mary Barile points out that "food establishment cookbooks," recipe compilations connected to restaurants or hotels, were sometimes sold as souvenirs at the establishment,[7] so the cookbook may have been available at Drummers' Home as well. "Housekeepers seeking reliable recipes, economical, as well as delicious and dainty, will find the contents of this little book helpful, simple and in reach of all," states the author in her brief introduction, which she signed simply as "Alice Roberts." Five of the recipes are directly credited to Drummers' Home, which may indicate that they were specialties. The one for biscuits on page 56 shows some of the challenges modern readers face with this cookbook.

"Drummers' Home" Baking Powder Biscuits

One large package Horseford's [*sic*] baking powder to fifty pounds of flour well sifted together. Then to one quart of this flour add one teaspoon of soda, one tablespoon lard; mix to a soft dough with buttermilk; roll out, cut and bake in a quick oven.

Converting *fifty* pounds of flour into homemade self-rising flour?! Someone with a large family making biscuits every day might not have blinked at that, but ordinary people would need to know how large a "large package" of Horsford's baking powder was, and then measure out one-fiftieth of that to go with a pound of flour. While most of the cookbook's recipes are in smaller proportions, many of the recipes lack details (here, how much buttermilk to make a "soft dough") that would help modern readers turn out a dish just like Miss Alice's. Still, there is much here to inspire. Despite the vague nature of the cookbook, the first three recipes I tried worked wonderfully and are "keepers" I'll make over and over again—Sweet Pickle Apples, Noodles for Soup, and Egg Balls.

Looking for the march of history on the cookbook's pages, the reader can tell that Roberts cooked from a pantry that was more modern than those of the cookbook authors before her. There is a marked jump in the number of ingredients that would have been purchased rather than grown. Roberts calls for many canned food products and a dozen name-brand ingredients. She is also connected to community: forty-six of the recipes are credited to twenty-four contributors. Locations for contributors aren't always mentioned, but some hailed from Augusta and Milledgeville.

Speaking of community, let's place Roberts and her recipes in a social context. Alice was born into the large farming family of James and Eleanor Gobert in Louisville.[8] Her tombstone gives her birth year as 1858, but other evidence points to 1853.[9] In 1874 Alice married twenty-four-year-old William C. D. Roberts of Milledgeville, who worked with his brother editing the Louisville newspaper *Jefferson News & Farmer* until 1875.[10] In 1879 Alice's father bought out the Roberts family shoe business for William to run.[11] In the 1880 census William is a "shoemaker," while Alice is "keeping house," and her retired father is the head of the household.[12] In 1884 William and Alice had a son, John.[13] Yet what looked like domestic stability didn't last.

An 1892 newspaper article refers to Alice as William's wife, but by the 1900 census he was a boarder living solo in Milledgeville.[14] The date is uncertain, but the couple divorced at a time when such things were rare. A few years later, another blow was the 1906 death of their twenty-three-year-old son from malaria.[15] John was buried in Sparta Cemetery just two blocks from Drummers' Home with a tombstone that reads "So many fond hopes lie buried here." But all hopes were not gone for Alice. She had already largely overcome the stigmas of the day regarding divorce, single motherhood, and women working outside the home. Then, in her own hotel on Christmas Day of 1912, Alice married W. H. Britt (1861–1934), a fifty-one-year-old divorced buggy salesman who later served as mayor of Sparta (1926–1930).[16] When Alice died in 1921 in her mid-sixties, she was buried in a grave next to her son.[17] Her tombstone defines her by her relationships: "Wife of William Hewell Britt, Mother of John Roberts." It also states, "She Hath Done What She Could." Indeed, she left behind a successful business that Britt took over with the help of his "new old wife." (After Alice died, Britt remarried wife number one.)[18] Although Drummers' Home ceased to be a hotel in the middle of the twentieth century, Alice's foodways legacy lives on in her recipes.

Lye Hominy (50–51)

One peck white selected corn, one peck of strong hickory ashes tied up in a strong thick bag or sack free from holes. Boil in a ten gallon pot full of water and cook until nearly done, till heart of corn begins to cook out in the pot. Then remove from the lye; wash until water is clear; then wash pot clean; put in the corn, then fill with water and cook till done and soft; then mash and fry in sausage grease or butter. This makes a delicious breakfast dish.

—Hester Allen, one of Drummers' Home Cooks[19]

Lafayette Gingerbread

Legend has it that George Washington's mother, Mary Ball Washington (1708–1789), once served pleasing gingerbread to Lafayette, and recipes for this treat named in his honor were later found in various American cookbooks. One wonders if Lafayette was served gingerbread in Sparta—and everywhere else he went. Sparta wasn't the only Georgia town to honor Lafayette in 1825. In Savannah, for instance, he stayed several nights in the Owens-Thomas House and addressed a crowd from the side balcony.[1] An article on Lafayette in the *New Georgia Encyclopedia* outlines his thirteen-day, four-hundred-mile tour of the state.[2]

LA FAYETTE GINGER CAKE.

One half pound of butter, a half pound of sugar, one pint of molasses, seven eggs, one and a half pounds of flour, four table-spoons of ginger, two and a half dozen cloves, two and a half dozen allspice, one small stick of cinnamon, and one teaspoon of soda dissolved in vinegar. The spices must be pounded together. Bake in pattie-pans.

A recipe from *Verstille's Southern Cookery* (1866), 108.

I've snapped photos of "Lafayette was here" markers across Georgia and up the Eastern Seaboard as far north as Niagara Falls. I was not expecting to see one in Olomouc, Czech Republic, yet found exactly that while wandering the streets during breaktime from a conference. A sign informed me that Lafayette was imprisoned there in the late 1790s. To my amusement, I returned to the conference venue to find that the refreshments placed out for the attendees included gingerbread! And the placard wasn't my only lesson that trip about how far-flung and interwoven history and foodways can be. I was also surprised to find that Royal Crown Cola is popular in the Czech Republic, and every can is graced with a picture of Claud Hatcher (1876–1933), the inventor from Columbus, Georgia. (Unfortunately, Hatcher is buried in Columbus's Riverdale Cemetery. It would have been more fun if he had been laid to rest near Coca-Cola inventor John Pemberton [1831–1888] in Linwood Cemetery less than three miles away.)

1. W. S. Kirkpatrick, "Now the Public Sees Where Lafayette Slept," *AC*, 20 March 1960.
2. Martha Keber, "Marquis de Lafayette in Georgia," *New Georgia Encyclopedia*, www.georgiaencyclopedia.org.

Cream Pie (78–79)

Three eggs, one cup sugar, one cup flour, two teaspoons cream tartar, one of soda dissolved in a little warm water. Sift cream tartar in the flour. This quantity makes two pies. Make them in thin tins. When cold, split and put in the cream. Cream for inside: One pint milk, one-half cup sugar, one-half cup flour, two eggs. Beat eggs, sugar and flour together; pour into milk when boiling. Season with vanilla.

—Aunt Florry Wilkins[20]

Sweet Pickle Apples (107)

Take one teacup vinegar, two of sugar, one teaspoon cloves and cinnamon mixed. If spices are ground put them in bag. Pare and core sweet apples; drop them in the syrup just as it comes to a boil and cook until tender, not soft. Put in a jar and pour syrup over them. They are ready to eat soon as cold. Try these, sisters, they are delicious.

Noodles for Soup (9)

Beat one egg light, add a pinch of salt and flour enough to make a very stiff dough, roll out in very thin sheet, dredge with flour, then roll up tightly. Begin at one end and shave down fine like cabbage for slaw, then throw them into the soup. Boil three or four minutes and serve.

Egg Balls (10)

Two hardboiled yolks of eggs, mix with the yolk of one raw egg and a little flour, roll the size of a hazelnut. Drop in soup and let cook about ten minutes.

"Drummer's Home" Favorite Dressing (33)

Twelve biscuits, four corn meal muffins, one large onion, one kitchen spoon fine cut parsley, one tablespoon butter, one pint sweet milk and one egg. Mix all thoroughly except parsley and the onions, and fry in hot grease until a golden brown. Remove from fire and add the onion, cut very fine, and the parsley. Season with salt and pepper. One pint of oysters drained, added to this recipe, instead of onion and parsley, makes a delicious oyster dressing. On state occasions add to the oyster dressing one teacup of pecans or old field walnuts. When the nuts are used leave out the butter.

Thomas Gingerbread

LaGrange educator Theodora Thomas (1905–1986) donated papers to the Troup County Archives that outlined the family genealogy, including the career of her great-grandfather, well-known bridge builder Horace King (1807–1885). Born into slavery, King earned enough money to purchase his freedom and built a strong reputation for his work as an architect and engineer.[1] Although he lived much of his life in Alabama, King moved his home and business to LaGrange in the early 1870s.

Thomas's collection includes sixteen family recipes.[2] A quarter of them are for gingerbread, a baked good that has been popular for centuries in forms both soft (sheet cake or drop cakes) and firm (cutout cookies, snaps, ginger-nuts).[3] In fact, gingerbread in some form appears in every single one of Georgia's nineteenth-century cookbooks.

As is often the case with manuscript recipe collections, the Thomas recipes are all undated. We'll use Theodora Thomas's birth year to settle gingerbread into our chronological exploration of Georgia recipes.

As is also sadly the case in many manuscript collections, the Thomas recipes are difficult to decipher due to aging paper and ink as well as damage caused by years of use. The most legible of the Thomas gingerbread recipes is shown here and is simply a list of ingredients with no method. It is scaled to feed a crowd, calling for two gallons of molasses and five gallons of flour! Interestingly, it also calls for cocoa. The recipe transcription below is from the most complete of the Thomas gingerbread recipes, although the original is faded enough that drastically adjusting the contrast on a digital photograph of the recipe was necessary to read it, and some words are still difficult to decipher; these are indicated by brackets.

Soft Ginger Cookies

1 cup of molasses.
1¾ " " sugar.
1¾ tsp. soda.
1 cup of sour milk.
½ " " shortening.
2 tsp. of ginger.
1 tsp. " salt.
Flour.

Add soda to molasses [and] beat. Add milk, shortening, ginger, salt, and flour. Enough flour must be ad[ded] to make mixture of right consiste[ncy] to drop easily from spoon. Let stand several hours to [thoroughly] chill. Toss ½ mixture on [board] slightly floured and roll lightly to ¼ ins thick, shape with round cutter. Bake on buttered [baking] sheets.

—Theodora Thomas Collection, 1890–1930, Troup County Archives, LaGrange[4]

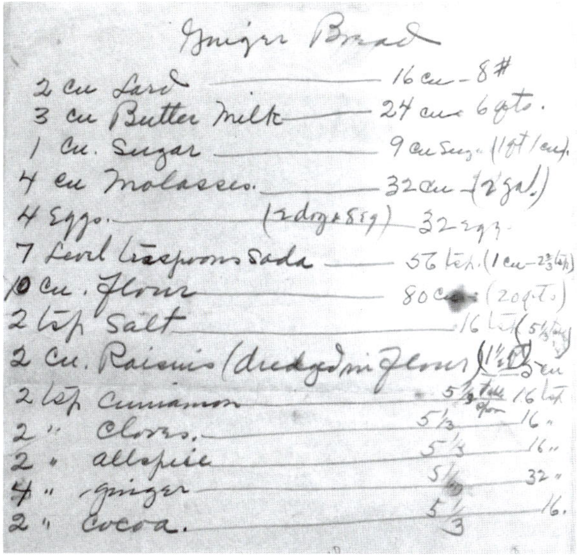
Ginger Bread
2 cu Lard — 16 cu – 8#
3 cu Butter milk — 24 cu 6 qts.
1 cu. Sugar — 9 cu Sug.
4 cu molasses — 32 cu (2 gal.)
4 Eggs — 32 egg
7 level teaspoons soda — 56 tea.
10 cu. Flour — 80 cu (20 qts)
2 tsp Salt — 16 t
2 cu. Raisins (dredged in flour)
2 tsp Cinnamon — 5⅓ — 16 tsp
2 " Cloves. — 5⅓ — 16 "
2 " allspice — 5⅓ — 16 "
4 " ginger — 5⅓ — 32 "
2 " Cocoa. — 5⅓ — 16.

Permission to include photograph of recipe is courtesy of the Troup County Archives.

Localism and Chicken

Regional food and culinary customs remain important because they are a collective communal expression of a location from the lives of the people who have lived there. Like sourdough starter, such customs and products need to be nurtured, keeping a part of their past in the present—without which they fail.

—Jake Tilson, *A Tale of 12 Kitchens*, 29

There's something about chicken that inspires Georgia foodways.[1] Is this ingredient so common and universal that Georgians have long been determined to creatively make it their own? There are several chicken dishes that modern Georgians feel are "ours."[2]

Brunswick Stew

Full disclosure—I made my entrance into this world in a hospital in Brunswick, Georgia, and therefore have a vested interest in the dish beloved in our state since deep in the 1800s. In my birth town, Mary Ross Waterfront Park features an iron cauldron immortalized on a cement pedestal that reads: "In this pot the first Brunswick stew was made on St Simon Isle July 2 1898." Georgia's foodways legacy is *cemented in.*

Why, then, in 1988 did the Virginia General Assembly pass a resolution honoring their Brunswick County as the official birthplace of this stew?! The Virginia stance is that in 1828 a cook named Jimmy Matthews created the dish to feed a hunting party with a combination of squirrel, bacon, onions, butter, and stale bread that later became a "fixture" at political gatherings.[3] The more I researched, the more I got a sinking feeling. If you and I were having a face-to-face foodways discussion right now, I might mumble the following and then quickly change the subject: In the 1800s, many Georgia sources referred to Brunswick Stew as a Virginia dish.[4]

But is it only about dates? Georgia has an old recipe. Ellen Verstille in 1866 included this recipe for chicken-based Brunswick Stew.[5] (See also 1928 section.)

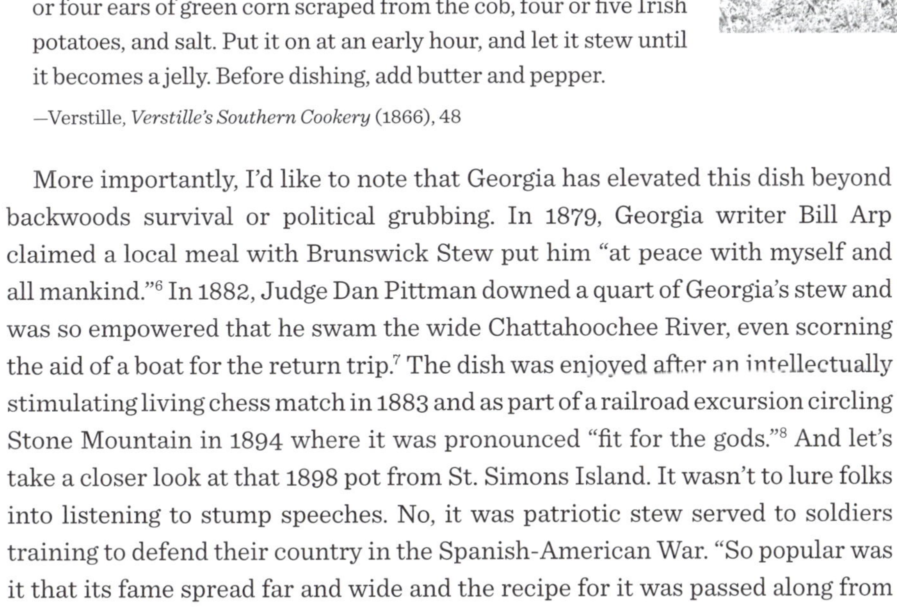

Brunswick Stew

Joint one chicken, and put it in a stewpan with sufficient water to cover it. Immediately add eight or ten tomatoes cut up, three or four ears of green corn scraped from the cob, four or five Irish potatoes, and salt. Put it on at an early hour, and let it stew until it becomes a jelly. Before dishing, add butter and pepper.

—Verstille, *Verstille's Southern Cookery* (1866), 48

More importantly, I'd like to note that Georgia has elevated this dish beyond backwoods survival or political grubbing. In 1879, Georgia writer Bill Arp claimed a local meal with Brunswick Stew put him "at peace with myself and all mankind."[6] In 1882, Judge Dan Pittman downed a quart of Georgia's stew and was so empowered that he swam the wide Chattahoochee River, even scorning the aid of a boat for the return trip.[7] The dish was enjoyed after an intellectually stimulating living chess match in 1883 and as part of a railroad excursion circling Stone Mountain in 1894 where it was pronounced "fit for the gods."[8] And let's take a closer look at that 1898 pot from St. Simons Island. It wasn't to lure folks into listening to stump speeches. No, it was patriotic stew served to soldiers training to defend their country in the Spanish-American War. "So popular was it that its fame spread far and wide and the recipe for it was passed along from friend to friend and from father to son."[9] A few years later, the stew of Macon's William K. Young (1869–1937) shone forth as the stuff of poetry:

Ah, Billie Young, how I envy you
That recipe by which you brew
The greatest dish that I ever knew,
That dear, delicious Brunswick stew.
When I partook of that heaping bowl,
I wished from the depths of my inner soul,
That Billie Young would ne'er grow ol',
And in Brunswick stew I'd always roll.[10]

I submit for the record that the true value in an old recipe isn't solely in its age but also in the power of its beloved traditions. Nay, in its ability to nurture body, mind, and soul. Perhaps Georgia's Brunswick Stew is not the oldest, but it is the most sublime. I rest my case.

Chicken Mull

Georgia claims another chicken stew. This one is pale and simple—chicken with onion, salt, pepper, and butter, then the whole thickened with crushed saltine crackers. Charles C. Doyle does a beautiful job exploring its history in his piece

"Mulling Over Mull," noting it as a specialty of Athens and giving a recipe, but I'll add some details. The earliest mention I could find of the dish is in a Danielsville newspaper from 1916.[11] In that first account, Chicken Mull is already a community dish, this one served at a "fishing frolic." (See 1840 section.) Like Brunswick Stew, Chicken Mull could be a stand-alone meal or served with barbecue.[12] The going price for a bowl in the early 1920s was twenty-five cents, but sometimes it was far cheaper.[13] A Depression-era newspaper scolded, "Sometimes boys steal chickens and have what they call a 'chicken mull' which also shows their allegiance to the evil side of life. Boys, if you are hungry ask for a piece of custard."[14] By midcentury, Chicken Mull was connected to tailgating parties for University of Georgia football games, particularly during the winning seasons of the 1940s.[15]

Doyle noted of this dish, "the familiarity diminishes sharply beyond a short radius of twenty-five miles from Athens."[16] A sprinkling of articles in early twentieth-century newspapers reveal a "Chicken Mull zone" in Northeast Georgia. Starting in Athens, one can drive an eighty-five-mile loop to visit the small towns most often linked to early newspaper mentions of Chicken Mull—Commerce, Carnesville, Royston, Danielsville, Colbert, and Hull. Georgians in this area may be surprised to learn that the village of Bear Grass all the way over in eastern North Carolina began an annual Chicken Mull Festival in 2013.[17] I probably used up my quota of smack talk in the Brunswick Stew portion of this section, so let me just state for the record that more than a century ago a Carolina newspaper called the dish "a Georgia special" and added, "it remains for the great state of Georgia to give us chicken mull."[18]

Country Captain

Country Captain is such the darling of historic foodways lovers that a slew of recent articles makes it difficult to write something new.[19] So how good is this chicken dish with its signature tomatoes and curry powder? Discussions of this dish often center around the Georgia town of Columbus, and one longtime legend is that a military general soon to pass through town wired ahead: "If you can't give me a party and have Country Captain, put some in a tin bucket and bring it to the train."[20] By the 1960s Sara Spano, food editor for the local newspaper, mused, "If you've lived here a long time you tend to think that everybody knows how to prepare this," and noted that the newspaper created a brochure to satisfy frequent inquiries about the recipe.[21]

Modern Country Captain recipes sometimes imply know-how for the dish was simply brought home from a mysterious sea voyage. The earliest Georgia evidence I could find is that in the early spring of 1880, a Country Captain recipe was passed along in American newspapers from the Northeast to the Midwest, reaching Georgia in May.[22] This version, however, was without tomatoes. Although not without contradictions in various sources, a more likely account of why this recipe is connected to Georgia is that Country Captain spread from Muscogee and Meriwether Counties in the early twentieth century. *Seasoned Skillets & Silver Spoons: A Culinary History of Columbus, Georgia* by Mary Hart Brumby (1914–2011) as well as local news articles of the day set the dish into a context of Georgia family and community.[23] The basics are that around 1906 Columbus matron Mary Bullard (1860–1943), daughter Mira Bullard Hart (1883–1977), and the family's cook, Arie Mullins (ca. 1875–1959), developed the Georgia version of the recipe from one in a 1906 cookbook by chef Alexander Filippini of New York's celebrated Delmonico restaurant.[24] (Thus the year for this section.) They worked with the recipe until it was one beloved by family and guests.[25] (Mullins, by the way, was a blue-ribbon-winning cook whose specialty was beaten biscuits.)[26] Beginning in 1920, area newspapers reported Country Captain served for special occasions.[27]

The Bullards were well connected, and eventually the social circles enjoying Country Captain extended to President Franklin D. Roosevelt, helping to secure the dish's fame. Following illness and paralysis in the early 1920s, Roosevelt began visiting Warm Springs to take advantage of naturally occurring thermal waters. Beginning in 1926 he helped open a therapeutic treatment center called the Georgia Warm Springs Foundation, which took over the old Meriwether Inn.[28] A former Inn cook from Fort Valley named Daisy Bonner (1902–1958) began cooking for Roosevelt whenever he was in town.[29] In his book *The President's Kitchen Cabinet: The Story of the African Americans Who Have Fed Our First Families, from the Washingtons to the Obamas*, Adrian Miller wrote, "Bonner took every opportunity to get FDR hooked on southern delicacies," mentioning such dishes as fried chicken, pigs' feet, turnip greens, hush puppies, and cornbread. Miller also mentioned Country Captain as a favorite for FDR.[30] Then one spring day in 1945, while Bonner was preparing his lunch, the president suddenly died. Standing in the kitchen afterwards, the stunned cook took up a pencil and wrote on the wall, "Daisy Bonner cook the 1st meal and the last one in this cottage for the President

Electric Range in Kitchen of the Little White House

The Dining Room
The Little White House, Warm Springs, Ga.

Staff at Roosevelt's Little White House near Warm Springs kindly gave their approval for including these postcards.

"It Tastes Like Chicken!"

Daisy Bonner feeding pig's feet to the president may surprise modern cooks, but like the terrapin discussed in the 1890 section, some proteins that now hardly seem like food at all once were delicacies. For instance, when plans were being made for president-elect William Howard Taft's January 1909 visit to Georgia, it was decided that the banquet would feature no fewer than a hundred opossums. The Atlanta Chamber of Commerce formed a 'Possum Committee.[1] Women began to sew plush toys upon hearing public arguments of "Billy 'Possum" named for Taft versus the "Teddy bear" named in honor of Theodore Roosevelt.[2] In the days leading up to the shindig, the newspaper reported that the prime hunting grounds of Worth County were "Possum Mad" with the efforts to locate enough animals to serve up.[3] One night a motorman in Macon even leaped from his streetcar into the shadows to catch one of the creatures—although when urged to send it north for the feast, he decided to eat it himself.[4]

Colonel Harry C. Fisher (1856–1926), onetime mayor of Newnan and "the Georgia Possum King," explained the finer points of opossum and outlined his plans to cook Taft's meal with his own hands, claiming, "Give us a 'possum-loving president and the white house will ring with peace and prosperity and joy for years to come."[5] On the fifteenth of January, Taft was pleased with the banquet, enjoying opossum with sweet potatoes and persimmon beer, and coming away with his own stuffed Billy 'Possum. In the end, however, it seems that the Georgia Possum King was spurned, and that caterer Charles Merritt had the honor of cooking Taft's meal—which also included soup from a 250-pound green turtle.[6] Merritt's recipe seems to have been hush-hush, although a month later it was reported that "the secret of the sweetness to the Taft 'possum is out."[7] Snowdrift brand shortening was the secret ingredient. (The oldest Georgia recipes I found for 'possum are in the 1894 cookbook of Annie Dennis[8]—roasted or stewed.)

1. "Near Menagerie Gathers," *AC*, 13 January 1909.
2. "Billy 'Possum Vs. Teddy Bear," *LE*, 13 January 1909.
3. "Worth County 'Possum Mad," *AC*, 9 January 1909.
4. "Caught This Fat 'Possum Out on Tattnall Square," *MT*, 13 January 1909.
5. "Many People Offer 'Possums for Taft," *Macon News*, 2 January 1909; "Hundreds of 'Possums for Taft," *AC*, 2 January 1909; "Fisher Cooks 'Possum for Pres.-Elect Taft," *AC*, 15 January 1909; "The Possum King," *Salt Lake (Utah) Herald-Republican*, 11 April 1909; "Harry C. Fisher Dies at Newnan," *AC*, 17 July 1926.
6. "Near Menagerie Gathers," *AC*, 13 January 1909.
7. "'Snowdrift' Used on Taft 'Possum," *AC*, 21 February 1909.
8. *Annie Dennis' Cook Book*, 184–185.

Roosevelt." The house is now known as Roosevelt's Little White House, a state historic site managed by the Georgia Department of Natural Resources, and Bonner's message is preserved for generations of visitors.

"When I first came to Warm Springs, I didn't know how to boil water," Bonner once admitted.[31] She later said, "I am studying hard to improve so that some day I may be the 'president of cooking.'"[32] After Bonner's death, prominent journalist Alice A. Dunnigan called her "a humble individual who had the imagination, the initiative and the aspiration to reach the top in her chosen field."[33] I am just sad that Bullard, Hart, Mullins, and Bonner never had a chance to learn about the creative homage recipe of Savannah bakery owner Cheryl Day for Country Captain Curry Hand Pies.[34]

Chicken Boudine

Orien Belle Andrews Cobb (1895–1987) was born in Greene County but later moved to Oconee County.[35] As a caterer of renown in nearby Athens beginning in the 1920s, she cooked for the inaugural parties of seven governors as well as for parties of four University of Georgia presidents.[36] One of her signature dishes still talked about in North Georgia was Chicken Boudine, graced with noodles, sherry, and mushrooms. Georgia cookbook author Rebecca Lang helped preserve Mrs. Cobb's legacy with her version of the recipe shared in her cookbook *Quick-Fix Southern*.[37]

Chicken Madeira

Daisy Smith Redman (1929–1983) of Savannah descended from a restaurateur at Old Tybee Depot.[38] Food historian Damon Lee Fowler wrote, "Her creative flair made her one of Savannah's most sought after caterers," adding that long after her death, her cooking remains "legendary."[39] One of her specialties was Chicken Madeira flavored with shallots, mushrooms, and wine. Thankfully, *Four Great Southern Cooks*, published in Atlanta in 1980, shared the recipe along with others by Redman.[40] Although no additional chicken specialties are mentioned, the other three cooks in the book are also distinguished Georgia cooks whose careers "in grand houses" fell within the period of this book. Beatrice Mize (1893–1994), raised in Habersham County and later well known in Atlanta's Sweet Auburn neighborhood, learned to cook on a woodburning stove and took inspiration from her Cherokee great-grandmother.[41] William "Junior" Mann (1904–1985) of Upson

County and Atlanta also learned to cook on an old-fashioned stove, building know-how through experience in various kitchens, travels with employers, and even one of Henrietta Dull's cooking schools.[42] (See 1928 section.) He cooked for Georgia governors and dignitaries.[43] Ruth Jenkins (dates unknown) grew up in McDuffie County and cooked for prominent families in Atlanta.[44]

Favorite Southern Recipes and a Haunted Lighthouse

Favorite Southern Recipes, 1912
Southern Ruralist newspaper
222 pages. 1,394 recipes including 203 from Georgia.

It was a dark and stormy night.

Actually, accounts just say that night was windy. Regardless, 129 steps made for a long, steep climb up the shadowy spiral staircase to the top of the lighthouse only for Annie Svendsen to discover that the mechanism for the light wasn't working. Her lighthouse-keeper husband was away, so she thought she was alone up there with the problem—until a man appeared out of the gloom. After waking from a faint, Annie discovered the light was working again. Since their arrival, they'd heard stories about Frederick Osborne, a keeper who died decades before due to a violent disagreement with his assistant. Perhaps he was dead but not gone.[1]

The informative St. Simons Island Lighthouse Museum gives today's visitors a chance to listen for ghostly whispers and learn about lighthouses while also offering a seagull's eye view of the Atlantic. And it is also one of the few public places in Georgia where you can walk into a historical kitchen and then later use an authentic recipe to taste a specific dish once made there.[2] The re-created living quarters show how the rooms might have looked soon after Carl Svendsen (1878–1935) arrived with his family to begin service as Principal Lighthouse Keeper (1907–1935).[3] One warm spring morning, my family toured the snug kitchen where Annie Baker Svendsen (1881–1983) once cooked. In the afternoon, we

The undated postcard of the lighthouse exterior was likely from the Svendsens' time, while the current photo of the lighthouse kitchen shows it in its restored form. Permission to publish these images is courtesy of the Coastal Georgia Historical Society.

strolled through Christ Church Episcopal Cemetery where live oaks draped with Spanish moss shade the graves of the Svendsens. That evening, we returned to the south end of the island, sitting beneath the looming 104-foot lighthouse as the sun set to read aloud spooky island stories.[4] Thanks to *Favorite Southern Recipes,* we picnicked on slices of Annie's Favorite Cake fragrant with orange. Past and present met in vivid (and delicious) ways.

Because the recipes in *Favorite Southern Recipes* are credited, we know that the fifty-eight Georgia counties represented include the Glynn County offerings of Annie Svendsen—Boston Baked Beans (35), Fruit Cake (151), and Favorite Cake (171). The recipes in this cookbook came from readers of the *Southern Ruralist* (1896–1930), a semimonthly newspaper that was published in Florida by Geo. W. Hastings & Company until 1899 and thereafter in Atlanta by the Southern Ruralist Company.[5] Several sources note that this cookbook was created as an enticement for subscriptions, yet according to *Publisher's Weekly* it was also offered for a price of fifty cents.[6] Interestingly, reminiscent of William and Rebecca White from the 1876 section, a husband-and-wife team was involved. Years before he became an editor for the *Georgia Market Bulletin,* Frank J. Merriam (1865–1939) was president of the Southern Ruralist Company while his wife, Lois Freeman Merriam (1888–1987), was editor of the Home

Department.[7] In the introduction, Lois explains the origins of the cookbook. "Prizes were offered for the three favorite recipes of any subscriber. The result was the offering of so many good recipes—many of them heirlooms, descending from mother to daughter for generations—and there was such an appreciative demand for copies of the RURALIST containing these recipes, it was decided to give these prize-winning delectables in book form."[8]

FAVORITE CAKE

One-half cupful of butter, one scant cupful of sugar, yolks of six eggs, two cupsful of flour, one heaping teaspoonful of baking powder, a fourth teaspoonful of salt, grated rind and strained juice of one large orange. Sift the baking powder, salt and flour together, cream butter and sugar, add the well-beaten yolks, orange juice, rind, then stir in the flour, mix to a smooth batter. Bake in moderate oven.—MRS. CARL O. SVENDSEN, *St. Simon Island Light House, Brunswick, Ga.*

Svendsen's recipe (171) makes just three cups of batter, perfect for a loaf pan. As noted with other baking recipes in the book, egg sizes were less standardized in the past; I find the recipe works best with three yolks from large eggs. And if you can get a wild sour orange from the Georgia coast (see 1863 section), a glaze from the juice and zest blended with powdered sugar nicely balances the cake's sweetness.

An issue of the *Southern Ruralist* from August 15, 1923.

PIE FOR DYSPEPTICS

Four tablespoonsful of oatmeal and one pint of water. Let stand a few hours, or till the oats are swelled. Then add two large apples, pared and sliced, a little salt, one cupful of sugar, one tablespoonful of flour. Mix all well together and bake in a buttered pie dish, and you have a most delicious pie.—MRS. H. O. KIRTON, *Rome, Ga.*

Anti-indigestion pie? This recipe (90) gave me pause because of the name but also because it sounded like an awful lot of water. Sure enough, the finished dish could have been named Apple Oatmeal Soup. We don't think of typographical errors in older sources, but they happened then too. Starting over, I swapped the first two quantities, sprinkling a couple of cups of oatmeal with four tablespoons of water, left them to soften, and then followed the recipe. Although it was more akin to a "crisp" than a pie, it worked and was enjoyable.

PERSIMMON CAKE

Strain two cupsful of persimmons through a sieve and set aside. For the batter, use one cupful of butter, two of sugar, four eggs (beaten separately), one cupful of milk, a teaspoonful of soda, two of cream of tartar, three cupsful of flour. Bake in layers. Filling: Beat the whites of two eggs until quite stiff and then stir in two cupsful of granulated sugar. Set the pan in another containing boiling water and cook until smooth like icing, stirring constantly. When done, remove from the fire and add the strained persimmons, then put between the layers of cake and on top, and you have an unusual and delicious cake.—MISS A. JONES, *Eatonton, Ga.*

Persimmons such as are needed for this recipe (140) grow wild in Georgia and are harvested in the autumn once they are ripe enough to fall from the tree.

Georgianne Cook Book and Advertising Recipes

The Georgianne Cook Book, 1916
Itasca Durham Hutcheson (6 August 1869–15 February 1951), compiler,
for the Hodgson Oil Refining Company, Athens
64 pages. 205 recipes.

I grew up seeing the old Hodgson Oil Company building near downtown Athens,[1] and assumed it was dedicated to petroleum. Not so. Through searches in old newspapers, I learned not only that it refined cottonseed for cooking oil and other products but also that it funded a small cookbook. The Hodgson Oil Refining Company, run by president Harry Hodgson (1874–1971), specialized in turning local cottonseed, "The Golden Heart of Cotton," into Georgianne salad and cooking oil as well as Gem White and Crystal Flake brands of shortening.[2] Ironically, it was in the autumn of 1915, the same year that the cotton-destroying boll weevil appeared in Georgia, that a local newspaper advertisement offered prize money for recipes from users of the new Georgianne oil: ten dollars for first place, five dollars for second place, and ten awards of one dollar each.[3] The contest was held at the local high school—graced with a display of Georgianne products in the Domestic Science Room—and judged by a panel that included a representative from the local State Normal School and Mrs. S. O. Hutcheson.[4] The latter became the spokesperson for Georgianne oil.

An article in mid-December of 1915 serves as a reminder to history researchers that word usage does change over time: "REFRESHMENTS SERVED AT REST ROOM THIS WEEK."[5] The Chamber of Commerce apparently called their gathering space the Rest Room, and it was here that Hutcheson offered Georgianne oil cooking demonstrations for more than four hundred people, with taste tests of doughnuts, cake, and fried potatoes.[6] She also gave presentations in other Georgia cities. Itasca Durham Hutcheson, who at that point had been the wife of local merchant, cotton warehouse owner, and bookkeeper Swepson O. Hutcheson (1853–1947) for thirty years, was a mother of six and apparently knew her way around a kitchen.[7] Itasca was active in the community, a founding

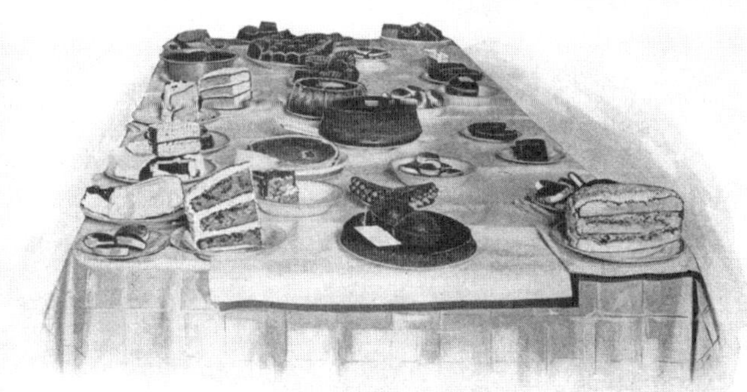

Photograph of Prize Winners' Exhibit in our recent contest among Athens' housewives for best recipes using Georgianne Cooking Oil.

Prize Recipes

WHITE CAKE.—*First Prize.*

Whites of seven eggs, two cups sugar, one teaspoon salt, two-thirds cup *Georgianne Cooking Oil,* four cups sifted flour, two teaspoons baking powder, one teaspoon flavoring, one cup of sweet milk or water.

Cream the sugar and oil together, add the salt, sift flour and baking powder together, beat whites of eggs well. Add flour and baking powder alternately with the milk or water to the sugar and oil. Lastly fold in the whites of eggs and add flavoring. Bake until cake is brown and leaves the pan.

MRS. TOM COMER.

NUT AND RAISIN CAKE.—*First Prize.*

Six eggs, two cups sugar, three and one-half cups flour, two heaping teaspoons baking powder, one cup sweet milk, three-fourths cup *Georgianne Cooking Oil,* one-half teaspoon salt, two pounds English walnuts, in hull or one pound shelled, one pound raisins, two large cocoanuts.

Cream *Georgianne Cooking Oil* with half sugar (1 cup), the yolks with half sugar, then mix together, add flour, then milk, cut up fruit and add last. Bake in four layers, put together with the grated cocoanut and icing.

MRS. A. L. MITCHELL.

ECONOMICAL FRUIT CAKE.—*Second Prize.*

Cream together two cups dark brown sugar and two-thirds cup *Georgianne Cooking Oil,* add one-half teaspoon salt and two teaspoons each of cinnamon, clove, allspice and grated nutmeg.

Mix all together thoroughly and add alternately two cups of sour milk and four cups of flour into which two teaspoons of soda has been sifted, and lastly one cup each of seeded raisins, figs cut fine, currants and nuts and one-half pound citron cut fine. Bake in moderate oven and keep at least one week before using. MISS HATTIE STEWART.

Plum Jelly

Use under-ripe acid plums. Wash fruit, and remove stems. Stick with a fork and put into a preserving kettle. Cover with water, and cook gently until the plums are boiled to pieces. Strain through a cheese cloth bag, and allow to drip over night. Measure juice, and allow one cup of DIXIE CRYSTALS Pure Cane Sugar to each cup of juice. Cook briskly until jelly begins to form. Skim, and pour into clean, hot jelly glasses. Seal with paraffin when cool.

Quince Jelly

Wash fruit, removing blemishes, and cut into small pieces. Do not pare, but remove core and seeds. Cover with water, and cook until tender. Strain through cheese cloth bag. Measure juice, and add 2/3 cup of DIXIE CRYSTALS Pure Cane Sugar for each cup of juice. Cook briskly until jelly forms. Skim, and pour into clean, hot jelly glasses. Seal with paraffin when cool. The quality of quince jelly is improved by an equal amount of tart apples.

These recipes from the undated fourteen-page cookbooklet *The Jelly Glass* are courtesy of Dixie Crystals, a sugar refinery that has been operating in Savannah since 1917.

CANDIES

Chocolate Pecan Fudge

2 cups white sugar **1 cup Borden's Sweetened Condensed Mik**
1 cup water **3 squares unsweetened chocolate**
1 cup GOLD MEDAL Pecans, chopped

Mix together sugar and water in large saucepan and bring to a boil. Add condensed milk and boil over low flame until mixture will form firm ball in cold water (235°—240°F.) Stir constantly to prevent burning. Remove from fire, add chocolate cut in small pieces, then the chopped Pecans. Beat until thick and creamy. Pour into buttered pan. When cool, cut in squares.

Mapleine Cream Balls

1 cup boiling water **1 pinch cream of tartar**
2 cups white sugar **1 tsp. butter**
2 tsps. white corn syrup **¼ tsp. Mapleine**
1 cup GOLD MEDAL Pecans, chopped

Add ingredients to the boiling water in the order named. Stir until sugar is dissolved. Place over fire and boil gently till soft ball forms in cold water. Remove from fire. Cool, add chopped Pecans; beat until creamy and form into balls.

Divinity Fudge

3 cups granulated sugar **¼ tsp. salt**
1 cup white Karo **1 tsp. vanilla**
½ cup cold water **1 cup chopped GOLD MEDAL Pecans**
2 egg whites

Combine Karo, water, salt and sugar, boil until a little tried in cold water is brittle. Beat egg whites stiff and gradually beat in the boiling syrup. Whip until it begins to stiffen, add vanilla and chopped Pecans, beat more and pour into a buttered pan. When cold cut in squares.

Chocolate Pecan Slices

2 squares unsweetened chocolate **1½ cups GOLD MEDAL Pecans**
1⅓ cups Borden's Sweetened Condensed Milk

Melt chocolate in double boiler; add condensed milk and stir over boiling water five minutes until mixture thickens. Cool for five minutes. Drop large tablespoonfuls of chocolate mixture into halved or chopped Pecans and work nut meats into surface. Form into roll. Let stand for 3 hours in ice box and cut in slices.

A page from an undated quad-fold Gold Medal Pecans pamphlet featuring fourteen recipes savory and sweet.

member of the Thoughts & Thimble Club and leader of the Girls' Extension Club at the local Young Women's Christian Association (YWCA).[8] While the Athens newspaper took a down-to-earth approach, promising that the demonstration was of "good things made out of a home product by home people," a Columbus newspaper advertisement for Georgianne oil referred to Itasca Hutcheson as "the well known teacher of Domestic science."[9]

We don't know Hutcheson's career path or exact connection with Hodgson Oil, but she was listed as "compiler" of the Georgianne cookbook. When it came out in February of 1916, there were two first-prize awards (White Cake, Nut and Raisin Cake) and two second-prize awards (Economical Fruit Cake, Nut Bread).[10] These and ten other winners are mentioned by contributor name in the cookbook. The remaining recipes are uncredited. Recipes from the cookbook were used in local Georgianne newspaper advertisements all month, and the cookbook itself was free with a thirty-cent quart of the oil.[11] Georgianne oil was mentioned in newspapers as late as 1922, and the Hutchesons eventually retired to Florida.[12]

As we've explored old Georgia cookbooks, we've seen ones curated by individuals and others created by committees. We've even seen hybrids. But we had not yet seen one created by a contest or a company. Georgianne oil is the earliest Georgia product I've found using a cookbook to help sell it, but it certainly wasn't the last. Dixie Crystals sugar (Savannah), Gold Medal Pecans (Columbus), and Sunshine/Pomona Pimientos (Griffin) are three companies that produced recipe booklets in the early twentieth century.

Home Brews and Steamed Puddings Fade from Use

It's time for a little dessert, so how about some pudding from scratch with a glass of homemade wine? Older Georgia cookbooks provide an array of recipes for both. By the 1920s, however, new cookbooks were no longer offering as many choices in these categories. Social and technological changes were afoot.

Home Brews and Spirits

Mary Edgeworth's 1859 cookbook could help readers create thirty-one alcoholic drinks with a fascinating array of ingredients. Her wine recipes called for blackberries, currants, oranges, and parsnips, while her beer recipes gained flavor from allspice, ginger, hops, molasses, and spruce. She also offered recipes for metheglin and mead (honey), cider (apples), and perry (pears). Ellen Verstille's 1866 cookbook included recipes for Muscadine Wine and Strawberry Cordial, and the next year Annabella Hill's cookbook added such possibilities as Tomato Wine and Crab Apple Beer. Ella Tennent's 1885 cookbook offered some novel alcoholic beverages made with persimmons, sweet potatoes, gooseberries, and raisins, while almost a decade later Annie Dennis shared a recipe for Lemon Beer. At least some of this variety reflects a desire to not waste produce during plentiful harvests.

The Famous Southern Persimmon Beer

Place carefully into a five or ten gallon keg a few pine tops for the double purpose of acting as a sort of filter and giving a sprucy flavor to the beer; make it draw well from a spigot bored about two inches from the bottom of the keg with a quarter or half an inch bit and fitted with a spile. Now put in persimmons well ripe (after frost) till the keg is one-fourth filled; fill up the keg with water (rain water is best). Then chip in a little bark of the sassafras root. Keep it in a warm place or near the fire, and in a few days it will have fermented and got clear, and you can draw off an agreeable, popular, and wholesome beverage. If it should not ferment well, a small quantity of yeast may be added.

—Dr. W. C. Bellamy, in Tennent, *House-Keeping in the Sunny South* (1885), 203

Tennent added that the same method could be used for Sweet Potato Beer, substituting boiled sweet potatoes for the persimmons. Mary Edgeworth, on the other hand, had a Persimmon Beer containing corn.[1]

Orange Cordial

Put into three quarts of brandy the chips of eighteen Seville oranges, and let them steep a fortnight in a stone bottle close stopped. Boil two quarts of spring water with a pound and a half of the finest sugar near an hour very gently. Clarify the water and sugar with the white of an egg then strain it through a jelly-bag and boil it near half away. When it is cold, strain the brandy into the syrup.

—Couper and Fraser Family Papers, 1810–1894, Georgia Historical Society, Savannah[2]

There were also recipes for fruit juices used as extracts and drink additives. Called shrubs, drinking vinegars, acids, or just "syrups," these may have been mixed with alcoholic beverages at times but were mainly added to water as an alternative to ever-popular lemonade.

Blackberry Vinegar

One gallon of fresh berries washed and picked. Pour over them a half gallon of good cider vinegar, let stand twenty-four hours; then strain. To each pint of juice add three fourths of a pound of sugar; boil half an hour and skim carefully. When cold, bottle and cork tightly. When used pour the depth of an inch in the glass, fill with water, pounded ice and season with nutmeg. This is a temperance drink.

—Mrs. E. McCarney, in Tennent, *House-Keeping in the Sunny South* (1885), 202–203

Did you notice the last sentence? The temperance movement encouraging abstinence from alcohol began in the United States during colonial times and gained support across the nineteenth century, particularly in religious and educational circles.

Temperance Punch

Boil a pound of sugar and half a pint of water until it spins a thread, taking care not to stir after the sugar is dissolved. After it has cooled, add the juice of six lemons and one quart of unfermented grape juice; cover and stand over night. When ready to serve, pour in a punch bowl with a piece of ice, and add any proportion of carbonated water desired.

—Wesleyan College Alumnae, *Macon Cook Book* (1909), 242

In the *Tested Recipe Cook Book* for the Cotton States Exposition of 1895, the instructions for Five O'clock Tea (107–108) call for adding rum to each teacup. Every one of Georgia's nineteenth-century cookbooks—yes, even the church ones—contain at least one recipe calling for alcohol. That said, however, recipes for making alcoholic beverage recipes decreased in cookbooks near the turn of the century. Then in 1920 the Eighteenth Amendment to the U.S. Constitution prohibiting alcohol took effect. (Thus the date for this section.) That was the end of all alcohol in Georgia's cookbooks for a while, right? Almost, but not completely. Henrietta Dull's 1928 cookbook included a series of fruitcake recipes, some of which would have been soaked in booze in years past but were now moistened by grape juice or black coffee.[3] The final fruitcake recipe, however, mentioned that wine might also be used—and her "Southern Hospitality" section included a handful of brandy-laced drinks and homemade wines.[4] In Harriet Colquitt's 1933 *Savannah Cook Book*, her recipe for Ambrosia wistfully states, "Of course, if a little wine could be poured over all, it would be so much the better."[5] Prohibition wasn't repealed until a few months after her book's publication, yet Colquitt added eleven alcoholic beverages to the last pages—although she did title that section "Gone Are the Days!"[6]

One might think that the end of Prohibition would see a surge in all types of alcohol recipes, but this generally isn't the case. Alcohol made something of a comeback as an ingredient, but twentieth-century cooks embracing canned soups and baking mixes were less likely to grow, harvest, and process ingredients to create their own alcohol.

Egg Nog

For one dozen eggs use one
quart double thick cream, nearly
one quart sour mash whisky and
two table spoons of rum.
To make—thoroughly beat the yolks
to a cream add a desert [*sic*] spoon of
sugar to each egg and whip
again, add whisky to taste (nearly
a quart) a little rum; the cream
should be whipped, add the cream,
then whites of eggs (well beaten)
to the bowl stirring slowly.

—Archibald W. Butt Scrapbooks, Georgia Archives, Morrow[7]

As with alcohol-soaked fruitcakes, social recipes such as punch and eggnog laced with purchased alcohol weathered Prohibition and continued in many Georgia recipe collections and cookbooks. The author of the above manuscript recipe, Augusta-born journalist and U.S. Army officer Major Archibald Butt (1865–1912), served as a military aide to presidents Theodore Roosevelt and William Howard Taft. In a 1910 letter to his sister-in-law, Butt describes serving the eggnog "made by my mother's old recipe" at a Washington gathering where "the people went wild about it when they ate it." Perhaps they partook using silver spoons, because Butt added, "It was too thick to be drunk."[8] Butt sailed on the maiden voyage of the RMS *Titanic* and went down with the ship on 15 April 1912.

And Now for a Little Pudding

Let's not forget the pudding portion of our dessert. When you saw the opening lines of this section, did you think to yourself, "Who would want wine with *pudding*?!" These days we tend to think of pudding as a simple chilled custard made from a mix, yet Georgia's early cookbooks gave pudding recipes that could be sweet or savory, cool or warm, custard-like or cake-like. In fact, these cookbooks often had something we rarely see in American cookbooks today—whole sections dedicated to puddings. As with make your own alcohol recipes, puddings went into a decline in Georgia cookbooks by the 1920s, just a few swept into general "Desserts" sections.[9] Why?

The Oxford Companion to American Food and Drink admits that puddings "fall into an extremely broad classification."[10] Many puddings have British roots, with the earliest being mixtures of whole grains along with chopped meats, vegetables, fats, and herbs cooked using the stomach or intestines of a slaughtered animal as a container. (Think of the notorious Scottish haggis.) In *Pride and Pudding: The History of British Puddings*, food historian Regula Ysewijn explores how such dishes helped use up food scraps and expanded the possibilities for early hearth cooks who owned just a single pot. Puddings evolved to various containers—earthenware dishes, hollowed-out vegetables or fruits, pastry crusts (once called "coffins"), tin molds, and even cloth bags. The food inside thickened and set during boiling, steaming, or baking.

Pease Pudding

Put a pint of split pease in a clean
cloth do not tie them up close
but leave a little room for them to
swell, put them on to boil in cold
water slowly till they are tender—
if they are good pease they will be
boiled enough in about 2½ hours
put them thru a sieve into a deep
dish adding to them an egg or two
an oz of butter pepper & salt. Beat
them well together for ten minutes
flour the cloth well put the pudding
in then tie it up as tight as possible &
boil it an hour longer
it is as good with roasted beef as with
boiled pork or roast pork.

—Recipe book of Evelyn Spalding (Sapelo Island), 1871, Duke University[11]

Just as containers evolved, so did the mixtures to be thickened. Although both Edgeworth (1859) and Hill (1867) offered savory puddings with meat and vegetables, increasingly puddings in Georgia cookbooks were made with processed grains such as flour, cornmeal, and white rice.[12] Additions of eggs, corn starch, or arrowroot powder helped thicken these refined grains. Some puddings were plain in texture, while others came to be dotted with dried or fresh fruits. (Think of the traditional English Christmas puddings that look like molded cakes.) Sweet puddings took the lead over savory ones.[13]

Banana pudding, chocolate pudding, rice pudding, and bread pudding have remained Georgia recipe favorites. One clue may be that these are usually cooked using simple methods. The old steamed and boiled cake-like puddings are more complicated. For these types of puddings, recipe writers like Annabella Hill (1867 section), Estelle Wilcox (1883), and Rebecca White (1876) needed long paragraphs to describe suitable containers and how to properly seal them.[14] Boiled and steamed puddings were cooked surrounded by moisture, yet an excess of moisture reaching the pudding itself could ruin it. On top of that, there was a time factor.

Boiled Indian Pudding, No. 1

Make a stiff batter, by stirring Indian-meal [corn meal] into a quart of boiling milk or water. Then stir in two tablespoonsful of flour, three of sugar, half a spoonful of ginger, or two teaspoonsful of cinnamon, and two teaspoonsful of salt, two tablespoonsful of fine chopped suet. Such puddings require a long boiling, say seven or eight hours. They require a good sauce for eating.

—Edgeworth, *Southern Gardener and Receipt Book* (1859), 208

Back in the days when a hearth or woodburning stove was used throughout the day for cooking and providing hot water as well as for household heat during cold weather, a pudding was smart. A cook could get the pudding going over gentle heat, then turn to other tasks around the house or farm, simply tending the coals now and then until suppertime when the pudding was warm and ready.[15] It was yesteryear's equivalent of the modern plug-in slow cooker. Then technological advances changed how we heat our homes and fuel our cooking. In addition, social changes meant that more people—including women—were off the farm and working outside the home. Long-cooking puddings were no longer cheap or handy.

Ah, but kitchen trends do come and go. Many of today's cooks wish to use sugar sparingly, and cake-like puddings often have less sweetener than other desserts. In fact, many of Georgia's old pudding recipes rely on a sauce to impart dessert-like sweetness, which is easily adjusted for each serving. If you are curious about old-fashioned puddings, know that there are newfangled tools, from nonstick pudding molds to small appliance steamers, that would make your foremothers jealous. Instructions for homemade alcohol and steamed puddings may be specialty recipes rather than general recipes today, but they offer rewards for the cooks willing to learn them.

For Woman's Work.

Seasonable Desserts.

PLUM PUDDING.

ONE POUND of raisins, one pound of currants, one-half pound of citron and lemon peel, nutmeg, ginger, two teaspoonfuls of saleratus, three eggs, three-fourths of a pound of bread crumbs, three-fourths of a pound of suet, one-half pound of flour, milk enough to wet all; tie in a cloth and boil for three hours.

SUET PUDDING.

One cup of molasses, one cup of suet, chopped, one cup of buttermilk, two and one-half cups of flour, one teaspoonful of soda, one cupful of raisins, one cup of currants, spices of all kinds. Steam four hours. For sauce use whipped cream.

COTTAGE PUDDING.

One egg, one-half cup of sugar, one tablespoonful of butter, one-half cup of milk, one cup of flour with one teaspoonful of baking power.

SAUCE.

One cup of hot water, one-half cup of sugar, one tablespoonful of butter, a pinch of salt, one-half tablespoonful of cornstarch dissolved in cold water. Season, and boil until clear. This sauce may also be used for the Suet Pudding, instead of the cream.

BREAD PUDDING.

One and one-half cups of bread crumbs, one-half cup of molasses, one teaspoonful of soda, dissolved in water, one cup of raisins, chopped; one-half cup of suet, chopped; cinnamon, cloves and allspice to taste, a little salt. Add enough hot water to dissolve the pudding. Steam or bake.

Pudding recipes from *Woman's Work* (Athens) 14.12 (December 1901): 11.

This tin for steaming pudding and bread features a tight-fitting lid that can latch and a center core that helps distribute heat. (The cooking chamber is 6 inches tall.)

Found in various sizes and shapes, some tins were intended for multiple cooking and molding uses including with chilled salads and frozen desserts. The second image shows the same tins opened and turned over with their lids in front. (The turban tin is 9½ inches in diameter while the wreath is 8.)

Woman's Club Cookbooks

Atlanta Woman's Club Cook Book, 1921
Atlanta Woman's Club, Mrs. Newton C. Wing and Mrs. J. A. Carlisle, editors
253 pages. 783 recipes.

Athens Woman's Club Cook Book, 1922
Athens Woman's Club, Mrs. Annie Mae Wood Bryant, editor
371 pages. 946 recipes.

The Georgia Clubwoman's Souvenir Collection of Prized Recipes, ca. 1938
Georgia Federation of Women's Clubs, Mrs. H. B. Ritchie, editor
239 pages. 614 recipes.

These cookbooks published between the two World Wars share features intriguing to history buffs. First, they include recipes spanning from historical to newfangled. Second, these cookbooks give recipes from households of famous Georgians and call upon cooking experts such as Henrietta Dull (1928 section) and Daisy Wright Mell (1894).[1] A little research reveals that many of the clubwomen and their spouses lived prominent lives themselves. Third, now that our exploration of twentieth-century Georgia cookbooks is well under way, we finally find a marked interest in recipes from—or at least inspired by—other countries and cultures. (The Atlanta cookbook's foreword states it specializes in "typical Southern recipes" yet reflects the "cosmopolitan character" of its membership.) Finally, these cookbooks often list contributors and their locations, so you may find older recipes from a specific Georgia community of interest.

These three cookbooks are also noteworthy because they reflect changes we saw brewing in earlier cookbooks. The first change involves a widening sense of community. Historian Jean E. Friedman, author of *The Enclosed Garden: Women and Community in the Evangelical South, 1830–1900*, noted that women's networks were formed primarily through family and place of worship. Social and charitable clubs drawing like-minded women from across a community were an early feature in the North, but the South needed a nudge from the aid societies and solicitation drives of the Civil War. This widening of attention is something we first sensed with Tennent's 1885 cookbook allied with the Phoenix Agriculture Club and drawing on far-flung recipe contributors. It bloomed a decade later with the 1895 Cotton States Exposition cookbooks put together by women who were often community leaders. The three cookbooks we are now discussing show the trend continuing to grow stronger.[2]

While the Exposition of 1895 was still open to the crowds, the Woman's Club of Atlanta drew up a charter.[3] In addition, seventeen social and literary clubs in

"In the past the food problem has always been considered one of economics. Cooking was considered an accomplishment of the nature of tatting, or trimming hats. There now succeeds the era of scientific study of food in relation to health. The exponent of food values is heard on every hand. The woman of today who wishes her family to be healthy is the woman who takes the time to learn something of the chemistry of food, physiology of the human body; the cost of food; and to a certain extent, the making of family budgets."
—*Athens Woman's Club Cook Book*[1] (1922), 21–22

1. By the way, this cookbook shared, on page 20, that married couples could expect to spend between $35 and $45 a month on food and $30 to $60 on rent.

various parts of the state soon came together to form the beginning of the Georgia Federation of Women's Clubs.[4] An early report states, "It is a great work these ambitious women of the federation have before them," and mentions improving education and civic conditions.[5] In the first few years, Federation members set about supporting the free kindergarten movement, education for females, the University of Georgia's Cooperative Extension program (formalized by the Smith Lever Act in 1914), and statewide library access. Also on their minds was "levelling social lines and bringing the woman of wealth into human sympathy with the self-supporting woman."[6]

Now that we know more about the woman's club movement, the second change we see in cookbooks of this time makes more sense. With Annabella Hill's 1867 cookbook, we saw an ideological shift regarding the authority of a cookbook author—from the efficient household-and-farmyard manager to the hands-on home cook. Mrs. Hill surely would have been proud of Ella Tennent and Annie Dennis. Through Jessup Whitehead and Alice Roberts, we saw that cookbook authority could also rest on professionalism, developed through the food service industry. In our contemporary times, cookbook authors are still using (and blending) these modes of authority, even if the surface has some new twists—the social media influencer, the cooking show host, and the celebrity restaurateur.

Another new source of authority was hinted at in 1895 with *The Atlanta Exposition Souvenir Cook Book* created by a Domestic Science Committee. Danielle Dreilinger's *Secret History of Home Economics* explains that "domestic science" soon came to be known as "home economics." While we may look back on this movement as old-fashioned, Dreilinger argues in her preface, "In its purist form, home economics was about changing the world through the household." Increased industrialization as well as improvements in literacy, education, communication, and travel pointed toward a need for science. In an increasingly interconnected world, women were becoming empowered to study problems, to enter community discussion, and to take part in solutions. Evidence of these changes can be found the woman's club cookbooks. They helped demystify new kitchen technologies, plus they introduced new concepts, such as "food value," "calories," and "vitamins." Where older cookbooks said "bake until done," club cookbooks offered baking tables to calculate time and temperature. If we could go back in time to ask Ella Tennent the whys and wherefores of her confident household advice, she might very well answer, "Because I know so!" or "All good housekeepers know that!" The women putting together the club cookbooks would be more likely to respond, "Because science tells us . . ."

The cookbooks include menus, recipes to serve large groups, and lists of food amounts needed for various-sized crowds. This recipe was one of many in these three sources intended for social gatherings.

Bird Nest Salad

Season cream cheese highly with cayenne pepper, a little onion and lemon juice and salt. Make into little balls representing eggs. Make nest of shredded lettuce. Put a spoonful of salad dressing in the nests, lay 4 or 5 eggs on top of this, sprinkle with paprika. These eggs may be tinted any delicate color.

—*Athens Woman's Club Cook Book* (1922), 99

SWEET POTATO SOUFFLE NO. 1.

1 cup nuts. ½ cup seeded raisins.
2 tbls. butter. ½ cup milk.
2 eggs. Flavored as desired.

Boil potatoes whole until very tender, peel and mash well, add sugar (about ½ cup for baking dish). Do not have batter too stiff. Bake slowly until light brown. Place marshmallows on top, return to oven long enough to melt slightly. Nicest served with mid-winter dinner and subject to many variations:

(b). Use half glass of jelly instead of sugar.

(c). Add bananas sliced instead of nuts and raisins.

(d). Stick an almond or cherry in marshmallows for fancy dish. Add any crystallized fruit with nuts and raisins.

(e). Omit milk, add 2 t-spoons baking powder and 1 cup cocoanut.

"PIG-IN-A-PEN."

Bake medium sized potatoes. When well done, peel, mash well, adding salt and pepper. To each potato add small all pork sausage cake (cooked). Mix thoroughly, make in cakes, brown in oven or refill potato cases with mixture. Can be served "en masse" as meat course.

POTATO CUSTARD.

2 small potatoes. 2 eggs.
1/3 cup butter. ¾ cup sugar.
1 t-spoon vanilla.

Boil tender, peel, mash; add eggs. butter, sugar and vanilla. Mix thoroughly (bake in rich crust and top with meringue).

POTATO PIE.

Peel and slice raw potatoes thin; cook tender in slightly salted water. Place all in baking dish, add spice, sugar to taste and a little butter. Top with rich crust and brown in moderate oven.

These potato recipes from the *Atlanta Woman's Club Cook Book* (1921), 22, are credited to Mrs. Oscar McKenzie of Montezuma, Georgia.

Favorites of Our President

"Con-a-Haney"

(Indian Corn Recipe)

1 quart old-fashioned hominy
2 quarts corn
½ pound nut meats, well broken
1 tablespoon butter
Salt and pepper to taste
Enough hominy water to moisten

Mix together, and cook in slow oven ½ an hour.

MRS. ROBERTA CAMPBELL LAWSON, President,
General Federation of Women's Clubs.

Venison Stew

Cut meat into small squares, roll in seasoned flour—salt and pepper (a wee bit of red pepper).

Have on stove a kettle or saucepan with boiling hot water. Drop meat in, a few pieces at a time. Do not stir until all pieces have been in long enough to "coat over." Stew slowly for 2 hours.

Be guided in amount of water used by quantity of meat which should be completely covered in the beginning.

This recipe was used by my grandmother in Old Indian Territory when venison was plentiful. Any tender meat can be so used.

MRS. ROBERTA CAMPBELL LAWSON, President,
General Federation of Women's Clubs.

The blend of old and new traditions in the club cookbooks is compelling. These two recipes are from *The Georgia Clubwoman's Souvenir Collection* (ca. 1938), 29.

THE FRIGIDAIRE—Just think, a refrigerator never damp! Never to have to watch out for the Ice-man's coming, to see that tickets or change are ready, or that we have been given correct weight—and then finally, perhaps to clean up after muddy feet. All these things are unnecessary with the Frigidaire. For several months we studied this delightful electrical contrivance at close range, the Frigidaire Company being kind enough to install it in our model kitchen at the Club House for that purpose, and we recommend it most heartily.

This snippet from the *Atlanta Woman's Club Cook Book* (1921), 245, shows how grateful some homemakers were for the advance of science and technology.

CAKES

"We will mix and bake the dainty cake
And beat the frosting light
The sweetest plan to please a man
Is through his appetite.

Even as women were embracing science and activism, older ideas hung on in Georgia cookbooks, as seen in this verse from the *Service Star Legion Cook Book* (1927), 72.

Exploring Further

The Congressional Club formed in Washington, D.C., in 1908 for the social benefit of the wives and daughters of many of the nation's officials. In 1927 it put out *The Congressional Club Cook Book: Favorite National and International Recipes*. There are now more than a dozen editions, and this is a good source if you wish to find recipes from the households of prominent Georgians. If instead you are looking for recipes from a home economics tradition, Augusta's Vera Stewart, a former home economics teacher turned cooking show host, wrote *The VeryVera Cookbook*.

Mrs. Stanfield and Georgia Cooking Schools

Mrs. Stanfield's Selected Recipes, 1927 and 1935. 52 pages.
White Lily Flour Cook Book, 1931. 98 pages.
White Lily Cooking Guide, 1934. 98 pages. 381 recipes.
Mrs. Stanfield's 52 Family Sunday Dinners, 1937. 144 pages. 465 recipes.
How to Work Wonders with Every Day Foods, 1939.

The list of cookbooks above is as complete as I could make it. I was only able to get my hands on three of the cookbooks, relying on online records to piece together the rest.[1] Some were published by companies, while others seem to be self-published. What they have in common is their author/compiler/editor: college-educated Elizabeth Stanfield, who taught cooking classes across the Southeast in venues such as schools, churches, and social clubs.[2] For a time she oversaw the model kitchen at Chamberlin-Johnson-DuBose, one of Atlanta's leading department stores.[3]

Elizabeth "Lizzie" Wynne was born in Georgia, likely in Pulaski County, in 1874.[4] A few months shy of her eighteenth birthday, she married Samuel H. Stanfield (1867–1946) in Floyd County, and the couple raised a family of four children in Rome, where he ran a shoe store.[5] By the 1920 census the couple lived in Atlanta, and Elizabeth's occupation was "hostess" of the War Camp Community Club, a place for the soldier who otherwise had "no place to go when in town, and must lounge about the streets seeking entertainment as best he can."[6] In 1925 Elizabeth Stanfield formed a liaison with the Frank E. Block food company to provide recipes for their advertisements.[7] The article announcing this partnership called Stanfield "one of the best known domestic science authorities of the south and specialist in the making of truly southern dishes." Her advertisements indicate she was already teaching cooking classes.[8] By the late 1920s she had written *Mrs. Stanfield's Selected Recipes*, supported by eight advertisers including the prominent brands Crisco shortening, Knox gelatin, Rumford baking powder, and White Lily flour.[9] By the 1930 census she was listed as a cooking school teacher.

Newspaper articles indicate Stanfield usually taught two-hour classes on multiple weekdays. Tuition in the 1920s was often a dollar for the series or around twenty-five cents per class.[10] Prices dropped to fifty or thirty-five cents for series classes during the Great Depression.[11] Near the start of World War II, at an age when most retire, Stanfield lectured as a nutrition expert.[12] The 1950 census finds the seventy-six-year-old living with her daughter, yet occupied forty hours per week sewing "for gift shops and private." She died in Atlanta in 1959.[13]

In the last part of the nineteenth century, cooking schools popped up across the country. The Boston Cooking School, established in 1879, still looms large in public memory in part due to the fame of cookbook author Fannie Farmer (1857–1915). Some cooking schools were brick-and-mortar institutions, while others were multiday events such as those offered by Elizabeth Stanfield. Still other cooking schools were a hybrid, periodically offered as part of an institution's curricula.

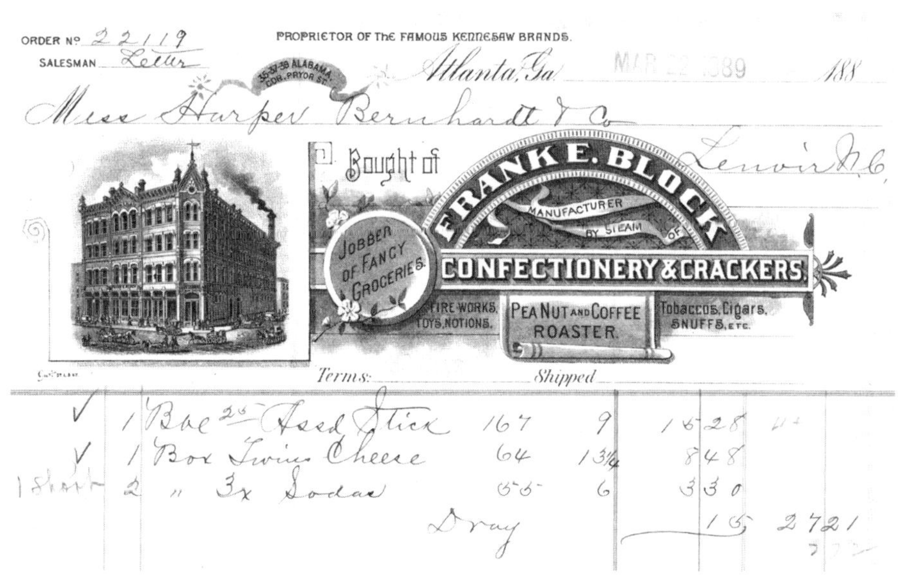

This 1889 invoice from the popular Block company shows its building once located downtown near what is now Underground Atlanta.

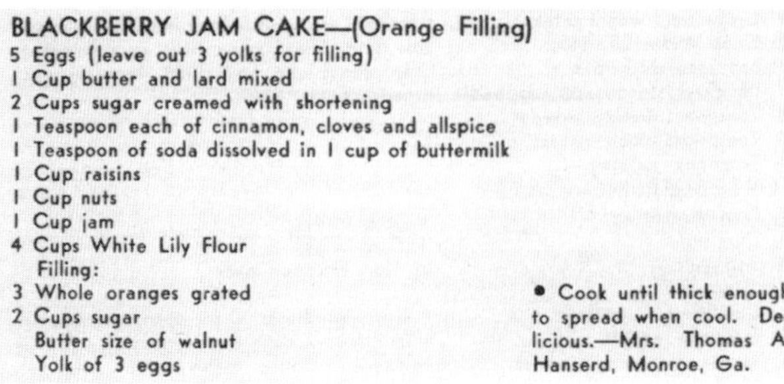

BLACKBERRY JAM CAKE—(Orange Filling)

5 Eggs (leave out 3 yolks for filling)
1 Cup butter and lard mixed
2 Cups sugar creamed with shortening
1 Teaspoon each of cinnamon, cloves and allspice
1 Teaspoon of soda dissolved in 1 cup of buttermilk
1 Cup raisins
1 Cup nuts
1 Cup jam
4 Cups White Lily Flour

Filling:
3 Whole oranges grated
2 Cups sugar
Butter size of walnut
Yolk of 3 eggs

• Cook until thick enough to spread when cool. Delicious.—Mrs. Thomas A. Hanserd, Monroe, Ga.

The cover of *The White Lily Cooking Guide* (1934) and a recipe from page 34, courtesy of Hometown Food Company.

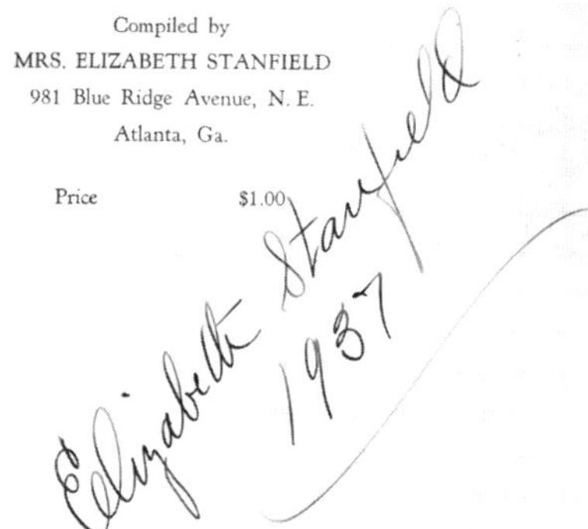

Compiled by
MRS. ELIZABETH STANFIELD
981 Blue Ridge Avenue, N. E.
Atlanta, Ga.

Price $1.00

Elizabeth Stanfield
1937

My copy of *Mrs. Stanfield's 52 Family Sunday Dinners* appears to be autographed. It offers seasonal menus with all the recipes needed to cook them, plus poems and advertisements. In her foreword (2), Stanfield told her readers, "The recipes are Southern Cooking; some having been used in our family for four generations."

The Extension Cooking School, for example, was part of the Athens Colored High and Industrial School, yet was also marketed to local women employed as cooks.[14] Regardless of the format, cooking schools began to be mentioned more frequently in Georgia newspapers by the 1890s. Sometimes a specific teacher isn't identified, or her name is given simply as "Mrs. ___," making it difficult to learn more about these experts and find their recipes. Three exceptions are Mrs. Stanfield, Mrs. Dull (1928 section), and Mrs. Habersham.[15]

Eliza "Leila" Mckay Elliott Habersham (1831–1901) was a Savannah institution unto herself.[16] In *The Savannah Cookbook*, food historian Damon Lee Fowler gives a short but moving portrait of her life.[17] Widowed during the Civil War, Mrs. Habersham supported herself and her children by moving back in with her mother and giving cooking lessons at their downtown home on the northeast side of Oglethorpe Square.[18] Terrapin Stew was one of Habersham's specialties and her recipe most commonly found in modern sources, the wording usually close to the version Harriet Ross Colquitt used to kick off her *Savannah Cook Book*. (See 1933 section.) This recipe even represented Georgia in Marion Brown's 1951 regional retrospective, *The Southern Cook Book*.[19] Thankfully, twenty-two-year-old Savannahian Caroline Woodbridge (1874–1960) took Mrs. Habersham's cooking classes in the spring of 1896, and her notes containing almost a hundred recipes can be found at the Georgia Historical Society.[20] There are recipes from others in the notebook, but more than a dozen clearly came from Mrs. Habersham, including this one:

Mrs. Habersham's Crabs à la St. Laurent

Put in a saucepan one tablespoonful of butter
& when melted stir in one " of flour.
Add slowly half a cup of milk stirring all
the while to keep it smooth. Add half a
cup of cream & cook until the sauce thickens
then stir in one cupful of boiled crabs
& two tablespoonsful of Parmesan cheese.
Season highly with salt & cayenne pepper
& after the mixture has simmered a few
minutes add one tablespoonful of sherry.
Meanwhile have pieces of readied toast cut
in squares and buttered. Spread these thickly with
mixture & sprinkle grated cheese on top.
Place them in a pan & put in a very hot
oven long enough to melt cheese. They
must be served *at once*. Garnish with
parsley or watercress.

—Caroline Lamar Woodbridge Papers, 1838–1867,
Georgia Historical Society, Savannah[21]

This eighteen-page program contains eleven recipes and promotes the event's eighty-three sponsors, from local eateries to national brand ingredients.

Exploring Further

There are thousands of old Georgia recipes out there, but not all of them work well. As a history buff but also a home baker looking for kitchen success, I treasure recipes from those who had substantial cooking experience and were also experts in effectively writing recipes and teaching cooking to others. In the research I conducted for this section as well as the 1921 section exploring home economics, I came to see that in addition to some of the cookbooks we have explored, online databases of old newspapers are a great way to find recipes from the pros—food columnists, food section editors, Cooperative Extension agents, school system nutritionists, or cooking school teachers. The next section, about Henrietta Dull, is a good example. And in recent years, cooking instruction has taken televised or video form with Georgia-related hosts such as cookbook authors Alton Brown, Paula Deen, Nathalie Dupree, Ginny McCormack, and Vera Stewart.

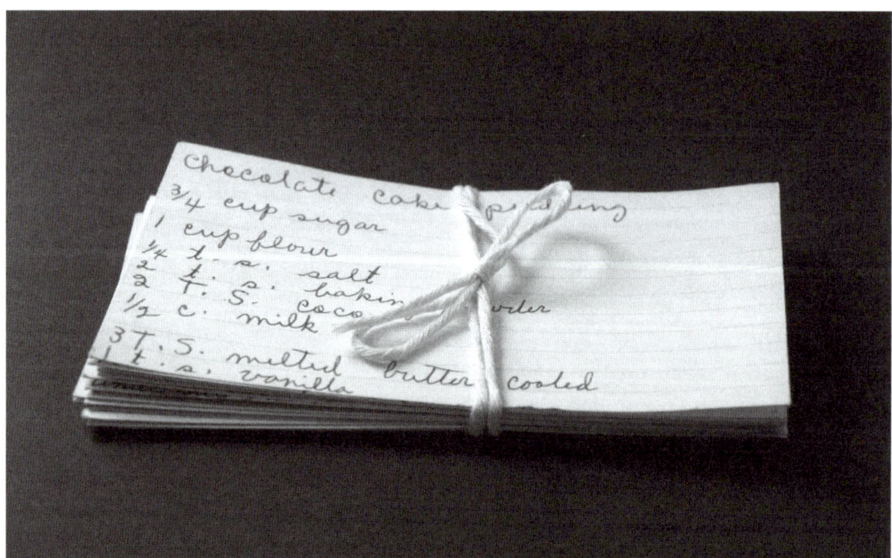

Mrs. Dull's Cooking Lessons

Southern Cooking, 1928 and 1941
Henrietta Celestia Stanley Dull (6 December 1863–28 January 1964)
The 1941 expanded edition has 384 pages and 1,282 recipes.

I married into a family with deep Georgia roots, yet their tradition of military service meant moves to far-flung places. In every new kitchen, however, was the same old tried-and-true cookbook—*Southern Cooking* by Mrs. S. R. Dull.[1] Four generations have used the battered green volume. To this day, my octogenarian father-in-law reaches for it every time he needs perfect frosting for coconut cake. At a church function when I mentioned I was writing this piece, a couple of elderly ladies exclaimed, "Oh, Mrs. Dull!" in the delighted way one does upon hearing the name of an old friend.

"Hennie" began life on a farm in Laurens County that she once said was located on "Hunger and Hardship Creek."[2] During the Civil War she was born to Ira and Mary Stanley at a place called Stanley Mill.[3] The family later moved to Flowery Branch in Hall County.[4] Henrietta married railroad clerk Samuel Rice Dull (born 1861) in Atlanta in 1887, and soon there were six children to raise.[5] When her husband's health prevented him from working in the late 1890s, she supported the family by selling baked goods and other foods to her church friends, which led to catering work as well as a job with the Atlanta Gas Light Company promoting newfangled gas appliances. Popular cooking demonstrations and various product endorsements soon followed.[6] Although she was a new widow in her late fifties at the time, Hennie's true fame began in 1920 when she began writing a column in the *Atlanta Journal* that would continue until 1945.[7] "Mrs. Dull's Cooking Lessons" columns usually followed a formula of a discussion and several recipes based on a theme—for example, a particular ingredient, picnic recipes, or holiday meals. Then there was a question-and-answer section where readers could ask for specific recipes or request tips about cooking challenges. In later years the column was often paired with a photo of young Atlanta matrons cooking.

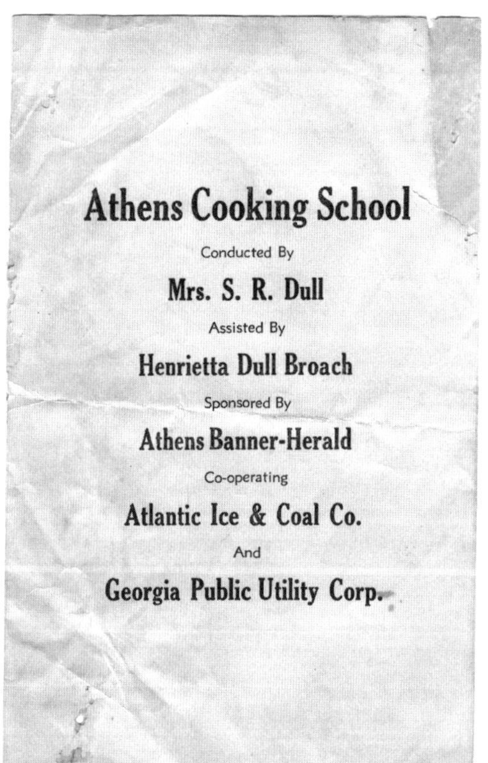

Athens Cooking School

Conducted By

Mrs. S. R. Dull

Assisted By

Henrietta Dull Broach

Sponsored By

Athens Banner-Herald

Co-operating

Atlantic Ice & Coal Co.

And

Georgia Public Utility Corp.

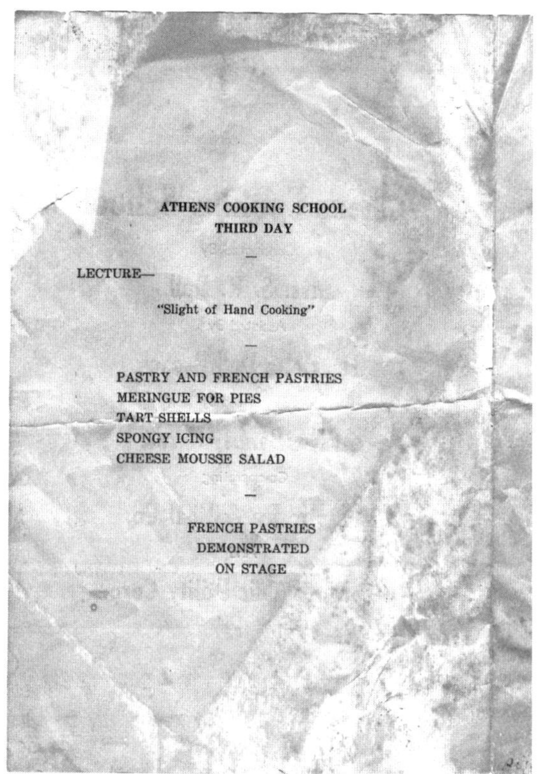

ATHENS COOKING SCHOOL
THIRD DAY

—

LECTURE—

"Slight of Hand Cooking"

—

PASTRY AND FRENCH PASTRIES
MERINGUE FOR PIES
TART SHELLS
SPONGY ICING
CHEESE MOUSSE SALAD

—

FRENCH PASTRIES
DEMONSTRATED
ON STAGE

At an Athens estate sale, I purchased a plastic bag stuffed with recipe clippings. They reeked so badly of mothballs that I had to air them in an out-of-the-way room next to an often-replenished tray of baking soda. The reward for my persistence, however, was a stash of Henrietta Dull clippings and this undated cooking demonstration pamphlet (cover and verso pictured). I don't know about you, but I'm curious about "Slight [*sic*] of Hand Cooking."

If you are interested in older foodways, the Dull cookbook is a great place to start. The recipes are modern in that most are in the format of a list of ingredients followed by the method. Measurements are standardized. And Dull combined hands-on cooking practice with an educator's know-how. For fans already deeply versed in *Southern Cooking*, it is nice to know additional Dull recipes are out there. The *Atlanta Journal* column published many recipes that did not find their way into the book yet are now available online through various databases. As early as 1918 she created a small cookbook for Mazo brand egg substitute.[8] She also contributed to cookbooks created by others—*The Atlanta Woman's Club Cook Book* (1921), *Service Star Legion Cook Book* (1927), and Sarah Field Splint's *65 Prize Recipes from the South* (1935). She sometimes provided recipes for products she endorsed.

BRUNSWICK STEW FOR FAMILY

1 fowl
1 quart of corn
1 quart of tomatoes
1 pint okra
1 pint butter beans
2 onions
Salt and pepper to taste

Method:: Boil chicken until it will leave the bones and be very tender. Pull meat from bones and cut into large cubes, return to the water in which it was cooked, add vegetables and cook down until a thick mixture. Cook slowly and stir often to prevent scorching.

All vegetables must be cut fine before adding. Bread crumbs may be added to thicken if necessary; use only the crumbs.

BARBECUE SAUCE

2½ lbs. of butter
2 quarts of apple vinegar
1 pt. of water
1 tablespoon of dry mustard
½ cup of minced onion
1 pint of Worcestershire sauce
1 pint of tomato catsup
1 bottle chili sauce (medium size)
2 lemons, juice only
½ lemon put in whole (seed removed)
3 cloves of garlic chopped fine and tied in bag
2 teaspoons of sugar

Mix all together, cook to season well. With a mop baste meat. This is used when meat is about three-fourths done. The sauce must be kept warm.

Here are a couple of Mrs. Dull's recipes from page 58 of the 1927 *Service Star Legion Cook Book*. Both this cookbook and her 1928 one contain exhaustive descriptions of pit barbecuing.

Not long before her death at age 100, Henrietta was asked which of the *Southern Cooking* recipes were her favorite.[9] She named brain croquettes, turnips, and ice cream made with sweet potato. Of these three, I have a hunch which one most contemporary readers would prefer:

Sweet Potato Ice Cream

1 cup mashed potatoes	2 egg whites
1 cup thick whipping cream	1 teaspoon vanilla
¾ cup sugar	½ teaspoon salt

Boil, mash and strain potatoes, then measure and let cool. Add to this half of the sugar, the salt and vanilla. Beat egg whites stiff, add the remaining sugar, and beat until it will hold its shape, a perfect meringue. Whip cream, add meringue and cream to potato mixture, folding together until well mixed. Pour into pan. Place in freezing zone of any mechanical refrigerator until frozen. This will freeze smooth. If the small pan is used it will freeze in about 60 to 90 minutes. More sugar may be added if a very sweet mixture is desired. Too much sugar makes the cream icy when frozen in refrigerators. This will serve six or eight. Chopped nuts and maraschino cherries may be used if desired.

Exploring Further

Kimberly Wilmot Voss's *The Food Section: Newspaper Women and the Culinary Community* helps with placing Georgia's newspaper-related cookbooks in a national context. Grace Hartley (1905–2000), originally from Pike County, succeeded Mrs. Dull at the *Atlanta Journal* and eventually wrote her own cookbook. Others connected to Georgia who blended journalism with writing cookbooks include:[10]

Jim Auchmutey (Atlanta)
Anne Byrn (Atlanta)
Harriet Ross Colquitt (1876–1962, Savannah)
Ben G. Cooper (1902–1983, Savannah and Atlanta)
Joseph E. Dabney (1929–2015, Columbus, Atlanta, and others)
Margaret Wayt DeBolt (1930–2009, Savannah)
Louise Dodd (1929–2010, Dublin and Macon)
Clara Eschmann (1917–2002, Americus and Macon)
Damon Lee Fowler (Savannah)

Annabella Hill (1810–1878, Atlanta)
Charleen McClain (1914–2003, Atlanta)
Violet Moore (1908–1992, Montezuma)
Martha Giddens Nesbit (Savannah)
Susan Puckett (Atlanta)
Sara Spano (1908–1998, Columbus)
Mildred Evans Warren (1909–1991, Perry)

The Refrigerated Ingredient That Refreshes

When You Entertain: What to Do, and How, 1932
Ida Bailey Allen (1885–1973) for the Coca-Cola Company
124 pages. 16 recipes.

As evening arrived during summer visits to my grandparents' house, we hung out on the porch watching the fireflies come out. Catching the yellow-green winks in a canning jar was a favorite pastime. And we might as well hang out outside. As soon as dusk began to settle, thrift-minded Grandpa Frey would twist the dial to silence the air conditioning unit and then throw open all the windows. The little southern house that had been pleasant a few minutes before quickly became a hot space, damp with the smell of surrounding weedy pasture and pines. Grandma's remedy was to stash glass bottles of Coca-Cola in the fridge. She had a hand-cranked ice crusher attached to the kitchen wall, so my brother or I would be dispatched to fill a small tumbler. We'd pop the metal bottle cap for her, and she'd sip her soda. I do mean sip. She'd pour just enough cola into the glass to froth halfway up the inside. A few minutes later, she'd pour a little more, nursing it along for a half hour of heat relief. Sure, there were many times our grandparents had family-size bottles of Coke or Tab, enjoyed during meals from large plastic cups. Cola for a stand-alone summer treat, however, was a leisurely occasion. That celebration spirit fizzes through the pages of a cookbook called *When You Entertain: What to Do, and How*. It was sponsored and copyrighted by Atlanta's

Coca-Cola Company in 1932 and dedicated to "The Pause That Refreshes," echoing the cola's early catchphrase.

The plain red hardback cookbook is small, barely over a hundred pages and about the size of your hand. Even though decades had passed since the drink's 1886 invention by Georgia's John Pemberton (1831–1888) and its initial promotion by Atlanta businessman Asa Candler (1851–1929), Coke fans were used to enjoying it poured for them during a visit to a soda fountain. Now the cookbook's readers were also encouraged to order Coke from their grocer: "In many cities you can buy Coca-Cola in what is known as the 'Six-Box,' that is, a carton containing six bottles of Coca-Cola."[1] Readers were even instructed how to chill the bottles.

The author was Connecticut cooking instructor and prolific cookbook author Ida Bailey Allen. She assured readers that for gatherings, "Coca-Cola is a happy innovation that is sure to find popular favor," and then suggested suitable menus, invitations, attire, themes, table decorations, dance steps, and amusements.[2] For example, one party game suggested for grown-ups is to place a book on a table in front of a guest, blindfold them, and then ask them to kiss the book without using their hands to guide them. As they lean over, the host stealthily replaces the book with a pan filled with flour.[3] (One hopes the guest didn't have asthma and wasn't wearing black velvet.) The cookbook offered menus for events from tea parties to picnics to midnight nibbles. (Spoiler alert: "Iced Coca-Cola" is recommended for each.) Although Georgia cookbooks later in the century would list Coca-Cola

COCA-COLA FLUFF

1 package prepared lime gelatin
⅔ cup boiling water
2 bottles Coca-Cola
1 cup whipped cream

Pour the boiling water over the gelatin; stir until dissolved; cool slightly; add the Coca-Cola, and stir until thoroughly mixed. Cool and place in the refrigerator. When the gelatin starts to congeal, beat with an egg beater until foamy; then fold in the whipped cream and chill. This recipe makes four servings.

Reprint permission courtesy of the Coca-Cola Company. Please note that bottles of Coke at this time were 6.5 ounces.

Menus for Formal Teas

1

Tiny Club Salad Sandwiches
Rolled Smoked Salmon Sandwiches
Olives *Salted Brazil Nuts*
Lemon Ice *Little Silver Cakes*
Tropical Coca-Cola Punch *Tea*
French Butter Creams

TROPICAL COCA-COLA PUNCH

⅔ pint shredded pineapple
½ cup lemon juice
6 bottles iced Coca-Cola
Cracked Ice
Sprigs of Mint

Combine ingredients in the order given; put ice in punch bowl and fill with punch; serve in small glasses or punch cups; garnish with sprigs of mint. This recipe makes twelve servings.

2

Open Lobster Paste Sandwiches with Olive Garnish
Cucumber Sandwiches *Rolled Parsley Butter Sandwiches*
Orange Ice *Frosted Lady Fingers*
Tea
Mints *Nuts*

as an ingredient in everything from barbecue sauce to ham glaze to cake, Allen's simple recipes were primarily for pairing the beverage with fruit. Try your Coke over ice cubes made from frozen lemonade!

At a time when many Georgians did not yet have electricity and depended upon home delivery of ice chunks for their wooden "ice box," Allen's recipes promoted the newfangled "mechanical refrigerator." The Great Depression was grinding along, but a cold cola could be a welcome home splurge for those of modest means and a show-off party offering for those who could afford kitchen innovations.

Exploring Further

There are several Coca-Cola cookbooks out there. One, *Classic Cooking with Coca-Cola,* is coauthored by Elizabeth Candler Graham, great-great-granddaughter of founder Asa Candler. Many cola recipes can be found in books by Georgia cookbook authors. Jim Auchmutey and Susan Puckett include a recipe for Coca-Cola Barbecue Sauce in *The Ultimate Barbecue Sauce Cookbook* (page 73). For accompanying ham, Cynthia Graubart's *Sunday Suppers* has a recipe for Cola-Dijon-Brown Sugar Glaze (185), while the popular Atlanta restaurant cookbook *Mary Mac's Tea Room 75th Anniversary Cookbook* by John Ferrell offers cola-based Raisin Sauce (64). The popular cocoa-and-marshmallow Cola Cake is one of the dessert recipes in the Junior League cookbook *Savannah Style* (228).

1933

The Savannah Cook Book and Local Flavor

The Savannah Cook Book, 1933
Harriet Ross Colquitt (28 July 1876–12 January 1962)
186 pages. 289 recipes.

"It makes my mouth water to write about it," Harriet Colquitt admitted in her cookbook's recipe for fried chicken on page 56. Of a rice recipe on page 70 loaded with fourteen ingredients, she quips, "No, don't add the kitchen stove. You will need that to cook it in." For a baked shrimp recipe on page 37, she instructs, "Dust a mere idea of nutmeg." At the time of the cookbook's publication, *Atlanta Constitution* writer Bessie Stafford noted that Colquitt's style was "intimate" and "informal."[1] A reviewer for the *Savannah Morning News* wrote, "Miss Colquitt is quite unconventional. . . . This gives her book a friendly, even an intimate quality far removed from the detachment of most cook books."[2] There are wonderful things about this approach, yet it also means that this is a historical cookbook that I would take special care with in a classroom setting.[3] Colquitt's work is from a time when racial discrimination was common, so scattered through the cookbook are images, quotes, and observations that, while they give us a window into another time, are problematic.[4]

The *Savannah Morning News* reviewer pointed out that the book was rich with "local flavor." With humor and an eye for detail, Colquitt's work embraced local and regional foodways traditions in a way no Georgia cookbook had before, which may have been why it lasted through at least nine editions and several publishing companies. Originally published in Savannah's bicentennial year, it celebrated parts of the city's history and culture. For instance, there are details of coastal life in the past such as the delicacy of palmetto hearts enjoyed whenever land was cleared of these small trees. Colquitt served up more than forty seafood recipes while also describing the seafood market and vendors that offered "a picturesque touch to streets that are fast losing their charm in the march of progress." She described old-fashioned oyster roasts and shared 1880s diary accounts of boating picnics. She gave soup recipes along with a description of the "Ritual of the Bird's Eye Pepper" where a host would first crush a spicy chili into each guest's bowl. Thanks to Colquitt we know what accompanied that bowl. "Rice is passed in the South with vegetable soups, just as grated cheese is passed in Italy with clear soups." She gave additional rice customs when she explained that in the old days this grain was never served with fish. Lamenting "the passing of the rice culture in this part of the country," Colquitt gathered thirty recipes using rice as well as two for cooking the rice birds (bobolinks) found in the fields where the grain grew. "Syllabub and Ambrosia always marked red letter days in my childhood, and were invariably the signs of company to dinner," Colquitt shared. Modern readers learn old-fashioned names for familiar ingredients—buckra yam (Irish potato), guinea squash (eggplant), and see-wee beans (butterbeans).[5]

Harriet "Hattie" Colquitt was born in Wayne County in 1876 to Walter Colquitt and Lilla Habersham Colquitt while they were "sojourning" near Jessup.[6] In her early years, Hattie moved with her family both to Washington, D.C., and to Atlanta, likely due to politics and extended family ties. Hattie's father served as the Chief of Internal Revenue under President Cleveland in the 1890s, and her uncle was Alfred Holt Colquitt (1824–1894), a Georgia governor and senator.[7] By the early 1900s, city directories show Hattie living in Savannah and working at the local newspaper. Although she briefly moved to France during the First World War to aid the Red Cross, she spent the first half of her life reporting Savannah's society and literary news.[8]

Around 1928, in her early fifties, Hattie made a career change that led to the cookbook. Long a member of the National Society of the Colonial Dames of America, she opened a popular tea room called Colonial Kitchens in the Colonial Dames House at 329 Abercorn Street.[9] (Now the Andrew Low House Museum, for a time it was home to Girl Scouts founder Juliette "Daisy" Gordon Low, who

Mosianna Milledge

Despite more "downs" than "ups," the marriage of Daisy and William Low officially lasted from their 1886 wedding to his death in 1905. During that time, Mosianna Ruth Delegal Milledge (1844–1909) served as household cook.[1] The widow of former Low house servant Tom Milledge (1818–1886), Mosianna would have been very familiar with the Low House where Harriet Colquitt ran her restaurant. Mosianna accompanied Daisy to England, where she was appreciated for her southern cuisine. She shared her expertise with "Queen of Cooks" Rosa Ovenden Lewis (1867–1952), who fed celebrities, noblemen, and royalty.[2] Mosianna's work paid off to the degree that she owned multiple Savannah properties to bequeath to her children.[3]

1. Cordery, *Juliette Gordon Low*; website for the Andrew Low House Museum, "Historical Figures: The Milledges," www.andrewlowhouse.com/explore/historical-figures.
2. Cordery, *Juliette Gordon Low*; Low House website (see note 1); *Birmingham Post* (Birmingham, England), 1 December 1952; Fielding, *Duchess of Jermyn Street*, 48.
3. Georgia Wills and Probate Records, 1742–1992, Chatham County, 8 July 1902, via Ancestry.com; Gabrielle Ware, "Forgotten Women Part 8: Mosianna Milledge," Georgia Public Broadcasting News, 9 December 2015, www.gpb.org/news/2015/12/09/forgotten-women-part-8-mosianna-milledge.

married Andrew's son, William.) In the cookbook's foreword, Colquitt explains, "we have had so many requests for receipts for rice dishes, and for shrimp and crab concoctions which are peculiar to our locality, that I have concentrated on those indigenous to our soil, as it were, begging them from housekeepers, and trying to tack our elusive cooks down to some definite idea of what goes into the making of the good dishes they turn out." Thanks to ample social connections, access to a professional kitchen, and writing experience, Colquitt published the cookbook in 1933 despite the woes of the Great Depression. Complete with drawings by Savannah history teacher and novelist Florence Olmstead (1875–1955), daughter of the Confederate Colonel Charles H. Olmstead who defended Fort Pulaski in the Civil War, the cookbook received many positive reviews.[10] It is not known how long the cookbook originally remained in print or when Colonial Kitchens served its last dish, but by the 1950 census Colquitt had moved to nearby Bluffton, South Carolina. There she died in 1962 at the age of eighty-five.[11]

Exploring Further

Love the combination of recipes and stories? The following authors share Georgia-connected recipes along with tales and lore: Johnathon Scott Barrett, Joseph E. Dabney, Nathalie Dupree, Clara Belle Hooks Eschmann, Lillian Britt Heinsohn, Luann Landon, and Betty Talmadge. Although Rick Bragg hails from East Alabama, his family moved in and out of West Georgia, as he explains in *The Best Cook in the World*. Similarly, the well-known Atlanta-born author of *The Pat Conroy Cookbook* spent much of his adult life in South Carolina, but his cookbook covers adventures in many places. Stories connected to foodways abound in the memoir *It Ain't All About the Cookin'* by Savannah's Paula Deen, whose classical southern restaurant turned out to be a kickoff to television work and many cookbooks. Georgia cookbook authors Hugh Acheson, Damon Lee Fowler, Rebecca Lang, Martha Giddens Nesbit, and Virginia Willis often embrace older traditions and give storied backgrounds for their recipes. (Psst—look for more books by these authors than just the ones listed in the bibliography.)

Duncan Hines and South Georgia's Winter Season

During the Great Depression, the job of a traveling salesman was no doubt challenging. Economy aside, those were the days before interstates, global positioning systems (GPS), and hotel reservations secured through a few clicks on a cell phone. One particular salesman, a Kentuckian temporarily transplanted to Chicago, felt that finding clean and pleasant restaurants was a never-ending trial. There were no online reviews or restaurant chains with reputations to uphold. While on the road, he experienced so many soggy dinners and dirty forks that he began requesting on-the-spot kitchen inspections. (To his lasting distaste, he once discovered a restaurant owner's cat snoozing atop a warm mound of bread dough.)[1] The salesman began keeping notes and swapping recommendations with other travelers. Fellow salesmen coveted this information, and soon he received so many requests for his restaurant list that he shared it via his annual Christmas cards. It only increased demand. Thus, in 1935, the salesman published his list in book form, titling it *Adventures in Good Eating*. The salesman's name? Duncan Hines (1880–1959). Did you just think to yourself, *Isn't that a brand of cake mix?* If so, you are correct. Although a century has passed since Duncan Hines first hit the road, his name is immortalized through a popular brand of home baking products. In fact, after he joined forces with entrepreneur Ray Park (1910–1993) in 1950, many food products and cooking tools were branded in honor of the man who for twenty-seven years published more than five million books guiding the travels of the American public.

Luckily for Georgians, one of Hines's publications was the 1939 cookbook *Adventures in Good Cooking and the Art of Carving in the Home*. Among the 466 recipes inside are four for dishes served at a family-owned inn and restaurant in the small town of Ashburn. Located in South Georgia along U.S. Highway 41, then a main artery between midwestern states and the sunny vacation spots, the restaurant was quaintly named The House by the Road and was owned by Robert Royal "Bob" Shingler (1897–1966) and his wife, Lillian "Lillie" Hughes Shingler (1887–1980).[2] Hines's cookbook contains recipes for the restaurant's Waffles, Sweet Potato Soufflé, Apple Sauce (covered with toasted marshmallows), and Guinea Squash Pie.[3] In addition to his books, Hines also wrote a syndicated newspaper column, *Adventures in Good Eating at Home*, and from time to time shared additional recipes there. A search through a national newspaper database turned up additional House by the Road recipes for Tasty Banana Bread and Cranberry Chiffon Pie.[4] While many of the restaurants praised by Hines fell into obscurity after his books ceased publication,[5] Bob and Lillie Shingler had a niece growing up next door who later married into a prominent political family. Leila Elizabeth "Betty" Shingler, born in 1923, married the future senator and Georgia governor Herman Talmadge (1913–2002).[6] In time she became a leading hostess in both Atlanta and Washington, D.C., ran a successful ham business, and wrote

"THE HOUSE BY THE SIDE OF THE ROAD," A TOURIST HOME, ASHBURN, GA. 3442-29

two cookbooks. The Shingler family and its recipes are explored in former Georgia first lady Betty Talmadge's 1977 book *How to Cook a Pig and Other Back-to-the-Farm Recipes.*

171. Waffles (Makes about 6)

INGREDIENTS	DIRECTIONS
2 egg yolks 1 cup milk 1½ cups cake flour—sifted 2 teaspooons sugar 1 teaspoon salt ¼ cup butter—melted	Stir to a smooth batter.
2 egg whites—beaten stiff 2 teaspoons baking powder	Fold in eggs and baking powder. Stir lightly Bake on a hot greased waffle iron, until brown.

The House by the Road, Ashburn, Georgia

—*Adventures in Good Eating* (2014)[7]

While we're discussing tourism, Thomasville in the far south of the state became a popular vacation spot during "the winter season." In the early part of the twentieth century, Lillie May Winstead Montgomery (1887–1965) opened the Terrace Room Tea House and, although she didn't land in his cookbook, she still earned a "thumbs up" from Hines.[8] It seems she wrote a cookbook called *Favorite Recipes*. No copy of this book is known to still survive, but thankfully North Carolina's Marion Brown included the following recipe in her 1951 *Southern Cook Book*.

SWEET POTATO SOUFFLE IN ORANGE BASKETS

SERVES EIGHT

6 sweet potatoes, medium or small	*Raisins*
½ teaspoon salt	*Grated rind 2 oranges*
1 lump butter	*Orange baskets*
1 egg	*Marshmallows*

Boil potatoes, peel and mash with potato masher or ricer, season with salt and butter; add beaten egg, raisins to taste, and the grated orange rind. Make little baskets of scooped out orange shells and fill with potato mixture. Top with marshmallow and bake until light brown.

Mrs. John S. Montgomery, from Favorite Recipes, *Terrace Tea House, Thomasville, Ga.*

Reprint permission courtesy of the University of North Carolina Press.

Exploring Further

It's no surprise that these two tourist-related recipes come from the southern part of the state. Although visitors have long flocked to Georgia's cities for culture, the coast for its shores, and the mountains for cool air and views, the southern part of the state was (and is) valued for its good weather in "the winter season." South Georgia, Northern Florida, and Southeast Alabama is a region known for wiregrass and pines as well as for hunting plantations with deep hospitality traditions. Some sources about the foodways in this region include:

- *African-American Life on the Southern Hunting Plantation,* by Titus Brown and James "Jack" Hadley
- *Bobwhite Quail & Buttermilk Biscuits: A Plantation Cooks for Company,* by Dianne Evans[9]
- *Born in the Kitchen: Plain and Fancy Plantation Fixin's,* by Flora Mae Hunter[10]
- *Georgia Pines Plantation Cookbook,* by Annie Laura Willis[11]
- *Pines and Plantations: Native Recipes of Thomasville, Georgia,* by the Vashti Auxiliary
- *Quail Country,* by the Junior League of Albany, Georgia
- *Riverview Plantation Cookbook,* by Peggy C. Cox[12]
- *Southern Plantation: The Story of Labrah, Including Some of Its Treasured Recipes,* by Lillian Britt Heinsohn[13]
- *The Southern Plantations Cook,* by Leslie Delaney and David McKim[14]

Old and New Recipes on the Georgia Home Front

Old and New Recipes from the South, 1943
The Junior League of Augusta
204 pages. 527 recipes.

When the title page talks about "Old and New Recipes from the South," they can indeed be found here. Although without the background information that historical foodways lovers crave, there is an antebellum Green Tomato Crisps recipe, an 1882 biscuit recipe, and, from the granddaughter of famed Georgia horticulturalist Prosper Jules Berckmans (see 1876 section), a turn-of-the-century cake recipe.[1] On the other end of the spectrum, there are also the type of midcentury recipes that lauded American cookbook author Julia Child (1912–2004) felt were for "assemblers" rather than true cooks[2]—gelatin-based Ginger-Ale Salad made with canned fruit, Graham Cracker Cake from soaking store-bought crackers, and dinner rolls with breakfast cereal as the main ingredient.[3]

Technological changes show up in this cookbook. Even though some of its elements seem old-fashioned, such as a traditional typeface and a sprinkling of the type of line drawings that had been in cookbooks for decades, here we finally have a community cookbook with the slick paper cover and plastic comb binding many of us find so familiar. (Doesn't every charity book sale have broken pieces of those bindings underfoot in the cookbook area?) While most of the pages are plain paper with black ink, there are a couple of full color advertisements featuring camera-perfect layer cakes. Speaking of advertisements, there are the expected banks and grocery stores, but now there are ads for air conditioning, the local movie theater, and radio shows.

Shifting social mores can also be seen in this cookbook. The front cover has a simple drawing of a Black woman in a floor-length dress, her hair tied in a cloth and a mixing bowl in her hands. Conversely, the back cover advertisement is a photograph of a grinning member of the WAFS—Women's Auxiliary Ferrying Squadron—in a regulation flight suit (complete with pants), one hand on her hip and one reaching up to light her Chesterfield cigarette. Inside the cookbook, a bakery advertisement proclaims, "You needn't bother to bake!" while a commercial laundry urged, "Let us do the washing."[4] Readers could call ahead to Sanford's Chicken Coop so that they could quickly pick up raw chicken pieces for cooking at home—or they could have fried chicken and ready-to-serve sides delivered.[5] Most of the married women who contributed recipes seem to be listed by their husband's names—but not all. Other recipes are credited to personal cooks, even though not all the cooks are listed with their surnames.

That's already a lot of social change glimpsed in one cookbook. And then there's the rapidly developing home front of World War II. There are multiple advertisements for war bonds, and the recipes are affected as well. One oatmeal cookie recipe is marked "victory recipe" because the oats reduced the amount of rationed wheat flour needed (174). The cookbook's "sugarless" recipes are not to prevent tooth decay or reduce carbohydrates but rather to utilize non-rationed ingredients such as maple syrup, crushed candy, or marshmallows. There are recipes for making meat stretch farther or even swapping it out with meatless dishes like the Lima Bean and Nut Loaf from Mrs. George P. Elliott on page 189. In addition, the new Camp Gordon training facility was nearby, and several of the recipes towards the back of the cookbook come from the wives of officers stationed there. This section contained the Pearl Harbor reminder: "With a prayer and a furtive tear, the army wife has sent her little tin box of recipes to storage along with her other treasures. A tear for the happy days in Manila, Hawaii, China and Panama—a prayer that her soldier may soon come home again and life take up where it left off that December Sunday in 1941."[6]

When those cooks took up life again, when the war was over at last, the world had entered the Atomic Age followed by the Space Age. Kitchens would soon reflect rapid changes in technology, manufacturing, communication, media, and transportation. In the two centuries before World War II, Georgia had ten cookbook authors.[7] During my research, I kept a list of Georgia cookbook authors after the war, and the current count is 190. Our state's kitchens and cooks have changed greatly across our history, but one thing for sure is that Georgia is rich with recipes.

Exploring Further

We saw in earlier sections that the Civil War led to an increased sharing of foodways. This is also true with World War II. One example is the 1948 cookbook *Secrets of Southern Cooking* by Ethel Farmer Hunter (1883–1969).[8] Hunter was born in Covington and lived in Atlanta for many years before moving to Chicago. "Mrs. Hunter had been collecting these recipes for 30 years. Friends urged her to put them into book form. Following her removal to Chicago she helped entertain war brides passing thru the city. Many of the brides, tasting the southern dishes, asked for and received individual recipes, and after the war they inquired as to when Mrs. Hunter would publish her kitchen secrets. Her manuscript was a result."[9] On a more personal level, there's *From Mother with Love: A Treasury of Recipes for Cooking and Living*. "The year is 1942. Young Selma Wight Beard, a warbride from Atlanta, moves to Miami with her enlisted husband and finds that she is as much a stranger to her own kitchen as she is to south Florida."[10] This account of home front life unfolds through advice and recipes passed from Rebecca Stewart Wight (1893–1977) to her daughter (1920–2021).[11]

Historical Cooking Adventures

On Savannah's shady Madison Square, one can visit the Green-Meldrim House, a Gothic Revival home constructed in the early 1850s and later pressed into service as General Sherman's headquarters during the Civil War.[1] At the Georgia Historical Society's research center just four blocks away, one can examine miscellaneous recipes from the house, most from the early twentieth century and donated in 1944.[2] (Thus the date for this section.)

As I carefully paged through the folder, Mabel's Delicious Honey-Cakes caught my eye. The recipe appeared on a half sheet of paper, the ingredient list carefully aligned using a typewriter. The collection's finding aid gave no indication of who Mabel might be, but the warm flavorings sounded appealing as autumn approached. I copied down the recipe and gave it a go. Here's the journal entry I wrote later that night.

> I just finished dealing with Mabel's Delicious Honey-Cakes, which turned out rather Halloweenish even if it is still September. Surprisingly, there's no flour in the recipe. I think now that it was accidentally left out. Since the recipe called for "chipped almonds," however, I tried using coarse almond flour in case that's what the recipe writer was getting at. "Bake in a large pan and spread thinly" seemed simple enough. I don't have much experience with almond flour, so I'm not sure what went awry, but the top formed a crust that baked almost immediately while the batter below was still barely warm. Then I got a whiff of burning honey. I tried covering the pan with foil, but the batter soon overflowed,

dripping like brown lava into the bottom of the oven. The house now smelling like one of the upper circles of Dante's Inferno, I put on oven mitts and hurried the scorched goo out into the dark, rainy night. Depositing the smelly pan on a stump to cool and soak in the rain seemed like a good idea, but while my two hands were still occupied with a heavy pan of molten batter, I walked face-first into the very sticky and thick webs of an orb weaver spider. I don't know where the large spider ended up. And I don't who Mabel was, but maybe her ghost was out there laughing at me.

In the introductory sections to this book, we talked about the fact that old recipes aren't always easy. As we draw to a close, I want to return to that idea and offer encouragement. That September night I was admittedly disappointed to be picking spider webs out of my wet hair rather than eating warm dessert, but while I dealt with the liner in the bottom of the oven, our whole family was laughing about the kitchen shenanigans. Historical recipes are *adventures*. And the story has a happy ending. First, somebody found Mabel's recipe delicious. The next morning, I discovered a deer enthusiastically licking the soggy contents of my pan. Second, I didn't give up but instead changed my approach. Mulling over old cookie recipes, I got to thinking about one from the papers of Dr. Stella Stewart

Mabel's Delicious Honey-Cakes just before they set off the smoke alarm.

Remember creative Georgia cook Susie King Taylor from the 1862 section who made custard with turtle eggs? This educator's account, *Reminiscences of My Life in Camp with the 33d United States Colored Troops, Late 1st S.C. Volunteers*, is the only known published Civil War memoir by a Black woman who served with the Union Army.[1] She was also a prize-winning cook and for a time worked for Charles Green (1807–1881) and his wife, Aminta Fisher Green (1835–1908), of the Green-Meldrim House.[2] In 2024, Savannah's Calhoun Square was renamed Taylor Square in Susie King Taylor's honor.[3]

1. Clinton, "Susie King Taylor," 130.
2. S. Taylor, *Reminiscences*, 112–113.
3. Evan Lasseter, "Taylor Square Officially Dedicated," *SMN*, 10 February 2024.

Permission to reprint this old postcard came from the staff at the Green-Meldrim House and its owner, St. John's Church.

Center (1878–1969) of Forsyth (Monroe County), an educator of national renown who wrote many books on how to effectively teach reading.[3] The instructions in her recipe archived at Mercer University include the words "have yourself a good time!" The encouragement was helpful, and so was the fact that her recipe is inspiringly flexible, giving a cook many options.

Taking a fresh look at Mabel's recipe, I realized that what originally excited me about it was the fact that it blends warm spices with citron. *The Book of Difficult Fruit* describes this citrus fruit as "mostly fragrant peel and thick pith, with dry vesicles at the center."[4] Candied citron peel was a popular baking ingredient in the 1800s but has so fallen from favor that we rarely see it anymore except at the end of the year when grocery stores sell tubs of greenish yellow cubes soaked in syrup for making fruitcake. Realizing the spice-plus-citron flavor combination needn't be locked to a single malfunctioning recipe, I pulled out my favorite never-fail oatmeal cookie recipe and changed the spice profile to match Mabel's—cinnamon, allspice, cloves, ginger, and nutmeg. I buy candied citron each Christmas and freeze it for working with historical recipes all year long, so I thawed and drained some of the tiny cubes before dredging them in flour, adding these instead of the usual raisins.[5] The results were fantastic, the citron transforming an ordinary cookie into one graced with jewellike flecks and soft lemony flavor.

When it comes to trying your hand at old recipes, know they may result in the occasional pan of scorched goo, yet embrace the flexibility and problem-solving skills needed to follow Dr. Center's good advice. Have yourself a cooking adventure and a good time!

Cookie Recipe

1 egg
1 cup of molasses or maple syrup. Molasses and maple syrup may be mixed to form one cup.
2 tablespoons of buttermilk or sweet milk
½ cup of Crisco or other shortening (a little more than ½ cup)
1 heaping teaspoon of soda stirred into the mixture
Pour all this mixture over the beaten egg
Add nutmeg, cinnamon, cloves, or any spices you like
Add flour to make a *very* stiff batter the consistency of soft biscuit dough.
[I use 2½ cups (320g)]
Drop in a well-greased flat biscuit pan and bake.

When done, place on a
dish towel to prevent
the cookies from sticking
together
Then eat them and have
yourself a good time!

—Stella Stewart Center Collection, 1904–1969, Mercer University, Jack Tarver Library, Macon[6]

This is how preserved citron looks. It should have a fresh and mild lemony flavor, but some brands are better than others.

Acknowledgments

I would first like to thank some "foundation builders." Food historian Damon Lee Fowler's writings on Georgia foodways made this book seem possible when I was still just daydreaming about it. And even though he didn't know me at first, he graciously answered periodic questions when I got stuck. Somehow Dr. Clifford Shillinglaw (1914–1979) of the Coca-Cola Company, assisted by Elisabeth Woodburn, managed to pull together an amazing collection of old Georgia cookbooks in the days before the Internet. This collection, now housed at the Atlanta History Center, was a huge boon to this project. Next, I would like to state that I am in awe of the dedicated people behind Georgia Historic Newspapers, the Georgia Newspaper Project, and the *New Georgia Encyclopedia*. The work you do is important and helped greatly with this book. And I am grateful to William "Doc. Bill" Thomas, who encouraged Georgians of Geechee and Cherokee descent to record their recipes, and who documented many recipes and traditions himself.

I am thankful to early readers who helped me find new perspectives (and typos): Jan Burkins, Rachel Clark, Cynthia Graubart, Lace Keaton, Evan Mathis, Michael Price, Pooya Rezai, Marshall Shepherd, Luciana Spracher, Brian Stone, Tamika Strong, Erin Zimmerman, and the Journey Class. I appreciate the encouragement.

Several people used their networks to help me make beneficial connections: Elizabeth Adams Thomas, Don Bower, Amanda Bright, Margaret Compton, Cindy Darden, Tim Foutz, James Guined, Rebecca Lang, Kaye Minchew, Russell Worth Parker, Jerry Shannon, Kathy Stone, Welch Suggs, Paul Van Wicklen, Janet Wright, and Noel Wright.

I am thankful for the expertise of various cooks, gardeners, genealogists, local "history-keepers," and others who shared special knowledge, including Millie Adams, Rogers Barde,

Cliff Brock, Paul M. Bulloch, Jan Burroughs, Laura Carter, Dale Couch, Charles B. Evans, Emily Formica, Eric Frey, Cleveland Gipson, Dusty Gres, Janice Hume, Greg Jarrell, Mandi Johnson, Suzanne Kantziper, Harriet Meyerhoff, Hans Neuhauser, Kevin O'Neal, Sylvia Pannell, John Preston, Gloria Pylant, Carolyn Henry Rader, Michelle Reaves, Penny Richards, Jennifer Smith, and Katie Smith.

People sometimes helped with loans or gifts of old kitchen tools, recipes, cookbooks, or other resources that made this book richer: John Albert, Carolyn Houseman Andrews, Alexander W. Barbee Jr., Laura Botts, Judy Byck, Janet Clark, Jacob Douylliez, Paula Eubanks, Cynthia Graubart, Phil and Sallie Hale, Susan Hoffius, Sandy Hudson, Amy Pontzer Jones, Amanda and Brandy Justice, Kaye Kole, Sarah Lamb, Brenda Mealing, Mary Rufo, Mary Stakes, Carolyn Steuer, Carl Stone, Ellen Stoneburner, Rita Trotz, JoAnn Wood, and Janet Wright.

Ever met one of those self-taught local historians who quietly go about making sure facts and stories about a community aren't lost forever? I'm grateful for the help of Mike Buckner (Talbot County), LeBon G. Abercrombie (Hancock County), and Eve B. Mayes (Clarke County).

I had very good experiences conducting research at various organizations, but sometimes staff really went the extra mile:

Ashantilly Center—Harriet Langford
Athens-Clarke County Library—Ashley Shull
Atlanta History Center—Leah Lefkowitz and Sue Verhoef
Bartow History Museum—Sandy Moore
Camden Archives and Museum (South Carolina)—Katherine H. Richardson
City of LaGrange Cemeteries—David Satterwhite
Cobb Landmarks & Historical Society—Trevor Beemon
Emory University Libraries—Kim Norman
Georgia Archives—Caroline Crowell, Linda Geiger, and Amanda Mros
Georgia Department of Natural Resources—Jan Mackinnon
Georgia Historical Society—Nate Pedersen
Georgia Military College—Joelle Trumbo
Georgia Public Library Service—Julie Walker
Georgia Southern University Libraries/Lane Library—Caroline Hopkinson
Juliette Gordon Low Birthplace—Kathryn White
Mercer University, Jack Tarver Library Special Collections—Daniel Williams
Middle Georgia Regional Library—Muriel Jackson
Roosevelt's Little White House—Jason Grantham
Savannah Municipal Archives—Luciana Spracher
Telfair Museums—Beth Moore
Traveler's Rest Historic Site, Georgia State Parks—Joshua Purdy

Troup County Archives—Clark Johnson
University of Georgia Archives—Gilbert Head
University of Georgia Libraries—Nan McMurray
Woodrow Wilson Presidential Library—Emily Kilgore

Many thanks to my editors, Nathaniel Holly and Lea Johnson, my copy editor Ann Marlowe, designer Erin Kirk, production manager Melissa Buchanan, and the rest of the staff at University of Georgia Press who have made this a wonderful experience.

A special thanks goes to Paula Eubanks, a community-minded and caring friend who knows how to encourage creative projects—and has a knack for cheerfully turning up when a need is great. Several times in my life, the need was great and there you were. Bless you. Also, to my supportive Wednesday Ladies—Nancy Carter, Marianne Causey, Cindy Darden, Sandy Hudson, Lane Norton, Charlalee Sedgwick, and Janet Wright. Last but not least, Sam Clark, Nikki Preston, Heidi Thomas, and Dominic Thomas for their never-ending encouragement.

Most of all, I am grateful to my husband, Brian, and son, Eli. From emotional support to overlooking me buying *another* old cookbook to patient stops at cemeteries and historical markers, you were always there for me during this decade-long project, and I love you.

ONE CUP 8OZ
3/4 CUP 6OZ
1/2 CUP 4OZ
2OZ

Appendix A

Guide to Measures and Temperatures

I have come across contradictory information, so the values below are not absolute but rather good starting places for working with a recipe.

Traditional Measures

Blade of mace = scant 1⁄4 teaspoon powdered mace
Bushel = 8 gallons (dry measure)
Coffee cup = about two tablespoons less than a standard cup
DO/do. = ditto or repeat
Drachm/dram = 3⁄4 teaspoon
Drop — 40 drops = one teaspoon
Firkin = 10 gallons
Fistful (flour or cornmeal) = 1⁄3 cup
Gill = 1⁄2 cup
Glass = 1⁄4 cup
Goblet = about two tablespoons less than a standard cup
Hogshead = large barrel, usually 63 gallons
Jack = 1⁄4 cup
Jigger = about 3 tablespoons

Lump Measurements:

- Lump of butter = 1 rounded tablespoon
- Size of an egg = 3 tablespoons
- Size of a goose egg = 6 tablespoons
- Size of a guinea or partridge egg = 2 tablespoons
- Size of a hazelnut = 1 teaspoon
- Size of a hickory/walnut = 1½ tablespoons
- Size of a quail egg = 1½ teaspoons
- Size of a turkey egg = 5 tablespoons

Noggin = ½ cup

Nutmeg (whole) = 2 teaspoons ground spice (stronger than the jar version)

Peck = 2 gallons (dry measure)

Pinch = amount lifted between thumb and first two fingers, scant ¼ teaspoon

Pint = 2 cups

Pottle = 2 quarts

Quarten = 1 quart

Quartern = a quarter (usually a quarter of a pint or ½ cup)

Saucer = 1 cup plus 1 tablespoon

Saucepan = small pan, 1 to 3 quarts

Spoons:

- Coffee spoon = ½ teaspoon
- Dessert spoon = 1 to 2 teaspoons
- Kitchen spoon = 1 teaspoon
- Soup spoon = 2 to 3 teaspoons, scant tablespoon
- Spoonful = 1 tablespoon
- Salt spoon = ⅛ to ¼ teaspoon

Stewpan = large pot, 4 to 10 quarts

Sugar, loaf (broken up): 1 pound = 1 quart

Teacup/teacupful = 4 to 6 fluid ounces, usually around 2/3 cup

Thimbleful = scant teaspoon

Tumbler (drinking glass) = 1 cup

Wine glass = around ¼ cup or four tablespoons

Many older sources state that ten unbroken eggs weigh a pound, which indicates older households expected to use eggs we now think of as "medium" size.

Oven Temperatures

Estimations and terms vary from source to source. Compare old recipes with modern ones before cooking.

Blood warm = 98°F
Touch warm = 100°F–115°F
Very cool = 225°F
Very slow = 250°F
Cool/slack = 275°F
Slow = 275°F–300°F
Moderately slow/very moderate = 325°F
Moderate/medium = 350°F
Moderately hot/quick = 375°F–400°F
Hot/quick/fast = 450°F–500°F
Very/extremely hot = 500°F or more

Appendix B

Abbreviations for Commonly Cited Georgia Periodicals

AB	*Athens Banner*
AC	*Atlanta Constitution*
ADH	*Athens Daily Herald*
AG	*Augusta Gazette*
AJ	*Atlanta Journal*
AJC	*Atlanta Journal-Constitution*
ATR	*Americus Times-Recorder*
AuC	*Augusta Chronicle*
BA	*Brunswick Advertiser*
BN	*Brunswick News*
CDE	*Columbus Daily Enquirer*
CE	*Columbus Enquirer*
CES	*Columbus Enquirer Sun*
CL	*Columbus Ledger*
CP	*Cherokee Phoenix* (New Echota)
DCS	*Daily Chronicle and Sentinel* (Augusta)
DG	*Darien Gazette*
DM	*Danielsville Monitor*
DS	*Daily Sun* (Columbus)
FM	*Friend and Monitor* (Washington)
GC	*Georgia Constitutionalist* (Augusta)

GJ	*Georgia Journal* (Milledgeville)
GWTGJM	*Georgia Weekly Telegraph and Georgia Journal & Messenger* (Macon)
JNF	*Jefferson News & Farmer* (Louisville)
LE	*Ledger-Enquirer* (Columbus)
MJ	*Marietta Journal*
MN	*Morning News* (Savannah)
MT	*Macon Telegraph*
MWT	*Macon Weekly Telegraph*
NGC	*North Georgia Citizen* (Dalton)
SB	*Southern Banner* (Athens)
SC	*Southern Cultivator* (Augusta/Athens)
SCDF	*Southern Cultivator and Dixie Farmer* (Atlanta)
SDG	*Savannah Daily Georgian*
SDR	*Savannah Daily Republican*
SEP	*Savannah Evening Press*
SFH	*Southern Farm and Home* (Macon)
SH	*Sandersville Herald*
SI	*Sparta Ishmaelite*
SMN	*Savannah Morning News*
SNP	*Savannah News-Press*
SS	*Sunny South* (Atlanta)
TB	*The Banner* (Athens)
UP	*Upson Pilot* (Thomaston)
UR	*Union & Recorder* (Milledgeville)
WC	*Weekly Constitution* (Atlanta)
WNA	*Weekly News and Advertiser* (Albany)
WT	*Weekly Telegraph* (Macon)

Notes

Rediscovering Georgia's Historical Recipes

1. Ellen Moseley (1830–1900) lived in Cleveland County. Her recipe and an exploration of it can be found in my *Preserving Family Recipes*, 134–139.

2. Sometimes old recipes don't work well with modern appliances. Powerful electric mixers, for instance, can ruin the texture of a recipe developed for hand mixing. On the other hand, labor-intensive recipes may find new life; food processors created a beaten biscuits renaissance. Trial and error are necessary.

3. In *Preserving Family Recipes*, 79, I compared a year of a nineteenth-century homemaker's magazine with a single issue of a contemporary one. The older magazine's 124 recipes called for 160 ingredients while the single modern issue offered 56 recipes calling for 199 ingredients. Although this is just one study, it points to a trend.

4. University presses in Georgia, South Carolina, and Kentucky have reproduced old cookbooks. Specialty presses include Andrews McMeel (American Antiquarian Cookbook Collection), Oxmoor House (Antique American Cookbooks), Applewood Books, and Bear Wallow Books. Entities that digitize old cookbooks and make them publicly available online include Feeding America, Google, HathiTrust, Internet Archive, and Project Gutenberg.

5. Kummer, *The Pleasures of Slow Food.*

6. See Pollan, *The Omnivore's Dilemma*; Rehak, *Eating for Beginners*; Schlosser, *Fast Food Nation.*

7. Borel et al., "The Future of Food"; Lidz, "Welcome to Farmtopia."

8. In "Keeping *Joy of Cooking* in the Family," John Becker, great-grandson of cookbook author Irma Rombauer, discusses how early American cookbook authors largely kept their personal information out of their work.

9. "Inflation Calculator," U.S. Official Inflation Data, Alioth Finance, www.officialdata.org.

10. Dennis and Wright, *Annie Dennis' Cook Book*, 184.

11. These days companies add molasses back in to create brown sugar, yet the analogy works.

12. My vita includes additional archives-related work I enjoyed greatly, but these were my full-time positions.

13. I will donate these materials to appropriate institutions.

14. K. Moss, *Seeking the Historical Cook*, 20.

Recipes in Context I: Old Recipes in Your Modern Kitchen

1. Blogger David Walbert explored cornstarch cake and reported that it "tastes lousy," which my experiments confirmed. See "1855: Cornstarch Cake," *David Walbert's Compendium of Instruction and Entertainment* blog, 17 September 2018. www.davidwalbert.com/dw/2018/09/17/1855-cornstarch-cake/#more-6046.

2. Chapter 3 of my book *Preserving Family Recipes* explores tips for working with difficult recipes.

3. For such tables see K. Moss, *Seeking the Historical Cook*, 9–11, 15–17.

4. Cotner interview, 25 July 2007.

5. Online searches for "hearth cooking," "reenactment," or "living history" along with your location may help you find groups and events. Staff at a nearby house museum, historical society, or state park may also know of programs.

6. Clifton, *One Hearth, One Pot*, 6.

7. Clifton, *Smith Plantation—Clarissa Clifton Food Blog*, http://roswellfam.com/market-posts.

Recipes in Context II: Cookbooks as History

1. V. Frey, "Yesteryear's Puddings," referencing Wilson, *Tested Recipe Cook Book*.

2. Genealogy and newspaper databases are available for home use by subscription, or you may be able to access them through your local library.

3. S. Williams, *Savory Suppers & Fashionable Feasts*, 11–12.

4. Arlie Mae Reaves Frey (1917–2000) was a lifelong resident of Cleveland County.

5. V. Frey, *Preserving Family Recipes*, 37.

6. Donovan et al., *The Thirteen Colonies Cookbook*, 233–252.

7. Kitchen Guild, *Tullie's Receipts*. The Atlanta Historical Society is now the Atlanta History Center.

8. Van Willigen, *Kentucky's Cookbook Heritage*, 7.

9. Both newspapers are quoted in a display advertisement from *AC*, 27 November 1904.

10. Dennis, *New Annie Dennis Cook Book* (1921 ed.), preface.

11. Mitchell, "Rhetoric of Celebrity Cookbooks," 527.

12. Theophano, *Eat My Words*, 6.

A Few Details about This Book

1. OCLC is a nonprofit global library organization, www.worldcat.org.

2. For ArchiveGrid, go to https://researchworks.oclc.org/archivegrid.

3. The PINES online catalog is at https://gapines.org.

4. *The Sifter*, created by Barbara Ketcham Wheaton, https://thesifter.org; *The Food Timeline*, created by Lynne Olver, www.foodtimeline.org.

1733, What Ingredients Did the Georgia Colonists Have?

1. Some sources use the spelling *Ann*. Period documents give the date as the first of February, 1733, but the New Style date is the twelfth. Of the original passengers, two toddlers died at sea.

2. Ferris, *Matzoh Ball Gumbo*. Colonial Georgia became home to both Sephardic and Ashkenazi Jews.

3. Manuscript, University of North Carolina, #00011, Series 3, Folder 43. Ten of the recipes are transcribed in *The Backcountry Housewife* by Moss and Hoffman.

4. For a list of foods, I gleaned the primary sources in *Georgia Journeys* by Temple and Coleman and in Moore's *A Voyage to Georgia*.

5. Reverend Boltzius of the Salzburger immigrants similarly noted this.

6. Bartram, *Travels*, 25; Sanders, *Guide to William Bartram's Travels*, 83; DeVorsey, "Indian Trails," *New Georgia Encyclopedia*, www.georgiaencyclopedia.org.

7. K. Moss, *Seeking the Historical Cook*, 12.

8. Yentsch, "Applying Concepts from Historical Archaeology."

9. Manuscript, #00011, Series 3, Folder 43, pages 80–81. Schmitt's life dates are unknown, but a document places her in Liberty County in 1804; see estate records for W. H. Sallett, Georgia Wills and Probate Records, 1742–1992, probated 10 June 1804, via Ancestry.com.

1734, Reverend Boltzius and Salzburger Beer

1. Carol Ebel, "Johann Martin Boltzius," *New Georgia Encyclopedia*, www.georgiaencyclopedia.org/articles/history-archaeology/johann-martin-boltzius-1703-1765/.

2. Bolzius, *Extract of the Journals*, 63. For ease of reading, the "long *s*" in which the lowercase *s* looks like a lowercase *f* has been updated. Multiple transcriptions are available of this source with slightly varied capitalization and spellings. Also, what we

now call fir trees grow in cooler climates and higher altitudes than coastal Georgia, and therefore the colonists were likely using a different conifer.

3. To purchase copies of the cookbook, visit the Georgia Salzburger Society Museum at 2980 Ebenezer Road, Rincon, Georgia 31326.

1736, Tomochichi's Oyster Roast

1. Thicknesse, *Memoirs and Anecdotes*, 29. For ease of reading, the historical "long *s*" that looks like a lowercase *f* has been updated, but spellings have been retained. There is a monument to Tomochichi in Savannah's Wright Square, where tradition says he was buried.

2. Manuscript, GHS 0602, Box 3, Folder 23, Item 257.

1763, Exotic Ingredients in the Backcountry

1. Cashin, *A Wilderness*, 25.

2. Hilliard, *Hog Meat and Hoecake*, 115–122.

3. Edgeworth, *Southern Gardener*, 243.

1773, Indigenous Nut Milk and the Expeditions of William Bartram

1. Bartram, *Travels*, 25. Spelling not corrected.

2. Manuscript, #01478, Heard Family Recipe Books, Series 3, Folder 214, Volume 69 (1828–1867), 109. Anna Edgar lived 1810–1891.

3. Manuscript, GHS 0857, Item 1. Anna White lived 1818–1852.

4. Ben Richmond, "The Forgotten Drink That Caffeinated North America for Centuries," 28 March 2018, www.atlasobscura.com/articles/what-is-yaupon-tea-cassina. The food section of the online magazine *Atlas Obscura* published *Gastro Obscura: A Food Adventurer's Guide*, edited by Cecily Wong and Dylan Thuras (New York: Workman, 2021). The book does not include cassina.

1774, Telfair Biskets on the Rise

1. Modern reprints of many early American cookbooks are available. Georgia author Christopher E. Hendricks and his mother, Sue, created a beautiful cookbook called *Old Southern Cookery* adapting Randolph's recipes.

2. See Charles J. Johnson, "Telfair Family," *New Georgia Encyclopedia*, www.georgiaencyclopedia.org/articles/history-archaeology/telfair-family.

3. Telfair Museums, www.telfair.org/visit/telfair-academy.

4. Donovan, *The Thirteen Colonies Cookbook*, 233–252.

5. Ibid., 234.

6. Manuscript, GHS 0793, Box 12, Folder 103, Item 426, Page 49. The handwriting is florid and the pages both worn and stained. Any errors in transcription are mine.

7. V. Frey, *Preserving Family Recipes*, 218; Figoni, *How Baking Works*, 287–301.

8. Civitello, *Baking Powder Wars*, 19.

9. Ibid., 18–20.

10. Figoni, *How Baking Works*, 288; Sandra L. Oliver, "Chemical Leavening," in A. Smith, *Oxford Companion*, 109–110.

11. I was unable to find life dates or significant biographical information about Jackson.

12. A copy of this pamphlet can be found at the Georgia Historical Society, Savannah, in GHS 1276, George Nowlan Saussy Correspondence and Papers, 1864–1910, Box 5, Folder 35.

1783, Springer Vinegar and Labor-Intensive Ingredients

1. Both Annabella Hill and Evelyn Spalding recommended using peach leaves with yeast. See 1867 and 1863 sections.

2. Manuscript, #00011, Series 3, Folder 43, page 93.

3. *SC* 27 (1869): 325. This article was shared from Mississippi.

4. Kimball, *Fannie's Last Supper*. There is a corresponding documentary.

1786, Chatham Artillery Punch, the Legendary Drink

1. Schmidt, *The Flowing Bowl*, interior of front cover. Because of the rare manuscript recipe and the book's age, the University of Georgia's copy of this book has moved from the Science Library, where most of the university's modern cookbooks are housed, to the Hargrett Rare Book and Manuscript Library. The recipe is similar to the one in Colquitt's *Savannah Cook Book*.

2. *Hutchinson* (Kans.) *News*, 26 April 1904.

3. *Philadelphia Inquirer*, 12 December 1965.

4. *SNP*, "Chatham Punch," 18 May 1986.

5. Robert White, "A Revolutionary Libation," *San Francisco Examiner*, 13 August 1986, 68. Paper place mats at the Pirates' House offer a recipe for making more than nine gallons of the punch.

6. Ralph McGill, "The Punch That Floored the Late Admiral Dewey," *AC*, 20 March 1944, 14.

7. Paddleford, *Great American Cookbook*, 264.

8. Colquitt, *Savannah Cook Book*, 167.

9. *AC*, 23 March 1893; *SMN*, 23 March 1893.

10. *Baltimore Sun*, 7 May 1885; Wondrich, *Punch*, 249; Tramazzo, *Bourbon and Bullets*, 193; *SMN*, 14 July 1879; *Darien Timber Gazette*, 18 July 1879.

11. A brief article from the *Baltimore Sun* on 7 May 1885 gives information from "the centennial edition" of the *Augusta Chronicle*. Although without specific measurements, it lists Chatham Artillery Punch ingredients as brandy, whisky, rum, sugar, lemon, and champagne.

12. DeBolt, *Savannah Sampler Cookbook*, 27.

13. *AC*, 30 April 1870.

14. *CDE*, 24 December 1876.

15. *Cedar Rapids* (Iowa) *Gazette*, 21 April 1883; *Hamilton County News* (Aurora, Neb.), 27 April 1883; *Omaha Daily Bee*, 7 November 1909.

16. *Meade* (Kans.) *Republican*, 16 March 1892; *Montgomery* (Ala.) *Advertiser*, 19 January 1902; *Los Angeles Times*, 20 October 1907.

17. *MN*, 21 March 1900.

18. *Indianapolis News*, 26 October 1909; *Yuma* (Ariz.) *Examiner*, 4 November 1909; *Warren* (Pa.) *Times Mirror*, 5 November 1909.

19. *Tampa Tribune*, 10 November 1909.

20. *AC*, 22 March 1900.

21. *MN*, 5 June 1890.

22. DeBolt, *Savannah Sampler Cookbook*, 27.

23. *MN*, 5 June 1890; *MN*, 29 January 1892.

24. *Omaha Daily Bee*, 7 November 1909.

25. *Washington Post*, 19 November 1911.

26. See note 6.

27. Fowler, *The Savannah Cookbook*, 47.

28. Ibid., 46–47.

29. *Pensacola News*, 30 August 1966.

30. Nichols, *The Geechee Cook Book*, 49.

31. Information about unprocessed collections is usually not public, so it is possible that the papers are waiting in some institution for an archivist's work time. Colleagues in likely institutions, however, kindly checked their lists of unprocessed materials without luck.

32. Sheehy and Wallace, *Civil War Savannah*, 1:348.

33. Margaret Branch Sexton (1869–1961) donated the book in honor of her deceased husband, James L. Sexton (1869–1934).

34. See note 6.

35. Wendell Brock, "'Joy' for a New Generation," *AJC*, 14 November 2019, E4–E5.

1806, Parsnip Wine and Newspaper Recipes

1. Debra Reddin van Tuyll, "Nineteenth-Century Georgia Newspapers," *New Georgia Encyclopedia*, www.georgiaencyclopedia.org/articles/arts-culture/nineteenth-century-georgia-newspapers.

2. Samuel Corbett, "For a Pipe," *AG*, 27 July 1799.

3. *Georgia Republican & State Intelligencer* (Savannah), 12 August 1803.

4. Pipes and Janowitz, "Op-Ed," 75; Theophano, *Eat My Words*, 155–156.

5. See note 1.

1809, Marble Cake, a Duel, and Recipe Names

1. Katherine E. Rohrer, "David B. Mitchell," *New Georgia Encyclopedia*, www.georgiaencyclopedia.org/articles/government-politics/david-b-mitchell-1766-1837.

2. Gilchrist, *Ordeals*, 191–193. Newspapers as far away as New York and Ireland later reported on the event.

3. Witt Callaway, "Dueling in Georgia," *New Georgia Encyclopedia*, www.georgiaencyclopedia.org/articles/history-archaeology/dueling-georgia.

4. Kitchens, *Ghosts of Grandeur*, 163–166.

5. Page 4 of the third edition states, "This book has been reprinted in its original form."

6. Egerton, *Southern Food*, 217.

7. Civitello, *Baking Powder Wars*, 24.

8. Byrn, *American Cake*, 40–24; Patent, *Baking in America*, 200. The earliest evidence of marble cake I have found is in newspaper reports from local fairs in the late 1850s. Recipes soon after treated it as a novelty, explaining what marble cake will look like when baked. The earliest known Georgia recipe was printed in the *Calhoun Weekly Times* on 6 June 1871, but the instructions would simply produce colored layers.

9. Verstille, *Southern Cookery*, 124.

10. The third edition contains a gingerbread recipe listed as 115 years old (page 78) and one for mincemeat listed as 150 years old (page 114). Depending on how soon the second edition of the cookbook followed the first and if these recipes were part of the first edition, it indicates these recipes were at least from the 1830s and 1790s, respectively.

11. Fowler's commentary in Hill, *Mrs. Hill's Southern Practical Cookery*, xxviii.

1838, Indigenous Foodways

1. *Cedar Rapids* (Iowa) *Gazette*, 23 January 1966.

2. These, according to Ray, *Ethnicity*, are the main groups associated with lands now within Georgia political boundaries. See pages 99–102, 114–119, 199–201, 224–226, and 254–255.

3. Despite Sequoyah (ca. 1770–ca. 1840) of the Cherokees creating a syllabary to transform spoken language into written words, my research turned up no written Cherokee recipes from before the twentieth century. The *Cherokee Phoenix* newspaper printed from 1828 to 1834 did include some recipes, but they were reprinted from mainstream newspapers in other locations. (See Ted Wadley, "Sequoyah," *New Georgia Encyclopedia*, www.georgiaencyclopedia.org/articles/history-archaeology/sequoyah-ca-1770-ca-1840.)

4. Kimmerer, *Braiding Sweetgrass*, 367–368. Zafar touches on a similar African concept called *sankofa* in *Recipes for Respect*, 5, 69–78.

5. This book was edited by Mary Ulmer and Samuel E. Beck, published by Mary and Goingback Chiltoskey, and copyrighted by the Museum of the Cherokee Indian.

6. Many newspaper articles as well as the cookbook mention this family connection. An editor's note for an autobiographical account by Lossiah called "The Story of My Life" in the Fall 1984 *Journal of Cherokee Studies* states that Chief John Ross was Lossiah's great-grandfather. My genealogical research was unable to determine Lossiah's connection.

7. Aubrey Jennings, "John Ross' Granddaughter Honored for Her Knowledge of Indian Lore," 25 May 1952, *Asheville* (N.C.) *Citizen-Times*.

8. Aggie Ross Lossiah death certificate, State of North Carolina, 1966, via Ancestry .com.

9. *Danville* (Va.) *Register*, "Mrs. Aggie R. Lossiah Dies: Beloved Cherokee Woman," 22 January 1966.

10. The spiral-bound book was edited by Georgia foodways enthusiast William "Doc. Bill" Thomas, who also edited *Foods of Georgia's Barrier Islands*, discussed in the 1863 section.

11. Murray, *Grits*, 59–62; Portman, "A Taste of Cherokee Cooking."

12. The website for I-Collective (Indigenous, Inspired, Innovative, and Independent) is www.icollectiveinc.org.

1840, Frolic Foods

1. *Milledgeville Federal Union*, 2 June 1840.

2. *NGC*, 13 August 1885.

3. Some advertisements for grocers and bakeries listed provisions intended for picnics, so this is an additional source of information. An article in the *Savannah Morning News* on 10 July 1904 offers an exhaustive list of picnic tools and utensils.

4. The same newspaper reported on 11 July 1879 that the picnic was a success with a mixed-race crowd between 600 and 1,000 people. There was music, dancing, and barbecue.

5. Southerners are sometimes chided for putting sugar in everything but their cornbread. Indeed, most of Georgia's historical cookbooks offer a wide array of sweets.

6. Eschmann, *Remember When—?*, 32–34. Additional pulled candy information can be found on page 193 of *The Athens Woman's Club Cook Book* (1922).

7. Mary Lane, "Cane Grindin' in Candy County," *AC*, 23 November 1947.

8. This program was supported by a grant from the Georgia Humanities Council.

9. Manuscript, GHS 2149, Book 4, unpaginated. A spider is a cast iron pan with long legs to straddle the coals of a fire.

1858, Elise's Tea Cakes

1. The specific copy in question is held by the Kenan Research Center, Atlanta History Center, MSS 139, Martha Lumpkin Compton Papers, 1832–1919, Box 1, Folder 1.

2. "Atlanta's Godmother Celebrates Birthday," *AC*, 26 August 1914; "Godmother of Atlanta Dead," *Kansas City Star*, 22 February 1917.

3. Harris, *High on the Hog*, 109; Wallace-Sanders, *Mammy*, 133–134.

4. Adele Alexander, *Ambiguous Lives*. The span between the 1860 and 1870 censuses is sometimes called "The Wall" for African American genealogy. Along with traditional research and hands-on cooking, foodways historian Michael W. Twitty (*The Cooking Gene*) used DNA tests to help him discover ancestral connections.

5. In addition to the Atlanta History Center collection cited in note 1, Emory University holds MSS 1074, Martha Lumpkin Compton Scrapbooks, 1832–1919. Governor Lumpkin's papers are held by various institutions as well.

6. This article by an Athens correspondent of the *Atlanta Constitution*, printed with the title "Martha Lumpkin" on 24 September 1893, was soon shared widely across the country in other newspapers. Microfilm copies from other places are often more legible than the original; see *Alameda* (Calif.) *Daily Argus*, 16 October 1893.

7. *AC*, 10 October 1902; *SMN*, 10 October 1902. Holt is buried in Athens's Gospel Pilgrim Cemetery in the southwest portion of Section F, while Compton is buried in Section 1 of Atlanta's Oakland Cemetery. Both women died before Georgia began keeping official death records. In the 1880 census, Thomas and Martha "Mattie" Compton are listed with a seven-year-old daughter from Thomas's previous marriage, who seems to have been adopted by Martha, according to Clarke County records for the couple's 19 December 1878 marriage as well as guardianship records from 23 October 1885 and 1 December 1890, via Ancestry.com. At the same address, 440 Lumpkin Avenue, the 1880 census also lists four Holts—Caroline (age 40), Molley (40), Susie (15), and Wilson (9). The Holts are all listed as Black except for Susie, who is "Mulatto."

8. *AB*, 7 March 1917.

9. Fulton County Wills, 16 April 1908, via Ancestry.com.

10. Bishop, "Speaking Sisters," 95.

11. Most modern baking recipes use the "creaming method," combining the fat with the sugar. Another method is to rub the flour into the fat with your fingers. Both work with this recipe. Georgia food writer Alton Brown's baking cookbook, *I'm Just Here for More Food*, is an excellent source to learn about mixing methods for baking.

12. The first mention of an eggbeater in a Georgia cookbook that I've been able to find is in Mrs. Hill's work from 1867 (page 15).

13. It is always possible that someone else wrote the recipe in the cookbook, but the handwriting seems to match Compton's other writings.

14. Knight, *Georgia's Landmarks*, 445.

15. *Chattanooga Daily Times*, 27 August 1915.

16. University of Georgia, "Buildings and Locations: Lumpkin House." *University of Georgia A-Z Index*, www.uga.edu/a-z/location/lumpkin-house.html.

17. Just down Cedar Hill, on the grounds of the UGA Center for Continuing Education & Hotel near its Lumpkin Street parking deck entrance, is a small stone monument erected by the Georgia Daughters of the American Revolution in 1930. It reads, "Here passed the old Indian trail used by the Creeks of the Savannah River Basin, the

Cherokees of Upper Georgia and Tennessee, and by trading parties of other tribes."

18. Although we don't know if Caroline retained contact with her parents after she was "gifted" to Martha, this is just one of many stories of enslaved parent/child separations that I came across during my research into antebellum recipes. It was a constant burr in my mind while my son and I baked Elise's Tea Cakes together.

19. Old recipes is a topic many would assume is benign, yet while researching this book I came across many disturbing stories of abuses and injustices that will always haunt me. Worse still, they were often told by people of the day with indifference, scorn, or even humor. As a parent, I share many uncomfortable truths of history with my son through museums, historic sites, and books, but I know him well enough to gauge how much he can handle, and I can be present when he wants to talk more about his thoughts—conditions that are unfortunately rare in the classroom.

20. To complicate matters, my five-times-great-grandparents were among the European Americans making a home in the 1770s in what became Clarke County.

1859, Mrs. Edgeworth's Antebellum Homestead

1. Egerton, *Southern Food*, 20.

2. Edgeworth, *Southern Gardener*, 186.

3. Starting in 1732 with the preparations for the colonists' arrival in early 1733.

4. Ferris, "Gender and Food," 59.

5. Veit, *Food in the Civil War Era*, 8; Barile, *Cookbooks Worth Collecting*, 97.

6. Egerton, *Southern Food*, 20.

7. W. Lewis, *Genealogy*, 247–249.

8. Fruitless searches were conducted in county cemetery records as well as in historic cemeteries in the areas of Spartanburg, S.C., Cartersville, Ga., and Fort Valley, Ga., for the graves of Mary and her second husband. There is a space between the graves of Joseph Michal and Sarah Michal, Mary's first husband and daughter, in Magnolia Cemetery in Spartanburg, so perhaps Mary is buried there. There are also unmarked open spaces in Rowland Cemetery where she may rest. The current owner of the former Edgeworth land in Peach County kindly let me know that there are no known graves on that land.

9. Mary is listed as 28 rather than 32 in the 1850 census and 42 rather than 52 in 1870. She was not found in the 1860 census.

10. According to the 1870 census, Salathiel Edgeworth was born around 1823, and multiple family trees on Ancestry.com gave his birthdate as 20 October 1823 but did not cite the source of this information. The 1880 census put his birth year around 1826.

11. W. Lewis, *Genealogy*, 239, 247.

12. *Weekly Mississippian* (Jackson), 30 September 1863.

13. W. Lewis, *Genealogy*, 247–249. Tombstone inscriptions were also used. A letter written by Mary's father in 1855 states that Mary was his eldest daughter; see John Sharpe

Rowland to William T. Lewis, 8 October 1855, William Terrell Lewis Papers (unprocessed), 1830–1896, Alabama Department of Archives and History, via Ancestry.com.

14. In various records and online family trees, the surname is spelled both Michal and Michael. Since Mary was alive when the tombstones were erected for family members with this surname and they all show "Michal," I stayed with this spelling. See *Western Star of Liberty* (Rutherford, N.C.), 8 December 1840; South Carolina, U.S., Compiled Marriage Index, 1641–1965, via Ancestry.com.

15. Appointments of U.S. Postmasters, 1832–1971, via Ancestry.com.

16. Sarah Frances Michal, 3 August 1837 to 12 August 1838, is buried in Magnolia Cemetery, Spartanburg, S.C. The tombstone's florid script is unclear in photographs, so that her dates are sometimes mistranscribed, but in person the grave markings are legible.

17. Members of the Lewis family also moved to the area. See Kitchens, *Ghosts of Grandeur*, 274–276.

18. Livingston, *Portraits*, 266–268. The Bartow County Genealogical Society's *Heritage Book* offers a brief but interesting account of the life of Jesse Richards (ca. 1853–1944), born enslaved on the Rowland plantation.

19. A marker was erected by the Etowah Valley Historical Society, and the facts related on this plaque are supported by census records, government documents, John Rowland's will, and newspaper articles. In the letter mentioned in note 13 there is some indication that, at least later on, Rowland or the whole family lived at Rowland Springs ten miles away from Etowah Valley; see also *Western Star of Liberty*, 8 December 1840. Census records indicate that Michal was a resident of Georgia in 1840, but his tombstone states he "died in Spartanburgh."

20. Rowland to Lewis (see note 13).

21. Currently, only sporadic copies of Cassville's *Georgia Pioneer* newspaper are known to exist from 1844.

22. *DCS*, 3 September 1849.

23. G. White, *Statistics*, 151.

24. The marker is located northeast of Cartersville. Rowland Springs Road SE crosses Canton Highway 20 and becomes Simpson Circle NE. Going north on Simpson, the marker is on the right side of the road past the left turn for Grand Georgian Court but before the intersection with Kay Road.

25. Cunyus, *History of Bartow County*, 178.

26. *Augusta Daily Constitutionalist*, 20 February 1851; *DCS*, 1 May 1851.

27. *CE*, 18 November 1851.

28. *Report on the Medical Department of the University of Pennsylvania, for the Year 1848*, 12, via Ancestry.com. Life dates for Salathiel's parents were pieced together from census and will documents via Ancestry.com.

29. Frances M. Smith, *Cincinnati Enquirer*, "About Our Ancestors: Rowland Family," 25 September 1927; Lewis, *Genealogy*, 250, 248.

30. Edgeworth, *Southern Gardener*, 479.

31. Information about Thornton was gleaned from census records and his work as well as K. Lewis, *Carolina Backcountry Venture*, 1–2, 272–273.

32. Edgeworth, *Southern Gardener*, vii.

33. A copy can be found in the Thornton clipping folder at the Camden Archives and Museum with a note that the original is found at the Caroliniana Library in Columbia (P2896).

34. Genealogical information in the Thornton file at the Camden Archives and Museum as well as online family trees in Ancestry.com point to the Thornton-Carpenter relationships with regularity, even if much of the information is not cited. The 1850 census for Lydia Thornton Carpenter, widow of Dan Carpenter, shows that she died in Houston County, Georgia. It should be noted, however, that not all the genealogical information found matched. This is not a surprise for those versed in genealogical research. The period in question is before vital records were kept by the state governments involved, as well as before everyone in a household was listed by name in the census.

35. Shirley Abbott, in Thornton, *Southern Gardener*, 9–10.

36. Despite plot location errors found online, Phineas Thornton's grave can be found in Section 6 of Camden's Quaker Burying Ground. Information about this cemetery is located on a historical marker at the front credited to the City of Camden.

37. Manuscript, Camden Archives and Museum, 2006.095.0017, Miller Family Letters, 1829–1833, and biographical vertical/clipping file for Thornton Family.

38. The Thornton house is located at the corner of Campbell and DeKalb Streets with the street address of 714 West DeKalb, Camden, South Carolina.

39. Edgeworth, *Southern Gardener*, x.

40. P. Thornton, *Southern Gardener*, 15.

41. Edgeworth, letter to Governor Joseph E. Brown, 26 March 1862, Georgia Archives, 001-01-005, Governor—Executive Department—Governor's Subject Files (Incoming Correspondence), 1781–2018, Document 288, Identifier C 115730.

42. The historical marker by the Etowah Valley Historical Society states that Brown was a frequent guest.

43. Relevant muster rolls and documents showing his service as a surgeon at the City Hall and Blind School Hospitals in Macon are available through Fold3 database.

44. *Georgia Weekly Telegraph* (Macon), 7 August 1868.

45. Last will and testament of Mary Edgeworth, October 1851, Wills Book B for Houston County, 1855–1896, via Ancestry.com.

46. Edgeworth, *Southern Gardener*, pages 108, 223, 144, and 169 respectively.

47. Sam Bowers Hilliard in *Hog Meat and Hoecake: Food Supply in the Old South, 1840–1860*, 178, points out that turnips were a "favorite of the new settler" because of the ease of planting and care as well as their long growing season.

1862, Civil War Make-Do Coffee

1. GHS 0318, Gordon Family Papers, 1802–1946, Box 1, Folder 6, Georgia Historical Society, Savannah.

2. Charles J. Johnson, "William Washington Gordon," *New Georgia Encyclopedia*, www.georgiaencyclopedia.org/articles/history-archaeology/william-washington-gordon-1796-1842. A monument to WW Gordon I can be found in Savannah's Wright Square.

3. Hoxie, *How Girls Can Help*, v.

4. Verstille, *Verstille's Southern Cookery*, 226.

5. *Cuthbert Enterprise and Appeal*, 12 August 1886.

6. The newspaper noted that the recipe came from an Ohio newspaper.

7. Burge, *Diary*, 122.

8. "Inflation Calculator," U.S. Official Inflation Data, Alioth Finance, www.officialdata.org/.

9. Andrews, *War-Time Journal*, 197.

10. Ibid., 340. In 1913 two of Andrews's recipes appeared in Rhodes and Hopkins, *The Economy Administration Cook Book*, 62. There seem to be two editions of this cookbook in the same year. The one published in Indiana by W. B. Conkey contains recipes by Andrews, while the one from New York published by Syndicate does not. I own the version published in New York, while the other is available online full text from Google Books.

11. S. Taylor, *Reminiscences*, 73.

1863, Geechee Foodways: Orienting within Recipe Collections

1. My parents, Robert W. "Bob" and Sharon Frey, arrived on Sapelo in 1968 with a son. I was born not long after. Our family lived there full-time only a few years but returned periodically for my father's work until his death in 1992. Many of the things he taught me can be found in my children's book, *The Living Shoreline*.

2. There were additional antebellum landowners who also left behind ruins or landscape changes, and Geechee settlements were once spread across the island.

3. During my childhood the settlement was known as Hog Hammock, but in recent years the older variant of the name was brought back.

4. The Geechee Kunda Cultural Arts Center website is www.geecheekunda.org; the Pin Point Heritage Museum website is https://chsgeorgia.org/PHM.

5. In particular, I am grateful for the kind friendships of Mrs. Annie Mae Green (1912–2000) and Mrs. Viola Johnson (1919–2001).

6. Georgia foodways enthusiast William "Doc. Bill" Thomas also edited *Cherokee Cooking*, discussed in the 1838 section. The Sapelo cookbook is currently out of print, but North Carolina cookbook author Nancie McDermott shared Bailey's Sapelo Island Pear Pie in *Southern Pies*, 99. Bailey's Pear Bread and Sapelo Island Hard Time Cake are found in McDermott's *Southern Cakes*, 114, 119.

7. Kim Severson, "Reviving a Crop and an African-American Culture, Stalk by Stalk," *New York Times*, 8 December 2020.

8. Manuscript, GHS 0750, Series 8, Box 2, Folder 14, Item 194.

9. Manuscript, Duke University, M:3677, Item 1, Mrs. Charles Spalding Recipe Book, 1871.

10. At the time of her death, Evelyn Spalding was a resident of Spalding County. See *Macon News*, 19 August 1898.

11. Spalding Recipe Book (see note 9), page 29.

12. Lower Altamaha Historical Society, "Behavior Cemetery," www.glynngen.com/cemetery/mcintosh/behavior. Hettie/Hattie may be a nickname.

13. Spalding Recipe Book (see note 9), page 22. It is difficult to tell if the word "brown" is underlined or crossed out. I find the recipe works with either brown or granulated sugar.

14. Ibid., 57. Evelyn's book does not include a recipe for wine sauce.

15. Alton Brown, "Homemade Marshmallows," Food Network, www.foodnetwork.com/recipes/alton-brown/homemade-marshmallows-recipe.

16. Bailey is one of four coauthors of Crook et al., *Sapelo Voices*.

17. Sapelo Island Cultural and Revitalization Society, https://sicars.org.

18. Non-Georgia writers include Kardea Brown, BJ Dennis, Valerie Erwin, Jesse Edward Gantt Jr., Veronica Davis Gerald, Charlotte Jenkins, Emily Meggett, Eva Segar, and Verta Mae Smart-Grosvenor.

19. The Ashantilly Center website is https://ashantillycenter.org.

1864, Wafers and Recipe Time Lags

1. Anastatia Sims, "Juliette Gordon Low," *New Georgia Encyclopedia*, www.georgiaencyclopedia.org/articles/history-archaeology/juliette-gordon-low-1860-1927.

2. Choate and Ferris, *Juliette Low and the Girl Scouts*, 4–5. No surname or additional information about Nancy could be found.

3. Jessica B. Harris, "Benne," in Edge, *Foodways*, 122. Benne treats are also popular in other southern coastal cities such as Charleston and New Orleans.

4. Byrd's Famous Cookies, "Byrd History," www.byrdcookiecompany.com/aboutus. The Benne Wafer was introduced after Benjamin Byrd Jr. took over the company in 1949. Recently, they have relegated the benne wafer to online sales only.

5. Colquitt, *The Savannah Cook Book*, 161.

6. Research is especially tricky because this seed has been known as bene, benne, benni, benniseed, bhene, sesame, sesamum, and simsim.

7. *Republican and Savannah Evening Ledger*, 2 May 1809.

8. Hess, *The Carolina Rice Kitchen*, 44.

9. Ibid., 45.

10. Irma Rombauer's encyclopedic *Joy of Cooking* is one of the few cookbooks that includes popcorn (790).

11. Tube- or straw-like wafers with and without fillings are sold today under brand names such as Barquillo, Cookie Straws, Pirouline, or Pirouette.

12. Trish Ainsworth, "Old Recipe to Be Used for Wafers," *SMN*, 6 February 1972. The museum is located at 10 East Oglethorpe Avenue, Savannah.

13. Harper Fowlkes House (Coastal Heritage Society), 230 Barnard Street, https://chsgeorgia.org/HFH#HISTORY.

14. You'll need 1.13 cups white sugar or 1.17 cups packed brown, 1.81 cups all-purpose flour, and one stick of butter.

1866, *Verstille's Southern Cookery* and the Influence of Travel

1. Judy Walker, "Of Cooks & Cookery—A Historic New Orleans Collection Exhibit Examines Crescent City Culinary Customs Through the Years," *New Orleans Times-Picayune*, 18 January 2007; Rien T. Fertel, "Cookbooks," *64 Parishes*, 5 April 2011, https://64parishes.org/entry/cookbooks.

2. Patout, "Corner of Creole and Cajun," 5.

3. I am indebted to cookbook author Cynthia Graubart for showing me her second edition cookbook linking Verstille to Georgia. I had looked into Verstille but was temporarily derailed by the "of Louisiana" on the first edition.

4. *WT*, 27 April 1852.

5. Instructions for making candles on page 236 call for "a piece of rosin the size of a partridge egg." Verstille's pancake recipe is on page 169. Annabella Hill (1867) also sometimes referred to "liquid sauce" for puddings. It likely meant a sauce that flowed easily even when cool, which would include things like maple or fruit syrup such as we use on pancakes today.

6. Considering name customs of the period such as those discussed in Jessica Harris's *High on the Hog*, 108, the two recipes familiarly using cooks' given names, Anne's Pudding (page 152) and Jinnie's Crullers (101), could very well be from Black cooks.

7. 1850 and 1870 census records support Ellen's birth state as Georgia. In the 1830 census before her birth and the 1840 one after it, her father is listed in Warren County. In her father's will, he refers to his other two children simply by their first names but to Ellen as "Ellen Jane," so she may have gone by a double name as is traditional in the South.

8. 1840 and 1850 censuses; *GJ*, 19 May 1818.

9. From family census records it seems likely that Ellen was born in Warren County, but this cannot be verified.

10. Muscogee County marriage records accessed via Ancestry.com; *WT*, 19 August 1851; Stiles, *Ancient Windsor*, 770–773; censuses 1820–1890; Jacobsen, *American Artists*.

11. The will of Charlotte Verstille, probated 4 May 1870 in Muscogee County and accessed via Ancestry.com, specifically mentions a portrait of her painted by her late father.

12. Rowland et al., History of *Beaufort County*; "Joseph Lawton, October 18, 1753–March 1815," by Thomas Oregon Lawton Jr., Allendale, S.C., Lawton Family Convention, ca. 1975 (the original paper is housed in the Lawton Genealogical File at the Georgia Historical Society, Savannah); online finding aid for the Tristram Verstille Papers (Bulk 1811–1860) at the South Caroliniana Library, University of South Carolina, Columbia.

13. William H. Sheldon Verstille appears with Tristram's family in the 1850 census, and there are many records in the 1840s and 1850s from Chatham County for both WHS and "Sheldon." Some family trees on Ancestry.com list him as son to Tristram and thus a brother-in-law to Ellen, but he appears in Stiles's Windsor history as the son of Sheldon, sixth child of William and Eliza, who died in 1821.

14. The 1840 census as well as multiple tax and land records place the Verstille family in Chatham County.

15. Catalog of the Officers and Students in Yale College, 1848–49, via Ancestry.com; *Edgefield* (S.C.) *Advertiser*, 28 April 1847.

16. *University of Georgia Centennial Alumni Catalog* (ca. 1885) 9:291–294, via Ancestry.com.

17. *DMN*, 30 March 1853; *SDG*, 4 June 1854; *CE*, 5 December 1854; *DMN*, 6 June 1855; *DMN*, 8 August 1855; *SDR*, 27 October 1856; *MN*, 16 December 1887.

18. 1870 census. According to Muscogee County records, Rosa Ellen Verstille later married Gustavus R. Glenn in 1875. An infant named Mary Verstille (1853–1854) is buried without a tombstone in Savannah's Laurel Grove Cemetery, but no records have been found connecting the child to Ellen.

19. 1850 census; *DMN*, 9 January 1851; *Prairie Blade* (Corsicana, Tex.), 29 February 1856; David Minor, "Wardville, Tex.," *Handbook of Texas*, Texas State Historical Association webpage, www.tshaonline.org/handbook/entries/wardville-tx; "Johnson County Post Offices," *Finders Keepers* (Johnson County Historical Society) 4.3–4 (1989); Brenda J. Edwards, "B. J.'s Corner: News and Notes," *Grandview* (Tex.) *Tribune*, 5 March 1999; [Lewis Publishing Company], *Lone Star State*, 92, 198.

20. *DS*, 13 August 1856.

21. *SDR*, 27 October 1856.

22. *DS*, 22 January 1857.

23. Keyword searches in the Georgia Historic Newspapers database, https://gahistoricnewspapers.galileo.usg.edu, were very helpful.

24. 1870 and 1880 census for Muscogee County gave Florence's age as 12 and 22 respectively. She later married Walter Johnson (*AC*, 24 January 1877). Her obituary (*CES*, 19 September 1890) suggests she was born in 1857. Her Columbus grave is currently marked with brickwork but no tombstone.

25. *Dallas Daily Herald*, 23 March 1859.

26. Will of William H. S. Verstille, Johnson County, Texas, probated 31 October 1861, via Ancestry.com.

27. *Opelousas* (La.) *Courier*, 27 January 1855.

28. "Avoyelles Heritage," *Marksville* (La.) *Weekly*, 9 August 1990 (this modern newspaper reprinted an unnamed 1890 publication); Avoyelles Parish probate records, 14 June 1862, via Ancestry.com.

29. *Avoyelles Pelican* (Marksville, La.), 12 July 1862 and 13 September 1862 are examples.

30. "Evergreen," historical marker erected by the Department of Culture, Recreation, and Tourism in 1985, Historical Marker Database, www.hmdb.org/m.asp?m=97455.

31. *New Orleans Daily News*, 10 April 1862; *Avoyelles Pelican*, 19 April 1962; Bergeron, *Louisiana Confederate Military Units*, 185.

32. Ramond L. Daye, "Author's Research Reveals Her Family's Connection to Johnson's Special Battalion in Civil War," *Avoyelles Today*, 28 January 2018, www.avoyellestoday.com/news-lifestyle/authors-research-reveals-her-family's-connection-johnson's-special-battalion-civil. This article reveals the work of writer Carol Siess Mills-Nichol.

33. Henry Lockhart left a will in Muscogee County probated 20 January 1862, accessed via Ancestry.com. He is buried in Linwood Cemetery, Columbus.

34. "Civil War Women's Riot," historical marker erected by the Georgia Historical Society and Georgia Department of Economic Development in 1956 on Broad Street between 13th and 14th Streets. http://georgiahistory.com/ghmi_marker_updated/civil-war-womens-riot.

35. Voucher number 21, paid 17 September 1864, via Fold3.com.

36. Shirley Abbott, in Hill, *Mrs. Hill's New Cook Book* (1985), 14.

37. *New Orleans Times-Democrat*, 3 October 1866; *DS*, 15 November 1866.

38. *Baton Rouge Tri-Weekly*, 13 November 1866.

39. The 1870 census shows members of the Robert/Roberts family living with the Verstille family. Charlotte Verstille also died this year (*DS*, 4 May 1870). She was shown living with the Lawton family in South Carolina in the 1860 census but had returned to Columbus.

40. Historic Linwood Cemetery website, https://linwoodcemetery.org/about-linwood. Verstille is buried in Section B, Lot 47.

1867, *Mrs. Hill's New Cook Book* for the Young and Inexperienced

1. Fowler, "Hill, Annabella Powell," 182.

2. The illustrations pictured here are found in Mrs. Hill's cookbook on pages 33 (fish knife and fork) and 148 (cow diagram).

3. Hill, *Southern Practical Cookery*, 12.

4. Ibid., 13.

5. Ibid., 12.

6. *In Joy and in Sorrow*, edited by Carol Bleser, was published in 1991 but remains one of the most helpful books in its field, along with the works of Catherine Clinton, Elizabeth Fox-Genovese, and Jean Friedman.

7. Quarterman, *The Home at the Bluff*, 52.

8. *AC*, 5 February 1878; *SS*, 9 February 1878.

9. Daughters of the American Revolution, *Lineage Book XXXII*, 52, via Ancestry.com.

10. Dawson, *Collection of Family Records*, 386–393; "Register of Marriage Bonds of Greensville County, Virginia, 1781-1808," *Tyler's Quarterly Historical and Genealogical Magazine* 2.1 (July 1920): 255.

11. Fowler's commentary in Hill, *Southern Practical Cookery*, 13. After comparing information from early Morgan County deeds with maps at the Georgia Archives, it seems that the Dawson family lived on a 500+-acre tract in the area between Big Indian Creek and Little Indian Creek, about six miles southwest "as the crow flies" from downtown Madison. For this rural location, one of the few public access points is Brenda Lane off Highway 83.

12. Manuscript, University of North Carolina, #00607; Morgan County, Georgia, Deed Book H, 1823–1824, via Ancestry.com.

13. Boykin, *Baptist Denomination*, 182; Falk, "Warrenton Female Academy." Attendance by Annabella's older sisters at the Academy was noted in a post to the Mordecai Female Academy blog by Penny L. Richards of the UCLA Center for the Study of Women; see http://mordecaischool.blogspot.com/2013/11/126-and-127-ann-and-mary-dawson.html.

14. *AC*, 5 February 1878.

15. Manuscript, University of North Carolina, #00607.

16. Hill, *Life and Services of Rev. John E. Dawson*, 10.

17. Accepted application #99634 for Thomas Hinman Moorer, Sons of the American Revolution Membership Applications, 1889–1970, accessed via Ancestry.com; Hardy, *Colonial Families*, 156–157.

18. Hardy, *Colonial Families*, 156–157.

19. Dawson, *Collection of Family Records*, 389.

20. G. White, *Historical Collections of Georgia*, 652.

21. *CE*, 18 November 1851.

22. A second politics-related bit of interest is that in 1863 Edward's younger brother, Joshua, was also an unsuccessful candidate for governor. He served in the United States Senate from 1871 to 1873. See *Biographical Directory of the United States Congress*, https://bioguide.congress.gov.

23. Felton, *Country Life*, 61.

24. Manuscript, University of Georgia, MS 81, Box 15, Folder 3. Felton's tea cake recipe is available online through the Digital Library of Georgia, http://dlg.galileo.usg.edu/do:guan_0081_harg0081-015-003.

25. Edge, *Foodways*, 182. The couple's daughter, Annabella Martha Hill (1843–1853), is in the 1851 school catalog for LaGrange Collegiate Seminary started by her uncle, Reverend John Dawson, in U.S. School Catalogs, 1765–1935, via Ancestry.com.

26. Fowler's commentary in Hill, *Southern Practical Cookery*, xv.

27. *AC*, 5 February 1878.

28. Ibid.

29. Van Willigen, *Kentucky's Cookbook Heritage*, 3; Hess, *Carolina Rice Kitchen*, 44; Hess, *Martha Washington's Booke of Cookery*, 6.

30. Fowler notes that there are discrepancies about Hill's death date on page xviii of his commentary. Her obituary in the *Sunny South* on 9 February 1878 gives the date as 29 January.

31. *AC*, 5 February 1878. In 2018, Troup County historian Forrest Clark Johnson (1950–2022) and LaGrange Cemeteries supervisor David Satterwhite helped me find the graves of the Hill family in Hill View Cemetery in Original Section A, Lot 108. Johnson noted that the grave marked "Annabella Hill" is for the daughter of Annabella and Edward. Mrs. Hill is in an unmarked grave immediately nearby.

1870, Wet Devil Sauce

1. Because I found the three letters in this portion of the recipe confusing, I sent a picture of the original to several colleagues familiar with old handwriting styles. In addition to the M E M ultimately chosen as the likely letters, other suggestions were M E W or N E W. The three letters could be initials or a nickname of the person paying for the recipe, or it may stand for "memorandum," a reminder of the expense paid. It is one more tricky reality of history research that even experienced professionals don't always agree on interpretations.

2. Manuscript, MS 1120, Box 1, Folder 7. On the family, see William Harris Bragg, "De Renne Family," *New Georgia Encyclopedia*, www.georgiaencyclopedia.org/articles/history-archaeology/de-renne-family.

3. Shephard, *Pickled, Potted, and Canned*, 107.

4. Ibid., 105.

5. Payne, *Housekeeper's Guide*, 33.

6. Research on the SS *Scotia* did not turn up useful information.

7. Dabney, *Smokehouse Ham*, 197–204, and *Lowcountry Cooking*, 203–215.

1873, Enclaves: From Congee to Flapper Food and Beyond

1. *A Night in Old Savannah Cook Book*, created by the Night in Old Savannah Committee in the late 1970s as part of a festival-type fundraiser for the Girl Scouts, also does this.

2. Self-published with a first edition in 1990 and a second in 2006. Cookbooks can be purchased at https://ccbaaugusta.com/cookbook.

3. See the Chinese Consolidated Benevolent Association website, https://ccbaaugusta.com/history.

4. *Savannah Morning News*, 25 September 1891, 11 November 1900, 8 May 1904; Night in Old Savannah Committee, *A Night in Old Savannah*, 17.

5. Manuscript, William Breman Jewish Heritage Museum, Mss 177, Container 1, Folder 10; tombstone in Oakview Cemetery, Albany, Georgia.

6. Greek Orthodox Cathedral (Atlanta), *Key to Greek Cooking*; St. Barbara's Philoptochos Society (Savannah), *Art of Greek Cooking*.

7. Manuscript, MC 97. With permission, the recipe transcript is from Bush, *Chattahoochee Cookin'*, 15.

1876, Georgia Horticulture and Recipes

1. County maps at the Georgia Archives helped locate the Edgeworth property and explore how it changed over time.

2. Okie, *The Georgia Peach*, 13.

3. Ibid. Also Bulloch, *The Georgia Peach Story*, 5.

4. McConnell, *Culinary History of Atlanta*, 8.

5. Ibid.

6. Meyers, "Fruitland Nursery," 55.

7. Tombstone, Summerville Cemetery, Augusta.

8. Alexa Lampasona, "Fruitland Augusta: From Peach Nursery to Peach Vodka." *AJC*, 4 August 2014. Other agriculturists initially started Fruitland, but Berckmans worked with his father and sons to further develop the property as a nursery.

9. Okie, *The Georgia Peach, 59–63*.

10. *Publications Georgia State Department of Agriculture* 21 (1895): 279.

11. *AC*, 1 April 1896.

12. *Canonsburg* (Pa.) *Daily Notes*, 19 August 1901.

13. *AC*, 18 May 1930.

14. Conroy, *Pat Conroy's Cookbook*, 42.

15. *New Orleans Times-Democrat*, 23 July 1867; *SB*, 7 July 1846; *Southern Literary Gazette* (Athens), 17 February 1849; *SB*, 18 July 1850. My research points to the east corner of College Avenue and Broad Street as the former location of White's store. Not surprisingly, the location is currently a Starbucks coffee shop.

16. Tombstone, Oconee Hill Cemetery, Athens; censuses 1850–1880; Mell and Mell, *Genealogy*. Interestingly, the Whites' daughter Annie (1849–1920) married into the Mell family, as did Georgia cookbook author Annie Dennis's assistant, Daisy Wright Mell.

17. *SFH*, January 1871, 108.

18. *SFH*, September 1870, 412.

19. *SFH*, April 1870, 312.

20. The database, available through the Digital Library of Georgia, is at https://gahistoricnewspapers.galileo.usg.edu.

21. See the Georgia Department of Agriculture website, https://agr.georgia.gov/gda-history.aspx. The publication was previously known as the *Market Bulletin* and *Farmers' Market Bulletin*.

22. Brown and Smith, *Best of Georgia Farms*. Two additional GDA cookbooks are listed in the bibliography.

23. Bryant and Fentress, *Pecans*.

24. 1920–1950 censuses. No additional information about Williams was found. Paddleford's life dates are based on her tombstone at Mill Creek Cemetery, Riley, Kansas.

25. Paddleford, *Great American Cookbook*, 271–272.

26. Carter, *Miss Lillian*; Jackson, *Soulfood Cookbook* (Peanut Butter–Raisin Sandwich Spread, 56). Ruth Jackson (1922–1985) was the cook for the Headstart program in Plains, according to the *Pensacola News*, 30 June 1978. Her life dates are from her New Lebanon Baptist Church Cemetery (Sumter County) tombstone.

27. Herbert Wilcox, "Goshen Onions Increase Cash for Farmers," *AC*, 9 June 1940.

1877, The Recipes and Three Pillars of Tunis Campbell

1. Russell Duncan, "Tunis Campbell," *New Georgia Encyclopedia*, www.georgiaencyclopedia.org/articles/arts-culture/tunis-campbell-1812-1891.

2. Tipton-Martin, *The Jemima Code*, 17.

3. Hogan, "Tunis G. Campbell."

4. Ibid., 411.

5. Duncan, *Freedom's Shore*.

6. *AC*, "Day of Terror Recalled," 9 February 1886.

7. 1888 Cambridge city directory; 1890 Boston city directory.

8. Although his son was buried in Everett/Woodlawn Cemetery in Boston in 1904, I could find no burial records for Campbell.

9. Lebo, *Difficult Fruit*, 219–225.

1880, *Choice Recipes of Georgia Housekeepers*

1. The preface refers to "MS collections" and "MS books." I interpret this as "manuscript."

2. *MJ*, 4 November 1880. A 2008 article in the *Augusta Chronicle* (Kelly Jasper, "Historic Church Ponders Future," 19 July 2008) gives more details about the congregation. In 1906 the congregation dedicated a new building at the same address and changed their name to Greene Street Presbyterian Church. Under this name they put out a third edition of the cookbook in 1916. (Details of a second edition are unknown.) The church divided into two congregations in 1991, and Greene Street Presbyterian Church dissolved in 2008.

3. *AC*, 28 October 1894.

4. Scarborough Puffs, page 61; White Sauce, page 28.

5. C. Fisher, *The American Cookbook*, 56–74; Barile, *Cookbooks Worth Collecting*, 44, 64–87; Elias, *Food on the Page*, 17–23.

6. Bower, "Our Sisters' Recipes," 137.

7. Introduction by A. Rutledge to 1979 reprint of Rutledge, *Carolina Housewife*, vii.

8. It is possible that the "Mr." was a typographical error for "Mrs."

9. On pages 89, 80, 84, and 113, respectively.

10. *AuC*, 10 May 1879 and 31 July 1879.

11. *Shole's Augusta City Directory*, 1877.

12. *Shole's Augusta City Directory*, 1886.

1882, Sans Souci Catsup and Georgia Restaurants

1. *WNA*, 1 July 1882.

2. *WNA*, 14 July 1883.

3. *WNA*, 29 June 1889 and 29 August 1891. John Mock (1846–1914) was from a prominent Catholic family in Dougherty County and is buried in Oakview Cemetery. His bar, restaurant, and ice cream parlor was located on Broad Street.

4. *WNA*, 1 July 1882.

5. Manuscript, MS 2326, Box 22, Folder 308.

6. Cookbooks featuring these restaurants are, respectively, Moye, *Bedingfield Inn Cook Book*; M. Coleman, *Frances Virginia Tea Room Cookbook*; Aycock and Kollock, *Recipes and Ramblings*, and Aycock, *Glen-Ella Springs*; Gaede, *Gottlieb's Bakery*; Lowenthal, *Johnny Harris Restaurant Cookbook*; Ferrell, *Mary Mac's*, and Lupo, *Southern Cooking from Mary Mac's*.

1883, The Chameleon *Dixie Cook-Book*

1. Estelle's name does not appear on the title page, and the volume is copyrighted by her husband.

2. A. Smith, *Food and Drink in American History*, 998.

3. "Estelle Woods Wilcox," Feeding America: The Historic American Cookbook Project, Michigan State University Library, https://d.lib.msu.edu/content/biographies?contributor_name=Wilcox%2C+Estelle+Woods.

4. For instance, in 1885 Alfred Wilcox is listed in the *Minneapolis City Directory* but also in the *Atlanta City Directory*.

5. "A Successful Business Woman," *Statesville* (N.C.) *American*, 16 November 1886.

6. A. Smith, *Food and Drink in American History*, 998.

7. Arkansas, Kansas, Nebraska, Rhode Island, and West Virginia are not represented.

8. Wilcox, *New Dixie Cook-Book*, 196, Spaghetti Butter recipe.

9. The Frozen Custard recipe on page 18 of the "Popular Dixie Dishes" section was credited to L. A. Clarkson, Atlanta, Ga. She was the publisher, and her recipe is the one Georgia-connected recipe to reappear in the 1889 cookbook, becoming an uncredited recipe called Custard Ice-cream on page 395.

10. "Michigan Profile: Meet Dr. Alvin Wood Chase, Cookbook Creator," Michigan History for Kids, Historical Society of Michigan, www.hsmichigan.org /alvin-wood-chase.

11. *SS*, 18 July 1891.

12. *Chicago Tribune*, 27 March 1917.

13. The earliest example of the advertisements seems to be *AC*, 2 March 1930. DeBoth, a food journalist and cooking school authority, hailed from Green Bay, Wisconsin. *Green Bay Press-Gazette*, 31 August 1959; *Madison* (Wisc.) *Capital Times*, 2 September 1959.

1885, *House-Keeping in the Sunny South* in a Time of Transition

1. A brief mention of the cookbook in the *Marietta Journal* on 26 March 1885 states, "Do not refuse to buy 'Housekeeping in the Sunny South,' because you have one published ten years ago." No evidence of an earlier edition has been found, so the article may have simply meant any older cookbook. The most recent article I found on the cookbook was by Sybil Williams, "Old Book Offers Helpful Recipes," *Marietta Daily Journal*, 28 February 1962. Several of Tennent's recipes were included in the 1978 *Savannah Sampler Cookbook* by Margaret DeBolt.

2. Shephard, *Pickled, Potted, and Canned*, 280–310.

3. Veit, *Food in the American Gilded Age*, 10–13.

4. *Southern Confederacy* (Atlanta), 17 July 1861; *Atlanta Daily Intelligencer*, 6 June 1869; *AC*, 6 August 1884, 3 January 1885, 25 January 1885.

5. A. Hill, *Mrs. Hill's New Cook Book* (1867), 14–16.

6. Kentucky Birth Records, 1852–1910, and Kentucky Marriage Records, 1852–1914, via Ancestry.com; 1860 census.

7. Mrs. Ella Ruth Tennent, "Pathetic Southern Romance of James G. Blaine," *SS*, 12 September 1903.

8. Kentucky Marriage Records, 1852–1915, via Ancestry.com.

9. Kentucky Death Records, 1852–1965, via Ancestry.com.

10. Online family trees and the 1900 census show that Ella may have had other children, but no documentation was found. The 1880 census lists Ella's child as a male, but later census and death records show that Virgie was a daughter and she later married Captain Dallas T. Ward of North Carolina. Her death certificate (17 June 1959, Richmond, Va.) indicates she was born in Cincinnati. Her Ohio birth is corroborated by various census records.

11. The Western and Atlanta Railroad put out promotional pamphlets in the 1880s, e.g., Jos. M. Brown, *Marietta: "The Gem City of Georgia"* (Buffalo, N.Y.: Matthews-Northrup, 1885).

12. *Bourbon News* (Paris, Ky.), 17 March 1882.

13. *Atlanta Weekly Intelligencer and Cherokee Weekly Advocate*, 13 July 1855.

14. *Atlanta Georgian and News*, 7 April 1911; Archibald Alexander, *Biographical Sketches*; A. Nevin, *Encyclopaedia of the Presbyterian Church*; *Edgefield* (S.C.) *Advertiser*, 7 March 1855; Temple, The *First Hundred Years*, 89.

15. 1850 census.

16. Gravestone of Gilbert Tennent Jr., Marietta City Cemetery.

17. Cobb County Probate Court, Marriage, vol. C, 1882–1890; *AC*, 24 December 1900.

18. *SCDF* 44.10 (October 1886): 413.

19. Cobb Land Trust, www.cobblandtrust.org/html/NUhist.htm. The ruins of the chapel are located at 1305 Powder Springs Road SW across from the entrance to Chapel Drive.

20. *SCDF* 44.10 (October 1886): 413.

21. Tennent's introduction; advertisement, *AC*, 17 October 1884.

22. The *Cartersville Courant*, 19 February 1885, shared a liver pudding recipe from the *Phoenix Agriculturalist* that also appeared on page 104 of Tennent's cookbook.

23. *SCDF* 45.4 (April 1887): 181.

24. Unfortunately, these four do not appear in the list of contributors, nor do census records and other period documents from Cobb County help with identification. Researcher Jessica B. Harris discusses honorifics such as "aunt" in *High on the Hog*, 108.

25. Temple, *The First Hundred Years*; D. Frey, *Marietta*. As far as I know, I am not related to Marietta author Douglas M. Frey.

26. Robert Taylor Nesbitt (1840–1913) and Rebecca Lanier Saffold Nesbitt (1845–1937), tombstones in St. James Episcopal Cemetery, Marietta.

27. *MJ*, 6 July 1899.

28. A. Hill, *Mrs. Hill's New Cook Book* (1867), 395.

29. Governor Treutlen Chapter, DAR, *History of Peach County*, 9.

30. *MJ*, 27 August 1885.

31. *MJ*, 7 March 1889, 4 January 1906, and 29 November 1906.

32. *MJ*, 20 August 1891 and 24 September 1908.

33. *MJ*, 13 October 1887; *SCDF* 45.4 (April 1887): 178. Very few issues of *Women's Work* still exist, but I can verify that volume 14 (January 1901) had the same publisher but a different editor.

34. *Abbeville* (La.) *Meridional*, 3 February 1887; *Staunton* (Va.) *Spectator*, 23 November 1887; *Concordia* (Kans.) *Empire*, 24 November 1887; *Orangeburg* (S.C.) *Times & Democrat*, 7 December 1887. It was a popular time for women's periodicals, according to researcher Lee Jolliffe's "Women's Magazines in the 19th Century," 129–130.

35. *MJ*, 13 October 1887.

36. *MJ*, 1 January 1891.

37. *Tennessean* (Nashville), 3 January 1892; *AC*, 11 September 1903.

38. *MJ*, 9 April 1908.

39. In terms of Marietta locations, Dr. Tennent placed newspaper announcements for a medical office on the west side of main public square (*MJ*, 17 June 1886). His office

was later on the south side in what was at the time the "Masonic Building" (*MJ*, 18 February 1892). The latter ad gives Tennent's residence as Cemetery Street. The 1900 census shows the couple living on Powder Springs Street, but the next year they moved to Roswell Street (*MJ*, 7 February 1901).

40. *MJ*, 4 February 1909. Ella's son and first husband were buried in Paris Cemetery, Kentucky, while her second husband is buried in Marietta City Cemetery. A grave has not been found for Ella Tennent.

41. Census and death records point to Georgia Anne Massey (1846–1910), married to printer John Andrew Massey (1843–1919). The couple lived in Marietta most of their lives, had five children, and are buried in Marietta City Cemetery.

42. "About the Stanley House," www.thestanleyhouse.com/about. Please note that the surname was spelled "Stephens" in a photo of the lumber company published by the *Marietta Daily Journal* on 5 January 1968.

43. "Club History," https://capitalcityclub.org/club-history.

1886, Lost Famous Baking Recipes

1. S. Morris, *Strolls About Athens*, 26. A "sequel" to *Strolls* was written many decades later by Dean William Tate (1903–1980) that includes information about Costa's ice cream shop mentioned in the 1898 section. Most legal documents as well as Laura's cemetery record refer to her as "McCray," while public sources such as the newspapers used the surname of her former master, Colonel John Billups.

2. Morris was a faculty member at the University of Georgia for over fifty years and at the time of his death had served as dean of the Law School for thirty years. *Macon News*, 25 January 1929; *Richmond* (Va.) *News Leader*, 25 January 1929.

3. *University of Georgia Centennial Alumni Catalog* 7: 361–364, via Digital Library of Georgia.

4. Woofter, "Phelps-Stokes Fellowship Studies," 11–12.

5. Gold Leaf flour was a product of the Cape County Milling Company, Jackson, Missouri. Its advertisements recalled that "Aunt Laura always used Gold Leaf Flour—that was one of her rules." *ATR*, 17 October 1924.

6. 1870, 1880, 1900, and 1910 census as Laura McCray; *TB*, 6 December 1913; "Ninety-Three Years Old and Still Baking Cakes," *AB*, 29 January 1910. McCray is buried on the east side of Section M, Gospel Pilgrim Cemetery (Athens).

7. "Ninety-Three Years Old and Still Baking Cakes," *AB*, 29 January 1910.

8. Mayes, "The Finest Cook," 34; *TB*, 6 December 1913.

9. Byrn, *American Cake*, 34.

10. Mayes, "The Finest Cook," 35; *AB*, 29 January 1910; *TB*, 6 December 1913

11. "Aunt Laura," *Miami (Fla.) Metropolis*, 17 December 1913.

12. Nicole Jankowski, "Eat Now or Forever Hold Your Piece: The Layered History of Wedding Cake," National Public Radio, 18 April 2017, www.npr.org/sections/thesalt

/2017/04/18/523787236/eat-now-or-forever-hold-your-piece-the-layered-history-of-wedding-cake.

13. George Justice, "Robert Toombs," *New Georgia Encyclopedia*, www.georgiaencyclopedia.org/articles/history-archaeology/robert-toombs-1810-1885/. My research did not turn up another likely "Mrs. Robert Toombs," and Tennent showed a tendency to include recipes from famous households.

14. Another famed Georgia baker I explored was Myra Miller (1811–1891) of Atlanta, but I was unable to find enough to write about her. Hopefully more sources will become available. See *AC*, 5 and 6 May 1891; McConnell, *Culinary History of Atlanta*, 58.

15. 1910 census; tombstones, Greenwood Cemetery, Cedartown; "President Wilson's Fruit Cake," *Concord* (N.C.) *Times*, 24 December 1913; "Georgia Woman Is Baking Xmas Cake for White House," *AC*, 14 December 1913.

16. Erick Montgomery, "Woodrow Wilson in Georgia," *New Georgia Encyclopedia*, www.georgiaencyclopedia.org/articles/history-archaeology/woodrow-wilson-in-georgia.

17. "Ellen Axson Wilson," About the White House: First Families, www.whitehouse.gov/about-the-white-house/first-families/ellen-axson-wilson.

18. *Concord* (N.C.) *Times*, 24 December 1913.

19. "Georgia Woman Is Baking Xmas Cake for White House," *AC*, 14 December 1913; Jennifer Giambrone for the White House Historical Association, "The Presidential Sweet Tooth," www.whitehousehistory.org/the-presidential-sweet-tooth.

20. The Woodrow Wilson Presidential Library & Museum in Staunton, Virginia, shares an adapted version of this recipe as "Jessie's Fruitcake" on their website at www.woodrowwilson.org/activities-page. I am indebted to their staff for information about the Rhodes/Hopkins cookbook. The fruitcake recipe is on pages 20–21 of the Syndicate Publishing Company version of the cookbook and is marked "Anna R. White," assumed to be the name of the person who originally shared the recipe with Mrs. Wilson.

21. "Miss Rankin—First Woman in M. C.," *Buffalo* (N.Y.) *Times*, 26 November 2016.

22. "What Will American Women Do With 1917?" *Louisville* (Ky.) *Courier-Journal*, 31 December 1916.

23. Krull, *Lives of Extraordinary Women*, 60–63.

24. Molly Moreland, "Jeannette Rankin," *New Georgia Encyclopedia*, www.georgiaencyclopedia.org/articles/history-archaeology/jeannette-rankin-1880-1973.

25. OnlineAthens, www.legacy.com/us/obituaries/onlineathens/name/mavis-allgood-obituary?id=19798266.

26. Manuscript, GHS 1256, Box 3, Folder 42.

1887, Jessup Whitehead and Fine Dining

1. Hewett and Crickmay, *Warm Springs of Georgia*.

2. *AC*, 26 June 1887.

3. Whitehead, *Whitehead's Family Cook Book*, v–vi.

4. "Professional Cookery Books," *AC*, 26 June 1887.

5. "He Was a Great Cook," *AC*, 14 May 1889; 1851 England Census and 1865 Kansas State Census, via Ancestry.com.

6. Consolidated List of All Persons of Class I, Subject to Do Military Duty in the Southern District, Davis County, Kansas, September through December 1863, via Ancestry.com. Whitehead also alludes to his service in some of his cookbooks.

7. Details of Whitehead's career can be found in his various cookbooks.

8. Whitehead, *American Pastry Cook Book*, 1.

9. Examples of newspaper ads are in *AC*, 3 July and 1 November 1887.

10. *Philadelphia Times*, 6 June 1886.

11. *AC*, 3 July and 5 November 1887.

12. The hotel ruins and a historical marker can be seen near the bend in the short Old Chimney Road SE to the east of Huntsville.

13. *AC*, 14 May 1889. Whitehead is buried in Huntsville's Maple Hill Cemetery.

14. Last Will and Testament of Jessup Whitehead, Madison County, Ala., 12 May 1889, via Ancestry. com.

15. "Sweetwater Park Hotel Destroyed by Fire," *Atlanta Semi-Weekley Journal*, 23 January 1912. A local history buff told me the resort was near the intersection of US Highway 78 and Sweetwater Road, but I was not able to verify this.

16. *AC*, 15 October 1885.

17. Richard Funderburke, "William H. Parkins," *New Georgia Encyclopedia*, www.georgiaencyclopedia.org/articles/arts-culture/william-h-parkins-1836–1894.

1890, Barbee's Terrapins and Prestige Ingredients

1. K. Moss, *Seeking the Historical Cook*, 13.

2. S. Williams, *Savory Suppers & Fashionable Feasts*, 122–126.

3. Yentsch, "Applying Concepts." Yentsch looked at cookbooks from northeastern states, yet Georgia's early cookbooks followed the same trends.

4. O'Connell, *The American Plate*, 167–168.

5. Van Willigen, *Kentucky's Cookbook Heritage*, 7.

6. "$24,000 a Year in Terrapins," *Rutland* (Vt.) *Daily Herald*, 10 October 1913; tombstone, Catholic Cemetery, Savannah.

7. "The New Route Opened," *MN*, 13 June 1890.

8. "Isle of Hope Postmaster," *MN*, 18 November 1894; Frederic J. Haskin, "The Terrapin Trust," *Waterville* (Me.) *Morning Sentinel*, 24 March, 1916; *MN*, 19 June 1893.

9. Mr. and Mrs. F. L. Martin, "Wilkes-Barre to Havana," *Wilkes-Barre* (Pa.) *Times Leader*, 3 May 1928.

10. *Springfield* (Ohio) *News-Sun*, 8 November 1912; "$24,000 a Year in Terrapins" (see note 6).

11. See note 10.

12. "Inflation Calculator," U.S. Official Inflation Data, Alioth Finance, www .officialdata.org.

13. Haskin, "The Terrapin Trust" (see note 8).

14. Ibid.

15. Ibid.

16. Martin and Martin, "Wilkes-Barre to Havana" (see note 9). The pavilion was along the Skidaway River on what is now West Bluff Drive near the end of Rosenbrook Avenue.

17. Haskin, "The Terrapin Trust."

18. Girl Scouts, *Centennial Receipt Book*, 3–4.

19. "Strange Effect," *Northern Wisconsin Advertiser* (Wabeno), 17 December 1903. It must have been an unpleasant journey.

20. "$24,000 a Year in Terrapins."

21. "Strange Effect" (see note 19).

22. Haskin, "The Terrapin Trust."

23. "Georgian Hatches Out Terrapin," *Omaha Morning World-Herald*, 19 October 1913; Martin and Martin, "Wilkes-Barre to Havana" (see note 9). Both articles agree Bryan hatched a terrapin in his hand. The earlier article indicated the Bryan terrapin may have gone elsewhere and therefore may not have been Toby.

24. See note 10.

25. Haskin, "The Terrapin Trust"; Martin and Martin, "Wilkes-Barre to Havana"; *MN*, 29 October 1892; B. Cooper, *Savannah's Cookin'*, 18. Accounts disagree on Toby's gender, but the majority indicate the terrapin was male.

26. Haskin, "The Terrapin Trust"; *MN*, 21 May 1895; *MN*, 17 November 1895.

27. P. Cooper, *Isle of Hope*. Page 18 has a picture of Toby.

28. "Old Caterer on Terrapin," *Owensboro* (Ky.) *Messenger-Inquirer*, 7 February 1898; City of Philadelphia, Register of Historic Places for 5706 Germantown Avenue, www .phila.gov/media/20210621133924/5706-Germantown-Ave-nomination.pdf; Viet, *Food in the American Gilded Age*, 104; Independent Presbyterian Church (Savannah), *Hints from Southern Epicures*, 10, 16.

29. Martin and Martin, "Wilkes-Barre to Havana." This article includes a "Southern Style" recipe, which differs from the one on the brochure by adding diced bacon, two tablespoons of flour, paprika, chopped hard-boiled eggs, and lemon.

30. "Hints to the Lovers of Terrapins," *Federal Union* (Milledgeville), 22 October 1834.

31. Haskin, "The Terrapin Trust."

32. Junior League of Augusta, *Old and New Recipes*, 43.

33. "Quick Thinking Saves Property," *Orangeburg* (S.C.) *Times and Democrat*, 16 October 1947.

34. Rita H. DeLorme, "A Pavilion and Family Worth Visiting," *Southern Cross* (Savannah), 24 February 2011.

1891, Recipes and Kitchen Innovation

1. Tombstone, Memorial Hill Cemetery, Milledgeville; 1850–1910 censuses. Mapp's needs may have been professional. The first announcement of the bread raiser in the local newspaper (*UR*, 25 August 1891) called Mary "Mrs. F. B. Mapp of the Milledgeville Hotel."

2. Description from Dough Riser, U.S. Patent No. 467,820 (US-0467820-A) on 26 January 1892. https://ppubs.uspto.gov/dirsearch-public/print/downloadPdf/0467820.

3. *Woman's Column* (Boston) 5.26 (25 June 1892); Handy, *World's Columbian Exposition*; Dodge, *Cotton States and International Exposition*.

4. Carlisle and Nasardinov, *America's Kitchens*, 79.

5. A similar hollowed-out-cake dessert from Georgia is Cinderella Pudding, widely shared in various newspapers by Marion Birdie Cobb Smith (1860–1919) of Athens, and collected in Rhodes and Hopkins, *Economy Administration Cook Book*, 264 (Syndicate edition); First Presbyterian Church (Athens), *Choice Recipes*, 80.

6. E.g., *Hartford* (Conn.) *Courant*, 10 September 1921. I hoped to discover the exact origins of this pan and whether it involved a person named Mary Ann, but I have had no luck.

7. E.g., *Washington Evening Star*, 7 November 1921.

8. In particular, Jessup Whitehead (see 1887 section) did this in some of his cookbooks. Whitehead, *The American Pastry Cook*, 34.

9. *Southern Sentinel* (Columbus), 23 July 1852.

1892, *Hints from Southern Epicures* and Foraged Ingredients

1. An online search for "rainbow cocktails" turns up many modern versions.

2. Sibley, *The Celestine Sibley Sampler*, 75.

1894, Annie Dennis and New Freedoms

1. 1850–1880 censuses.

2. W. Davidson, *A Rockaway in Talbot*, 1:399–401.

3. Bleser, *In Joy and in Sorrow*; Clinton, *Tara Revisited*.

4. Printed letter from Peter Early Dennis, *UP*, 4 February 1860; W. Davidson, *A Rockaway in Talbot*, 1:309.

5. *UP*, 16 January 1860.

6. Confederate records, 2 March 1862, Muster Roll for PE Dennis, via Fold3.com; W. Davidson, *A Rockaway in Talbot*, 4:90–92.

7. *CDE*, 31 December 1878 and 2 January 1879; *GWTGJM*, 11 November 1879 and 16 December 1881.

8. W. Allen, *Travelers' Official Railway Guide*.

9. W. Davidson, *A Rockaway in Talbot*, 1:312.

10. *CDE*, 2 January 1879; *GWTGJM*, 11 November 1879; *Macon Weekly Telegraph and Messenger*, 31 October 1884; *MWT*, 27 October 1885; *MWT*, 3 November 1885; *WC*, 25

October 1887; *MWT*, 1 November 1887; *Columbus Daily Enquirer-Sun*, 10 April 1888. One advertisement for *The New Annie Dennis Cook Book* lists some of Dennis's fairs and premiums; see *AC*, 22 March 1902.

11. Sutherland, *Cookoff*, 27.

12. *WC*, 25 October 1887.

13. Bleser, *In Joy and in Sorrow*; Dorsey, *Reforming Men and Women*.

14. *SS*, 9 June 1894; *AC*, 25 July 1894.

15. "The Women Named Who Are to Lead in the Good Work of Upbuilding the Woman's Department of the Exposition," *AC*, 23 April 1894; "Women's Department of the Exposition," *AC*, 5 August 1894.

16. "Wonderful Woman: Annie Dennis of Talbotton, and Her Work," *AC*, 27 October 1895.

17. Evelyn Hanna, "Syllabub and Nondescripts," *AC*, 15 June 1944.

18. *AC*, 15 June 1902; *Athens Daily Banner*, 19 August 1902.

19. *AC*, 11 and 15 June 1902.

20. *AC*, 28 March 1913. I found no connections between William King and the King Hardware Store.

21. Georgia Death Certificate, 18 May 1920, via Ancestry.com.

22. "Miss Annie Dennis Dies While on Trip to Attend Wedding," *AC*, 20 May 1920.

23. Her grave is in Jasmine Section, Row G, Lot 2.

24. "Many Proposals Found in Papers of Famous Cook," *AC*, 4 September 1921 and 28 March 1913.

25. 1860–1940 census records; tombstones, Linwood Cemetery, Columbus, Georgia; "Arminius Wright Final Rites Today," *AC*, 3 August 1927; W. Davidson, *A Rockaway in Talbot*, 1:114–115; manuscript, Columbus State, MC 42.

26. Manuscript, Columbus State University, MC 42, Box 1, Folders 1, 3, 9, and 12.

27. W. Davidson, *A Rockaway in Talbot*, 1:312.

28. Manuscript, University of Georgia, MS 1791(m).

29. J. Nevin, *Prominent Women of Georgia*, 60–61, 162–163.

30. Manuscripts, University of Georgia, MS 1791, Box 1, Folders 1–11; MS 2480, Box 1, Folder 1.

1895, The Cotton States and International Exposition: A Tale of Two Cookbooks

1. Roth and Kemph, *Piedmont Park*, 9.

2. One would certainly hope a cookbook would not be poisonous, yet the Poison Book Project was created to keep a database of nineteenth-century books with green covers containing arsenic; see https://sites.udel.edu/poisonbookproject. The *Tested Recipe Cook Book* is not on the list, but it is not known if the cover has been tested.

3. Roth's introduction to the 1984 reprint, xii–xiii.

4. 1850 census; Kenan Research Center, Atlanta History Center, Personality Subject File for Mrs. Henry Lumpkin Wilson, profile by Lollie Bell Wylie. The Wilsons are buried in Atlanta's Oakland Cemetery, Section 3, Block 92, Lot 4.

5. *AC*, 12 April 1896.

6. See Carey Olmstead Shellman, "Nellie Peters Black," in Chirhart and Wood, *Georgia Women*, 1:297–317.

7. Chuck Perry, "Atlanta Journal-Constitution," in *New Georgia Encyclopedia*, www.georgiaencyclopedia.org/articles/arts-culture/atlanta-journal-constitution; tombstone, Oakland Cemetery, Atlanta.

8. See Roth's introduction to the 1984 reprint of *Tested Recipe Cook Book*, xiii.

9. I later discovered that this cookbook also appears in Cook, *America's Charitable Cooks*, 52.

10. 1900 census and additional sources listed below.

11. *Topeka* (Kans.) *Plaindealer*, 8 December 1899.

12. Lamb, *Howard University Medical Department*; *Washington Evening Star*, 17 July 1933; tombstone, Columbian Harmony Cemetery, Washington, D.C.

13. *Washington Bee*, 21 March 1908.

14. Dunbar Circle, First Annual Report of the Dunbar Circle, 1907, https://credo.library.umass.edu/view/full/mums312-b002-i172; *Washington Evening Star*, 21 March 1908. She is buried in Columbian Harmony Cemetery, Washington D.C.

15. Horizon (firm), *Horizon* 3.3 (ca. May 1908), in W. E. B. Du Bois Papers (MS 312), Special Collections and University Archives, University of Massachusetts Amherst Libraries, http://credo.library.umass.edu/view/full/mums312-b287-i003.

16. An excellent source for helping to put this cookbook in context is *Race and the Atlanta Cotton States Exposition of 1895* by Theda Perdue.

17. *Washington Evening Star*, 16 May 1899.

18. Edward Hatfield, "Auburn Avenue," *New Georgia Encyclopedia*, www.georgiaencyclopedia.org/articles/counties-cities-neighborhoods/auburn-avenue-sweet-auburn; Linda Hall, "Historically Black Colleges and Universities Initiative," *New Georgia Encyclopedia*, www.georgiaencyclopedia.org/articles/arts-culture/historically-black-colleges-and-universities-initiative.

19. Leroy Davis, "John Hope," *New Georgia Encyclopedia*, www.georgiaencyclopedia.org/articles/education/john-hope-1868-1936; Derrick Alridge, "W. E. B. Du Bois in Georgia," *New Georgia Encyclopedia*, www.georgiaencyclopedia.org/articles/history-archaeology/w-e-b-du-bois-in-georgia; Alexa Benson Henderson, "Alonzo Herndon," *New Georgia Encyclopedia*, www.georgiaencyclopedia.org/articles/business-economy/alonzo-herndon-1858-1927. These men were also involved with the Niagara Movement. Schools are listed by their current names.

20. 1880 and 1900 censuses; Washington DC Marriage Records, 1810–1953, via Ancestry.com; 1900 Washington, D.C., city directory.

21. Wright and Hawkins, *Centennial Encyclopedia*; Woodlawn Cemetery records, Washington, D.C.

22. Online finding aid for the papers of her brother, William Joiner, at Howard University, Moorland-Spingarn Research Center, Washington, D.C., 10-1-2015, https://dh.howard.edu/finaid_manu/111.

23. 1900 and 1910 censuses; *Washington Evening Star*, 15 July 1896.

24. *Washington Evening Star*, 16 November 1906.

25. *Washington, D.C., Compiled Marriage Index, 1830–1921*, via Ancestry.com; 1930 census.

26. In 1930, Ohio's Daisy Alice Kugel (1878–1940), an instructor for two years at Spelman College, published a collection of recipes called *Recipes for Food Classes*. These are the only other older recipes related to Georgia's HBCUs found through my research. Hopefully more will be donated or made available over time. *Sandusky* (Ohio) *Register*, 17 December 1940; tombstone, Oakland Cemetery, Sandusky.

27. Although likely served during our book's time period yet still protected by copyright, recipes for the creamy gelatin dessert called Quilly beloved by Martin Luther King Jr. can be found online. Food writer Poppy Cannon published one in "What Food Appeals to Dr. Martin L. King Jr.," *Hartford Courant*, 14 January 1968. (Although there are versions of Cannon's article as early as December of 1967 in various newspapers, this one prints the recipe in a clear format.)

1897, The Georgia Mystery Cookbooks File and Mrs. Bell

1. Advertisement for Franklin Publishing House, *AC*, 22 December 1890.

2. George M. Downs obituary, *AC*, 4 December 1939.

3. Wesleyan College Alumnae, *Macon Cook Book*, 221.

4. *Chattanooga News*, 19 March 1919.

5. "Famous Bell House Ends Its Career," *AC*, 17 June 1897.

6. Census records for 1900 and 1910 give Bell's birth year as around 1850; Westview Cemetery, Section 5.

7. *AC* and *AJ*, 3 March 1914.

8. I hoped to find a marriage certificate for the Bells as well as more information about the life of John Bell but was disappointed. The Civil War and Reconstruction not only wreaked havoc with lives but also the documents that recorded them.

9. *AC* and *AJ*, 3 March 1914; tombstone, Westview Cemetery, Atlanta.

10. Tombstone of Emma's daughter, Willie Bell Cutler (1867–1941), Westview Cemetery, Atlanta.

11. Hugh Park, "Around Town," *AC*, 22 November 1951.

12. "Permanent Club Formed by Bell House Boys," *AJ*, 9 March 1914.

13. Ibid. "Gas Street Lamp Lighting to Salute Bell House Boys," *AC*, 16 November 1951, gives the starting year of Bell House as 1878.

14. I. S. Jonas, "Bell House Boys," *AC*, 12 February 1893; "Permanent Club Formed by Bell House Boys," *AJ*, 9 March 1914.

15. Richard Funderburke, "Early Victorian Architecture," *New Georgia Encyclopedia*, www.georgiaencyclopedia.org/articles/arts-culture/early-victorian-architecture-overview.

16. "Gas Street Lamp Lighting" (see note 13).

17. Hugh Park, "Around Town," *AC*, 22 November 1951.

18. "Famous Bell House Ends Its Career," *AC*, 17 June 1897. Many newspaper articles listed the Bell House Boys at various times and hinted at professions.

19. Ibid.

20. "Signal Tribute Paid to Beloved Founder of the Bell House," *AC*, 13 April 1917.

21. See the club's recipe for Orange Jelly Baskets in the 1885 section.

22. "Great Contest for Saturday," *AC*, 29 July 1907; O. B. Keeler, "'Cap' Joyner," *AJ*, 5 January 1925.

23. Sidney Ormond, "Bell House Boys Lose to Capital City Club," *AC*, 14 July 1907.

24. I. S. Jonas, "Bell House Boys," *AC*, 12 February 1893.

25. "Some Mid-Day Reveries of Old Bell House Days," *AC*, 29 July 1907.

26. "Bell House Head Cook Falls Dead One Week After Mrs. Bell Dies," *AC*, 11 March 1914; "'Aunt Malinda,' Bell House Cook, Is Dead," *AJ*, 11 March 1914.

27. Census records 1880–1910.

28. Her birth year on census records varied from 1850 to 1861. A tombstone has not been found.

29. Wilkes, *Famous Recipes* and *Mrs. Wilkes' Boardinghouse Cookbook*; Gibson, *Boarding House Reach*, and Welch-Bafile, *Smith House History Cookbook*; F. Brown, *Dillard House*, respectively. The well-known Blue Willow Inn became a restaurant in 1990 but was never run as an inn or boardinghouse. Owners Louis and Billie Van Dyke wrote a popular cookbook. Juliann Angert, "Social Circle's Iconic Blue Willow Inn Restaurant to Experience Gentle Rebirth Soon," *Morgan Citizen* (Madison), 13 November 2023.

1898, Georgia's Turn-of-the-Century Community Cookbooks

1. Edge, *Foodways*, xix.

2. "History of Emmanuel," www.emmanuelathens.org/history.

3. Boles, "Stirring Constantly," 55.

4. In 2019 I approached Archives & Special Collections Coordinator Ashley Shull about starting a local cookbook collection, and she immediately grasped the importance. She began working on institutional support as well as cataloging and storage details while I started collecting. In 2022 we gave a presentation on the new collection for the annual Georgia Libraries Conference. From a professional point of view, one of the biggest challenges of old cookbooks is that they often require original cataloging, but

an in-house database can offer intellectual control over the collection until it can be cataloged over time.

1902, *Drummers' Home Cook Book* and the Town Hotel

1. Lane, *The Rambler in Georgia*, xiv.

2. Many sources state that the hotel became Drummers' Home in 1897. It was renovated that year, yet old newspapers note the hotel was run by Roberts as early as 1892 (*AC*, 27 August 1892). One newspaper noted that Drummers' Home was established in 1891 (*Punxsutawney* (Pa.) *News*, 22 July 1891), while the hotel name seems to have existed as early as 1890 (*AC*, 21 April 1890). A helpful history of the building can be found in Rozier's *Houses of Hancock, 1785–1865*, 54–59. See also Linley, *Architecture of Middle Georgia: The Oconee Area*, 141.

3. Jean Thwaite, "Old Sparta Hotel to Get a New Life?" *AC*, 24 April 1975. The apostrophe in the hotel name is in various positions depending on the source. In all but one recipe on page 33, in the cookbook it is spelled "Drummers'."

4. Ibid.

5. Celestine Sibley, "A Drummer Remembers the Old Days," *AC*, 21 June 1978.

6. *News & Farmer* (Louisville), 14 August 1902 and 7 July 1904.

7. Barile, *Cookbooks Worth Collecting*, 117–120.

8. 1850 and 1860 censuses.

9. Alice's death certificate with information provided by her brother lists her birth date as 1853, and Jefferson County marriage records and the census show her father remarrying in 1855 with Alice belonging to the previous marriage, all via Ancestry.com.

10. *JNF*, 14 January 1875.

11. *News & Farmer* (Jefferson), 30 January 1879.

12. *JNF*, 30 January and 18 April 1879.

13. Sparta Cemetery tombstone.

14. *Thomasville Daily Times Enterprise*, 8 September 1892.

15. *SI*, 5 October 1906.

16. Sparta Cemetery tombstone; Rozier, *Houses of Hancock*, 58.

17. *SI*, 20 May 1921; Sparta Cemetery, Section D, Lot 57.

18. Rozier, *Houses of Hancock*, 58.

19. The 1900 census lists Allen as a forty-eight-year-old Black widowed mother of two.

20. No information was found for Wilkins. Her Ham Pudding recipe is on page 28.

1905, Thomas Gingerbread

1. Thomas French and John S. Lupold, "Horace King," *New Georgia Encyclopedia*, www.georgiaencyclopedia.org/articles/arts-culture/horace-king-1807-1885.

2. Seven additional recipes are for foods helpful for feeding the sick.

3. Cost, *Ginger East to West*.

4. Manuscript, MS-2008.05, Folder 1.

1906, Localism and Chicken

1. The Quota Club of Macon put out a 1948 cookbook called *Recipes of the Deep South* that includes a wonderfully descriptive recipe for fried chicken on pages 106–107 from Harriett Pritchett Stevens Crumwell (ca. 1872–1969). Although I was unable to find someone to grant permission to reprint it, I want my readers to know about this recipe. *MT*, 10 December 1948; *MT*, 4 and 6 July 1968.

2. Although it's not a chicken dish, more than one lover of old recipes has asked me about a sweet potato casserole recipe from the household of Senator Richard B. Russell (1897–1971). The only recipe in the Russell papers at the University of Georgia's Richard B. Russell Library for Political Research and Studies is one from his cook, Modine Thomas (1916–1991), for baked onions. And, to answer the other question I often get, rosin or turpentine potatoes do not appear in any old Georgia cookbooks that I know about. See Caroline Hatchett, "The Elusive Roots of Rosin Potatoes," *Bitter Southerner*, 22 November 2022, https://bittersoutherner.com/feature/2022/the-elusive-roots-of-rosin-potatoes.

3. Virginia bills and resolutions before the year 1994 are not available online, but House Joint Resolution No. 2, Designating Brunswick Stew Day at the General Assembly (agreed to by the Senate 28 February 2002 and the House of Delegates 4 March 2002) echoes the language of the 1988 resolution. https://lis.virginia.gov/cgi-bin/legp604.exe?021+ful+HJ2ER.

4. Tennent, *House-Keeping*, 48; *Macon Republic*, 8 January 1845; *DCS*, 16 November 1859; *SMN*, 21 August 1871; A. Smith, *Oxford Companion*, 72.

5. Smith's *Oxford Companion* notes that Georgia's version of the stew is made with a combination of beef and pork, yet the other nineteenth-century Georgia recipes I was able to find also called for using chicken, such as the Independent Presbyterian Church's *Hints from Southern Epicures* (1892), 9, and the 1898 *Hapeville Presbyterian Cook Book*, 32.

6. Bill Arp, "From the Field," *UR*, 8 July 1879.

7. *AC*, 25 June 1882.

8. *AC*, 25 October 1883; *AC*, 3 May 1894.

9. "Socially Speaking," *CL*, 22 September 1946.

10. "Annual Barbecue Bar Association Was Huge Success," *MT*, 26 August 1909. Neither the article nor the poem was credited.

11. *DM*, 7 April 1916.

12. *DM*, 29 June 1917 and 20 June 1919.

13. *DM*, 19 June 1921.

14. *Cleveland Courier*, 22 May 1931. I assume he meant a piece of custard pie.

15. *AC*, 1 September 1941; *Greenville* (S.C.) *News*, 27 August 1942; *Richmond* (Va.) *Times Dispatch*, 27 September 1942; *Knoxville* (Tenn.) *Journal*, 5 September 1946; *D*, 2 September 1952.

16. Doyle, "Mulling Over Mull," 55.

17. Portman, "How to Make Chicken Mull."

18. *Greenwood* (S.C.) *Index-Journal*, 11 March 1923. Another recipe is in Graubart, *Chicken*, 42–43.

19. One thorough recent account can be found in Graubart, *Chicken*, 46–48.

20. Latimer Watson, "Columbus Carousel," *CL*, 10 June 1949.

21. Sara Spano, "'Country Captain' Revisited," *CL*, 14 February 1968.

22. One example can be found in *Buffalo Commercial* (N.Y.), 31 March 1880; *UR*, 25 May 1880.

23. Brumby, *Seasoned Skillets*, 96–98.

24. Filippini, *The International Cook Book*, 558–559.

25. Cynthia Graubart, "What Is Country Captain—and Why It's a Southern Classic," *Southern Living*, 25 January 2020, www.southernliving.com/food/meat/chicken/what-is-country-captain. It is difficult to know where credit lies with this recipe. Mrs. Bullard's granddaughter claimed Bullard was "a wonderful cook" in an article by Terry Donahue ("Country Captain Was a Presidential Favorite," *Tampa Tribune*, 22 October 1987). Little is known about Arie Mullins. Her funeral notice (*CL*, 8 December 1959) states she was born in Harris County but lived in Columbus for fifty years. She is buried in Columbus's Porterdale Cemetery, but no birth year is listed in their records. Her birth year varied with each census between 1866 and 1880, but it was given in the Georgia Death Index as circa 1875.

26. "Negroes Given Prize Awards" [Chattahoochee Valley Exposition], *CE*, 14 October 1933; "Roll 'Em Until They Blister," *CL*, 31 July 1952.

27. "Messrs. M. J. Ellis and J. B. Harrold Entertained in Columbus," *MN*, 27 July 1920; "Mrs. William Hart, Hostess," *LE*, 15 March 1921 and 17 April 1921.

28. Ashley Aultman, "Franklin D. Roosevelt and the Spirit of Warm Springs," National World War II Museum, New Orleans, 12 April 2021, www.nationalww2museum.org/war/articles/franklin-d-roosevelt-little-white-house-warm-springs.

29. Miller, *The President's Kitchen Cabinet*, 53–54, 136–139. Some of Bonner's recipes can be found online, but authenticity and copyright could not be ascertained.

30. Terry Donahue's article "Country Captain Was a Presidential Favorite" in the *Tampa Tribune*, 22 October 1987, also mentioned this.

31. "Little White House Cook Dead," *Pittsburgh Courier*, 17 May 1958.

32. Alice A. Dunnigan, "Washington Inside Out," *Pittsburgh Courier*, 23 April 1960.

33. Ibid.

34. Day, *Cheryl Day's Treasury of Southern Baking*, 228–229.

35. 1920–1930 censuses.

36. "Mrs. Orien A. Cobb, 92, Athens Caterer of Statewide Renown," *AC*, 22 November 1987.

37. Lang, *Quick-Fix Southern*, 129.

38. "In Memory of Mrs. Daisy Smith Redman," *SMN*, 2 January 1983.

39. Damon Lee Fowler, "Remembering Daisy Redman and Chicken Madeira," *Recipes and Stories* blog, 6 October 2014, www.damonleefowler.com/blog/posts/24056. His post includes the recipe.

40. DuBose, *Four Great Southern Cooks*, 25. Damon Lee Fowler included the recipe in *The Savannah Cook Book*, 146–147.

41. U.S. Society Security Death Index for Beatrice I. Mize, via Ancestry.com; obituary for Beatrice Mize, *AC*, 2 May 1994.

42. Tombstone, Cedar Grove Cemetery, Thomaston.

43. Helen Moore, "4 Great Cooks Record a Heritage of Southern Cooking," *Charlotte* (N.C.) *Observer*, 25 June 1981.

44. There is evidence of several women by the name of Ruth Jenkins in Atlanta; more information could not be ascertained.

1912, *Favorite Southern Recipes* and a Haunted Lighthouse

1. U.S. Lighthouse Society, *Lighthouse Keeper's Research Catalog*, https://archives.uslhs.org; *BA*, 6 and 13 March 1880; Wes Wolfe, "Old Tales Shed Light on Local Specters," *BN*, 25 October 2018; Larry Hobbs, "Ghost of Lighthouse's Past Still Inspires a Good Yarn Today," *BN*, 2 November 2019. Osborne lived from 1841 to 1880 and is buried in Brunswick's Oak Grove Cemetery. Most of the lighthouse ghost stories I found simply involved mysterious sounds. This seems to be the most dramatic of the stories, and some accounts say this tale was famous during the time of the Svendsens, but my research turned up only recent retellings. Scholars often disdain ghost stories, but for history education purposes they can be a fun way to spark interest in the past and start a discussion about how research and verification work.

2. Similar experiences may be possible with the Telfair kitchen (45), Union Nesbitt Chapel (167), the Robert Toombs House (177), and the boyhood homes of presidents Jimmy Carter (145) and Woodrow Wilson (178).

3. U.S. Lighthouse Society, *Lighthouse Keeper's Research Catalog*, https://archives.uslhs.org.

4. *BA*, 6 and 13 March 1880; N. Roberts, *Georgia Ghosts*; Farrant, *Ghosts of the Georgia Coast*; Hobbs, *Coast Tales*; Roberts, *Georgia Ghosts*.

5. Library of Congress, Washington, D.C., https://www.loc.gov/item/sn96027427.

6. *Publisher's Weekly* 83.9 (1 March 1913), 786.

7. *AC*, 27 November 1904 and 6 June 1937; *Southern Ruralist* 30.10 (15 August 1923); *LE*, 8 April 1939; tombstones, Westview Cemetery, Atlanta.

8. Food historian Joseph Vehling (1879–1950) is sometimes associated with this cookbook, as a copy was part of a collection he donated to Cornell University. There is evidence of a 1929 edition under the title *Our Favorite and Tested Recipes*, but this could not be confirmed.

1916, *Georgianne Cook Book* and Advertising Recipes

1. The Hodgson Oil building, located at 286 Oconee Street southeast of downtown, is now owned by the University of Georgia. The once-faded lettering on the side of the building has been restored. See 1898 section about the cookbook's printer, McGregor Company.

2. *Oil Miller and Cotton Ginner* (Atlanta) 24.6 (June 1926): 11; T. Larry Gantt, "Lard Making in Athens," *AB*, 4 July 1922; *AB*, 16 December 1915; tombstone, Oconee Hills Cemetery, Athens; *AC*, 22 September 1971; 1910 and 1920 censuses. The company also made fertilizers.

3. *ADH*, 26 November 1915; "Timeline," University of Georgia Extension, https://extension.uga.edu/about/our-history/timeline.html; *AB,* 12 January 1916.

4. *ADH*, 12 January 1916.

5. *AB*, 15 December 1915.

6. *AB*, 15 and 16 December 1915; *ADH*, 16 December 1915. The Rest Room was located on Clayton Street in downtown Athens.

7. Censuses for 1860–1880 and 1900–1920; Oconee County Probate Court Marriage Records, 1875–2010, with marriage date 8 November 1885, via Ancestry.com; *Oconee Enterprise* (Watkinsville), 9 August 1889; 1912 Athens city directory; tombstone inscriptions, Evergreen Cemetery, Jacksonville, Florida. There was a helpful but uncited newspaper article clipped for a scrapbook and later posted to Ancestry.com with the headline "Couple Observes Golden Wedding." Itasca Hutcheson was not a contributor to either of Athens's early community cookbooks discussed in the 1898 section.

8. *ADH*, 24 March 1914; 13 August 1914; and 13 January 1916.

9. *ADH*, 12 January 1916; *LE*, 29 February 1916.

10. *ADH*, 15 February 1916.

11. Ibid.

12. *AB*, 4 July 1922; censuses 1930–1950.

1920, Home Brews and Steamed Puddings Fade from Use

1. Edgeworth, *Southern Gardener*, 264.

2. Manuscript, GHS 0265, Folder 10.

3. Dull, *Southern Cooking*, 253–254.

4. Ibid., 254, 241–242.

5. Colquitt, *Savannah Cook Book*, 113–114.

6. Ibid., 167–172.

7. ac. 1977-0600M, ah00607. This is available online via the Virtual Vault, https://vault.georgiaarchives.org/digital/collection/adhoc/id/45.

8. His mother was Pamela Robertson Boggs Butt (1836–1908). Jeffrey Wells, "Archibald Butt," *New Georgia Encyclopedia*, www.georgiaencyclopedia.org/articles/history-archaeology/archibald-butt-1865-1912/; Butt, *Taft and Roosevelt:*

The Intimate Letters of Archie Butt, 247–248; Pamela Butt tombstone, Magnolia Cemetery, Augusta.

9. Mary Norwak's *English Puddings: Sweet & Savoury* states that "pudding" is now an alternative term for dessert in England, and she helpfully explains some English pudding traditions that were still evident in Georgia cookbooks long after the colonial period.

10. A. Smith, *Oxford Companion*, 481.

11. Manuscript, M:3677, Item 1, pages 20–21. See 1863 section for information about Spalding.

12. Verstille's puddings were mostly sweet, while Hill offered savory puddings in her meats section.

13. Edgeworth combined puddings with pies, as did Tennent (1885) and Roberts (1902). Verstille (1866) and Wilson (1895) combined puddings with custards. Hill (1867), *Choice Recipes of Georgia Housekeepers* (1880), the 1898 church cookbooks, and *Southern Ruralist* (1912) all had separate pudding sections. Dennis (1894) and Bell (1897) put puddings under the general "desserts" heading, which became the trend farther into the twentieth century.

14. Hill, *Mrs. Hill's New Cook Book*, 256–257; Wilcox, *Dixie Cook-Book*, 225–226; Mrs. Wm. N. White, "Household Department Domestic Receipts," *Southern Farm & Home* (Macon), March 1870, 178.

15. Some puddings required additional time to set as they cooled or for the pudding's surface to dry, but most of the work was done once the pudding was cooked.

1921, Woman's Club Cookbooks

1. Henrietta Dull's recipes can be found in *Atlanta Woman's Club Cook Book*, 59, 223–224, while one of Daisy Wright Mell's recipes is in *Athens Woman's Club Cook Book*, 218.

2. Nellie Peters Black, whom we met in the 1895 section, was an early leader, and the *Atlanta Woman's Club Cook Book* contains a special memorial recipe section for her on pages 207–208, as she died not long before its publication.

3. Croly, *Woman's Club Movement*. A description of the Georgia Federation spans pages 356–369.

4. The seal of the Georgia Federation of Women's Clubs celebrates 1896 as their founding date. Please note that with various clubs "woman's" and "women's" were both used.

5. Croly, *Woman's Club Movement*, 358.

6. Ibid., 360.

1927, Mrs. Stanfield and Georgia Cooking Schools

1. Ashantilly Center (Darien) owns the 1927 edition. I own the 1934 and 1937 cookbooks. OCLC's WorldCat and Library of Congress online catalogs provided information for the others. As far as I can tell, *Mrs. Stanfield's Selected Recipes* and

The White Lily Cooking Guide have different titles and introductory pages, but the menus and recipes are the same. These cookbooks are currently under copyright and permission to reprint could only be found for the White Lily recipes.

2. 1840 census; *AC*, 10 May 1925, 11 June 1925, and 16 July 1959.

3. *AC*, 5 November 1925.

4. 1870, 1880, 1910 censuses. Some sources show Elizabeth's maiden name without the *e*, but her parents' tombstones are both spelled with it.

5. Georgia Marriage Records from Select Counties, 1828–1978, via Ancestry.com; 1910 census; *AC*, 16 July 1959.

6. *LE*, 24 April 1921.

7. *AC*, 13 September 1925. Businessman Frank E. Block (1844–1920) started a simple Atlanta grocery in the 1860s, yet eventually built "the largest and oldest manufacturer of chocolates, confectionery and biscuits in the Southern States" according to *AC*, 6 May and 16 December 1883, 15 November 1911, 13 May 1915, and 14 February 1920. Block's best-known product was Kennesaw Saltines (*AC*, 18 May 1907). In 1927 the company sold "its plant, equipment, trade-marks, and good will to the National Biscuit company" (*AC*, 3 May 1927).

8. *AC*, 9 October 1925.

9. Although it offers no publication information, the earliest known copy has "1927 edition" on the title page. The 1935 edition was published by J. Allen Smith & Company of Knoxville.

10. *AC*, 16 May 1926, 26 September 1926, 22 March 1927, 23 October 1927, and 2 May 1928.

11. *AC*, 9 October 1931, 25 October 1931, 5 February 1933, and 8 October 1934

12. *AC*, 17 November 1942.

13. She is buried in Atlanta's Crest Lawn Cemetery, Section 15. "Mrs. Elizabeth Stanfield, Author of Cookbook Series, Dies at 84," *AC*, 16 July 1959.

14. *Athens Weekly Banner*, 7 February 1913.

15. Although she wasn't as well known as Stanfield, Dull, and Habersham, Augusta native and longtime Decatur resident Ethel Kalbfleisch Pierce Lewis (1887–1975) taught cooking classes across North Georgia in the 1930s; a program from one of her classes is shown in this section. 1900–1950 censuses; *AC*, 13 July 1975.

16. 1860 census; *SMN*, 1 May 1901; tombstone, Laurel Grove North, Savannah. Using tombstones, census records, and newspaper articles, I verified ties between Leila Habersham and 1933 cookbook author Harriet Colquitt through Colquitt, Habersham, and Elliott families, but they are more elaborate than can be outlined here.

17. Fowler, *The Savannah Cookbook*, 55.

18. Habersham's teaching space was located in the Elliott-Huger House at 204 East State Street, but the building is now gone.

19. M. Brown, *The Southern Cook Book*, 161–162.

20. Fowler (in Hill, *Mrs. Hill's Southern Practical Cookery*, 453) notes that Nellie Gordon also recorded Habersham recipes that are now in the collection of the Juliette Gordon Low Birthplace.

21. Manuscript, GHS 0878, Folder 4.

1928, Mrs. Dull's Cooking Lessons

1. Over the years, Grosset & Dunlap (New York), Ladies Home Journal (New York), and Cherokee Publishing (Atlanta) have reprinted the cookbook. In 2006 the University of Georgia Press reprinted the 1941 edition with a foreword by Georgia food historian Damon Lee Fowler.

2. Frank Wells, "U.S. Official Pays a Call on Mrs. Dull," *AC*, 17 September 1963; 1860 and 1870 censuses; Anne Byrn, "The Godmother of Southern Cooking (with Gas)," *Bitter Southerner*, http://bittersoutherner.com/henrietta-dull-southern-cooking.

3. Stanley Mill, now Chappell's Mill, is located off Highway 441 about halfway between Dublin and Irwinton.

4. Frank Daniel, "Mrs. Dull Not Dull at 100," *AJ*, 6 December 1963.

5. Georgia, U.S. Marriage Records from Select Counties, 1828–1978, via Ancestry.com; 1900–1950 censuses.

6. The undated pamphlet pictured in this section for the Athens Cooking School may have been from a series Dull offered in the summer of 1917; see "Interesting Lectures by Mrs. S. R. Dull of Atlanta," *Athens Daily Herald*, 6 July 1917.

7. Damon Lee Fowler in foreword to Dull, *Southern Cooking*.

8. *Anniston* (Ala.) *Star*, 24 May 1918.

9. Daniel, "Mrs. Dull Not Dull at 100" (see note 4). Dull is buried in Section 14 of Atlanta's Westview Cemetery.

10. McClain's work was based mostly in Texas and Tennessee, but her 1952 *Holland's Southern Cookbook* was published in Atlanta.

1932, The Refrigerated Ingredient That Refreshes

1. I. Allen, *When You Entertain*, 120.

2. Ibid., 40.

3. Ibid., 107. The Tropical Coca-Cola Punch recipe is from page 62 and the Fluff recipe from 82. Only the cola recipes are included in the cookbook, not the other foods mentioned in Allen's menus.

1933, *The Savannah Cook Book* and Local Flavor

1. Bessie S. Stafford, "The Savannah Cook Book Contains Savory Old-Fashioned Receipts," *AC*, 19 March 1933.

2. Jane Judge, "The Savannah Cook Book by Harriet Ross Colquitt," *SMN*, 12 February 1933.

3. In the 1858 section and its endnotes, I briefly discuss the challenges of knowing how much to share with a given audience when teaching history.

4. Tipton-Martin's *The Jemima Code*, Sharpless's *Cooking in Other Women's Kitchens*, and Kytle's *Willie Mae* are helpful for examining various aspects of the *Savannah Cook Book*. See also Bentley, "In Service."

5. This paragraph refers to, in order, Palmetto Cabbage (94), Sea Food section commentary (34), Old Fashioned Picnic (174–175), the Ritual of the Bird's Eye Pepper (8), Rice and Hominy Dishes section commentary (73), Syllabub and Ambrosia (113), Vegetables section commentary (89), and Yams (97).

6. Certificate of Death, South Carolina, death date 12 January 1962, via Ancestry.com; "Miss Colquitt, Editor and Author, Dies," *SEP*, 13 January 1962.

7. Barton Myers, "Alfred H. Colquitt," *New Georgia Encyclopedia*, www.georgiaencyclopedia.org/articles/government-politics/alfred-h-colquitt-1824-1894; Richard H. Clark, "The Two Colquitts," *AC*, 29 April 1894; 1880 census; "Walter W. Colquitt Dies Suddenly," *AC*, 19 December 1913.

8. U.S. Passport Applications, 1795–1925, application date 22 October 1918, via Ancestry.com; "Miss Harriet Ross Colquitt," *SEP*, 13 January 1962. Please note that according to clippings in a biography file at the Georgia Historical Society (Savannah), there were two articles about Colquitt's death from the *Savannah Evening Press* on 13 January, 1962.

9. 1930 census; *SEP*, 13 January 1962; Bessie S. Stafford, "The Savannah Cook Book Contains Savory Old-Fashioned Receipts," *AC*, 19 March 1933.

10. Hawes, "Memoirs of Charles H. Olmstead"; tombstone, Laurel Grove North Cemetery; "Three Talented Sisters," *SMN*, 23 September 1950.

11. She is buried in Laurel Grove Cemetery (North), Savannah, Lot 488.

1935, Duncan Hines and South Georgia's Winter Season

1. Hatchett, *Duncan Hines*, 85. While this incident is horrifying from a diner's point of view, it must have been cozy indeed for the cat.

2. Tombstones at Rose Hill Cemetery, Ashburn.

3. The book has no page numbers, but the recipes are numbered. The House by the Road recipes are 120, 243, 246, and 260. In 2014, the University Press of Kentucky released a version of Hines's cookbook and in that volume the Waffles are recipe 171.

4. *Tampa Times*, 2 June 1949; *Star Tribune of Minneapolis*, 10 November 1950.

5. Although I found postcards of the House by the Road dated as early as 1915, as well as a newspaper article promoting the establishment as late as 1967 in the *Houston Journal* (Perry), 8 June 1967, it is unclear exactly when the restaurant opened and closed. The year after Lillie Shingler's death, however, the *Atlanta Constitution* carried an advertisement in its 15 November 1981 issue publicizing an auction to sell the property.

6. *AJC*, 9 May 2005; *New York Times*, 12 May 2005.

7. Recipe reprint permission courtesy of University Press of Kentucky.

8. Tombstone, Laurel Hill Cemetery, Thomasville; "Terrace Tea House," *Tallahassee Democrat*, 25 November 1941.

9. The author cooked for the Gillionville Plantation (Dougherty County) as well as Greenwood Plantation and Willow Oak Plantation (both in Thomas County).

10. Hunter was born in Thomas County.

11. This cookbook is from Grady County.

12. For those looking for recipes from Black cooks, the *Riverview Plantation Cookbook* includes recipes by Lillie J. "Miss Tekie" Harris (ca. 1914–1982) of Mitchell County, who cooked there for twenty-five years. Georgia Death Index via Ancestry.com.

13. Labrah was located in Thomas County.

14. The Delaney/McKim cookbook covers multiple counties—Burke, Camden, Dougherty, Early, Houston, and Jefferson.

1943, *Old and New Recipes* on the Georgia Home Front

1. Green Tomato Crisps from Mrs. Charles Bowen, page 78; Easter Sugar Biscuits from Miss Marguerite Mustin, claimed to be first made by Mrs. S. B. Carpenter on 4 April 1882, page 23; and Lizzy Scott's Wedding Cake by Miss Mary Alice Berckmans, page 13. Please note that this cookbook's recipes are all under copyright.

2. Fitch, *Appetite for Life*, 346.

3. Ginger-Ale Salad from Mrs. Cooley, Sandersville, page 124; Graham Cracker Cake from Mrs. Ferdinand Phinizy, page 125; Delightful All Bran Rolls from Mrs. Charles W. Bowen, page 95.

4. Claussen's Bakery, no address, page 20; Hulse Laundry, no address, page 186.

5. Advertisement for Sanford's Chicken Coop, 1326 Greene Street, page 184.

6. This passage on page 181 refers to December 7, 1941, when the Japanese attacked Pearl Harbor and precipitated the entry of the United States into World War II.

7. The line is a little blurry between the roles of author and editor, and it is not always clear which cookbooks are by committee, which cookbooks were widespread enough to have an impact on Georgia foodways, and which cookbook authors came here after their works were already done. I am counting Edgeworth, Verstille, Hill, Tennent, Dennis, Bell, Roberts, Stanfield, Dull, and Colquitt.

8. Obituary, *AC*, 19 September 1969.

9. "Chicagoan Tells of Southern Cooking," *Chicago Tribune*, 5 September 1948.

10. Wight and Beard, *From Mother with Love*, back cover.

11. U.S. Social Security Death Index, 1935–2014, via Ancestry.com; obituaries in *AC*, 3 February 1977 and 3 January 2021

1944, Historical Cooking Adventures

1. Green-Meldrim House, 14 W. Macon Street, https://greenmeldrimhouse.org. This section involves two undated recipes, so chronologically I fitted it into the year that the Meldrim Family Papers were gifted to the Georgia Historical Society, knowing it was also a time when Stella Center was active in her career.

2. Manuscript, GHS 1288, Box 5, Folder 38.

3. Obituary, *Tampa Bay Times*, 13 January 1969.

4. Lebo, *Difficult Fruit*, 332.

5. There used to be several companies selling tubs of citron, but the only brand I've seen in stores recently produces cubes that are unpleasantly slick and taste somehow soapy. Candied citron may also be ordered online.

6. Manuscript, PP0171, Box 9, Folder 22.

Bibliography

Manuscript Collections

Atlanta History Center, Kenan Research Center

MSS 139, Martha Lumpkin Compton Papers, 1840–1959, undated.

MSS 690F, Clifford A. Shillinglaw Cookbooks, 1820s–1880, undated.

Camden Archives and Museum, Camden, South Carolina

2006.095.0001–0019, Mary Medonis Collection, Miller Family Letters, 1829–1833.

Columbus State University Archives and Special Collections, Columbus

MC 42, Wright Family Papers, 1819–1930.

MC 97, Mitchell Family Papers, 1900s–1999.

MC 154, Alfonso Biggs Collection, 1880–2000.

Duke University, Durham, North Carolina

David M. Rubenstein Rare Book and Manuscript Library

M.3677, Mrs. Charles Spalding Recipe Book, 1871.

Emory University, Atlanta

Stuart A. Rose Manuscript, Archives, and Rare Book Library

MSS 151, Means Family Recipe Book, Alexander Means Papers, 1824–1863.

MSS 1074, Martha Lumpkin Compton Scrapbooks, 1832–1919.

Georgia Archives, Morrow

001-01-005, Governor—Executive Department—Governor's Subject Files (Incoming Correspondence), 1781–2018.

Archibald W. Butts Scrapbooks, ac. 1977-0600M, ah00607.

Georgia Historical Society, Savannah

GHS 0265, Couper and Fraser Family Papers, 1810–1894.

GHS 0318, Gordon Family Papers, 1802–1946.

GHS 0602, Owens and Thomas Family Papers, 1837–1954.

GHS 0750, Spalding Family Papers, 1772–1940.

GHS 0793 (Deposit), Telfair Family Papers, 1751–1875, 1909.

GHS 0857, Anna Matthews White Composition Notebook, 1828–1832.

GHS 0878, Caroline Lamar Woodbridge Papers, 1838–1867.

GHS 1256, Edward Varner Family Papers, 1730–1965.

GHS 1276, George Nowlan Saussy Correspondence and Papers, 1864–1910.

GHS 1288, Meldrim Family Papers, 1809–1973.

GHS 2149, Anderson Family Papers, 1869–1923.

Mercer University, Macon

Jack Tarver Library—Archives, Special Collections, and Digital Initiatives

PP0171 Stella Stewart Center Collection, 1904–1969.

Troup County Archives, LaGrange

MS-2008.05, Theodora Thomas Collection, 1933–1978.

MS-23, Edith B. Hines Papers, 1890–1930.

University of Georgia, Athens

Hargrett Rare Book and Manuscript Library

MS 81, Rebecca Latimer Felton Papers, 1851–1930.

MS 1120, De Renne Family Recipes and Remedies, 1860–1949.

MS 1791, Augusta Amelia (Daisy) Wright Mell Papers, 1869–1944.

MS 2326, Murrell Family Papers, 1832–1977.

MS 2480, Mell-Rutherford Family Papers, 1874–1930.

University of North Carolina, Chapel Hill

Louis Round Wilson Special Collections Library

#00011, Alexander and Hillhouse Family Papers, 1758–1998.

Dorothea Cristina Schmidt Recipe Book, undated.

#00607, Douglas Watson Porter Papers, 1819–1862.

#01478, Stephen D. Heard Papers, 1758–1889.

William Breman Jewish Heritage Museum, Atlanta

Norman L. Estroff Reference Library

Mss 177, James and Ethel Montag Family Papers, 1844–2008.

2022.005.002, Bertha Kayton Rosenheim Recipe Book, undated.

Books and Journal Articles

Acheson, Hugh. *A New Turn in the South: Southern Flavors Reinvented for Your Kitchen*. New York: Clarkson Potter, 2011.

Alexander, Adele Logan. *Ambiguous Lives: Free Women of Color in Rural Georgia, 1789–1879*. Fayetteville: University of Arkansas Press, 1991.

Alexander, A[rchibald], ed. *Biographical Sketches of the Founder and Principal Alumni of the Log College*. Princeton, N.J.: J. T. Robinson, 1845.

Alexander, Kelly. *Peaches*. A Savor the South Cookbook. Chapel Hill: University of North Carolina Press, 2013.

Allen, Ida Bailey. *When You Entertain: What to Do, and How*. Atlanta: Coca-Cola Company, 1932.

Allen, William F., ed. *Travelers' Official Railway Guide for the United States and Canada*. New York: National Railway Publication Company, 1882.

Alumnae of Shorter College. *Sweets and Savouries*. Rome, Ga.: W. T. Sherard, 1915.

Andrews, Eliza Frances. *The War-Time Journal of a Georgia Girl, 1864–1865*. 1908. Lincoln: University of Nebraska Press, 1997.

Arellano, Gustavo. "How Southern Food Has Finally Embraced Its Multicultural Soul." *Time*, 26 July 2018. https://time.com/5349518/southern-food-culture.

Arp, Bill. *See* Smith, Charles H.

Ashantilly Center (Darien, Ga.). *Ashantilly Cookbook*. Waverly, Iowa: G & R, ca. 2005.

Athens Woman's Club. *Athens Woman's Club Cook Book*. Edited by Annie Mae Wood Bryant. Athens, Ga.: McGregor, 1922.

Atherton, Lewis E. *The Southern Country Store, 1800–1860*. Baton Rouge: Louisiana State University Press, 1949.

Atlanta Junior League. *The Cotton Blossom Cook Book*. Atlanta, 1947.

Atlanta Woman's Club. *Atlanta Woman's Club Cook Book*. Edited by Mrs. Newton C. Wing and Mrs. J. A. Carlisle. Atlanta: [Johnson Dallis Co., 1921].

Auchmutey, Jim. *Smokelore: A Short History of Barbecue in America*. Athens: University of Georgia Press, 2019.

Auchmutey, Jim, and Susan Puckett. *The Ultimate Barbecue Sauce Cookbook*. Marietta, Ga.: Longstreet, 1995.

Aycock, Barrie. *Glen-Ella Springs: Recipes and Remembrances*. Nashville: Favorite Recipes, 1997.

Aycock, Barrie, and John Kollock. *Recipes and Ramblings from Glen-Ella Springs*. Turnerville, Ga.: Panther Creek, 1992.

Bailey, Ida D., comp. *The Atlanta Exposition Souvenir Cook Book: A Safe Guide to Ordering and Cooking*. Washington, D.C.: R. L. Pendleton, 1895.

Barile, Mary. *Cookbooks Worth Collecting*. Radnor, Pa.: Wallace-Homestead, 1994.

Barrett, Johnathon Scott, ed. *Cook & Tell: Recipes and Stories from Southern Kitchens*. Macon, Ga.: Mercer University Press, 2017.

Barringer, Mrs. [Maria Massey]. *Dixie Cookery; or, How I Managed My Table for Twelve Years*. Boston: Loring, 1867.

Bartow County Genealogical Society. *Bartow County Georgia Heritage Book*. 2 vols. Cartersville, Ga.: The Society, 1995–1998.

Bartram, William. *The Travels of William Bartram*. Edited by Francis Harper. Athens: University of Georgia Press, 1998.

Becker, John. "Keeping *Joy of Cooking* in the Family, with John Becker and Megan Scott." *Salt and Spine* podcast, 31 March 2020. www.saltandspine.com/episode/john-becker-megan-scott.

Beecher, Catharine. *Miss Beecher's Domestic Receipt Book*. New York: Harper, 1846.

Bell, Emma. *One Hundred Choice Dishes for One Hundred Cents*. Atlanta: Franklin Printing and Publishing, 1897.

Bennett, Chris. *Southeast Foraging*. Portland, Ore.: Timber, 2015.

Bentley, Rosalind. "In Service: A Heavy Legacy Born of Domestic Work." *Gravy* (Southern Foodways Alliance). www.southernfoodways.org/in-service.

Bergeron, Arthur W., Jr. *Guide to Louisiana Confederate Military Units, 1861–1865*. Baton Rouge: Louisiana State University Press, 1996.

Bethlehem Methodist Church (Bethlehem, Ga.), Wesleyan Fellowship. *Bethlehem's Kitchen Secrets*. Kansas City, Mo.: Bev-Ron, 1951.

Bishop, Marion. "Speaking Sisters: Relief Society Cookbooks and Mormon Culture." In Bower, *Recipes for Reading*, 89–104.

Bleser, Carol, ed. *In Joy and in Sorrow: Women, Family, and Marriage in the Victorian South, 1830–1900*. New York: Oxford University Press, 1991.

Boles, Frank. "'Stirring Constantly'": 150 Years of Michigan Cookbooks." *Michigan Historical Review* 32.2 (Fall 2006): 33–62.

Bolzius, Johann Martin, and Philipp von Reck. *An Extract of the Journals of Mr. Commissary Von Reck, Who Conducted the First Transport of Saltzburgers to Georgia: and of the Reverend Mr. Bolzius, One of Their Ministers. Giving an Account of Their Voyage to, and Happy Settlement in That Province*. London: M. Downing, 1734.

Borel, Brooke, et al. "The Future of Food: How to Feed a Hungry Planet in the Digital Age." *Popular Science* 287.4 (October 2015): 35–41.

Bower, Anne L. "Our Sisters' Recipes: Exploring 'Community' in a Community Cookbook." *Journal of Popular Culture* 31.3 (Winter 1997): 137–151.

——, ed. *Recipes for Reading: Community Cookbooks, Stories, Histories*. Amherst, Mass.: University of Massachusetts Press, 1997.

Boykin, Samuel. *History of the Baptist Denomination in Georgia*. Vol. 2. Paris, Ark.: Baptist Standard Bearer, 1881.

Bragg, Rick. *The Best Cook in the World: Tales from My Momma's Table*. New York: Alfred Knopf, 2018.

Brewer, Priscilla J. *From Fireplace to Cookstove: Technology and the Domestic Ideal in America*. Syracuse, N.Y.: Syracuse University Press, 2000.

Brown, Alton. *I'm Just Here for More Food: Food x Mixing + Heat = Baking*. New York: Stewart, Tabori & Chang, 2004.

Brown, Eleanor, and Bob Brown. *Culinary Americana: Cookbooks Published in the Cities and Towns of the United States of America During the Years from 1860 Through 1960*. New York: Roving Eye, 1961.

Brown, Fred. *The Dillard House Cookbook and Mountain Guide*. Atlanta: Longstreet, 1996.

Brown, Fred, and Sherri M. L. Smith. *The Best of Georgia Farms Cookbook and Tour Book*. Atlanta: CI Publishing, 1998.

Brown, Marion Lea. *The Southern Cook Book*. Chapel Hill: University of North Carolina Press, 1951.

Brown, Titus, and James "Jack" Hadley. *African-American Life on the Southern Hunting Plantation*. Charleston, S.C.: Arcadia, 2000.

Brumby, Mary Hart. *Seasoned Skillets & Silver Spoons: A Culinary History of Columbus, Georgia*. Columbus: Columbus Museum Guild, 1993.

Brunvand, Jan Harold, ed. *American Folklore: An Encyclopedia*. New York: Garland, 1996.

Bryan, Mrs. Lettice. *The Kentucky Housewife*. Cincinnati: Shepard & Stearns, 1839.

Bryant, Barbara, and Betsy Fentress. *Pecans: Recipes & History of an American Nut*. Recipes by Rebecca Lang. New York: Rizzoli, 2019.

Bryant, Pat, and Ingrid Shields. *Georgia Counties: Their Changing Boundaries*. 2nd ed. Atlanta: Georgia Department of Archives & History, 1983.

Bulloch, Paul Milner. *The Georgia Peach Story*. Woodland, Ga.: Old South Farm Museum and Ag Learning Center, ca. 2010.

Burge, Dolly. *The Diary of Dolly Lunt Burge, 1848–1879*. Edited by Christine Jacobson Carter. Athens: University of Georgia Press, 1997.

Busbee, Mary Beth. *Guess Who's Coming to Dinner: Entertaining at the Georgia Governor's Mansion*. Atlanta: Peachtree, 1986.

———. *Mary Beth's Sampler: A Georgia Cookbook*. With Jan Busbee Curtis. Atlanta: Conger, 1976.

Bush, Rebecca, ed. *Chattahoochee Cookin': The Cookbook*. Columbus, Ga.: Columbus Museum, 2015.

Butt, Archibald. *Taft and Roosevelt: The Intimate Letters of Archie Butt*. Garden City, New York: Doubleday, Doran, 1930.

Byrn, Anne. *American Cake: From Colonial Gingerbread to Classic Layer, the Stories and Recipes Behind More than 125 of Our Best-Loved Cakes from Past to Present*. New York: Rodale, 2016.

Campbell, Tunis G. *Hotel Keepers, Head Waiters, and Housekeepers' Guide*. Boston: Coolidge and Wiley, 1848.

———. *Sufferings of the Rev. T. G. Campbell and His Family in Georgia*. Washington: Enterprise, 1877.

Carlisle, Nancy, and Melinda Talbot Nasardinov. *America's Kitchens*. With Jennifer Pustz. Boston: Historic New England, 2008.

Carter, Lillian. *Miss Lillian and Friends: The Plains, Georgia Family Philosophy and Recipe Book*. As told to Beth Tartan and Rudy Hayes. New York: A & W, 1977.

Cashin, Edward J., ed. *A Wilderness Still the Cradle of Nature*. Savannah: Beehive, 1994.

Central Congregational Church (Atlanta) Ladies Union. *Good Things to Eat*. Atlanta: [Hubbard & Bolton], 1915.

Central Georgia Genealogy Society. *First Hundred and Ten Years of Houston County, Georgia (1822–1932)*. Chelsea, Mich.: Bookcrafters, 1983.

Central Presbyterian Church (Atlanta). *The Southern Housekeeper: A Book of Tested Recipes*. Atlanta: Franklin Printing and Publishing, 1898.

Chase, A. W. *Dr. Chase's Third, Last and Complete Receipt Book and Household Physician; or, Practical Knowledge for the People*. Atlanta: Rowland, 1888.

Chiltosky, Mary. *See* Ulmer, Mary.

Chinese Consolidated Benevolent Association of Augusta. *Favorite Recipes of the Augusta Chinese Community*. 2nd ed. Augusta, Ga.: Privately published, 2006.

Chirhart, Ann Short, and Betty Wood, eds. *Georgia Women: Their Lives and Times*. 2 vols. Athens: University of Georgia Press, 2009–2014.

Choate, Anne Hyde, and Helen Ferris. *Juliette Low and the Girl Scouts: The Story of an American Woman, 1860–1927*. Garden City, N.Y.: Doubleday, Doran, 1928.

Choice Recipes of Georgia Housekeepers. *See* Second Presbyterian Church, Augusta.

Civitello, Linda. *Baking Powder Wars*. Urbana: University of Illinois Press, 2017.

Clarke, Erskine. *Dwelling Place: A Plantation Epic*. New Haven, Conn.: Yale University Press, 2005.

Clifton, Clarissa. *One Hearth, One Pot: For Love of Food and History*. Charlotte, N.C.: Clarissa Clifton, 2010.

Clinton, Catherine. "Susie King Taylor." In Chirhart and Wood, *Georgia Women*, 130–146.

———. *Tara Revisited: Women, War, and the Plantation Legend*. New York: Abbeville, 1995.

Coleman, Feay Shellman. *Nostrums for Fashionable Entertainments: Dining in Georgia, 1800–1850*. Savannah: Telfair Academy of Arts and Sciences, 1992.

Coleman, Mildred Huff. *Frances Virginia Tea Room Cookbook*. Atlanta: Peachtree, 1981.

Colquitt, Harriet Ross, ed. *The Savannah Cook Book: A Collection of Old Fashioned Receipts from Colonial Kitchens*. Charleston, S.C.: Colonial, 1933.

Congressional Club. *The Congressional Club Cook Book: Favorite National and International Recipes*. Washington, D.C., 1927.

Conroy, Pat. *The Pat Conroy Cookbook: Recipes of My Life*. With Suzanne Williamson Pollack. New York: Nan A. Talese, 2004.

Cook, Margaret. *America's Charitable Cooks: A Bibliography of Fund-Raising Cook Books Published in the United States, 1861–1915*. Kent, Ohio: Cookery Bibliography, 1971.

Cooley, Angela Jill. *To Live and Dine in Dixie: The Evolution of Urban Food Culture in the Jim Crow South*. Athens: University of Georgia Press, 2015.

Cooper, Ben Green. *Savannah's Cookin'*. Mableton, Ga.: Ben Green Cooper Press, 1967.

Cooper, Polly Wylly. *Isle of Hope, Wormsloe and Bethesda*. Charleston, S.C.: Arcadia, 2002.

Cordery, Stacy A. *Juliette Gordon Low: The Remarkable Founder of the Girl Scouts*. New York: Viking, 2012.

Corriher, Shirley O. *BakeWise: The Hows and Whys of Successful Baking*. New York: Scribner, 2008.

———. *CookWise: The Hows and Whys of Successful Cooking*. New York: William Morrow, 1997.

Cost, Bruce. *Ginger East to West*. Rev. ed. Reading, Mass.: Aris, 1989.

Cotner, Dennis. Interview with the author, Williamsburg, Va., 25 July 2007.

Cotter, Colleen. "Claiming a Piece of the Pie." In Bower, *Recipes for Reading*, 51–74.

Cox, Eugenia Barrs, ed. *Low Country Cooking*. Hinesville, Ga.: Liberty County Historical Society, 1988.

Cox, Peggy C. *Riverview Plantation Cookbook*. Tallahassee, Fla.: Rose Printing, 1984.

Croly, Mrs. J. C. *The History of the Woman's Club Movement in America*. New York: H. G. Allen, 1898.

Crook, Ray, et al. *Sapelo Voices: Historical Anthropology and the Oral Traditions of Gullah-Geechee Communities on Sapelo Island, Georgia*. Carrollton, Ga.: State University of West Georgia, 2003.

Cunyus, Lucy Josephine. *The History of Bartow County, Formerly Cass*. Cartersville, Ga.: Tribune Publishing, 1933.

Dabney, Joseph E. *The Food, Folklore, and Art of Lowcountry Cooking*. Nashville: Cumberland House, 2010.

———. *Smokehouse Ham, Spoon Bread, and Scuppernong Wine: The Folklore and Art of Southern Appalachian Cooking*. Nashville: Cumberland House, 1998.

Davidson, Marty. *Grandma Grace's Southern Favorites: Very, Very Old Recipes Adapted for a New Generation*. Nashville: Rutledge Hill, 2005.

Davidson, William H. *A Rockaway in Talbot: Travels in an Old Georgia County*. 4 vols. West Point, Ga.: W. H. Davidson, ca. 1983–1990.

Davis, Robert S., and Ted O. Brooke. *Georgia Research: A Handbook for Genealogists, Historians, Archivists, Lawyers, Librarians, and Other Researchers*. 2nd ed. Atlanta: Georgia Genealogical Society, 2012.

Dawson, Charles C. *A Collection of Family Records with Biographical Sketches and Other Memoranda of Various Families and Individuals Bearing the Name Dawson, or Allied to Families of That Name*. Albany, N.Y.: J. Munsell, 1874.

Day, Cheryl. *Cheryl Day's Treasury of Southern Baking*. New York: Artisan, 2021.

DeBolt, Margaret Wayt. *Georgia Entertains: A Rich Heritage of Fine Food and Gracious Hospitality*. With Emma Rylander Law and Carter Olive. Nashville: Rutledge Hill, 1983.

——, comp. *Savannah Sampler Cookbook*. With Emma Rylander Law. Atglen, Pa.: Whitford, 1978.

DeBoth, Jessie Marie. *Modernistic Recipe-Menu Book of the DeBoth Homemakers' Cooking School*. Chicago, 1929.

Deen, Paula. *It Ain't All About the Cookin': A Memoir*. With Sherry Suib Cohen. New York: Simon and Schuster, 2007.

——. *The Lady & Sons Savannah Country Cookbook*. New York: Random House, 1997.

Delaney, Leslie, and David McKim. *The Southern Plantations Cook*. St. Simons Island, Ga.: Saint Simons Publishing, 1999.

Dennis, Annie E. *The New Annie Dennis Cook Book*. Rev. ed. Atlanta: Mutual, 1915.

Dennis, Annie E., and Daisy A. Wright. *Annie Dennis' Cook Book: A Compendium of Popular Household Recipes for the Busy Housewife*. Atlanta: American Publishing and Engraving, 1894.

Dietrich, Paul Henry. *The History of Rowland Springs, Cartersville, Georgia*. Cleveland, Tenn.: Carroll Printing, 2014.

Dodd, Louise. *Eating from the White House to the Jailhouse*. Memphis: Wimmer, 2004.

Dodge, P. S., comp. *Official Guide to the Cotton States and International Exposition*. Atlanta: Franklin Printing and Publishing, [1895].

Donovan, Mary, et al. *The Thirteen Colonies Cookbook*. New York: Praeger, 1975.

Dorsey, Bruce. *Reforming Men and Women: Gender in the Antebellum City*. Ithaca, N.Y.: Cornell University Press, 2002.

Doyle, Charles C. "Mulling Over Mull: A North Georgia Foodways Localism." In *Cornbread Nation 5: The Best of Southern Food Writing*, edited by Fred W. Sauceman, 55–61. Athens: University of Georgia Press, 2010.

Dreilinger, Danielle. *The Secret History of Home Economics*. New York: W. W. Norton, 2021.

Dubose, Fred. *Four Great Southern Cooks*. Atlanta: DuBose Publishing, 1982.

Dull, Mrs. S. R. *Southern Cooking*. Atlanta: Ruralist Press, 1928. Reprint with 1941 additions, Athens: University of Georgia Press, 2006.

Duncan, Russell. *Freedom's Shore: Tunis Campbell and the Georgia Freedmen*. Athens: University of Georgia Press, 1986.

Dupree, Nathalie, and Cynthia Graubart. *Nathalie Dupree's Favorite Stories & Recipes*. Layton, Utah: Gibbs Smith, 2019.

DuSablon, Mary Anna. *America's Collectible Cookbooks: The History, the Politics, the Recipes*. Athens: Ohio University Press, 1994.

Ebenezer Baptist Church (Atlanta). *Edibles from Ebenezer*. Edited by Mary Nell Hollis Glenn. Olathe, Kans.: Cookbook Publishers, 1986.

Eberhard, Wallace B. "Sarah Porter Hillhouse: Setting the Record Straight." *Journalism History* 1.4 (Winter 1974–75): 133–136.

Edge, John T., ed. *Foodways*. Vol. 7 of *The New Encyclopedia of Southern Culture*. Chapel Hill: University of North Carolina Press, 2007.

———. *A Gracious Plenty: Recipes and Recollections from the American South*. New York: G. P. Putnam's Sons, 1999.

Edgeworth, Mrs. Mary L. *The Southern Gardener and Receipt Book, Containing Valuable Information, Original and Otherwise, on All Subjects Connected with Domestic and Rural Affairs, Gardening, Cookery, Beverages, Dairy, Medicinal, Veterinary and Miscellaneous*. Rev. 3rd ed. Philadelphia: J. B. Lippincott, 1859.

Egerton, John. *Southern Food: At Home, on the Road, in History*. New York: Knopf, 1987.

Elias, Megan J. *Food on the Page: Cookbooks and American Culture*. Philadelphia: University of Pennsylvania Press, 2017.

Emmanuel [Episcopal] Church (Athens, Ga.). *The Home Cook Book*. Norwalk, Ohio: Laning Printing, 1898.

Engelhardt, Elizabeth S. D. *A Mess of Greens: Southern Gender and Southern Food*. Athens: University of Georgia Press, 2011.

Erwin, Valerie. "A Geechee Girl Speaks." In *Cornbread Nation 6: The Best of Southern Food Writing*, edited by Brett Anderson, 282–285. Athens: University of Georgia Press, 2012.

Eschmann, Clara Belle Hooks. *Remember When—? Family, Friends, and Recipes*. Macon, Ga.: Mercer University Press, 1998.

Evans, Dianne. *Bobwhite Quail & Buttermilk Biscuits: A Plantation Cooks for Company*. Memphis: Wimmer Brothers, 1984.

Falk, Stanley L. "The Warrenton Female Academy of Jacob Mordecai, 1809–1818." *North Carolina Historical Review* 35.3 (July 1958): 281–298.

Farmer, Fannie Merritt. *The Boston Cooking-School Cook Book*. Boston: Little, Brown, 1896.

Farrant, Don. *Ghosts of the Georgia Coast*. Sarasota, Fla.: Pineapple Press, 1998.

Felton, Rebecca Latimer. *Country Life in Georgia in the Days of My Youth*. Atlanta: Index Printing, 1919.

Ferrell, John. *Mary Mac's Tea Room 75th Anniversary Cookbook*. Kansas City, Mo.: Andrews McMeel, 2019.

Ferris, Marcie Cohen. *The Edible South: The Power of Food and the Making of an American Region*. Chapel Hill: University of North Carolina Press, 2014.

———. "Gender and Food." In Edge, *Foodways*, 58–62.

———. *Matzoh Ball Gumbo: Culinary Tales of the Jewish South*. Chapel Hill: University of North Carolina Press, 2005.

Fielding, Daphne. *The Duchess of Jermyn Street*. New York: Penguin, 1964.

Figoni, Paula. *How Baking Works: Exploring the Fundamentals of Baking Science*. 2nd ed. Hoboken, N.J.: Wiley, 2008.

Filippini, Alexander. *The International Cook Book*. Garden City, N.Y.: Doubleday Page, 1906.

First Baptist Church (Albany, Ga.), Building Fund Association. *The Baptist Cook Book*. Columbus, Ga.: Gilbert Printing, 1907.

First Presbyterian Church (Athens, Ga.), Young Ladies Missionary Society. *Choice Recipes*. Athens, Ga.: Atkinson & Smith, 1910.

First Presbyterian Church (Dalton, Ga.), Woman's Auxiliary. *Dalton Cook Book*. 4th ed. Dalton, Ga.: A. J. Showalter, 1923.

First Presbyterian Church (Rome, Ga.), Ladies Aid Society. *The New South Cook Book*. Rome, Ga.: T. E. Clement, 1905.

Fisher, Abby. *What Mrs. Fisher Knows About Old Southern Cooking*. San Francisco: Women's Co-operative Printing Office, 1881. Reprinted in facsimile with commentary by Karen Hess. Bedford, Mass.: Applewood, 1995.

Fisher, Carol. *The American Cookbook*. Jefferson, N.C.: McFarland, 2006.

Fisher, Carol, and John Fisher. *Pot Roast, Politics, and Ants in the Pantry: Missouri's Cookbook Heritage*. Columbia: University of Missouri Press, 2008.

Fitch, Noël Riley. *Appetite for Life: The Biography of Julia Child*. New York: Doubleday, 1997.

Fowler, Damon Lee. *Classical Southern Cooking: A Celebration of the Cuisine of the Old South*. New York: Crown, 1995.

———. "Hill, Annabella Powell." In Edge, *Foodways*, 182.

———. *The Savannah Cookbook*. Salt Lake City: Gibbs Smith, 2008.

Foxfire. "Foxfire's Book of Wood Stove Cookery." Special issue, *Foxfire* 15.4 (Winter 1981).

Fox-Genovese, Elizabeth. *Within the Plantation Household: Black and White Women of the Old South*. Chapel Hill: University of North Carolina, 1988.

Franklin, Linda Campbell. *300 Years of Kitchen Collectibles*. 5th ed. Iola, Wisc.: Krause, 2003.

Frey, Douglas M. *Marietta: The Gem City of Georgia; A Celebration of its Homes, a Portrait of its People*. Marietta: Cobb Landmarks and Historical Society, 2010.

Frey, Valerie J. *The Living Shoreline*. Illustrated by Alan Reid. Athens: University of Georgia Press, 2021.

———. *Preserving Family Recipes: How to Save and Celebrate Your Food Traditions*. Athens: University of Georgia Press, 2015.

———. "Yesteryear's Puddings: A Timeless Treat." *Georgia Connector* 7.1 (2016): 77–81.

Friedman, Jean E. *The Enclosed Garden: Women and Community in the Evangelical South, 1830–1900*. Chapel Hill: University of North Carolina, 1985.

Gaede, Sarah. *Gottlieb's Bakery: 100 Years of Recipes or 100 Years of "Is it Fresh?"* With Irving and Isser Gottlieb. Memphis: Wimmer, 1983.

Gallay, Alan, ed. *Voices of the Old South: Eyewitness Accounts, 1528–1861*. Athens: University of Georgia Press, 1994.

Georgia Department of Agriculture. *The Essential Market Bulletin Cookbook: A Refreshing Take on a Century of Southern Cooking*. [Atlanta: Georgia Department of Agriculture, 2022.]

———. *Seasons of Georgia: Kitchen Keepsake Cookbook*. Boca Raton, Fla.: Phoenix Media Network, 2007.

Georgia Farm Bureau, Women's Committee. *A Legacy of Georgia Cooking*. Memphis: Wimmer Cookbooks, 2010.

Georgia Federation of Women's Clubs. *The Georgia Clubwoman's Souvenir Collection of Prized Recipes*. Athens, ca. 1938.

Georgia Military College, Bulldog Club. *Old Capitol Cook Book*. 3rd ed. Milledgeville, Ga.: Georgia Military College, [1973].

Georgia Salzburger Society. *Ye Olde Time Salzburger Cook Book: A Book of Recipes and Remedies Used by the Early Salzburgers*. 1925. Rincon, Ga.: Georgia Salzburger Society, ca. 1963.

Gibson, Dot Rees. *Boarding House Reach: Famous Smith House Recipes*. Waycross, Ga.: Dot Gibson Publications, 1981.

Gilchrist, James P. *A Brief Display of the Origin and History of Ordeals: Trials by Battle; Courts of Chivalry or Honor; and the Decision of Private Quarrels by Single Combat; Also, a Chronological Register of the Principal Duels Fought from the Accession of His Late Majesty to the Present Time*. London: Privately printed, 1821.

Gillespie, Kevin. *Fire in My Belly: Real Cooking*. With David Joachim. Kansas City, Mo.: Andrews McMeel, 2012.

Gilman, Edward F., and Dennis G. Watson. "*Nyssa Ogeche*: Ogeechee Tupelo." University of Florida Extension Service, Publication #ENH-579. https://edis.ifas.ufl.edu/publication/ST420.

Girl Scouts of the United States of America. *Centennial Receipt Book: Juliette Gordon Low, Hostess and Homemaker, 1860–1960*. New York: Girl Scouts of the U.S.A., 1960.

Glasse, Hannah. *The Art of Cookery Made Plain and Easy*. Facsimile of 1805 edition, with notes by Karen Hess. Bedford, Mass.: Applewood, 1997.

Goldenson, Suzanne. *The Open-Hearth Cookbook*. With Doris Simpson. Rev. ed. Chambersburg, Pa.: Alan C. Hood, 2006.

Gordon, Arthur. *How Sweet It Is: The Story of Dixie Crystals and Savannah Foods*. Savannah: Savannah Foods & Industries, 1992.

Gottlieb. *See* Gaede.

Governor Treutlen Chapter, Daughters of the American Revolution. *History of Peach County, Georgia*. Atlanta: Cherokee, 1972.

Graham, Elizabeth Candler, and Ralph Roberts. *Classic Cooking with Coca-Cola*. Nashville: Hambleton-Hill, 1994.

Grant, Donald L. *The Way It Was in the South: The Black Experience in Georgia*. 1993. Athens: University of Georgia Press, 2001.

Graubart, Cynthia Stevens. *Chicken*. Chapel Hill: University of North Carolina Press, 2016.

———. *Sunday Suppers*. New York: Oxmoor House, 2017.

Greek Orthodox Cathedral of the Annunciation (Atlanta). *The Key to Greek Cooking*. Atlanta: Privately published, 1974.

Green, Thomas A., ed. *Folklore: An Encyclopedia of Beliefs, Customs, Tales, Music, and Art*. Santa Barbara, Calif.: ABC-CLIO, 1997.

Greene Street Presbyterian Church (Augusta). *Choice Recipes of Georgia Housekeepers*. 3rd ed. Augusta, Ga.: Ridgely-Wing-Tidwell, 1916.

Gregory, Annie R. *The New Dixie Receipt Book*. Atlanta: D. E. Luther, 1902.

Grovner, Yvonne J., Cornelia Walker Bailey, and Doc. Bill [William Thomas]. *The Foods of Georgia's Barrier Islands: A Gourmet Food Guide of Native American, Geechee and European Influences on the Golden Isles*. Gainesville, Ga.: Privately printed at Georgia Design & Graphics, 2004.

Grubb, Alan. "House and Home in the Victorian South: The Cookbook as Guide." In Bleser, *In Joy and in Sorrow*, 154–175.

Handy, Moses Purnell, ed. *World's Columbian Exposition, 1893, Official Catalogue*. Chicago: W. B. Conkey, 1893.

Hapeville Presbyterian Church. *The Hapeville Presbyterian Cook Book*. Atlanta: Franklin Printing and Publishing, 1898.

Hardy, Stella Pickett. *Colonial Families of the Southern States of America: A History and Genealogy of Colonial Families who Settled in the Colonies Prior to the Revolution*. New York: Tobias A. Wright, 1911.

Harris, Jessica B. *High on the Hog: A Culinary Journey from Africa to America*. New York: Bloomsbury, 2011.

Hartley, Grace. *The Grace Hartley Cookbook: Selected Southern Favorites from Over Forty Years of Recipes from the Atlanta Journal*. Garden City, N.Y.: Doubleday, 1976.

Hatchett, Louis. *Duncan Hines: How a Traveling Salesman Became the Most Trusted Name in Food*. Lexington: University Press of Kentucky, 2014.

Hawes, Lilla Mills. "The Memoirs of Charles H. Olmstead, Part 1." *Georgia Historical Quarterly* 42.4 (December 1958): 389–408.

Hearn, Lafcadio. *La Cuisine Creole: A Collection of Culinary Recipes, from Leading Chefs and Noted Creole Housewives, Who Have Made New Orleans Famous for Its Cuisine*. 2nd ed. New Orleans: F. F. Hansell, 1885.

Heinsohn, Lillian Britt. *Southern Plantation: The Story of Labrah, Including Some of Its Treasured Recipes*. New York: Bonanza/Hearthside, 1962.

Hendricks, Sue J., and Christopher E. Hendricks. *Old Southern Cookery: Mary Randolph's Recipes from America's First Regional Cookbook Adapted for Today's Kitchen*. Guilford, Conn.: Globe Pequot, 2020.

Henry County [Alabama] Historical Society. *Wiregrass Cooking Through the Years: An Historical Way of Life in Southeast Alabama, 1600–1982*. Abbeville, Ala.: Henry County Historical Society, 1981.

Hess, John L., and Karen Hess. *The Taste of America*. 1972. Champaign: University of Illinois Press, 2000.

Hess, Karen. *The Carolina Rice Kitchen: The African Connection*. Columbia: University of South Carolina Press, 1992.

——, ed. *Martha Washington's Booke of Cookery*. New York: Columbia University Press, 1981.

Hewett, D. F., and G. W. Crickmay. *The Warm Springs of Georgia, Their Geologic Relations and Origin: A Summary Report*. With the Georgia Department of Forestry and Geological Development. Washington, D.C.: U.S. Government Printing Office, 1937.

Hill, Mrs. A. P. *The Life and Services of Rev. John E. Dawson*. Atlanta: Franklin Steam Publishing House, 1872.

——. *Mrs. Hill's New Cook Book, a Practical System for Private Families, in Town and Country; with Directions for Carving and Arranging the Table for Dinner, Parties, etc. Together with Many Medical and Miscellaneous Receipts Extremely Useful in Families*. New York: Carleton, 1867; New York: G. W. Dillingham, 1886. Editions are nearly identical.

——. *Mrs. Hill's New Cook Book*. Combined with the 1863 *Confederate Receipt Book* and with a preface by Shirley Abbott. Birmingham, Ala.: Oxmoor House, 1985.

——. *Mrs. Hill's Southern Practical Cookery and Receipt Book*. Facsimile of 1872 edition with commentary by Damon L. Fowler. Columbia: University of South Carolina Press, 1995.

Hilliard, Sam Bowers. *Hog Meat and Hoecake: Food Supply in the Old South, 1840–1860*. Carbondale: Southern Illinois University Press, 1972.

Hines, Duncan. *Adventures in Good Cooking and the Art of Carving in the Home: Famous Recipes*. Bowling Green, Ky.: Adventures in Good Eating, 1939. Many of Hines's recipes were reprinted in 2014 by the University Press of Kentucky as *Adventures in Good Eating*, edited by Louis Hatchett.

Hobbs, Larry. *Coast Tales: True Historic Stories from Georgia's Golden Isles*. Brunswick, Ga.: Brunswick News, 2019.

Hogan, Richard. "Tunis G. Campbell, Sr. (1812–1891)." *Journal of African American Studies* 18.4 (2014): 409–416.

Hooker, Richard J., ed. *A Colonial Plantation Cookbook: The Receipt Book of Harriott Pinckney Horry, 1770*. Columbia: University of South Carolina Press, 1984.

Hoxie, W. J. *How Girls Can Help Their Country: The Handbook for Girl Scouts*. 1913. Bedford, Mass.: Applewood, 2013.

Hudson, Charles M., ed. *Black Drink: A Native American Tea*. Athens: University of Georgia Press, 1979.

——. *The Southeastern Indians*. Knoxville: University of Tennessee Press, 1976.

Hunt, Sharon Kaye. *"My" Official Georgia Geechee Cookbook: Geechees, Low Country Cooking and History Facts*. Privately published via Xlibris, 2015.

Hunter, Ethel Farmer. *Secrets of Southern Cooking: A Collection of Heirloom Recipes Long Treasured by the Old Families of the South*. Chicago: Ziff Davis, 1948.

Hunter, Flora Mae. *Born in the Kitchen: Plain and Fancy Plantation Fixin's*. 4th ed. Tallahassee, Fla.: Pine Cone Press, 1979.

Hutcheson, Mrs. S. O., comp. *The Georgianne Cook Book*. Athens: McGregor Company, 1916.

Independent Presbyterian Church (Savannah), Flower Committee. *Hints from Southern Epicures*. [Cincinnati: A. H. Pugh], 1892.

Jackson, Ruth. *Ruth Jackson's Soulfood Cookbook, Plains, Georgia*. Memphis: Wimmer Brothers, 1978.

Jacobsen, Anita. *Jacobsen's Biographical Index of American Artists*. Carrollton, Tex.: A. J. Publications, 2002.

James, Virginia E. *Arnold & McCord's Key to Good Cooking*. Atlanta, 1890.

——. *Mother James' Key to Good Cooking*. Chicago: Preston, 1895.

Jennings, Matthew, ed. *The Flower Hunter and the People: William Bartram on the Native American Southeast*. Macon, Ga.: Mercer University Press, 2014.

Jolliffe, Lee. "Women's Magazines in the 19th Century." *Journal of Popular Culture* 27.4 (Spring 1994): 125–140.

Jones, Sharon Foster. *The Atlanta Exposition*. Charleston, S.C.: Arcadia, 2010.

Junior League of Albany, Georgia. *Quail Country*. Albany, Ga.: Smith House, 1983.

Junior League of Augusta, Georgia. *Old and New Recipes from the South*. 3rd ed. Augusta, Ga.: The League, 1943.

Junior League of Savannah, Georgia. *Savannah Style*. Memphis: Wimmer Brothers, 1980.

Kamp, David. *The United States of Arugula: How We Became a Gourmet Nation*. New York: Broadway, 2006.

Karatassos, Pano. *Modern Greek Cooking*. New York: Rizzoli, 2018.

Kennedy, Jackie. *Diverse Power, Place and Plate: Culture and Cooking in West Georgia*. Virginia Beach, Va.: Donning, 2016.

Kimball, Christopher. *Fannie's Last Supper: Re-creating One Amazing Meal from Fannie Farmer's 1896 Cookbook*. New York: Hyperion, 2010.

Kimmerer, Robin Wall. *Braiding Sweetgrass: Indigenous Wisdom, Scientific Knowledge, and the Teachings of Plants*. Minneapolis: Milkweed, 2013.

King, Alveda. *GG's Home for the Holidays Cookbook: Sweet Savory Bites from Our King Family Kitchen to Yours*. With Jan Horne. Atlanta: Stanton, 2017.

Kitchen Guild of the Tullie Smith House Restoration, eds. *Tullie's Receipts: Nineteenth-Century Plantation Plain Style Southern Cooking and Living*. Atlanta: Atlanta Historical Society, 1976.

Kitchens, Michael W. *Ghosts of Grandeur: Georgia's Lost Antebellum Homes and Plantations*. Virginia Beach, Va.: Donning, 2012.

Knight, Lucian Lamar. *Georgia's Landmarks, Memorials and Legends*. 2 vols. Atlanta: Byrd, 1913–1914.

Krull, Kathleen. *Lives of Extraordinary Women*. San Diego, Calif.: Harcourt, 2000.

Kugel, Daisy Alice. *Recipes for Food Classes*. Spelman College Bulletin. Atlanta: Atlanta University Press, 1930.

Kuhn, Clifford M., Harlon E. Joye, and E. Bernard West. *Living Atlanta: An Oral History of the City, 1914–1948*. Athens: University of Georgia Press, 1990.

Kummer, Corby. *The Pleasures of Slow Food: Celebrating Authentic Traditions, Flavors, and Recipes*. San Francisco: Chronicle, 2002.

Kytle, Elizabeth. *Willie Mae*. New York: Knopf, 1958.

Lamb, Daniel Smith, ed. *Howard University Medical Department, Washington D.C.: A Historical Biographical and Statistical Souvenir*. Washington, D.C.: R. Beresford, 1900.

Landon, Luann. *Dinner at Miss Lady's: Memories and Recipes from a Southern Childhood*. Chapel Hill, N.C.: Algonquin, 1999.

Lane, Mills, ed. *The Rambler in Georgia*. Savannah: Beehive, 1973.

Lang, Rebecca. *Quick-Fix Southern*. Kansas City, Mo.: Andrews McMeel, 2011.

LaRowe, John E., ed. *Somethin's Cookin' in the Mountains*. Clarkesville, Ga.: Soque, 1982.

Lawton, Christopher R., Laura E. Nelson, and Randy L. Reid. *Seen/Unseen: Hidden Lives in a Community of Enslaved Georgians*. Athens: University of Georgia Press, 2021.

Lebo, Kate. *The Book of Difficult Fruit*. New York: Farrar, Straus and Giroux, 2021.

Le Guin, Magnolia. *A Home-Concealed Woman: The Diaries of Magnolia Wynn Le Guin, 1901–1913*. Edited by Charles A. LeGuin. Athens: University of Georgia Press, 1990.

Leslie, Miss [Eliza]. *Directions for Cookery, Being a System of the Art in Its Various Branches*. Philadelphia: E. L. Carey & A. Hart, 1837.

Levitas, Earlyne S. *Secrets from Atlanta's Best Kitchens*. Charleston, S.C.: Walker, Evans & Cogswell, 1971.

Lewis, David Levering. *W. E. B. Du Bois: Biography of a Race*. New York: Henry Holt, 1993.

Lewis, Edna. "What Is Southern?" *Gourmet*, January 2008. Reprinted in *Reader: Ideas and Information on Arts and Culture* (Grantmakers in the Arts) 19.3 (Fall 2008): 4.

Lewis, Kenneth E. *The Carolina Backcountry Venture*. Columbia: University of South Carolina Press, 2017.

Lewis, William Terrell. *Genealogy of the Lewis Family in America, from the Middle of the Seventeenth Century Down to the Present Time*. Louisville, Ky.: Courier-Journal Job Printing, 1893.

[Lewis Publishing Company]. *The Lone Star State: A Memorial and Bibliographical History of Johnson and Hill Counties, Texas*. 1892.

Lidz, Franz. "Welcome to Farmtopia." *Smithsonian* 46.2 (May 2015).

Lincoln, Waldo. *American Cookery Books, 1742–1860*. Rev. by Eleanor Lowenstein. Worcester, Mass.: American Antiquarian Society, 1954.

Linley, John. *Architecture of Middle Georgia: The Oconee Area*. Athens: University of Georgia Press, 2014.

Livingston, John. *Portraits of Eminent Americans Now Living, with Biographical and Historical Memoirs of Their Lives and Actions*, vol. 4. New York: Cornish, Lamport, 1854.

Long, Lucy M. "Culinary Tourism: A Folkloristic Perspective on Eating and Otherness." *Southern Folklore* 55.3 (1998): 181–204.

Longone, Janice Bluestein, and Daniel T. Longone. *American Cookbooks and Wine Books, 1797–1950*. Ann Arbor: William L. Clements Library of American History, University of Michigan, 1984.

[Longstreet, Augustus Baldwin]. *Georgia Scenes, Characters, Incidents, &c., in the First Half Century of the Republic*. 2nd ed. New York: Harper, 1845.

Lossiah, Aggie Ross. "The Story of My Life as Far Back as I Can Remember." Edited by Joan Greene. *Journal of Cherokee Studies* 9.2 (Fall 1984): 89–99.

———. *See also* Ulmer, Mary, and Samuel Beck.

Lowenthal, Julie Donaldson. *Johnny Harris Restaurant Cookbook*. Gretna, La.: Pelican, 2014.

Lundy, Ronni, ed. *Cornbread Nation 3: Foods of the Mountain South*. Chapel Hill: University of North Carolina Press, 2005.

Lupo, Margaret. *Southern Cooking from Mary Mac's Tea Room*. Atlanta: Cherokee, 1993.

Lynn, Kristie, and Robert W. Pelton. *The Early American Cookbook: Authentic Favorites for the Modern Kitchen*. Georgetown, Del.: William H. McCauley, 2000.

Mallon, Thomas. *A Book of One's Own: People and Their Diaries*. New York: Ticknor & Fields, 1984.

Marzolf, Marion. *Up from the Footnote: A History of Women Journalists*. New York: Hastings House, 1977.

May, Kathy L. *Molasses Man*. New York: Holiday House, 2000.

Mayes, Eve B. "'The Finest Cook in All the South!' Aunt Laura Billups of Athens." *Athens Historian* 18 (2018): 29–39.

McClain, Charleen, ed. *Holland's Southern Cookbook*. Atlanta: Tupper & Love, 1952.

McConnell, Akila Sankar. *A Culinary History of Atlanta*. Charleston, S.C.: American Palate, 2019.

McCrary, Wiley, Janet McCrary, and Amy Paige Condon. *Wiley's Championship BBQ: Secrets Old Men Take to the Grave*. Layton, Utah: Gibbs Smith, 2014.

McDermott, Nancie. *Fruit*. A Savor the South Cookbook. Chapel Hill: University of North Carolina Press, 2017.

———. *Southern Cakes: Sweet and Irresistible Recipes for Everyday Celebrations*. San Francisco: Chronicle, 2007.

———. *Southern Pies: A Gracious Plenty of Pie Recipes from Lemon Chess to Chocolate Pecan*. San Francisco: Chronicle, 2010.

McFeely, William S. *Sapelo's People: A Long Walk into Freedom*. New York: Norton, 1994.

McGrath, Frances. *The Pirates' House Cook Book*. Asheville, N.C.: Biltmore Press, 1961.

McIntyre, Pam, comp. *The Original Vidalia Onion Cookbook*. Vidalia, Ga.: Vidalia Chamber of Commerce, 1981.

McMurtrie, Douglas C. *A History of Printing in the United States*. Vol. 2, *Middle & South Atlantic States*. New York: R. R. Bowker, 1936.

———. "Pioneer Printing in Georgia." *Georgia Historical Quarterly* 16.2 (June 1932): 77–113.

McRee, Patsie. *The Kitchen and the Cotton Patch*. Atlanta: Cullom & Ghertner, 1948.

Mell, Patrick Hues, and Annie R. White Mell. *The Genealogy of the Mell Family in the Southern States*. Auburn, Ala.: J. Munsell's Sons, 1897.

Mellinger, Marie, and Mary Nikas. *Out of Old Fields: A Wild Edibles Cookbook*. Rabun Gap, Ga.: Hambidge Center, 1975.

Meyers, Christopher C. "Fruitland Nursery: A 'Horticultural Mecca.'" *Georgia Historical Quarterly* 99.1–2 (Spring/Summer 2015).

Miller, Adrian. *The President's Kitchen Cabinet: The Story of the African Americans Who Have Fed Our First Families, from the Washingtons to the Obamas*. Chapel Hill: University of North Carolina Press, 2017.

Mitchell, Christine M. "The Rhetoric of Celebrity Cookbooks." *Journal of Popular Culture* 43.3 (2010): 524–539.

Mixon, Myron. *Smokin' with Myron Mixon: Recipes Made Simple from the Winningest Man in Barbecue*. New York: Ballantine, 2011.

Moore, Francis. *A Voyage to Georgia*. London: J. Robinson, 1744. Republished by Fort Frederica Association (Jacksonville, Fla.: Allied Graphics, 2002).

Moore, Violet. *Hearth Cookery: Authentic Recipes from America's Past*. Montezuma, Ga.: Privately published, ca. 1974.

Morgan, Philip, ed. *African American Life in the Georgia Lowcountry: The Atlantic World and the Gullah Geechee*. Athens: University of Georgia Press, 2010.

Morris, Patricia. *Georgia's Lighthouses*. Charleston, S.C.: Arcadia, 2008.

Morris, Sylvanus. *Strolls About Athens During the Early Seventies*. 1912. Athens, Ga.: Athens Historical Society, 1969.

Moss, Kay K. *Seeking the Historical Cook: Exploring Eighteenth-Century Southern Foodways*. Columbia: University of South Carolina Press, 2013.

Moss, Kay, and Kathryn Hoffman. *The Backcountry Housewife: A Study of Eighteenth-Century Foods*. Gastonia, N.C.: Schiele Museum of Natural History, 2001.

Moss, Robert F. *The Lost Southern Chefs: A History of Commercial Dining in the Nineteenth-Century South*. Athens: University of Georgia Press, 2022.

Moulton, Gary E. *John Ross: Cherokee Chief*. Athens: University of Georgia Press, 1978.

Moye, Mrs. L. M., ed. *The Bedingfield Inn Cook Book*. Lumpkin, Ga.: Stewart County Historical Commission, 1966.

Murray, Erin Byers. *Grits: A Cultural & Culinary Journey Through the South*. New York: St. Martin's Press, 2018.

National Council of Negro Women. *The Black Family Reunion Cookbook*. New York: Fireside/Simon & Schuster, 1991.

———. *The Historical Cookbook of the American Negro*. Compiled and edited by Sue Bailey Thurman. 1958. Boston: Beacon, 2000.

Nelson, Bobbe Hickson. *A Land So Dedicated: The History of Houston County, Georgia*. Perry, Ga.: Southern Trellis, 1998.

Nelson, Bobbe, and Nanette Green. *The New Perry Hotel: A Century of Southern Hospitality*. Perry, Ga.: New Perry Hotel, 1994.

Nesbit, Martha Giddens. *Savannah Entertains*. Charleston, S.C.: Wyrick, 1996.

Neuhaus, Jessamyn. *Manly Meals and Mom's Home Cooking: Cookbooks and Gender in Modern America*. Baltimore: John Hopkins University Press, 2003.

Nevin, Alfred, ed. *Encyclopaedia of the Presbyterian Church in the United States of America*. Philadelphia: Presbyterian Encyclopaedia, 1884.

Nevin, James B., ed. *Prominent Women of Georgia*. Atlanta: National Biographical Publishers, 1928.

Nichols, Gene. *The Geechee Cook Book: Savannah, Georgia*. Savannah: Southern Printers of Savannah, 1973.

Night in Old Savannah Committee. *A Night in Old Savannah Cook Book: An Introduction to a World of Cookery*. [Savannah: Privately printed, ca. 1983.]

Norwak, Mary. *English Puddings: Sweet & Savoury*. London: Grub Street, 2004.

O'Connell, Libby H. *The American Plate: A Culinary History in 100 Bites*. Naperville, Ill.: Sourcebooks, 2014.

Okie, William Thomas. *The Georgia Peach: Culture, Agriculture, and Environment in the American South*. New York: Cambridge University Press, 2016.

Owen, Mrs. De Witt C. *Chafing Dish Delicacies*. Dixon, Ill.: Rogers & Owen, [1890s].

Paddleford, Clementine. *The Great American Cookbook: 500 Time-Tested Recipes*. Adapted by Kelly Alexander. New York: Rizzoli, 2011. This is a revised edition of *How America Eats* (New York: Scribner, 1960).

Patout, Gerald. "At the Corner of Creole and Cajun: Musings of a Louisiana Cookbook Collector." *Repast* 31.3 (2015): 5.

[Payne, Arthur Gay]. *Housekeeper's Guide to Preserved Meats, Fruits, Vegetables, &c.* London: Crosse & Blackwell, 1889.

Perdue, Theda. *Race and the Atlanta Cotton States Exposition of 1895*. Athens: University of Georgia Press, 2010.

Phipps, Frances. *Colonial Kitchens, Their Furnishings, and Their Gardens*. New York: Hawthorn, 1972.

Pipes, Marie-Lorraine, and Meta F. Janowitz. "Op-Ed: The Influence of New Technologies, Foods, and Print Media on Local Material Culture Remains in Nineteenth-Century America." *Northeast Historical Archaeology* 42 (2013), article 6.

Plemmons, Nancy, and Tony Plemmons. *Cherokee Cooking from the Mountains and Gardens to the Table*. Edited by Doc Bill [William Thomas]. Gainesville, Ga.: Privately printed at Georgia Design & Graphics, 2000.

Pollan, Michael. *The Omnivore's Dilemma: A Natural History of Four Meals*. New York: Penguin, 2006.

Ponce de Leon Baptist Church (Atlanta), Ladies' Aid Society. *The Gate City Cook Book*. Atlanta: Privately published, 1915.

Portman, Jed. "How to Make Chicken Mull." *Garden and Gun*, 24 February 2015. https://gardenandgun.com/recipe/how-to-make-chicken-mull.

———. "A Taste of Cherokee Cooking." *Garden and Gun*, 7 July 2017. https://gardenandgun.com/articles/taste-cherokee-cooking.

Purvis, Kathleen. *Pecans*. A Savor the South Cookbook. Chapel Hill: University of North Carolina Press, 2012.

Quarterman, Elizabeth Walker. *The Home at the Bluff*. With *Reminiscences of a Country Boy* by Luther H. Quarterman. Flemington, Ga.: Privately published, 1961.]

Quota Club of Macon, Georgia. *Recipes of the Deep South*. Privately published, 1948.

Raiford, Matthew. *Bress 'n' Nyam: Gullah Geechee Recipes from a Sixth-Generation Farmer*. Woodstock, Vt.: Countryman, 2021.

Randall, Alice, and Caroline Randall Williams. *Soul Food Love: Healthy Recipes Inspired by One Hundred Years of Cooking in a Black Family*. New York: Clarkson Potter, 2015.

Randolph, Mary. *The Virginia House-Wife*. Washington, D.C.: Davis and Force, 1824.

———. *The Virginia Housewife; or, Methodical Cook*. 1836. Philadelphia: E. H. Butler, 1860. Reprinted in facsimile with introduction by Janice Bluestein Longone. New York: Dover, 1993.

Ravenel, Lydia T. *Plantation Recipes of the Tugaloo River Valley Circa 1850*. Edited by Marty B. and Nancy T. Fleming. Toccoa, Ga.: Traveler's Rest State Historic Site, ca. 1990.

Ray, Celeste, ed. *Ethnicity*. Vol. 6 of *The New Encyclopedia of Southern Culture*, edited by Charles Reagan Wilson. Chapel Hill: University of North Carolina Press, 2007.

Rehak, Melanie. *Eating for Beginners: An Education in the Pleasures of Food from Chefs, Farmers, and One Picky Kid*. Boston: Houghton Mifflin Harcourt, 2010.

Rhodes, Susie Root, and Grace Porter Hopkins, eds. *The Economy Administration Cook Book*. New York: Syndicate, 1913.

———. *The Economy Administration Cook Book*. Hammond, Ind.: W. B. Conkey, 1913.

Roberts, Mrs. A. E. *Drummers' Home Cook Book*. Norwalk, Ohio: Laning, 1902.

Roberts, Nancy. *Georgia Ghosts*. Winston-Salem, N.C.: John F. Blair, 1997.

Robinson, Sallie Ann. *Gullah Home Cooking the Daufuskie Way*. With Gregory Wrenn Smith. Chapel Hill: University of North Carolina Press, 2003.

Rombauer, Irma S., and Marion Rombauer Becker. *Joy of Cooking*. 13th ed. Indianapolis: Bobbs-Merrill, 1975.

Ronald, Mary. *The Century Cook Book*. New York: Century, 1895.

Rose, Jessica, and Stephen Rose. *The Peach Truck Cookbook*. New York: Scribner, 2019.

Roth, Darlene, and Jeff Kemph, eds. *Piedmont Park: Celebrating Atlanta's Common Ground*. Athens, Ga.: Hill Street, 2004.

Rowland, Lawrence Sanders, Alexander Moore, and George C. Rogers, Jr. *The History of Beaufort County, South Carolina*. Vol. 1, *1514–1861*. Columbia: University of South Carolina Press, 1996.

Rozier, John. *The Houses of Hancock, 1785–1865*. Decatur, Ga.: Auldfarran, 1996.

Russell, Malinda. *A Domestic Cook Book: Containg a Careful Selection of Useful Receipts for the Kitchen*. 1866. Introduction by Janice Bluestein Longone. Ann Arbor, Mich.: Longone Center for American Culinary Research, William L. Clements Library, University of Michigan, 2007.

Rutledge, Sarah. *The Carolina Housewife; or, House and Home by a Lady of Charleston*. Charleston: W. R. Babcock, 1847. Facsimile, with commentary by Anna Wells Rutledge. Columbia: University of South Carolina Press, 1979.

Salkin, Allen. *From Scratch: Inside the Food Network*. New York: Putnam, 2013.

Sanders, Betty Bird Foy. *Favorite Recipes of Georgia's First Lady*. Atlanta: Georgia Power Company, 1965.

Sanders, Brad. *Guide to William Bartram's Travels: Following the Trail of America's First Great Naturalist*. Athens, Ga.: Fevertree Press, 2002.

Schaefer, Christina Kassabian. *The Hidden Half of the Family: A Sourcebook for Women's Genealogy*. Baltimore: Genealogical Publishing, 1999.

Schenone, Laura. *A Thousand Years Over a Hot Stove: A History of American Women Told Through Food, Recipes, and Remembrances*. New York: W. W. Norton, 2003.

Schlosser, Eric. *Fast Food Nation: The Dark Side of the All-American Meal*. Boston: Houghton Mifflin, 2001.

Schmidt, William. *The Flowing Bowl: When and What to Drink*. New York: C. L. Webster, 1892.

Second Presbyterian Church (Augusta). *Choice Recipes of Georgia Housekeepers*. New York: Trow's Printing & Bookbinding, 1880.

Service Star Legion, Atlanta. *Service Star Legion Cook Book*. Atlanta: [Ben Franklin Press], 1927.

Shapiro, Laura. *Perfection Salad: Women and Cooking at the Turn of the Century*. Farrar, Straus, and Giroux, 1986.

Sharpless, Rebecca. *Cooking in Other Women's Kitchens: Domestic Workers in the South, 1865–1960*. Chapel Hill: University of North Carolina Press, 2010.

Sheehy, Barry, and Cindy Wallace. *Civil War Savannah*. Vol. 1, *Savannah: Immortal City*. Austin, TX: Emerald Book Company, 2011.

Shephard, Sue. *Pickled, Potted, and Canned: How the Art and Science of Food Preserving Changed the World.* New York: Simon & Schuster, 2000.

Shorter College. *See* Alumnae of Shorter College.

Sibley, Celestine. *The Celestine Sibley Sampler.* Edited by Sibley Fleming. Atlanta: Peachtree, 1996.

Simmons, Amelia. *American Cookery.* Hartford, Conn.: Hudson & Goodwin, 1796.

Smith, Andrew F., ed. *Food and Drink in American History: A "Full Course" Encyclopedia.* 3 vols. Santa Barbara, Calif.: ABC-CLIO, 2013.

———. *The Oxford Companion to American Food and Drink.* New York: Oxford University Press, 2007.

Smith, Charles H. [Bill Arp, pseud.]. *The Farm and the Fireside: Sketches of Domestic Life in War and Peace.* Atlanta: Constitution, 1892.

Smith, Eliza. *The Compleat Housewife; or, Accomplish'd Gentlewoman's Companion.* London: J. Pemberton, 1727.

Smith, Elizabeth Wiley, and Sara S. Carnes. *The History of Hancock County, Georgia.* Vol. 1, *History, Heritage, and Records.* Vol. 2, *Ancestors, Families, and Genealogies.* Washington, Ga.: Wilkes, 1974.

Smith, Jane Webb. *Georgia's Legacy: History Charted Through the Arts.* Athens: Georgia Museum of Art, University of Georgia, 1985.

Smith, T. J., ed. *The Foxfire Book of Appalachian Cookery.* Rev. ed. Chapel Hill: University of North Carolina Press, 2019.

Southern Ruralist. Favorite Southern Recipes. [Atlanta: Southern Ruralist Company, 1912].

Spano, Sara. *Sara's Recipes Through the Years.* Kearney, Neb.: Morris Press, 2009.

Splint, Sarah Field. *65 Prize Recipes from the South.* Chicago: Swift, 1935.

St. Barbara's Philoptochos Society (Savannah). *The Art of Greek Cooking.* Savannah: Privately published, ca. 1978.

St. John's Episcopal Church (Savannah), Ladies of the Bishop Beckwith Society for the Benefit of the Manual Training School. *Favorite Recipes from Savannah Homes: A Collection of Well Tested and Practical Recipes.* Savannah: Morning News, 1904.

St. John's Episcopal Church (Savannah), Rector's Aid Society. *The Ever Ready Cook Book.* Savannah: Privately published, 1910.

St. Paul's Church (Albany). *The Southwest Georgia Cook Book: Selected Recipes of Proven Merit.* Albany, Ga.: Privately published, 1924.

Stanfield, Elizabeth. *How to Work Wonders with Every Day Foods.* Hutchinson, Kans.: Carey Salt, 1939.

———. *Mrs. Stanfield's 52 Family Sunday Dinners.* Atlanta: Privately published, 1937.

———. *Mrs. Stanfield's Selected Recipes.* Knoxville: J. Allen Smith, 1935.

———. *White Lily Cooking Guide.* Knoxville: J. Allen Smith, 1934.

———, ed. *White Lily Flour Cook Book,* Knoxville: J. Allen Smith, 1932.

Stevens, Mrs. M. F. *Kitchen Lore: Being a Few Choice Recipes*. Atlanta: Foote & Davis, n.d.

Stewart, Vera. *The VeryVera Cookbook*. Winter Park, Fla.: Story Farm, 2018.

Stiles, Henry Reed. *History and Genealogies of Ancient Windsor, Connecticut*. Rev. ed. Hartford, Conn.: Case, Lockwood & Brainard, 1892.

Stuntz, Stephen Conrad, comp., and Emma B. Hawks, ed. *List of the Agricultural Periodicals of the United States and Canada Published during the Century July 1810 to July 1910*. Washington, D.C.: U.S. Government Printing Office, 1941.

Sullivan, Buddy. *Sapelo: People and Place on a Georgia Sea Island*. Athens: University of Georgia Press, 2017.

——. *Thomas Spalding: Antebellum Planter of Sapelo*. Privately published, 2019.

Sutherland, Amy. *Cookoff: Recipe Fever in America*. New York: Viking, 2003.

Talmadge, Betty. *How to Cook a Pig and Other Back-to-the-Farm Recipes: An Autobiographical Cookbook*. New York: Simon & Schuster, 1977.

Tate, William. *Strolls Around Athens*. Athens, Ga.: Observer, 1975.

Taylor, Nicole A. *Watermelon & Red Birds: A Cookbook for Juneteenth and Black Celebrations*. New York: Simon & Schuster, 2022.

Taylor, Susie King. *Reminiscences of My Life in Camp with the 33d United States Colored Troops*. Boston, 1902.

Telfair Academy Guild. *The Artful Table: Menus and Masterpieces from Telfair Museums*. Savannah: Telfair, 2011.

Temple, Sarah Blackwell Gober. *The First Hundred Years: A Short History of Cobb County, in Georgia*. Atlanta: Walter W. Brown, 1935.

Temple, Sarah B. Gober, and Kenneth Coleman. *Georgia Journeys: Being an Account of the Lives of Georgia's Original Settlers . . . from . . . 1732 until . . . 1754*. Athens: University of Georgia Press, 1961.

Tennent, Mrs. E. R., ed. *House-Keeping in the Sunny South*. Atlanta: Jas. P. Harrison, 1885.

Terry, Elizabeth. *Savannah Seasons: Food and Stories from Elizabeth on 37th*. New York: Doubleday, 1996.

Theophano, Janet. *Eat My Words: Reading Women's Lives Through the Cookbooks They Wrote*. New York: Palgrave, 2002.

Thicknesse, Philip. *Memoirs and Anecdotes of Philip Thicknesse, Late Lieutenant Governor of Land Guard Fort, and Unfortunately Father to George Touchet, Baron Audley*. Dublin: Graisberry & Campbell, 1790.

Thomas, William "Doc. Bill." *Northeast Georgia Cuisine: A Gourmet Guide to the Southern Appalachian Mountains*. Gainesville, Ga.: Privately printed at Georgia Design & Graphics, 1999.

Thornton, Ella May, comp. *Finding-List of Books and Pamphlets Relating to Georgia and Georgians*. Atlanta: Georgia State Library, 1928.

Thornton, P[hineas]. *The Southern Gardener and Receipt Book*. 2nd ed. Newark, N.J.: A. L. Dennis, 1845. Reprinted in Antique American Cookbooks library edition, with introduction by Shirley Abbott. Birmingham, Ala.: Oxmoor House, 1984.

Tillery, Carolyn Quick. *Southern Homecoming Traditions: Recipes and Remembrances*. New York: Citadel Press, 2006.

Tilson, Jake. *A Tale of 12 Kitchens: Family Cooking in Four Countries*. New York: Artisan, 2006.

Tipton-Martin, Toni. *The Jemima Code: Two Centuries of African American Cookbooks*. Austin: University of Texas Press, 2015.

———. *Jubilee: Recipes from Two Centuries of African American Cooking*. New York: Clarkson Potter, 2019.

Tramazzo, John C., and Fred Minnick. *Bourbon and Bullets: True Stories of Whiskey, War, and Military Service*. Sterling, Va.: Potomac, 2018.

Tucker, Martha Goode. *Housekeeping Diary of an Antebellum Lady*. Milledgeville, Ga.: Colonial Dames of America in the State of Georgia, 1990.

Twitty, Michael W. *The Cooking Gene: A Journey through African American Culinary History in the Old South*. New York: Amistad, 2017.

———. *Rice*. A Savor the South Cookbook. Chapel Hill: University of North Carolina Press, 2021.

Tye, Diane. *Baking as Biography: A Life Story in Recipes*. Montreal: McGill–Queen's University Press, 2010.

Ulmer, Mary, and Samuel E. Beck, eds. *Cherokee Cooklore: Preparing Cherokee Foods*. Drawings by Goingback Chiltosky. Photos of Aggie Lossiah by Juanita Wilson. Cherokee, N.C.: Mary and Goingback Chiltosky, 1951. This volume, titled *Cherokee Cooklore: To Make My Bread* on the cover, is copyrighted by the Museum of the Cherokee Indian.

United States Department of Agriculture. *Report of the Commissioner of Agriculture for the Year 1870*. Washington, D.C.: U.S. Government Printing Office, 1871.

———. *Report of the Commissioner of Agriculture for the Year 1887*. Washington, D.C.: U.S. Government Printing Office, 1888.

Van Dyke, Louis, and Billie Van Dyke. *The Blue Willow Inn Cookbook: Experiencing the South*. Saint Simons Island, Ga.: Saint Simons Press, 1996. There are several editions and versions of Blue Willow Inn cookbooks.

Van Willigen, John. *Kentucky's Cookbook Heritage: Two Hundred Years of Southern Cuisine and Culture*. Lexington: University Press of Kentucky, 2014.

Vashti Auxiliary. *Pines and Plantations: Native Recipes of Thomasville, Georgia*. Thomasville, Ga.: Vashti Auxiliary, 1976.

Veit, Helen Zoe, ed. *Food in the American Gilded Age*. East Lansing: Michigan State University Press, 2017.

———. *Food in the Civil War Era: The South*. East Lansing: Michigan State University Press, 2015.

Verstille, Mrs. E. J. *Verstille's Southern Cookery: Comprising a Fine Collection of Cooking and Other Receipts Valuable to Mothers and Housekeepers*. New York: Owens & Agar, 1866.

Volo, James M., and Dorothy Denneen Volo. *Family Life in 17th- and 18th-Century America*. Westport, Conn.: Greenwood, 2006.

Voss, Kimberly Wilmot. *The Food Section: Newspaper Women and the Culinary Community*. Lanham, Md.: Rowman & Littlefield, 2014.

Wallace-Sanders, Kimberly. *Mammy: A Century of Race, Gender, and Southern Memory*. Ann Arbor: University of Michigan Press, 2009.

Wallach, Jennifer Jensen, ed. *Dethroning the Deceitful Pork Chop: Rethinking African American Foodways from Slavery to Obama*. Fayetteville: University of Arkansas Press, 2015.

Warren, Mildred Evans. *The Art of Southern Cooking*. Garden City, N.Y.: Doubleday, 1969.

Waters, Alice. *The Art of Simple Food: Notes, Lessons, and Recipes from a Delicious Revolution*. New York: Clarkson Potter, 2007.

Waters, Andrew, ed. *On Jordan's Stormy Banks: Personal Accounts of Slavery in Georgia*. Winston-Salem, N.C.: John F. Blair, 2000.

Weaver, Dexter. *Automatic Y'all: Weaver D's Guide to the Soul*. With Patrick Allen. Athens, Ga.: Hill Street, 1999.

Webster, Mrs. A. L. *The Improved Housewife; or, Book of Receipts, with Engravings for Marketing and Carving*. 19th ed. Boston: Phillips & Sampson, 1853.

Welch-Bafile, Freida. *The Smith House History Cookbook*. Dahlonega, Ga.: Smith House, 2015.

Wesleyan College Alumnae. *Macon Cook Book*. 1909. Macon, Ga.: Burke, 1936.

Westinghouse Electric Corporation Home Economics Institute. *Delicious Foods and How to Cook Them with Your Westinghouse Electric Range*. Mansfield, Ohio: Westinghouse Electric Corporation, 1945.

Westminster Presbyterian Church (Savannah). *The Savannah Cook Book*. Savannah: Morning News, 1909.

Wetmore, Ruth Y. "The Green Corn Ceremony of the Eastern Cherokees." *Journal of Cherokee Studies* 8.1 (Spring 1983): 46–57.

White, George. *Historical Collections of Georgia*. New York: Pudney & Russell, 1855.

———. *Statistics of the State of Georgia: Including an Account of Its Natural, Civil, and Ecclesiastical History*. Savannah: W. Thorne Williams, 1849.

White, Max E. *The Archaeology and History of the Native Georgia Tribes*. Gainesville: University Press of Florida, 2005.

White, William N. *Gardening for the South, or the Kitchen and Fruit Garden*. New York: C. M. Saxton, 1856. The 1859 edition (New York: A. O. Moore) is now reprinted on demand by Forgotten Books of London.

Whitehead, Jessup. *The American Pastry Cook*. Chicago: Jessup Whitehead, 1894.

———. *Cooking for Profit*. 3rd ed. Chicago: Jessup Whitehead, 1893.

———. *The Hotel Book of Breads and Cakes*. Chicago: Jessup Whitehead, 1894.

———. *Hotel Meat Cooking*. 7th ed. Chicago: Jessup Whitehead, 1901.

——. *Whitehead's Family Cook Book and Book of Breads and Cakes*. Chicago: Jessup Whitehead, 1891.

Wight, Rebecca Stewart, and Selma Wight Beard. *From Mother with Love: A Treasury of Recipes for Cooking and Living*. Atlanta: Peachtree, 1984.

Wilcox, Estelle Woods, comp. *Centennial Buckeye Cook Book*. Marysville, Ohio: J. H. Shearer, 1876. Reprinted with introduction and appendices by Andrew F. Smith. Columbus: Ohio State University Press, 2000.

——. *The Dixie Cook-Book*. Rev. ed. Atlanta: L. A. Clarkson, 1883.

——. *The New Dixie Cook-Book*. Atlanta: Dixie Cook-Book Publishing/L. A. Clarkson, 1889.

Wilkes, Sema. *Famous Recipes from Mrs. Wilkes' Boarding House in Historic Savannah*. Memphis: Toof Cookbook Division, 1976.

——. *Mrs. Wilkes' Boardinghouse Cookbook*. Berkeley, Calif.: Ten Speed, 2001.

Williams, Susan. *Savory Suppers & Fashionable Feasts: Dining in Victorian America*. New York: Pantheon, 1985.

Williams, Victoria. "Great Cake." George Washington's Mount Vernon. www.mountvernon.org/library/digitalhistory/digital-encyclopedia/article/great-cake.

Williams-Forson, Psyche A. *Building Houses Out of Chicken Legs: Black Women, Food, and Power*. Chapel Hill: University of North Carolina Press, 2006.

Willis, Annie Laura. *Georgia Pines Plantation Cookbook*. Tallahassee: Florida, 1988.

Willis, Virginia. *Bon Appétit, Y'all*. Berkeley, Calif.: Ten Speed, 2008.

——. *Secrets of the Southern Table*. Boston: Houghton Mifflin Harcourt, 2018.

Wilson, Mrs. Henry Lumpkin (Mary Elizabeth Monk), ed. *Tested Recipe Cook Book*. Atlanta: Foote & Davies, 1895. Reprinted as *The Atlanta Exposition Cookbook*. Athens: University of Georgia Press, 1984.

Wondrich, David. *Imbibe!: From Absinthe Cocktail to Whiskey Smash*. Rev. ed. New York: Perigee, 2015.

——. *Punch: The Delights (and Dangers) of the Flowing Bowl*. New York: Perigee, 2010.

Woofter, Thomas Jackson, Jr., et al. "Phelps-Stokes Fellowship Studies, No. 1: The Negroes of Athens, Georgia." *Bulletin of the University of Georgia* 14.4 (December 1913).

Works Progress Administration Writers' Program. *Georgia: A Guide to Its Towns and Countryside*. Athens: University of Georgia Press, 1940.

Wright, Richard R., and J. R. Hawkins, eds. *Centennial Encyclopedia of the African Methodist Episcopal Church*. Philadelphia: A. M. E. Church, 1916.

Yentsch, Anne. "Applying Concepts from Historical Archaeology to New England's Nineteenth-Century Cookbooks." *Northeast Historical Archaeology* 42 (2013), article 8.

Yoder, Ruth. *Montezuma Amish Mennonite Cookbook*. Montezuma, Ga.: Yoder's Catering Service, 1988.

Ysewijn, Regula. *Pride and Pudding: The History of British Puddings Savoury and Sweet*. London: Murdoch, 2016.

Zafar, Rafia. *Recipes for Respect: African American Meals and Meaning*. Athens: University of Georgia Press, 2019.

———. "The Signifying Dish: Autobiography and History in Two Black Women's Cookbooks." *Feminist Studies* 25.2 (1999): 449–469.

Zehr, Farrel J., ed. *The Pecan Cookbook*. Americus, Ga.: Koinonia Farm, 1967.

Food and Kitchen Index

General Index